Rules of Engagement

Rules of Engagement

Trademark Strategies, Protection and Enforcement in China

Paolo Beconcini

Wolters Kluwer

Published by:
Kluwer Law International B.V.
PO Box 316
2400 AH Alphen aan den Rijn
The Netherlands
Website: www.wklawbusiness.com

Sold and distributed in North, Central and South America by:
Wolters Kluwer Legal & Regulatory U.S.
7201 McKinney Circle
Frederick, MD 21704
United States of America
Email: customer.service@wolterskluwer.com

Sold and distributed in all other countries by:
Turpin Distribution Services Ltd
Stratton Business Park
Pegasus Drive, Biggleswade
Bedfordshire SG18 8TQ
United Kingdom
Email: kluwerlaw@turpin-distribution.com

Printed on acid-free paper.

ISBN 978-90-411-8254-8

e-Book: ISBN 978-90-411-8280-7
web-PDF: ISBN 978-90-411-8281-4

Printed in the United Kingdom.

To my splendid and patient wife Wiji and our brilliant son Domizio,
the force behind all!

About the Author

A sought-after authority on IP litigation in China, Paolo regularly appears in Chinese courts and attends IPR raids on local counterfeiters. His record of success in patent infringement lawsuits includes a landmark case once designated “case of the year” by several IP journals. He leads business intelligence teams that pursue evidence of counterfeiting operations, particularly in China’s automotive and mechanical industry, but also in its fashion industry.

He is frequently invited to speak at conferences devoted to the growing field of Chinese IP, and has been actively involved in field projects, including trademark and patent enforcement training programs for Chinese civil servants. Paolo is regularly interviewed on China IP matters by media around the world such as *The Wall Street Journal*, CNN, Bloomberg, *La Tribune* and Il Sole24 Ore, to name a few.

In China, where intellectual property disputes routinely involve multiple cultures, Paolo’s fluency in five languages, including Mandarin, helps him navigate international borders, and creates confidence in his clients. Paolo represents US and European clients in confronting the myriad crosscultural challenges – legal, commercial, political – that threaten patent and trademark assets.

Table of Contents

Preface

No matter how the Chinese economy performs in the next five years, it has become a country that no one can ignore. Intellectual property protection is one of the hottest topics. Any foreign company needs to study this book for survival, prosperity and to hold competitive advantage. China is a ruthless and tough market where IP control can mean the difference between a fortune made and a fortune lost. This book is the ultimate playbook for success.

Western legal and business professionals are often frustrated and resigned when dealing with intellectual property, and specifically trademark protection in China. The 2015 American Business in China and Business Climate Survey of the American Chamber of Commerce reports that most foreign business operators believe that the Chinese intellectual property system is inefficient and ineffective. Consequently, the apparently unstoppable rise of trademark theft and counterfeiting in China has always been blamed on the ruthless and aggressive Chinese. The China blame game has been then amplified by western media. The result is that, with few exceptions, foreign businesses and professionals could not see that some of their trademark problems were due to failure to prepare, failure to understand and lack of proper preparation. Most publications on trademark law in China are traditional law textbooks reaching out to a very limited number of practitioners. Also, these law books tend to be compartmentalized to the legal sphere and the analysis and practical tips can at most help lawyers to solve a specific legal issue, but will not help them and their clients to conceive and implement wider and effective trademark strategies in China. At the same time, business books on brand management in China treat the legal aspects of the brand protection very marginally, so that trademark protection and enforcement occupy a very marginal position in the planning of business strategies. This book bridges this gap.

Foreign legal practitioners, businessmen and IP managers need support in formulating concrete and effective strategies based on a more comprehensive source of knowledge about trademark protection and enforcement in China. The relevant market needs access to knowledge that is not compartmentalized and scattered, but comprehensively treated and presented in a practical manner. This book presents comprehensive strategic approaches to dealing with trademark protection and enforcement in

China, challenge common legal thinking, and propose new and deliver creative strategic solutions to old unresolved problems.

This book is the result of 15 years of field experience in trademark protection and enforcement in China and offers a comprehensive, interdisciplinary and strategic guide to deal with trademark challenges in China. The book also details state of the legal and business strategies adopted by foreign companies when dealing with trademark theft and counterfeiting in China.

The book offers a unique strategic perspective on Chinese trademark law and practice for a number of reasons; the author is not only a lawyer specialized in Chinese trademark protection and enforcement but also an anticounterfeiting investigator and manager of investigative teams. He has also worked as part of the enlarged in-house teams of major foreign companies running their trademark enforcement coordination programs in China, thus gaining insight into various companies' IP management processes. These different positions have given to the author the insight and perspective needed to elaborate and produce comprehensive and interdisciplinary trademark protection and enforcement strategies in China. The author is a businessman, developing software solutions for the management of anticounterfeiting cases in China, thus gaining direct and personal understanding of the challenges of doing business in this country.

Ultimately, it is this broad perspective and the specific professional experience of the author that allows the book to challenge consolidated legal thinking on certain aspects of trademark protection and enforcement in China, while proposing new and more creative solutions to what appear to be unsolvable problems.

The book's aim is to provide professionals with one reliable, practical and insightful source of knowledge that will help them succeed in China's trademark business and challenge the legal interpretations and use of Chinese law from the point of view of the business and through the lenses of consolidated IP management theories and processes.

2016, Beijing, People's Republic of China and Irvine, California, USA.

List of Abbreviations

AIC	Administration for Industry and Commerce
AQSIQ	Administration of Quality, Supervision, Inspection and Quarantine
C2C	Consumer-to-Consumer
CEO	Chief Executive Officer
CTMO	China Trademark Office
EU	European Union
GAC	General Administration of Customs
HQ	Head Quarter
IACC	International AntiCounterfeiting Coalition
IP	Intellectual Property
IPR	Intellectual Property Rights
MNC	Multi-National Company
MOFCOM	Ministry of Commerce of the People's Republic of China
OECD	Organization for the Economic Cooperation and Development
OEM	Original Equipment Manufacturer
PRB	Patent Reexamination Board
PRC	People's Republic of China
PSB	Public Security Bureau

R&D	Research and Development
SAIC	State Administration for Industry and Commerce
SCNPC	Standing Committee of the National People's Congress
SIPO	State Intellectual Property Office
SME	Small-Middle Enterprises
SPC	Supreme People's Court
STMA	State Tobacco Monopoly Administration
TRAB	Trademark Reexamination and Adjudication Board
TRIPS	Trade-Related Aspects of Intellectual Property Rights
TSB	Technical Supervision Bureau
WIPO	World Intellectual Property Organization
WTO	World Trade Organization
VIN	Vehicle Identification Number
PoA	Power of Attorney

CHAPTER 1

An Introduction to Trademark Protection and Enforcement in China

Western culture and approach to business issues and challenges is different from that of the Chinese. Western companies have shown a certain degree of understanding when making "local customization" one of the driving forces behind their penetration of the Chinese markets.[1] At the same time, a less open-minded attitude has characterized the strategic approach to intellectual property (IP) and in particular, trademark challenges in China. Foreign investors seem in most cases to assume that Chinese laws and legal/business culture are similar to those in the West. Little efforts have been made to explain that this is not the case. The result is that most foreign brands trademark strategies in China were based on inaccurate, if not utterly wrong, legal and business premises. This has resulted in most, if not all western companies of all sizes, committing and often repeating legal mistakes. What is most interesting though, is that in spite of the emergence of clear "blunder patterns" repeating no matter the size and type of the foreign companies, their reactions do not appear to have changed, thus making the repetition of such mistakes look like the work of the devil. In practice, though, it seems that foreign rights holders may not have wanted to accept that in many instances they were the primary cause of a trademark theft or a counterfeiting action, and rather preferred loading the blame onto the Chinese legal system. This erroneous, post-colonial approach to China IP and business challenges continues to the date this book is being written.

Western companies have come to play the IP game in China without knowing or understanding the rules, and once they started losing the game, they began complaining that the rules were wrong! If that happened to kids playing some board or role games, it would likely end up in a quarrel! It is not the task of this book to find an explanation for such a strange contradiction in the Westerners approach to doing

1. Michael Silverstein, The $10 Trillion Prize, Captivating the Newly Affluent in China and India (Harvard Business Review Press 2015).

business in and with China. However, this uncontestable fact is one of the reasons why we are still having severe IP problems in China. In practice, the contradiction is there and continues to produce mistakes, which in turn continue repeating themselves in almost identical patterns. So, who is wrong here? It cannot only be China's fault. In defense of western investors, it can be stated that part of the problem has been caused by the legal profession. Why were we attorneys not able to convey the right message to our western clients? It could be objected here that lawyers, especially foreign lawyers specialized in China IP laws have been writing and communicating a lot about the Chinese legal differences. They have surely learned to loudly repeat some mantras, such as "file your IP rights in China timely" to avoid theft or be tough and enforce your IP rights in China because "courts are not as bad as they say." However, such messages are really slogans without a real body if taken outside a more strategic analysis of what China IP really looks like, when you put away the "western lenses."

In sum, either we have decided to ignore the rules and expect China to apply our own from the west, or the legal knowledge we got was not contextualized in a business approach to trademark challenges, which deprived us the opportunity to correctly exploit such law in our clients' favor.

It is time that trademark issues and challenges in China are treated within a comprehensive strategic approach, i.e., similar to the IP management approach most large companies have adopted for patents. More systematic approaches, where the legal is but one of the components of a complex solution, will be the best way for companies to overcome the current deadlocks, thus improving their business in China overall. This book wants to make two things clear: One is that there are rules in China. They may not be perfect and certainly they may be applied somewhat inconsistently, but there are rules nonetheless. It is every western company's duty to learn these rules before playing the game! Second, once the rules are learned, as well as the methods for their effective legal interpretation and application, it is important to place them in a strategic context, where these rules become functional to the realization of concrete business strategies.

It is in fact important to understand that trademark challenges are fore and foremost business rather than legal issues. If a supplier or distributor has appropriated himself of the principal's trademark, that is fore and foremost a business problem. It is first an issue of whether the right holder has chosen the right business model for the distribution of his products in China, and it concerns the relation between two companies and how they have set up their distribution business, before becoming as well a legal issue regarding the violation of the trademark law. If the foreign company in the examples gets a legal solution, this alone may not solve the underlying business problem. Therefore, the legal solution can only be part of a bigger strategic approach to the business challenge. Seen under a broader strategic point of view, a legal solution that could make sense legally may not be viable from a business point of view.

This is what this book is about. It helps foreign practitioners in China get it right when approaching business challenges involving trademark rights. To do this, the book will look at typical trademark challenges, how they have been traditionally approached, why they failed, and how they can be tackled today by using a strategic comprehensive approach in which business and law come together as integral part of the solution. It is hoped that certain "metropolitan legends" about China and its IP system will be partly refuted and effective knowledge channeled to the readers as well as the awareness to be better prepared when facing China trademark challenges.

The result of this multidisciplinary approach to trademark challenges like trademark grabbing and trademark counterfeiting, produces a set of rules of conducts to be observed by foreign right holders when dealing with trademarks in China. These rules are not just the rules of law. Knowledge of the rules of law is but one of the rules of engagement to succeed over trademark infringers. Rules of engagement are more generally strategic rules of conduct that provide guidance as to how to learn, understand and approach trademark challenges in China in an objective and more correct manner. They will help obtaining a correct knowledge of facts, assess the dangers and risks, and help design the legal and business reaction strategies that will reduce or eliminate the risks connected to trademark theft and counterfeiting in China. Knowledge and mastery of these rules of engagement will help foreign investors to be better prepared when doing business in China, thus preventing or reducing the risk of trademark theft, while tackling more efficiently and with longer lasting effects the issues of trademark infringement and trademark counterfeiting.

§1.01 A BRIEF HISTORY OF IPR INFRINGEMENT IN CHINA

The mention of protection of IP in China evokes in most foreign practitioners a feeling of frustration and resignation. It is like talking of breathable air on the moon, it just does not exist. The 2015 American Business in China White Paper and the related 2014 Business Climate Survey of the American Chamber of Commerce in China seem to support the assumption that most foreign business operators believe that the Chinese Intellectual Property Rights (IPR) system is inefficient and ineffective.[2] The cited reports list IP protection as seventh out of the nine greatest risks facing United States (US) businesses in China. IP ranks ahead in importance of deterioration of bilateral relations and behind the global economic slowdown. The people taking the survey saw IPR protection not as much as a macroeconomic or political problem, but rather as a pure legal concern. However, the author believes that other nonlegal factors, such as corruption are viewed also as a negative factor affecting IPR protection inefficacy in China. The fact that this is not reflected directly by the survey is because corruption is normally treated as a business topic of its own, rather than a practice affecting businesses horizontally, all other concerns being legal, economic or political. Another interesting set of data emerging from the survey are those reporting that 54% of respondents rated China's IP enforcement "ineffective" in 2014 and 14% rated it "totally ineffective." Also, there were fewer respondents answering "don't know" compared to 2009. This means that the perception and negative direct experience have become more widespread among the American business operators.[3] European Union

2. AmCham China, 2015 American Business in China White Paper (16th ed., AmCham China 2015); *see also* AmCham China, 2014 China Business Climate Survey Report (AmCham China 2014).
3. Mark Cohen, Going Sideways on China IP...?, http://chinaipr.com/2014/05/11/going-sideways-on-chinese-ip/ (accessed May 30, 2016). For more information on this point, *see also* U.S.

(EU) surveys mirror those of the Amcham and confirm that most westerners doing business in China have negative views of its IPR system.[4] By reflection, the information about China IPR conveyed to the general public in the west, including all those businesses that have not as yet started to move to China but are in the process or are planning to do so, will also receive mostly negative views and reports.

In the last decades, Western countries have been reacting against these perceptions by initiating government led pressure activities (political pressure,[5] threat of trade sanctions[6]) or by starting institutionally sponsored cooperation programs with the main aim of changing the China IP system to comply with their own standards.[7] Institutions have been created to increase external pressure on China to change the system to a more western format.[8] These approaches may have brought about critical legislative improvements in China.[9] However, they have not had any major influence on the enforcement of the laws and their application and have not brought about much concrete benefits to foreign investors so far. This explains why industrial groups of interests and Multi-National Companies (MNCs) have since long started parallel lobbying efforts to obtain better trademark protection in China on a one-to-one basis. This lateral kind of pressure has also mostly focused on enforcement and has indeed succeeded in pushing Chinese authorities to double their enforcement efforts in these past years. However, in both cases, the result has been the same. Higher volumes of enforcement have not brought about the end of counterfeiting, as sovereign pressure has not been able to prevent trademark theft and counterfeiting. In practice, and in

Department of State Bureau of Economic and Business Affairs, 2015 Investment Climate Statement, http://www.state.gov/e/eb/rls/othr/ics/2015/241518.htm (May 2015). *See also* The Office of the United States Trade Representative, 2015 Special 301 Report, https://ustr.gov/sites/default/files/2015-Special-301-Report-FINAL.pdf (April 2015).

4. European Commission Staff Working Document, *Report on the protection and enforcement of intellectual property rights in third countries*, SWD (2015) 132, https://euipo.europa.eu/ohimportal/documents/11370/0/Report+on+the+protection+and+enforcement+of+intellectual+property+rights+in+third+countries (July 1, 2015).
5. The US have used negotiating pressure with China in relation to the US support to China's becoming part of the WTO. For an overview of the intergovernmental relations concerning China's access to WTO and the TRIPS agreement, *see* Mikahelle Schiappacasse, Intellectual Property Rights in China: Technology Transfers and Economic Development, Vol. 2, Buffalo Intellectual Property Law Journal, 164, 176 (2004). For an overview of the WTO dispute between the US and China on the latter's failed implementation of the TRIPS agreement, *see* Donald P. Harris, The Honeymoon Is Over: Evaluating The U.S.-China WTO Intellectual Property Complaint, Vol. 32, No. 1, Fordham International Law Journal, 96 (2008).
6. Ellen Nakashima, U.S. Developing Trade Sanctions against China for Cyberthefts, Washington Post https://www.washingtonpost.com/world/national-security/administration-developing-sanctions-against-china-over-cyberespionage/2015/08/30/9b2910aa-480b-11e5-8ab4-c73967a143d3_story.html (August 30, 2015). *See also* Charles Baum, Trade Sanctions and the Rule of Law: Lessons from China, Vol. 1, Stanford Journal of East Asian Affairs, 46, 54 (2001).
7. Reference can be made to the recently established "IP Key," a joint IPR cooperation effort between the EU Commission, the Office for Harmonization (OHIM) and the Chinese Ministry of Commerce. IP Key is the continuation of an older cooperation project between the EU and China known as IPR2 project. For more information, *see* www.ipkey.org, www.ipr2.org.
8. *Ibid.*
9. The effect of external sovereign pressure on China has been disputed. Most Chinese will deny that legislative changes were imposed by foreign governments, and rather sustain that they were the natural consequence of the changes of China's economic policies and structures.

spite of such external forms of pressure on China, foreign companies have continued to suffer from trademark theft, trolls and counterfeiting. Actually, as we shall see below, the phenomena of trademark theft and counterfeiting have more and more extended from larger foreign companies and reputed brands to businesses of any form and size.

The typified reaction from the West starts with the assumption that there is something wrong with China. China IP has to be changed to look like and work as the IP systems in the west. The first problem with such an approach is that it ignores the fact that IP is not just a legal issue. IP rights are first and foremost a business issue. The abstraction of the IPR dialogue from its natural business context may just result in sterile discussions. There is in fact no doubt that in practical terms, years of IPR unilateral threats and dialogue initiated from the West have brought little to fruition.[10]

More serious, and with negative consequences for foreign businesses, is the fact that such an approach will prevent them from learning more about how business is done in China and how its legal system works. This governmental or MNC pressure on China's authorities has rather encouraged scapegoating China as a way to justify the failure of such lobbying attempts or their enforcement strategies. The legal profession is also to be blamed. The messages we have given to foreign companies were political, rather than business oriented. We have been often carried along by the blame game, thus failing to inform and guide businesses through China's legal and business peculiarities. When it comes to protecting trademark rights and more in general all IP rights in China, we should abandon the political lenses, learn the rules and play the game according to the laws and practice we have in place here, rather than those we would like to have.

If we narrow this discussion down to trademark protection in China, an overview of the recent history of trademark theft and infringement, read without biased lenses, shows that the first reason for the failure of western companies to secure proper trademark portfolios was due *in primis* to their lack of knowledge of Chinese trademark laws and practice, their naivety when doing business in China, the blind trust in local partners without understanding the Chinese ways and thus taking the needed precautions. If foreign companies deny they have made mistakes, then they will be bound to repeat them again, and this is what has often happened to our businesses here in China. Therefore, the fundamental lesson here is "knowledge-first." Chinese IP and civil laws are all well translated into English and are quite accessible in addition to the relevant case law. There are plenty of examples from which others could learn. Nonetheless, we still nowadays continue to repeat the same mistakes and to blame China for it. Phenomena such as trademark theft and trademark trolls have repeated themselves in the last decade with increasing frequency. However, in the West, instead of wondering whether we foreigners were maybe doing something not quite right, we have spent most of our energy blaming China. Such common negative experiences have indeed contributed to create a shared perception that all that was wrong was the Chinese legal

10. Andrew C. Mertha, The Politics of Piracy, Intellectual Property in Contemporary China, 4 (Cornell Paperbacks 2005). One of the reasons for such failure is that local economic interests in China tend to prevail over foreign trade pressure.

system. This has prevented companies from doing some critical work, consider mistakes and adjust their strategies to concrete business and legal parameters.

The author is not here to justify China at all costs. As the readers shall see through this book, there are plenty of examples of bad legislation and bad decisions, all attributable to a less than ideal legal system. The goal of this book is to concretely help foreign businesses get it right with IP in China, based on the legal system as it is. It is not the goal of this book to discuss the system in itself and how it can be improved, but rather to help others understand and use it more efficiently as it is, thus reducing such a critical risk factor of doing business in China. A brief history of trademark protection in China over the last 20 years shall be an introduction to the major topics of this book which are trademark theft, trademark infringement and counterfeiting. A historic perspective will also put such topics in context with the ever changing business environment in China.

[A] On the Origins of Trademark Theft

Trademark theft, also referred to as trademark squatting, grabbing and hijacking, occurs when a Chinese party files and registers a trademark identical to that of a foreign right holder who did not timely register or has completely neglected the registration in China of that trademark right. A review of a number of trademark theft cases involving famous foreign brands, starting at the end of the nineties and continuing to this very day, has brought this phenomenon to global attention. Outraged western media reports and popular reactions mostly blamed Chinese thieves and the Chinese legal system as solely responsible for such occurrences. Meanwhile, the spread of the internet in China allowed Chinese thieves to extend their reach to less famous brands, all the way down to completely unknown and new foreign brands not even yet present in China. Again, the critical reaction to this phenomenon has been political and directed towards the Chinese government for not taking measures to prevent it. The latest effects of such debate are reflected by some new provisions of the trademark law of 2014 which are aimed at reducing the economic incentives of stealing trademarks with the purpose of filing troll lawsuits as a move to pressure the legitimate right holder to buy back the stolen trademark at a very high price. Practically, the only reform that could stop this phenomenon, which requires the trademark system to switch the determination and award of trademark ownership and exclusivity from a first to file ownership to first to create/use model is not foreseeable anytime soon in the near future. Therefore, the protection of trademarks in China against theft is left to an array of legal tools actionable by the usurped right holder after the stolen trademark has been applied for registration or has been already registered. In this context, the same outraged reactions have accompanied many decisions of the Chinese trademark authorities denying, for example, recognition of well-known status to foreign trademarks, or to resort generously to presumptions of bad faith intent by the grabber as ground for oppositions and invalidations.

It is certainly true that the Chinese system, especially by adopting the first to file principle, exposes itself to the risk of grabbing. However, we cannot blame China for making such a choice. It is a legally available form of rights acquisition, common to Western countries as well, such as the US for patent rights for instance. It is actually a choice that provides a certain degree of certainty as to trademark ownership in the country with most trademark filings per year in the world.[11] It is in fact disputable that there would be less trademark grabbing in China if we had no first to file system. First, switching to a first to create/use system will also not prevent the grabbing of trademarks. Trademark thieves can still file other's brands in China. Again, the focus is on reaction rather than prevention. In this context, it is therefore disputable again whether the usurped right holder will have the ability to prove his prior use. The critical issue here is the fact that ownership can only be disputed before a Chinese civil court. Such a procedure is longer and surely more expensive than a trademark opposition or invalidation. Also, due to the peculiarities of the Chinese civil procedure in the matter of acquisition of evidence formed abroad. Evidence of use outside China would have to be acquired in legalized form, i.e., through a complex process involving notaries in China and abroad as well as the Chinese consular authorities in the country of evidence formation. Only such formally assumed evidence can enter a civil dispute on trademark ownership. If we consider this current situation, it makes little economic sense to switch to a first-to-use system in China.

Other tools such as screening of applicants and filed documents are already in place but, as in other trademark systems, play only a marginal role in prevention. No trademark system has an interest to dry out trademark filing by putting too many obstacles in front of the applicants. No legal system wants to make the exercise of a right practically difficult, without nullifying the effective existence of that right. Trademarks are important tools in all economies, and restricting the access to trademarks based on the identity of people or other filtering tools may in the end prejudice more the applicants in good faith than the ones in bad faith.

The focus switches therefore to the efficacy of the legal tools provided by the Chinese law to recover stolen trademarks. This topic will be analyzed in depth in the chapter dedicated specifically to trademark theft and remedial strategies. Here it is sufficient to say that remedies such as opposition and invalidation require certain amount of evidence, also in a given form if acquired outside of China, and that bad faith cannot be easily presumed unless certain evidentiary burdens have been met by the opposing or invalidating party as to the existence of at least a certain reputation of the stolen brand or that of certain links between the prior right holder and the grabber. Foreign brands have since long complained that the law was not clear and surely insufficient to protect trademark rights, and that trademark authorities have misused it to protect Chinese economic interests. The trademark law is far from perfect, but that is true for all legal systems in the world. Until a few years ago, we may have with reason criticized the Chinese authorities for being too slow in adapting the law to the changes of business practices. However, this is no longer true. Laws have been changed and

11. According to WIPO in 2014, the trademark applications in China amounted to two million two hundred thousand, of which 1,997,014 filed by Chinese resident, 107,520 by nonresident and 140,355 by abroad applicants. *See* WIPO Statistical Country profiles http://www.wipo.int/ipstats/en/statistics/country_profile/profile.jsp?code=CN (2014).

now more and more judicial interpretations by the Supreme People's Court (SPC) have been issued in clarification of many disputed legal interpretations. Also, administrative regulations are constantly updated to face new challenges and improve the protection of trademark rights. Recently, the trademark administrative bodies have utilized corrective interpretational tools that have increased the number of successful recovery actions by foreign right holders against trademark thieves.

In this very first chapter, a number of cases and trends in the history of trademark grabbing will be presented in order to isolate certain common patterns and prove that aside from certain malfunctions of the trademark system, a substantial amount of responsibilities for such historic failures laid with the brands, which had not properly anticipated the risks and dangers of the Chinese legal system and had adopted ineffective strategies and reactions to the theft of their rights.

This overview will highlight a number of critical issues and errors affecting the trademark strategy of many foreign companies in China. It will also be evident that such critical errors are not attributable to the Chinese legal system, and could have been avoided had the foreign parties obtained good knowledge of the Chinese law, its application, and more generally, the way business is done in China. More and better knowledge of these features will surely help foreign brand owners to prepare strategy that realistically consider and elaborate the risks of the Chinese legal and business landscape, without assumptions or wishful thinking, as has been so often the case in the past.

It is important to notice that the following is only a selection of a large number of cases that involved famous foreign brands in China since the nineties. We selected a number of examples with the aim of introducing some relevant concepts and issues that will later be covered by the book. The list is therefore not exhaustive of all the stories of trademark theft still circulating in the west. At the end of the chapter, we will mention some more cases for the sake of completeness and reference them for those who wish to research them in more depth.

Ultimately, the information about each case can be collected from many newspaper articles and online publications in both Chinese and English. For this reason, we did not quote all of them here.

[B] The 1990s

At its very beginning, the phenomenon of trademark was characterized by cases of trademark theft implemented by Chinese competitors, often small and medium enterprises operating in the same industry as the foreign company, producing the same kinds of goods. This type of trademark theft has thereafter remained a constant, with hundreds of Western companies facing such challenges right up to the current decade.

Ferrari – 1995

On January 4, 1995, Jiajian Business Department applied to China's Trademark Office for the registration of the "Graphics of Running Horse" mark. Within the legal contestable period, FERRARI Corporation submitted an opposition application to the

Trademark Office against the "Graphics of Running Horse" application, claiming its similarity to the famous "FERRARI and Running Horse" graphic logo. However, such logo had not been registered in China and the China's Trademark Office and the State Trademark Review and Adjudication Board (TRAB) rejected the opposition. Not satisfied with the ruling, FERRARI Corporation took the State TRAB to the No. 1 Intermediate People's Court in Beijing.

FERRARI Corporation claimed that the "FERRARI" and "FERRARI and Graphics of Running Horse" trademarks both constituted its famous logo, enjoying a good reputation on the world scene, and being very familiar to the relevant consumers in China. The "Graphics of Running Horse" trademark owned by Jiajian Business Department was to be seen as similar to the above-said trademarks owned by FERRARI Corporation in respect of the same goods.

After a hearing, the No. 1 Intermediate People's Court in Beijing judged that FERRARI Corporation did not provide evidence proving the above trademarks' use in China and the establishment of a well-known reputation. It just submitted the certificates of the registration of relevant trademarks in China and abroad, and the catalog of products in foreign countries, which was insufficient to prove that these trademarks were popular to the relevant public in China or enjoyed a good reputation. Therefore, the court dismissed FERRARI Corporation's request for recognizing "FERRARI and Graphics of Running Horse" trademark as a "well-known trademark."

In such early decisions, both the TRAB and the administrative judges adopted a very formalistic approach to the law. They required a very high degree of notoriety for the brand to be considered well known and hinged this notoriety on intensive use of the brand during a long period of time. We must not forget the rules for the determination of well-known status of trademarks at that time. Today, any administrative body dealing with opposition or invalidation matters, as well as civil court, can declare a trademark to be well known. However, back in the nineties, the determination of well-known trademark could be made only by a special administrative body at the end of a lengthy procedure. This explains the high formalistic approach by the trademark authorities in this case. It was rumored in those years that the trademark authorities were considering well known only those foreign brands that had been intensively used in China for over a decade.

In such a case, the brand owner should have first considered whether it should have occupied the class of goods coming into question in this case by his own timely application. This would have prevented the act of theft and the following embarrassment of the running horse of Ferrari being considered unknown to the relevant Chinese public. A brand owner should know the law and its application at any time. The situation of the recognition of well-known status in 1995 should have been considered by Ferrari as a factor in determining the construction of its portfolio. Blaming the Chinese authorities for applying the law to the extent known at that time seems to only serve the purpose of covering up internal planning mistakes. A careful knowledge and China focused planning of the filing strategy, use and enforcement of that trademark adapted to the peculiar circumstances is a must in order to avoid such mistake. It is also important to observe that the Chinese legal peculiarities as to the application of the law, the level of evidence required to obtain well-known recognition and how this was to be first obtained, were not kept secrets and could have been known and correctly appreciated by Ferrari as by any foreign company coming to China.

Hermes – 1995

A 15-year famous trademark battle started in 1995 when Guangdong-based clothing company Dafeng Garment Factory applied to the Chinese Trademark Office for the registration of the trademark "爱玛仕" (AI Ma SHI) for clothing products. The application later passed the board's preliminary review and was announced to the public.

Hermes had registered its English name and pattern in China back in 1977, but it never registered its Chinese name as a trademark. The French company filed opposition against the trademark board in 1997 over the trademark "爱玛仕, " claiming its similarity to the Chinese name of Hermes "爱马仕" based on both visual and phonetic similarity. Indeed the two trademarks have the same pronunciation and differ only for the central character. Even that one is actually almost identical in both names. The trademark board rejected Hermes' appeal and approved the Chinese company's registration in 2001.

In 2009, Hermes once again took action against the registered hostile trademark by filing a request for its invalidation, arguing that its Chinese name had enjoyed a high reputation around the world since the 1970s and asking the board to cancel the disputed trademark. However, Hermes' application was rejected for a second time. At the time of filing the invalidation, the sole argument left to Hermes was that of filing invalidation grounded on the assumption that its trademark had been well known prior to the date of filing of the hostile mark back in 1997. In fact, trademark invalidation is subjected to a five-year statute of limitation counting down from the date of registration of the hostile trademark. The only exception is an invalidation based on an unregistered well-known trademark, which is not subjected to any statute of limitation. In this case, Hermes had decided to move back against the hostile trademark well over eight years after its registration and had thus no choice but using well-known ground as the main and only argument to support its invalidation request. Also, it argued that the disputed trademark was an imitation of its Chinese name and was obtained through "deceptive means." With retrospective insight, it was an action doomed to failure for several reasons. It hinged the whole success on the weakest of its arguments, the well-known status of its Chinese trademark. It was indeed a weak argument because back then, as most brands did and many still do today, Hermes had failed to really effectively use and establish its Chinese name in the Chinese market. It was not realistic to expect the trademark examiners to believe the contrary. The action lacked also perspective, likely due to the poor knowledge Hermes had collected of its counterpart. The resorting to the argument of bad faith registration by deceptive means, confused means with intentions and was a very weak argument. It would likely be a weak argument today as well. We will amply discuss these legal issues in the following chapters.

Therefore, it was no surprise that the invalidation was rejected. The decision stated that most of the evidence presented by Hermes took place after the disputed trademark had been registered. I think this is self-explanatory of the very bad legal judgment of Hermes in planning this action. Also, the evidence consisted mainly in media reports about the Chinese name of Hermes in Hong Kong, and therefore this was failing to prove Hermes was well known among consumers on the Chinese mainland. Besides, Hermes also failed to provide evidence showing the disputed trademark had been acquired illegally. It is evident from this short summary that Hermes response to the theft had been mostly a gut reaction based on mere legal considerations. Hermes had failed to properly assess and apply the three main rules of engagement we will discuss here in this book. It did not properly assess its own alleged prior right's strengths and weaknesses (First Rule of Engagement: Know yourself). It failed to properly assess the status and weaknesses/strengths of the infringer (Second Rule of Engagement: Know Your Enemy), and eventually, it also missed several legal points (i.e., delayed invalidation, use of illicit means to determine the bad faith intent), which turned in the presentation to the trademark authorities of a rather weak case (Third Rule of Engagement: Know the Battlefield).

Castel – 1998

This case is an example of a troll action based on a stolen trademark. Although this case will be dealt with in more details in the following chapters, we provide an outline of the facts here.

In this case, a trademark infringement lawsuit was filed against the notorious French winemaker "Castel Frere" by the Chinese wine distributor Panati Wine (Shanghai) Co., Ltd regarding the Chinese trademark Kasite (卡斯特), a phonetic rendition of Castel in Chinese.

The origin of the case dates back to the late 1990s, when Wenzhou-born entrepreneur (and allegedly famous trademark-squatter) Li Daozhi, started the wine distribution company Panati Wine to introduce initially Spanish, then French wines to the Chinese wine market. He also started applying for the registration of trademarks like the Chinese name Kasite in 1998. Castel began bottling to China in 1999, and the Chinese translation of its name was known as Kasite by Chinese wine consumers. In reaction to the theft, the French company successfully submitted nonuse cancellation request in 2005, nevertheless losing the appeal filed by Li.

The trademark infringement lawsuit was filed by Li in 2009, claiming a compensation of CNY 40 million (over USD 5 million) from Castel for its unlawful use of the trademark Kasite, and the case ended up with the landmark judgment coming from the Wenzhou Higher People's Court, according to whom Castel had to stop using the Chinese trademark Kasite on its wines and, more important, to pay a fine of CNY 33.73 million (over USD 5 million) to Panati Wine and its owner Li Daozhi.

After the initial verdict, both plaintiff and defendant submitted appeals, and the case was brought before the Zhejiang Provincial Higher Court, which upheld the first instance judgment, ordering to Castel to publish an apology. The case was then brought to the SPC for a retrial. Meanwhile, Castel not only had lost the use of its established Chinese name but also had continued suffering economic losses related to the theft. In 2016, the SPC issued a judgment cutting down the damage awards from the original CNY 33 Million to merely CNY 500,000 (equivalent to USD 90,000). Although the attorneys of Castel claimed this to be a victory, in practice it was Pyrrhic one: the damage to the brand had long since been made and damages had been suffered independently from the liquidation of the original damage award. Most harmful however, was the loss of the trademark "Kasite" along with its good will. All this simply because Castel had not registered its brand or identified the existence of a trademark with that name in a timely manner. Doing either of these things could have helped the wine maker to choose another one long before "Kasite" had turned into a company asset.

Land Rover – 1999

In 1999, Geely, a large Chinese car company registered three trademarks covering the phrase "陆虎" (Lu Hu) in class 12 covering goods such as cars, sports cars and motors. The characters literally mean continental tiger. Land Rover claimed to have been using them since the early 1990s, and that Geely had registered them in bad faith, openly challenging the first to file Chinese system. While one of these marks had been registered in the meanwhile, two were opposed by Land Rover.

After a failed attempt to reach an agreement for the transfer of the trademarks to Land Rover, the latter also filed an invalidation action against Geely's mark in 2004 based on bad faith and likelihood of confusion. In July 2010, after a six-year battle and a first instance rejection of Land Rover's claims in the opposition, the invalidation was also rejected by the TRAB. Land Rover brought evidence of use of the trademark 陆虎 trademark, but it was not sufficient to support the claim that their "continental tiger" trademark was well known before Geely registered it in 1999.

Geely's mark had previously survived two nonuse cancellation actions in 2004 and 2006, and a lawsuit filed to overturn the TRAB decision is now still pending.

This case is a typical example of trademark theft by a large competitor with preventive aims. Geely had thus hampered the further expansion of Land Rover by forcing the latter to give up the use of a trademark that was gaining foothold in the Chinese market. It is also typical of such cases, where the thief was a large competitor, to see attempts at negotiated solutions. It is easy to see now how such negotiations never had a chance to succeed because there was no amount of money Land Rover could have paid that would have convinced Geely to remove a far more valuable commercial advantage. Maybe, only the offer of a joint partnership could have persuaded Geely to give up its prey. However, that was not the wish of Land Rover, which was not ready to give in to such business blackmail. In the end, negotiation served the purposes of Geely more than the interests of Land Rover, which had thus weakened the following invalidation action. Such an action should have been filed before opening negotiations, so that it could have been used as a sort of leverage for Land Rover to obtain some concessions.

In conclusion, during this first phase in the nineties, grabbers appeared to be legitimately registered companies with competing interests, largely motivated by the intention of free riding famous brands for quick illicit profit or to prevent foreign brands from further expanding their business in the Chinese market. They targeted the portion of foreign brands that had not yet been registered or used intensively as trademarks in China in the same classes of products and services occupied by the corresponding foreign brand.

[C] Trademark Theft Evolves

Since the beginning of the twenty-first century, trademark theft sees the emerging of even more "ruthless" cases of trademark theft, not only perpetrated by competitors using other's trademarks to increase sales or launch their own products, but also from companies which were not apparently competitors of the foreign brands. For instance, in some cases, famous brands were registered in classes which were not traditionally related to the famous brands products or services. This resulted not only in the theft of such trademarks, the Chinese name or parts of logos, but also in the theft of the official foreign name in different classes, concerning totally dissimilar kinds of products, and regardless of the danger of nonassociation between trademark and product made by the consumer. The intent of these new wave of thefts seemed to be aiming at exploiting the "less-prudent" part of the public, a large group of the population which trusts more the trademark itself (or more in general, something which "sounds familiar") than the kind of goods to whom such brand is normally associated.

Moreover, an additional new trend seems to find roots in the very beginning of the new century – trademark thefts coming from individuals ("serial" thieves looking for a profitable agreement rather than a real commercial exploitation of the trademark) rather than companies. By 2005, this trend will become the predominant for of trademark grabbing.

Pfizer – 2001

Pfizer, Inc. hit it big with its blockbuster drug, Viagra, in the US and many other countries. It had also been targeting China as a large market for Viagra for years, as it is shown by the investment of over 500 million dollars in the People's Republic of China (PRC) for production facilities as well as the opening of a research and development center in Shanghai. In spite of such investments and expansion plans in China, Pfizer had neglected applying the Chinese name of Viagra, Weige (伟哥) (which means "Great Older Brother"), for trademark registration in China. Such name was coined and accepted spontaneously by the Chinese market as the official Chinese name for Viagra, in spite of the effort of Pfizer to impose WaiAike (万艾可) as the official name of the medicine. Pfizer registered the Chinese name WaiAike (万艾可), a transliteration of Viagra, but it never reached the popularity and appeal of Weige. On the other hand, Weige was owned by a Chinese pharmaceutical company, who first registered the mark when the Chinese media coined it as a transliteration of Viagra. Despite many attempts to challenge the Weige mark, Pfizer has been unsuccessful in gaining ownership of the mark. Pfizer's difficulties illustrate a method that is frequently used by trademark squatters to infringe on a trademark owner's rights. Because English trademarks are commonly referred to by a Chinese transliteration, once an unofficial Chinese-language name gains popularity, a Chinese entity may obtain a registration for that name before the original trademark owner can do so. The risk of such type of squatting is increased by the natural intricacies of the Chinese language. There are in fact numerous similar characters, forms and sounds, that can be combined to create similarly looking and sounding combinations of characters for one English name! Meanings can also be engineered and thus manipulated, like in the case of Weige v. WaiAiKe. This creates great opportunities for trademark squatters. Trademark squatters can thus manipulate the form, sound or meaning of a trademark so that they can register confusingly similar marks of their own.

Soon after Pfizer officially launched Viagra in the US in 1998, Viagra pills were illegally smuggled into China. Thus, Viagra became very popular in China as soon as it had become available in the US and Europe. It was therefore at the very beginning of the nineties, when Viagra had not yet entered the Chinese market, that the Chinese media coined the transliteration Weige. Pfizer failed to realize that because of the US media coverage of the launch of Viagra in the mid to late 1990s, the Chinese media would not use the word "Viagra," but instead would give the product a Chinese transliterated name. Still nowadays, many foreign companies fail to appreciate the difference between markets in which English is the native or dominant language and markets in which the native population does not speak English or other western languages. In China as well as in other Asian countries, consumers will likely refer to a foreign product's name with a local colloquial name, no matter how famous or prestigious the foreign name may be worldwide. It is obvious that due to the dominance of Chinese language in China, Chinese media and consumers will always use a Chinese transliteration of an English trademark rather than the English word itself, more so if the English name is visually and phonetically unattractive to Chinese consumers. This practice in China even applies to the most famous international brands in the world, including Coca-Cola and McDonald's, whose Chinese names are more well known as trademarks than their English one. Given the dominance of Chinese language, Pfizer could have predicted that once Viagra became a frequent topic of discussion in the international media, the Chinese media and Chinese consumers - not Pfizer - would give Viagra a Chinese name (Weige), which was a transliteration of the English word. This transliteration occurred before Pfizer attempted to register a Chinese trademark for Viagra in China.

Once Pfizer realized that Weige had become so popular in the Chinese speaking world, it immediately sought for its registration as a trademark in China but was obstructed by prior competing applications. One month after Pfizer's launch of Viagra in the US in April 1998, several Chinese companies filed trademark registrations for Weige with the Chinese Trademark office. Viamen in particular, filed the first application for Weige on May 20, 1998. Pfizer applied for its Weige trademark in China less than four months later. Viamen's application was therefore the first, and was awarded the Weige trademark on June 21, 2002. Pfizer filed an objection, but the TRAB affirmed the decision of the Trademark Office. Considering that by 2002 the brand equity of the

Weige trademark was estimated to be between USD 85 and USD 120 million,[12] the decision of the TRAB had awarded Viamen a significant business and financial asset. In October 2005, Pfizer appealed the TRAB decision by filing an administrative lawsuit with the Beijing First Intermediate People's Court on the grounds that it owned the rights to the Weige trademark in China. It argued that even though its trademark application was later in time, Weige had achieved fame as Pfizer's trademark under the well-known trademarks doctrine in China. Pfizer further claimed that this fame was achieved prior to Viamen's application and created rights in Pfizer and Viamen's unauthorized use of the Weige trademark violated Article 10 of China's Anti-Unfair Competition Law. In January 2007, the Beijing court rejected Pfizer's claim that it owned the famous trademark Weige, and in July 2009, Pfizer lost its final appeal on this issue in the SPC.

Aside from questionable litigation choices, for instance the decision not to pursue a stronger strategy on ownership's claims through civil litigation, the major lesson that a foreign company can learn from this case is the following: it is strategically critical to choose and control the use of the Chinese transliterations of a brand, and that it is never too soon to do so. Even if a foreign company is not planning to launch a product in the Chinese market at present, it should still plan ahead by selecting immediately, along with the birth of the original English brand, its Chinese transliteration and make sure that such name is applied for trademark registration along with the English one, and that it is also used in China. If there is not an actual business, the company should still make sure to refer to that Chinese name when dealing with Chinese business partners, at exhibitions in China, on business cards, websites etc. In the Viagra case, the cultural error of Pfizer was that of having neglected the fact that Chinese consumers would have coined their own name of Viagra if Pfizer neglected the job. In substance, the selection and use of a trademark are first and foremost a business issue. Pfizer had failed to properly analyze and assess the use of a Chinese name for its product and had to pay dear business consequences for that. The recovery of the stolen trademark was only the legal aspect of a larger business issue.

Haagen-Dasz – 2003: A Winning Case[13]

On June 3, 2003, a Chinese company and apparel factory applied to register "Haager-Dasz" as a trademark for clothing items. The application was preliminarily approved for registration and opposed by Haagen-Dazs. One of the challenges here was that the goods of the stolen trademark were in a class of goods (clothing in class 25) rather different from that of the original brand (ice cream in class 30). In order for the original brand owner to succeed, two conditions were required and are still required today in

12. Daniel C. K. Chow, Lessons from Pfizer's Disputes over Its Viagra Trademark in China, 27 Maryland Journal of International Law 82 (2012). *See also* Yahong Li et al., Viagra in China: A Prolonged Battle Over Intellectual Property Rights, Asia Case Research Center & Columbia Business School, 10 (2010).
13. A similar case was the one involving the theft of the "Chivas"(Scotch Whiskey) brand by a Wenzhou businessman in 2003, also for goods in class 25. The story of this case seems quite a faithful copy of the Haagen-Dazs case.

such a case: (i) the two disputed brands are identical; and (ii) the allegedly squatted one is well known or enjoys a certain reputation in China. The trademark board found that the materials provided by Haagen-Dazs failed to prove that it had been "well known with China's relevant public and lacked high reputation." "Haager-Dasz" was thus granted registration. The classification of goods has, in fact, the purpose of distinguishing the origin of products so that in principle, even two identical marks can coexist if they were filed in different classes. The only exception is the well-known trademark, whose notoriety reduces the gap in goods/classes differences in the eyes of a consumer. Even identical marks can coexist on disparate goods like this, and since the clothing company was first to file this application, it would ordinarily be entitled to this registration.

In the revision before TRAB, the American rights holder made many efforts to prove a certain degree of notoriety in China that could bridge the gap between the classes in dispute. However, TRAB ruled for the clothing company, finding that General Mills' well-known brand argument was unconvincing. As too many times seen in the cases quoted above, the problem is not that the marks are dissimilar or even that the foreign brand is not famous, but rather that the foreign company had insufficient evidence to prove its well-known status at the time of the theft.

After the TRAB ruled against General Mills, the administrative decision was appealed to Beijing's First Intermediate Court, which has exclusive jurisdiction over these appellate cases. The court ruled the other way, exceptionally striking down the TRAB decision. The ruling was based on the assumption of class proximity and notoriety. It is possible for an ice cream and food company to have a line of merchandising products including clothing. If a certain degree of popularity is proved, such assumption of class proximity due to a consideration of actual business model in which chain stores of a world brand expand into merchandising, can indeed become effective against trademark theft. However, as we shall see, few brands can claim to be able to use such arguments to win their rights back. Most Small-Middle Enterprises (SMEs) brands will be too far unknown to enjoy such a broader protection.

Sony Ericson – 2003

In March 2003, Liu Jianjia submitted his application to the Chinese Trademark Office for the registration of the trademark "索爱" (Suo Ai). On August 7, 2004, the Trademark Bureau approved the registration of the disputed trademark in class 9 for video-disc players, amplifiers and other products. In June 2005, Sony Ericson China applied for revocation of the disputed Trademark, holding that the trademark "索爱" is a famous trademark in China owned by Sony Ericson China. In November 2007, the invalidation of Sony Ericson China was rejected by the TRAB.

Sony Ericson China filed an appeal with the No. 1 Intermediate People's Court of Beijing and claimed that before the application date for registration of the disputed trademark "索爱," had been deemed by the relevant public as the abbreviation for the well-known trademarks "索尼爱立信" and "Sony Ericsson," and the disputed trademark was solely and definitely symbolizing the Sony Ericson Group (including Sony Ericson China) and its products. Sony Ericson alleged that the applicant had filed the trademark with the unfair intent of preventing the competition to use its legitimate prior rights when doing business in China. The appellant argued that the registration and use of the disputed trademark would cause confusion or misunderstanding in the relevant public regarding the source of the products.

The No. 1 Intermediate People's Court of Beijing affirmed that since December 2002 to the application date for registration, news reports and comments of different types of "索爱" mobile phone and other "索爱" electronic products had appeared on various websites, and the manufacturer of these products is Sony Ericson or Sony Ericson China. This means that in daily life, "索爱," as the abbreviation for "索尼爱立信," has been widely used by the relevant public and media, and has been recognized by the consumers since the establishment of the Sony Ericson China and the appearance of its electronic products. "索爱" has become a symbol of product source and quality, which will naturally affect Sony Ericson China, and it can be deemed as Sony Ericson China's use of this trademark. Thus, "索爱" had become a trademark used by Sony Ericson China, and the hostile applicant should have known that given that he had been engaged in the trade of electronic products for many years. Therefore, the court overruled the TRAB decision and sent the case back to TRAB. That was not the end of the story though.

The holder of the registered trademark filed an appeal with the High People's Court of Beijing and claimed that the administrative judgment was based on a wrong interpretation of the evidence provided by Sony Ericson. In particular, it maintained that Sony Ericson China had never used the disputed trademark according to the laws of China.

The High People's Court of Beijing held that, the claim of Sony Ericson China was based on the news reports and comments about the use of "索爱" for mobile phones and other products on some websites, and according to these news reports and comments, the manufacturer of these "索爱" products is Sony Ericson or Sony Ericson China. However, the court observed that these news reports or comments were not from Sony Ericson China, but by third parties. However, there was no evidence in the case that by the application date for registration, Sony Ericson China had conducted any manufacturing, selling or advertising activity involving the name "索爱" for mobile phone products, and up to about October 2007, Sony Ericson China had not officially taken any action to acknowledge and recognize "索爱" as the abbreviation for its company name or for its mobile phones or other electronic products. Since Sony Ericson China had never used "索爱" as its trademark for commercial purpose, the affirmation made by the first instant court was found to be flawed and was overruled. The trademark of the third party thus became a fully valid trademark.

Like in Pfizer, Sony Ericsson had not approached the issue of a Chinese transliteration with due caution and attention to the Chinese market. The trademark 索尼爱立信 of Sony Ericsson is a sound transliteration of the English name of the company. It is a long trademark that has no particular appeal from a marketing point of view. Typically foreign companies will let their local Chinese lawyers suggest a Chinese name transliteration. Normally this starts very casually when their foreign trademark or trade name has to be translated for administrative filing purpose. As in many other cases, the transliteration is mostly based on the faithful reproduction of the sounds of the trade name in English. Sony Ericsson is a long name and therefore it was transliterated with four characters. Such transliteration is indeed acceptable for use as a trade name in all administrative filings including trademark filings. Is it also an attractive brand for potential Chinese consumers and customers? In the present case, it evidently was not, given that the same Sony Ericsson admitted that the specialized press and the internet were using the abbreviation 索爱 to refer to the products of Sony Ericsson. This case shows that many foreign companies do not give sufficient thoughts to their branding strategies in China and do not make sufficient efforts to create Chinese names and trademarks that are appealing to their Chinese targeted market. The result is that the market finds the right name. In this case, a four characters' name, with little attractiveness was reshaped into a more Chinese-friendly format by shortening it to two characters, both referring to syllables SO and ER of Sony Ericsson. It is in fact very common in China to shorten name combinations by using the characters that most distinguish the two combined names: for example, the Beijing-Tianjin Highway is called Jing-Jing Highway!

In summary, the trademark challenge in this case was again first and foremost a business challenge. Sony Ericsson had failed to properly, and in a timely manner, conceive and protect an appealing Chinese brand, and had let the market choose one while failing to recognize that and secure it by filing for trademark first. There is little room to criticize the final decision of the Beijing Higher Court, in that there was indeed no direct evidence of the use of "索爱" by Sony Ericsson and at that time in particular, notoriety was recognized only if there had been an intensive use of the trademark by the holder.

Remy Martin – 2003 and Chanel – 2004

In both cases, Chinese parties had filed for the registration of Chinese names corresponding identically to those of the foreign companies, but in classes of goods different from those of the foreign brand. For instance, in the Remi Martin Case, the "usurper" had registered the name 人头马 (Ren Tou Ma) on January 3, 2003, designating the goods in class 9 for computers, and portable computers, while Remy Martin was registered for alcohol products. In the Chanel case, the usurper had applied for the registration of "香奈儿CHANEL及图" (Xiang Nai Er CHANEL & Device) in class 19 designating the goods ceramic tiles and tiles in 2004, while Chanel's cited marks were registered in Classes 3, 18, 25 on goods such as perfumes, clothes, bags, etc. In both cases, the goods of the stolen applications were different from those of the classes of goods of the original trademarks. In both cases, the decisive legal issues were the notoriety of the original trademarks and whether such notoriety was strong enough to bridge the gap between different classes, and create a presumption that the hostile applicant should have known he was stealing a famous brand. The two cases had a very different outcome: Remy Martin argued that the claimed goods of "Ren Tou Ma" were similar to those of the cited marks, even though they fall in different international classes. The arguments centered on the assumption that people who buy alcohol, or clothing also buy computers because these are all products of daily use of a normal person. Both the Trademark Office and TRAB recognized to Remy Martin a certain degree of notoriety but refused to extend the existing trademark registration to goods of class 9. The TRAB stated that "it doesn't mean that the protection on well-known marks should be expanded unlimitedly, and instead, the protection must follow the rule of fair competition and consider the interests of the trademark owners and consumers." The evidence submitted by Remy Martin could only prove the wide and continuous usage and promotion of Remy Martin's cited marks on alcohol products, but not on computers or similar goods. As a result, the relevant public in China still can distinguish Ren Tou Ma from the cited marks, and likelihood of confusion does not exist.

In the Chanel case, the French company was able to overrule the initially unfavorable decision of the Trademark Office. The TRAB concluded that Chanel's well-known trademark "Xiang Nai Er" in Chinese, has been widely acknowledged among Chinese consumers, and the well-known status of CHANEL in Chinese is such that the opponent can be presumed to be in bad faith when filing that trademark. In this case, the degree of notoriety recognized to Chanel was sufficient to bridge the gap between the classes at issue.

What makes these cases interesting is first of all the fact that, unlike the Sony Ericsson case, the hostile applicants here were not competitors but professional squatters driven by the occasional motive of trying to make some money by exploiting someone else's famous brand. These cases heralded a new wave of hostile trademark grabbing of reputed brands in different classes. As we shall see, this phenomena further evolved to extend to less famous brands until it degenerated in the actual and most insidious form of trademark squatting that appropriates unfairly of "any" foreign brand even when not famous. Eventually, these two matters are interesting from a mere legal point of view in that they exemplify the legal challenges of proving notoriety and how each decision on a trademark notoriety may vary in its conclusions depending on the degree of such notoriety as perceived by the trademark examiners. It is obvious that trademark law is not rocket science. Subjective impressions and perceptions play an important role and may produce different decisions in apparently similar cases. Such legal technicalities will be more thoroughly analyzed in the following chapters.

New Balance - 2004

On April 24, 2015, Guangzhou Municipal Intermediate People's Court in south China's Guangdong Province ruled that Xinbailun Trade (China) Co., the local sales company for the well-known US sports brand New Balance, must pay the equivalent of USD 16 million for infringing the trademark rights of Zhou Yuelun, a Chinese individual and the owner of the Chinese trademark "Xin Bai Lun" in class 25. In addition to the very high damage compensation and, in order to avoid further consumers' confusion, the Court ordered the Chinese affiliate of New Balance to stop using the "Xin Bai Lun" trademark to manufacture and sell its product in China and required them to publicly apologize for the harm caused to Mr Zhou. The story of this now famous trademark theft and infamous trademark troll infringement lawsuit dated from the end of the nineties. The very recent appeal judgment on June 23, 2016, confirmed the infringement but substantially reduced the damages to an equivalent of about USD 800,000.[14]

The plaintiff, Mr Zhou, registered the trademarks "Bai Lun" in China since 1996 for "clothes, footwear, and headgear" of class 25 of the Chinese Classification System. The name used by the New Balance affiliate was "Xin Bai Lun." "Xin" means "New" in Chinese and "Bai Lun" is a phonetic translation of "Balance." In 2004, Zhou applied to register the trademark "Xin Bai Lun" in class 25, and the application was granted in January 2008. Zhou had an established brand of men's shoes using the names "Bai Lun" and "Xin Bai Lun" that were sold in local Chinese department stores. In 2004, New Balance opposed the registration of Zhou's "Xin Bai Lun" arguing that New Balance had been using an identical version of the mark "Xin Bai Lun," since 2003. The Chinese Trademark Office rejected their opposition and as a result, Zhou's "Xin Bai Lun" was registered in class 25 for clothing, shoes and hats. In spite of the fact that at that time Mr Zhou owned the rights to the "Bai Lun" and "Xin Bai Lun" marks, New Balance continued to use the marks in China on its products and packaging without Mr Zhou's consent. Mr Zhou thus filed a trademark infringement lawsuit that led to the famous 2015 judgment against New Balance.

In the lawsuit, the plaintiff Mr Zhou claimed that New Balance was using "Xin Bai Lun" on shoes without his authorization, and New Balance's unauthorized use led customers to believe that all shoes so marked were Bai Lun shoes. The alleged unauthorized use encompassed also the use of the name "Xin Bai Lun" on New Balance's official China website as well as by printing "Thank you for buying Xin Bai Lun products" on the stores' receipts in China. Zhou maintained that New Balance's behavior hampered his ability to build and develop his own brands "Bai Lun" and "Xin Bai Lun" in China. New Balance rebutted that "Xin Bai Lun" was used in good faith as part of its name and was a direct transliteration of the English "New Balance." New Balance further argued its use of "Xin Bai Lun" as a sale label predated the plaintiff's use of "Xin Bai Lun" in commerce.

The Court opined that the defendants should have known that the "Bai Lun" and "Xin Bai Lun" marks had previously registered in the name of the plaintiff. Furthermore, the Court found that New Balance opposed the registration of the plaintiff's trademark application for "Xin Bai Lun" in 2007, and obviously was aware of the dispute. Finally, the Court determined that since New Balance was aware of the existence of the trademarks of "Bai Lun" and "Xin Bai Lun," and since New Balance continued to trade on the plaintiff's registered trademarks, they did so in bad faith. In view of these findings, the Court rejected New Balance's argument for fair use and first use. The Court also rejected New Balance's argument that "Xin Bai Lun" is a translation of the company name, finding that a proper translation for New Balance should have been "Xin (new) Ping Heng (balance)," which is also the name of the New Balance affiliate, Xin Ping Heng Athletic Shoe, Inc. Finally, the Court pointed out that New Balance previously used another name "Niu Ba Lun" which is the phonetic translation

14. 庭审直击 | 判了：”新百伦”赔偿周乐伦500万元，http://mp.weixin.qq.com/s?__biz=MjM5NzU5ODEzNw==&mid=2665201136&idx=2&sn=872f542cbd63e14da5adce56b5e77b4a&scene=5&srcid=06231vECVvuI4hICGVHH7kcK#rd (June 23, 2016).

of New Balance and therefore found New Balance's argument that "Xin Bai Lun" is the company's name in Mandarin is not supported.

New Balance in this case has committed a number of errors that were common to other cases. As in the previous cases, the lack of knowledge of the Chinese trademark business and legal aspects prevented New Balance from efficiently and timely selecting a proper Chinese name and branding strategy and a certain amount of bad counseled actions likely caused New Balance to fail in protecting such right or even more important, to take appropriate remedial measures. The author does not know the details of the case and can only speculate as to the very early history of the commercial relation between New Balance and its local distributor. However, certain facts from the case and the author's experience of foreign businesses in China allows for some remarks: At the time of entry in the Chinese market New Balance had not conceived any branding strategy for a Chinese name, thus neglecting one important step for successful market penetration. Even if considerations had been made about the Chinese name, there had not been any diligent fact finding. In particular, failure to discover the existence of the "Bai Lun" trademark since 1996, created the base for a bad name selection. A thorough due diligence may have helped selecting another name and trademark which would have avoided the above-described blunders. It often happens that foreign brands entering the Chinese market put little focus on the branding of their Chinese name. Often, the selection of a Chinese name is left to the local staff not correctly guided in a more structured selection process, encompassing trademark conflict verifications, and competitors' monitoring. The Chinese distributor, thus left without specific instructions, will take such important branding and legal decisions. This is a mistake foreign companies should avoid. Selection of a Chinese brand is not second in importance to the selection of their original foreign brand. The cases presented in this chapter and this case in particular, have shown the dire consequences for such mistakes. In this particular matter, another serious mistake was committed when it was decided to continue using Mr Zhou's trademark "Xin Bai Lun" after it had successfully overcome New Balance opposition and become a registered trademark. The error here was to have based the whole opposition and recovery action on flimsy facts. Proper fact finding and in-depth investigations could have provided important information which could have helped determining whether there was a serious risk of a troll action. Knowledge of the "enemy" is one of the three golden Rules of Engagement we will present in this book. Deep knowledge of the counterpart and his business and a thorough intelligence analysis of the facts by experienced professionals that can understand trademark issues in China, could have provided New Balance with appropriate counseling. Lack of proper fact finding and intelligence analysis can lead to wrong decisions with disastrous consequences. Blaming Mr Zhou or the legal system in China will only be of comfort for those who have to save their jobs after such blunders. However, it will not help others avoiding similar mistakes in the future. Foreign companies must accept the fact that they have been making mistakes in China and that lack of trademark protection cannot be blamed only on the Chinese legal system. Only when westerners recognize their mistakes, will they learn from them and understand what needs to be done in order to succeed in their trademark challenges in China. Many authors writing about this case have put the blame on first to file. However, as we explained above, even if there was a first-to-use system in place in China, the outcome of this case would likely not have been any different. The foreign brand had not been the first-to-use brand in China! Even if that had been the case, New Balance had still failed to register that brand and could not have stopped the counterpart to file it as it did. At that point, the dispute was unavoidable anyway. In practice, New Balance should have proved its prior use of the trademark and its prior ownership! Therefore, New Balance can mostly blame itself for this bad case.

Tesla – 2006

In September 2006, Mr Zhan Baosheng, a Chinese businessman, applied for the "Tesla" trademark for goods of class 12 such as "land, air and sea transport vehicles" and was granted registration in June 2009. Another individual, Mr Qiao Weiwei also had registered with success the trademark "TESLA MOTORS," but the trademark covered only rail vehicles, sleighs, airplanes and ships.

As a result of the above prior right, "Tesla" was rejected by the Chinese authorities in its application for the "Tesla" trademark in 2009. This situation had caused delays in Tesla's plan to expand to the Chinese market, including its plan to open a flagship store in Beijing. After 2009, Mr Zhan additionally filed Tesla in other classes as well its Chinese transliteration.

Mr Zhan Baosheng claims he had planned producing electric cars already in 2002, and had chosen the name Tesla in honor of the scientist who invented the alternating current. Tesla, after realizing the mistake committed by forgetting to register its Chinese trademark before it was stolen, started negotiating a settlement with the usurper. Tesla had started offering USD 50,000 and ending the negotiation with a USD 300,000 offer. In 2012, these negotiations failed, while in 2013 Tesla Motors was able to negotiate the transfer of Mr Qiao's trademark. Also, Tesla had to face another challenge, common to many foreign companies in China: Domain name registration was another challenge for Tesla Motors. Mr Zhan had also registered three Tesla domain names: tesla.com.cn, teslamotors.com.cn and tesla.cn, and he used them by filling them with Chinese text, photos of cars and even a T-shaped logo that looks like the one on Tesla models. This created very serious problems to Tesla, which is reliant on web sales.

Meanwhile Tesla had filed cancellation for nonuse against the stolen trademark of Mr Zhan and a copyright infringement lawsuit against Mr Zhan including copyright claims directed against the stolen domain names.[15] However, Mr Zhan appealed such decisions and hit Tesla motors with a troll lawsuit demanding the equivalent of USD 4 million in damage compensation for Tesla trademark infringement. At that time, Tesla shares at the New York Stock Exchange dropped of 1.6%![16] For this reason, Tesla Motors intensified negotiations with Mr Zhan and the parties reached an agreement in

15. INTA, China: Tesla Settles with Chinese Citizen, Vol. 69, INTA Bulletin, 19 (October 15, 2014).
16. Bloomberg News, Tesla sued by businessman claiming China trademark rights, http://www.bloomberg.com/news/articles/2014-07-07/tesla-sued-in-china-for-trademark-infringement (July 9, 2014).

August 2014, agreeing to settle the dispute "completely and amicably." The amount of the settlement was not disclosed.

This case is most interesting in that it shows a more aggressive and to a certain degree a more practical approach to the problem by the foreign brand owner. Tesla has indeed adopted modular and multilevel approaches which at the end obtained the elimination of the threat. Whether this was done without losses, it cannot be said because of lacking data. What remain to be remarked here is that such full-fledged approach, i.e., filing several legal actions to recover the brand to put the infringer under pressure is a good tactic if you are a company like Tesla. Such approach would be less realistic for SMEs or in general companies with tighter budgets. It would be interesting to consider what another company, would have done in such a case, without having the resources of Tesla at its disposal to fight the infringer. This is actually one of the main topics this book will focus on.

[D] Trademark Theft and Nonfamous Brands: The Internet Revolution

The cases reported above are a small selection of the many cases of trademark theft involving famous foreign brands. In the very early nineties, Mars and Kellogg's were among the first prominent victims of trademark theft and infringement. In those cases, the matter was not much that of theft of an identical trademark, but the sale and use of confusingly similar brands, almost a joke of the original one. We can cite here the cases of Lacoste against Crocodile International and that involved Nike and Qiaodian, regarding the Jordan and logo, which saw many failed attempts to invalidate the Chinese Jordan brand. At the same time, the case escalated when Michael Jordan also sued Qiaodan for theft of image and name rights. All these cases ended up in a debacle for the foreign right holders. Similar in legal nature was the Adidas v. Adivon case that started in 2008 and ended in a settlement after five years of battles started in 2008. We can also mention the cases of Mazda in 2010, Tom Ford in 2012 and Victoria's Secret in 2015. The last to come to a negative decision for the right holder was the very famous IPhone case in 2016.[17]

With the ever growing number of trademarks filed in China every year, making China the first country in the world for numbers of trademarks, with ever tightening time constraints for examiners to review filings and procedures, leaving an examiner with about 20 minutes per file,[18] it is indeed possible that trademark theft, especially if it hits SMEs, will often go unchecked for a long time and once detected, remedies may not be sufficient for a just recovery of the stolen brand. It is in such a scenario, together with all the "ignorance" factors which affect foreign trademark strategies as seen in the

17. The usurper in this case had registered the trademark IPhone in China on leather goods back in 2010. Apple started fighting back this registration in 2012 without success. *See* more information in http://money.cnn.com/2016/05/04/technology/apple-trademark-lawsuit-china.

18. Such calculation can be made if each year we count the number of total filings divided by the number of available examiners and the average working time for each examiner, which are all available public data.

example above, that the internet has played the ultimate prank of foreign trademark holders.

In 2005, the trademark database went online. Within a few years, a new profession was born: professional grabbers.

The internet allows professional grabber to monitor foreign companies, see them all with a left click on the screen and couple these results with the corresponding data available in the Trademark Office database. Nothing could be simpler. By sitting at a desk, with no particular preparatory costs, any individual and organization can prevent thousands of foreign companies from entering the Chinese market by simply anticipating them and filing their trademark first in China. The availability of the Trademark Office database online has opened new possibilities to grabbers. Not only famous brands but also any foreign company can become the victim of a serial trademark thief. The motivations and the organizations of grabbers and the strategies to prevent such thefts or recover the stolen trademarks will be the object of the third chapter of this book. It is thus here important to remark how trademark grabbing went from being a "luxury" problem of famous foreign brands to a plague affecting even the least famous ones all over the world. Although the Chinese laws have changed in the last few years and started addressing this issue, it still remains a serious problem, especially because there are no legal ways to prevent it. It will be critical for foreign brands to fine-tune their strategies based on realistic assessments of the business environment and the law, rather than on a resigned repetition of certain common mistakes that surely help infringers to do their job, and do not allow administrative authorities to offer a better protection. For the vast majority of the victims, small-middle enterprises with little access to knowledge or certain more expensive legal remedies, such knowledge of the existence of business and legal strategies to bring about effective solutions in China, becomes even more important. That is why this book was written.

§1.02 A SHORT INTRODUCTION TO TRADEMARK COUNTERFEITING

Counterfeiting of goods and art is as old as the world. When it comes to China, the phenomena of recognized counterfeiting starts in the eighteenth century, when China started to trade with the west. Rich American businessmen ordered counterfeit paintings of George Washington and famous battles of the war of independence from Chinese craftsmen, to the consternation of the legitimate authors.[19] Counterfeiting in China has been linked by westerners, to a tenet of the traditional Confucian education, requiring students to copy and recite works of great role models. Such view is very simplistic and does not consider the complexities of China. It is indeed reductive to attribute the emergence of counterfeiting as imitation of role models, with counterfeiting of goods. As some authors have pointed out, there is no honor in copying industrial

19. Eric Jay Dolin, Debate Jibes Ignore Chinese Counterfeiting's long History, http://blogs.reuters.com/great-debate/2012/10/24/debate-jibes-ignore-chinese-counterfeitings-long-history/ (October 24, 2012).

goods for daily use.[20] Even at the time in which Chinese painters were commissioned to paint portraits of George Washington back in the nineteenth century, emulation of role models was not really the point. The point was simply that there were westerners that found it economically convenient to pay a Chinese painter to obtain a good copy of a popular but expensive western work, and for the Chinese a good occasion to make money in a growing mercantile Asian society. It is also true that certain ways of copying have also a cultural component, like in the case of the cultural dimension of the "Shanzhai" phenomenon. "Shanzhai" is a word coined in the mid years of the new Millennium that refers to the act of counterfeiting in the economic and legal sense. However, very quickly it evolved to incorporate a figurative meaning projecting a cultural dimension of copying, intended as the philosophy of being inspired by the better ones to design and create cheaper and localized version of a more famous product or work.[21] However, this cultural dimension plays no role at all when we refer to the counterfeit of industrial products. Therefore, the major factors influencing the steady growth of the submerged economy of counterfeiting are first and foremost related to the economic and industrial development of China and with the structure of its laws and administrative enforcement system. The latter is of great influence in the practical way foreign brands tend to enforce trademark rights against counterfeiters.

Counterfeiters are moved by economic factors. This explains, for instance, why different types of consumer goods are counterfeited in certain regions: textile and fashion in the south, automotive in the east, heavy machined goods in the east and north east of China. These geographical separations reflect in fact the original industrial substrate of China. At the same time, new regions develop. Foreign companies establish new factories in the cheaper west, and you then see counterfeiting hubs growing around these new industrial areas. In sum, counterfeiting follows the official and legitimate industrialization processes. This applies also to the trading of counterfeit goods. Guangdong is traditionally the heart of China wholesale and distribution system with large seaports in Shenzhen and Zhuhai, and with the largest markets and exhibitions in Guangzhou. Many goods manufactured elsewhere will then pass through wholesalers and traders in these southern cities, because it is there where legitimate consumer goods transit to overseas destinations. The current manufacturing overcapacity of many Chinese factories in the north east and north west of China, including the many steel factories now out of business, may in part be reconverted to making fakes to keep entrepreneurs and even the State earning money as well as keeping workers able to bring a salary home every month. This parallel running of legitimate and illegitimate/counterfeiting business is what characterizes China's economy nowadays. At the same time, these parallel lines meet very often, in that public and private business finds common economic interests in having counterfeiting running unhindered. For years, automotive spare parts were faked in Zhejiang province. Certain regions in that province were relying of automotive spare part

20. Harry Yang, Is Counterfeiting a Part of Chinese Culture?, Vol. 19 China IP Journal, http://www.chinaipmagazine.com/en/journal-show.asp?id=264 (August 2007).
21. Ling Jiang, Call for Copy-The Culture of Counterfeit in China, Vol. 2, No. 2, Journal of Chinese Economics, 73, 78 (2014).

counterfeiting to support their local economy. A high level of protectionism ensured the economic stability of whole regions and their technological improvement. More recently, the same region saw more and more legitimate businesses emerging and producing legal spare parts, thus giving an opposite spin to the local economy. This motivated the local authorities to begin a cleanup of the counterfeiters in these regions so as to protect legitimate jobs and economy. Infringers left this region and moved to poorer ones where their economic services were needed! This explains again how important is to know the real factors feeding and supporting counterfeiting so as to plan long-term strategies which may obtain better success than those adopted so far. We cannot thus separate the illegal economy of counterfeiting from the legal one that runs next to it.

Another important and critical factor that emerges in the recent history of China's counterfeiting is the role of the enforcement authorities and how they have influenced the strategic goals and enforcement plan of foreign brand owners instead of the contrary. In order to plan effective enforcement strategies, a foreign company must abandon the law books and understand how anti-counterfeiting really works in China. This is a topic that will be discussed in detail in Chapter 4. At this stage, we will just make some very general observations on this topic, so that the reader can start gaining some basic conceptual knowledge. From the mid-nineties and the new economic policies started by Deng Xiaoping in full swing, the State apparatus had started reacting to external international pressure to enforce IP rights by assigning often overlapping and concurring IP enforcement functions to several administrative bodies and by launching centralized campaigns against counterfeiters to react to specific crisis, mostly caused by mounting external pressures by either States and international organizations, or by well-coordinated foreign industrial lobbies. Another factor has influenced the way foreign brands have enforced trademark rights in China over all these years: investigative companies. These have played since the end of the nineties a major role in the counterfeiting business. Even without mentioning how many such companies are led and motivated by illegal intents, to the point of conniving with infringers to ensure a limitless number of raid-able targets to both parties' interest, they all have created privileged relations with the enforcing authorities. Such investigators have thus been deciding what and how to enforce IP rights in China and not their clients. Outside any possible real control over their sources and strong of their local relations with the enforcing authorities, these private businesses have been a major engine in the anti-counterfeiting arena in China.[22] They and not their clients have determined the real enforcement agendas. They have selected the type of cases they would uncover and bring them to justice, and they have worked the administrative agency into accepting such claims and raid targets, in some cases even through illicit incentives. Western brands managers aboard do not know all of this, or have at most a vague idea. They may even believe they retain control of their enforcement strategies; however, they have been forced to set goals and agendas by third parties: investigative

22. Martin K. Dimitrov, Piracy and the State – The Politics of Intellectual Property Rights in China, (Cambridge University Press 2009) offers examples of how private investigators work in China and how they may illegally collude with public officials.

companies and public officials. What is most surprising is that such a system has been passively accepted by brand owners. They also accept the fact that by supporting such a corrupted system, they only help its perpetration and survival, while at international fora and before their own government they plea to press China to change it. It is also surprising to see how for years this whole thing has remained the same. The question therefore is whether there are alternatives to such inefficient and corrupted enforcement systems! How can brands help China bring about a change in the way State bodies enforce trademark rights? This is what we will discuss in Chapter 4.

CHAPTER 2

Know the Rules and Play the Game

§2.01 RULES OF ENGAGEMENT: CONCEPTS AND CONDITIONS FOR SUCCESSFUL TRADEMARK PROTECTION AND ENFORCEMENT IN CHINA

Rules of Engagement are strategic rules. They are the sum of legal and business knowledge about China trademarks. The mastery of these rules will help businesses, lawyers as well as businessmen and women to view trademark challenges in China in a comprehensive strategic manner that will supply them with effective business solutions to the most typical China trademark challenges. These rules are of general application and can positively help any kind of business to gain a more objective and factual knowledge of the trademark laws of China and their practical application so that they can learn how to exploit them in their favor, finding practical, business solutions, avoiding the mistakes they had committed in the past and preparing for newly emerging challenges. By adopting a strategic approach to trademark challenges in China, practitioners of all kinds will be in a better position to use and control their Chinese counsel, thus playing a really active and leading role in the creation, shaping and execution of trademark protection and enforcement strategies in China. Knowledge and use of the appropriate rules of engagement will show that there still are creative solutions to trademark challenges in China, without need to give in to resignation. The Rules of Engagement start from the apolitical acceptance of Chinese law as it is and not as it should or could be. Rules of Engagement are not based on wishful thinking and start from the acceptance that westerners have made mistakes and that it is time they take new paths to correct them. The Rules will be accepted and understood as they are in order to build strategies that will be adapted to the Chinese business and enforcement reality, so that companies will have the possibility to build mid-term strategies that will indeed make their business successful. Rules are myth busters. This means that in certain cases, consolidated and practically standard response to a trademark challenge may be abandoned for what at first may appear less advantageous to the typical legal practitioner, but that will surely reveal of great benefit to the client's business when seen in a comprehensive strategic perspective.

There are, in sum, three major Rules which are complementary and inseparable from each other:

- Know your strength: Set your strategic goals before you take action and after you have collected all the needed information.
- Know the enemy: Collect all the facts about the opponent and investigate him/her at 360 degrees. The solution of a case may lay in a small fact that you would ignore if you were to look only with the lenses of a lawyer!
- Know the battlefield: Acquire full knowledge of the local law and practices. Learn litigation tactics and exploit them in your favor. Accept the local law as it is without prejudice; this will help you make better and more effective use of it.

It is therefore time for legal practitioners, managers and businessmen/women to put on a new pair of lenses and observe the known problems and challenges in the field of trademark protection and enforcement in China from a different point of view!

[A] General Principles of Conducts when Enforcing IP Rights in China

There is little doubt that IPR enforcement cannot be considered as an isolated occurrence both in space and time. A company should see an act of trademark theft or trademark infringement not as an isolated episode to be dealt with through legal measures only, but as part of the company's way of doing business in China, more precisely as the symptom of some malfunction with the company's business strategy and its implementation. In fact, a trademark infringement is not only the expression of the illicit intentions of a third party to gain unjust economic advantages, but also the measure of what is going wrong with the overall company's business. IPR in general should not be perceived only as passive assets filed to prevent competitors from illicitly advantaging themselves of a technical breakthrough or a growing good will. IPR are active tools of business and are the measure of the success of such a business. Trademarks in particular, are the base upon which a company can measure its status in the market and its ranking in such market in respect to competitors. Trademarks are commercial tools that open up new business relations and facilitate penetration into new markets. Eventually, trademarks are the tool to win customers' fidelity by granting the brand legal stability and certainty of origin.

Within this context, an act of infringement is not just a matter of law, but fore and foremost it is a business matter. Why did an infringer choose my brand instead of another one? Why now and not before? If the infringer is a present or a former licensee or distributor, the infringement will be a clear sign that something is wrong with the actual distribution and retail model, or with the selection of local business partners. If the infringement is the isolated act of an competitor, it may indicate its intent to prevent your expansion and signal to you that his business is in turn expanding; if the infringement is taking the form of widespread counterfeiting, it may signal that your brand is gaining popularity or that you have not taken the issue seriously and your brand is already diluting. In sum, a trademark infringement is like the symptoms of an illness but not necessarily the principal and only cause of it. Furthermore, an infringement in a country may be linked to other parallel acts of infringement elsewhere, forcing the right holders to elaborate strategies that consider how the enforcement in a certain jurisdiction will affect the business in others. Eventually, each act of trademark infringement occurs within a country's legal system. Strategies will have to balance the cross-border enforcement choices with the peculiarities of all the legal and business systems involved. A strategy that wins an infringement lawsuit in China may not automatically result in a beneficial effect for other jurisdictions affected by the Chinese infringement! The challenge here is that the Chinese legal system will have to be considered and used so as to obtain the desired objectives beyond the Chinese borders as well.

All this explains why trademark protection and enforcement in China cannot be based on a simple illegal action/legal reaction operation but on a more complex strategic planning that extend the equation to business and managerial factors. Trademarks are tools that a company can use, among others, to implement its business strategy. As such, protection and enforcement of trademarks must be contextualized within the business models and strategy of the company. How does this translate into decision and actions? What do an in-house trademark attorney and his external counsel need to know and do in a concrete case of trademark theft or infringement in China?

IP enforcement is not a random activity but the implementation of a larger IP protection plan, which in turn is functional to the overall business strategy of a company. The trademark infringer is someone with an aggressive plan to expropriate the right holder of the economic benefits derived by a legal form of monopoly. Enforcement is the institutionalized act of force to counter such aggression. Trademark litigation is substantially a conflict and a manifestation of force. In fact, when an infringement dispute is settled, lawyers speak of "peaceful resolution of the matter." Such a conflict cannot be won in a single battle, and a general strategy should be the first step before deciding which tactical options may be available and suitable to win such final act of forced confrontation and win it in a way that will benefit the right holder for a long time.

In order to understand the shortcomings of a mere legal approach to trademark protection in China, and to appreciate the complex nature of trademark protection and enforcement as part of an overall business strategy, some parallels and comparisons may be of help. For instance, we may try to look at litigation trademark disputes as wars and battles. Obviously, IP enforcement is not war and the parallel has nothing to do with matters of principles. The parallel here is offered only as an example of how certain rules of engagement are common to other fields of life and that any person, without being a lawyer can understand them in that they are rules of conducts dictated by common sense. The following parallel will show that, like in war, having a good case does not mean being able to win it, and that even winning a lawsuit may not end the infringement and cure the underlying business problems. In summary, like in war mandatory proscription does not make a good fighting army, packing a case and filing a lawsuit may not be the best strategy against a trademark infringement.

Now roll the drums and unfurl the flags!

Imagine you are a general of the Napoleonic era in command of a veterans' division. You know your troops are of good quality. They have fought before. They have been issued the best weapons available and are fairly motivated and in good spirit for the planned campaign. You have been ordered to occupy a certain position ahead in enemy territory. The staff at Army Head Quarter (HQ) have given you reassurance that there may be but little enemy activities in front of you. However, you worry because you have not been made part of the overall campaign goals by your superiors. What you know goes as far as your eyes can see. Eventually, you have but a general sketch of the Army's position once you will reach your destination. Meanwhile, you have studied the available maps of this hostile territory and have heard reports from locals about the terrain and the alleged presence of enemy forces. You know there are risks, but you are confident that your division will be able to fend off any threat and reach its destination as ordered. Early in the morning, you issue the marching order. Cautiously, you distribute your forces in formations ready for sudden deployment in case of contact with enemy troops. Squadrons of light dragoons are deployed on your flanks to search for enemy positions ahead, while a line of infantry skirmishers is deployed to screen off your troop's main body. All seem in order and you are confident about your own strength. The morning of the march is gray and a thick fog lies over the unknown fields and woods. The ground is marshy and your artillery train bogs down immediately while soldier's boots fill with murky water. You order your infantry to move along, and leave a rearguard to accompany the artillery train.

After a few hours of marching, reports from different regiments and battalions start coming in. You learn that the terrain is swampy, and that some of the units on the far right flank had detached and lost contact with your troop's main body. The fog confuses the troop's movement, and some of the battalions in the center moved into some thick woods and lost cohesion. You had not seen those large woods marked on your maps. Also, the map did not tell you that the main highway where the artillery train was supposed to ride is actually a thin countryside trail interspersed with jagged rocks. Wheel and spikes give way and slow down the progress of the guns. Suddenly, to your consternation, skirmishers report that there is a stream in front of your marching lines and that also was not marked in your maps. Scouts inform you and your staff that the stream is actually very small and fordable in several points, but the embankment on your side is very steep. The muddy condition makes it difficult for loaded troops to get down to the shore in good order, and it will be a challenge for both cavalry and artillery to get down to the bank. Due to the seasonal rains, the stream current is rather strong. You and your troops will have to cross it with water knee high!

It takes time to move your units across the stream. It is also confirmed that on your right flank, the confusion of the morning has resulted in the delayed march of some of the other companies. The fog hangs still and thick, even in the early afternoon, and the terrain ahead cannot be crossed without difficulty. Now with a small river and a high embankment on your back and an unknown country ahead, your units resume the march. Meanwhile, your worries about possible enemy activities increase. Small skirmishes break out on your left flank. For hours you have not had any news of one of the squadrons of your light dragoon on the left flank, maybe due to increasing enemy presence in that position. You send out a reinforced scouting unit on your left. After a while, the fire on that side of the fields intensifies. Reports of enemy concentration on the left make you switch part of your center to that side. The available artillery is brought up to support your infantry advance. Suddenly, you find yourself engaged by the enemy, whose forces you cannot estimate. You start feeling frustrated and increasingly worried. Reports of musketry are clearly heard from the right flank as well. Artillery fire opens against your right flank. At this point in time, you have neither idea of the terrain in front of you, nor of the strength and position of your enemy. Also, you have not been informed of the overall general strategy of this campaign by your supreme commander, and you have therefore no general guidance as to whether you should engage the enemy and under which circumstances. Should you retreat behind the stream and assume a defensive position? Should you scout all flanks to determine where the bulk of the enemy forces are? Should you accept engagement under the present conditions?

The critical point from the example is that at the outset of the march, your general had very little information about the opponent and the terrain. However, he had to march off and execute orders. Acting without knowledge of critical facts has been the main reason for the above-described crisis and delays of an effective response. Most of all, the general loses the initiative! He can only react impromptu. All this is eventually made worse by the fact that he has no indications about the mission's general strategy and final goals. Can he retreat to a better position or accept engagement with the enemy under uncertain conditions? What can he do to strengthen his knowledge and take effective decisions? How can he gain again initiative and lead the battle to a desirable conclusion? As a leader you are presented with several challenges: what are your ultimate goals? How strong is the enemy? What are the relevant features of the battlefield? Which features are favorable and which are unfavorable relative to position and strengths/weaknesses?

Now transport this battle scene to today's time in China. Instead of being a general in Napoleon's "Grand Armee" you are the Chief Executive Officer (CEO) or the GM or the IP counsel/general counsel of a European or American company. Among your tasks is that of protecting, managing and exploiting the company's IP assets. Even if the time, the context and the scenarios are completely different (peacetime, business disputes, IP rights, legal procedures and rule of law), you can still draw lessons from such an example that could well serve you in the more peaceful IP battles of today's China. It is in fact possible to see that from a conceptual point of view, the same questions and challenges faced by that French general are the same as yours.

You run or have supervision over the IP portfolio of a solid western company. You have a strong team of experienced patent and trademark attorneys who know the ups and downs of China IP at least in general lines. Meanwhile, you have been informed that there is a Chinese company infringing a trademark or a patent of your company. You check your patent and trademark rights. They seem in order. You are not only familiar with their prosecution history and know possible weaknesses but are also aware of their strength, and that they are ready to be deployed against any treat of infringement in the best interest of the company. You are now informed that a Chinese company has started selling a copy of your patented solution in China or a copy of your product and trademark both in China and abroad. Your in-house staff in Shanghai or Beijing or wherever it may be located, start feeding you with information. All is rather generic and not much intelligence can be gained from it. However, you now have a target. The product of the alleged infringer has been purchased in China and verified at your HQ. From your glass tower in the western hemisphere, you start contacting your Chinese counsel. The latter will feed you with some legal information about enforcement, damage recovery, costs etc., which will be of course major factors to be considered when deciding enforcement. In the best of cases, your evidence collection may even bring in some interesting intelligence. Your Chinese lawyer will confirm the infringement based on the legal standards of infringement examination in China and you will now face the momentous decision. Considering that the infringed patent or trademark is indeed a key asset for your company, and that aside from that actual infringer others are or may be doing the same, you decide to enforce by filing a lawsuit. Your troops are ready, you think you have identified the enemy and have prepared your weapons for an attack. You even feel that you can indeed move comfortably well in China. You had expected so much more differences between the legal systems of China and your country. The preparation phase was also not as complicated and long as you had expected. Also, it took but a couple of months to prepare all that was apparently needed. You think you have enough knowledge now of the enemy and the battlefield to go. And so you go.

Like in the military example described above, the risks of IP litigation in China, as on the real battlefield, are mostly hidden. A few months' preparation of IP enforcement in China is often insufficient to really discover the traps and tricks hidden behind the case façade. Knowledge of the law is useful but it is not enough to help you prepare a winning strategy if you do not know how this law is interpreted and applied by each court, especially in a country where there are no legally binding judicial precedents. More than the law, you should have studied the ways of infringers in China, past battles and others' defeats and learn from them. Another problem, and in the author's experience, the most critical one, is that your decision to act is based on the sudden infringement and all your preparations and operations are focused on the infringement itself. What about a master-plan? What are your final goals? Is the lawsuit as it has been conceived and prepared, suitable to achieve those goals? Have all possible parties been included as defendants? Have you considered that they may escape liability even in case of a favorable judgment? Is a trademark or patent lawsuit alone sufficient to stop the infringement?

There is nothing worse than winning a "Pyrrhic victory," a victory that has no benefits and brings about no real change aside from bleeding out your budget and leave you with no money for what was really needed to be done. However, settling a case does not necessarily mean you will lose the war in the end. An infringer that cannot be stopped by warning letters may be stopped by filing a well-thought lawsuit, independently from whether the lawsuit will be won or settled. Therefore, the first lesson to be learned by our generals is that they should work closely with the HQ, the board, to make sure that whatever they intend to do in China will have a benefit for the overall business strategy of the company.

Goal setting will therefore be the first critical factor to be considered when deciding whether and how to take enforcement action. If the right goals are set, it will then be possible to efficiently measure the success of a strategy. Once a grand strategy is ready and goals are clear, the IP general will be in a better position to take decisions even at the time of distress because he knows what the ultimate goals are. In this respect, winning a lawsuit, collecting damages are rather tactical than strategic goals. Strategic goals have to do with the broader implementation of the company business strategy.

Second, our IP general should be more careful about the knowledge of the legal environment in China and its enforcement system. This is what we can define as the battlefield. Knowledge of the battlefield requires intensive preparatory work, such as engineering of effective forum shopping strategies, study of courts case law, identification and consideration of possible influence by local factors, availability of preliminary measures etc. For this, he needs to select experienced lawyers who can understand his business needs and present him with the law in a way that he can effectively use it in its enforcement plan.

Eventually, an IP general should always demand more facts. Facts are everything because they are the most solid base for decisions. Knowing that there is an infringer and acquiring the infringing goods is not enough to build up a solid case. Fact finding and investigations need not only to identify evidence sources and acquire such evidence, but to build it into a more comprehensive enforcement strategy finalized to the preset strategic goals. Knowledge of the infringer, i.e., the enemy in the battlefield, is most crucial to the success of the enforcement plan. Investigations cannot be therefore left to investigative companies alone, as it is normally the case in China. The right holder together with his counsel must be the leader of the investigative team.

In conclusion, a general counsel or an IP counsel or the business owner of a foreign company should act not only as a Napoleonic general on a battlefield, but also as Napoleon himself. His task is not just to win a patent or trademark battle but a patent or trademark campaign, where a specific battle is but an aspect of the whole issue.

[B] First Rule of Engagement: Strategic and Tactical Goal Setting

Goal setting is not winning a lawsuit or successfully obtaining the cancellation of a hostile trademark. These are tactical achievements which could assist the right holders in achieving their goals through enforcement. In fact, winning an opposition procedure may not deter others from filing similar hostile trademarks again, just as winning an infringement lawsuit and obtaining compensation may not bring about the cessation of an infringing act, or more generally, a solution to a business problem related to the infringement (i.e., distribution structure that favors infringements). Strategic goals are business goals. If trademarks are legal tools functional to a better and more effective implementation of a company overall business strategy, their protection and enforcement must be conceived and executed in the function of such strategy. For instance, if one of the trademarks registered in China by a foreign company is infringed, that company should refrain from investing resources in enforcing it, if it has not been recently used or its abandonment has been already decided. However, an enforcement by proper legal means should be seen as unavoidable if, for instance, that trademark, although not currently used on any company product, is meant to be licensed/sold to a third party or due to be reactivated soon. Even if the trademark does not produce immediate revenues to the company, it is an active asset that is going to be monetarized in one way or another. Failing to protect such trademark could result in an economic loss and could damage future business relations. In that case, the goal is to protect future investments and enforcement is functional to this goal.

Setting strategic goals is a most critical task in that their achievement and the degree in which such goals have been achieved or not achieved, will be the measure of the success of the overall IP strategy of the rights holder. For instance, if the goal of a company's anti-counterfeiting strategy is to eradicate infringements in China, a successful raid against one single counterfeiter's factory will not automatically achieve this goal. Setting the right goals at the base of any act of exploitation of an IP right, even in the negative sense (enforcement, oppositions, cancellations etc.), is as delicate as fixing the price of a new product at the time of market launch. Setting the right strategic goals shows the degree of understanding of an IP right value and its relation to the company's business. Setting the right goal will then help the right holder in selecting the most appropriate and effective legal tools to protect such right and the underlying business interests. Practical examples may help giving substance to abstract conceptual constructions.

A US company produces canned food products. It is a quite well-established business with a long history in its country of origin. For some years, its products were imported into China in small quantities by some local Chinese distributors. More recently, expansion plans have brought this company to expand its market in China by increasing distribution. Consequently, the US Company begins filing for the protection of its various trademarks in China. As it happens to many foreign companies, one of its core brands had been registered with success by a local company in southern China. The first strategic blunder here was to let too much time pass between the very first sales of its products few years earlier in China and the filing of trademark applications for the brands used on those products. As we shall see in more details, China recognizes protection only to registered trademarks and ownership of a trademark is based on the first-come-first-serve rule (known better as "First-to-File" principle). In that case, the southern China Company filed for the trademark in question long before the original US owner. The first reaction of the US prior right holder was to file cancellation of the stolen trademark based on the bad faith of the Chinese company. Although the most direct and natural legal reaction to a perceived violation of the law, it was not necessarily the best way about this matter. Cancelling such a trademark is indeed an option, and probably the most "natural" option from a legal point of view, especially if seen from the perspective of an American company. The US law allows cancellation based on bad faith and that is what the Company would have done if the case was in the US. However, the Company was rightly cautioned to first clearly think of its business goals and review the local law carefully, before deciding whether cancellation of registration in bad faith was the best options. After a long process of acquaintance with the law and review of the company business goals, it was agreed that any action against the trademark usurper would have to be seen as part of the ongoing process of further expansion of the brand and its products in the Chinese market. This then allowed the formulation of tactical goals: elimination or neutralization of the opponent's threat as a way to achieve the preceding strategic goal!

Put in such context, the cancellation action becomes a tactical tool to achieve a strategic goal. Also, from this higher level of abstraction, we can see other options, not necessarily legal ones, which could help achieve the same tactical and strategic goals. As to the first aspect, i.e., the choice of a legal tool to eliminate or neutralize a threat, the Company was informed that unlike the US, bad faith is not always an available legal ground for trademark cancellation, because it requires the claimant to prove a certain degree of recognition of the trademark among the relevant Chinese consumers of that product. Knowledge of the fighting ground is indeed critical to implement goal setting. Although bad faith is now more often recognized and accepted as ground of cancellation, others options were considered. One available option was that of filing cancellation for nonuse for three consecutive years of the stolen trademark. However, before selecting either of these forms of cancellation, knowledge of the hostile grabber was of key importance. Only by determining the size and nature of the threat, could an effective tactical decision be taken. Investigation revealed that the infringer was using the trademark only for some of the products covered by the trademark registration, and that it was using it only in a small supermarket in its hometown. It was also discovered that the supermarket belonged to that same company. No products with the grabbed trademark were sold elsewhere in China. This information, analyzed in light of the set tactical goals, revealed that the risk of the usurper to fight back was very limited, and it could be easily contained and that the US Company could have rather safely continued to market its products in China without much worry of a reprisal from the usurper, while proper cancellation tools were filed. In this respect, the strategic goal in its broadest terms was already achieved by simply collecting more information. The client was advised that it was safe to continue sell in and expand its market to the rest of China.

In this context, the activation of the legal remedy will have the localized tactical value of immobilizing the infringer, thus reducing the risk of a counterattack through a trademark infringement lawsuit. In such circumstances, considering the length of any legal proceedings, it would be of minor relevance whether legal action succeeded or not, in that the achievement of the strategic goals would not solely depend on that cancellation. In this case, the grabber was in no condition and had no intention to go after the Company and just wanted to keep its small business running at its local supermarket. Under this condition, it was decided that a partial cancellation for nonuse was the best way to go to keep the target at bay while continuing the penetration of the whole Chinese market. The outcome of the cancellation was favorable to the US entity. The stolen trademarks were indeed cancelled for 90% of the goods, which the thief had neglected to market and sell. This had automatically reduced the strength of the stolen trademarks, by limiting their protection and economic value to very few goods which were sold in extremely low quantities in one local supermarket. At the same time, while enforcing the cancellation tactic, the US entity was advised to consider other possible preventive legal measures in case of a later counterattack by the trademark hijacker. A review of the local news during investigation had reported that the target company had been accused in the past of selling substandard quality food and beverages and had thus been investigated and fined by local authorities. Considering that the products protected under the stolen trademarks belong to safety-sensitive group of consumer products, tests were run on samples purchased at the beginning of the case. Some of the products ingredients found in the packaging were different from the ingredients listed in the labels. This provided the US entity with a strong deterrent against the trademark grabber. Eventually, based on all the successful partial cancellations and the quality tests results conducted on some of the infringers' products, it was decided to approach the target company to negotiate a transfer at zero costs, which the client succeeded in doing!

Something that we can learn from this case is that the legal solution that appeared to be the most appropriate at the beginning of the case was later abandoned from a more complex and cross-disciplinary action once the right holder strategic goals were duly selected, facts thoroughly investigated and evidence collected. The success of such a modular strategy was granted ultimately by a legal action which was outside the range of the IP tools. Resorting to such a tactic encompassing other legal fields, in this case that of product quality and safety, was possible only because the foreign company had been provided with a clear set of rules of engagement that were followed thoroughly and consistently. First, the company set a strategic goal/exploitation model for its trademark rights compatible with its business strategy in China. Second, it had thoroughly familiarized itself with the enemy, its strengths and weaknesses. Third, it had familiarized itself with the battlefield, the law and its interpretations, with an open-minded approach. The last step was to put all these factors together and select the means available to achieve the set goals. Another example will help to drive these points home.

Although this book focuses on trademark protection, certain concepts such as goal setting are common to all IP rights, and patent infringement cases can also provide a definition and substantiation of the concept of strategic goals' setting. Here is one such example. A leading European company in the biochemical sector was informed that a number of Chinese competitors were allegedly manufacturing and selling the former's patented technical solution. Information about the infringing behavior was acquired through sales staff in China. Samples of the infringing product were purchased through investigators from what appeared to be the most dangerous of the various infringers in a form suitable for judicial use. The European company had in fact decided to sue the larger and most dangerous of the various infringing companies first. The lawsuit was then prepared and filed in the court where the infringing product samples had been purchased. The patentee had also decided to claim statutory compensation, i.e., he left to the court the decision of how to determine economic damages.[23] After a few years of legal battle, both the judge of first instance and the

23. Article 60 of the Patent Law provides for the methods of calculation of damage compensation: Losses of the patentee, illegal profit of the infringer or royalty fee equivalents. If none of these can be proved by the plaintiff, the plaintiff himself or the court ex officio will determine damage compensation based on the circumstances of the case and the available evidence within a fixed

Appeal Court confirmed the patent infringement and the liability of the infringers to cease production and pay damage compensation for the equivalent of USD 130,000.

If we look at the facts above, we would believe this to be a case of successful IPR enforcement. The legal battle was won. The problem here is that the troubles started only after the case had been won in court. In sequence: the infringers completely ignored the judgment and went on infringing. The market was as flooded with their product as it was before the lawsuit, if not more. Second, the patent of the European company, whose nullification procedure had been pending since the beginning of the civil case, was eventually invalidated by the Beijing Higher Court. What went wrong? Lots of things went wrong, and most of them had to do with lack of a clear strategic goals, and bad preparation. This is an example where the rights holder had followed the rules of the law in China, but not the broader Rules of Engagement.

The major problem was the lack of clear goals to determine the success or failure of the adopted strategy. Seen the other way round, the chosen strategy proved to be unsuccessful because it did not achieve any clear goals, and because the right holder had not set itself clear strategic goals. The patentee had assumed that the material act of infringement of the patent was enough ground to obtain a successful enforcement. This may be true in some European countries, but it is surely not the case in China, where local as well as economic, legal and political factors may alter the effects of a favorable judgment. The client had assumed that winning the lawsuit was in itself the strategic goal. However, as the examples show, winning a lawsuit may be a tactical goal, but it is not the end of an enforcement strategy.

Second, the rights holder had not prepared the case properly, thus ignoring the other Rules of Engagement. He had not properly considered and understood the opponents' structure, business model and strengths. The original infringing party, even before the filing of the lawsuit, had started transferring the manufacturing operations involving the infringed patented solution to another company of the same group. The patentee had been so focused on the original target that it missed this development and failed to react to the legal changes in time. In this way, the enforcement action was addressed in substance against the wrong legal party. This was a tactical mistake by the patentee that would ultimately result in the futility of its court victories. In fact, by the time the judgment was issued the original infringer was indeed complying with the court order to cease and desist from infringement and nothing else could be done. At the same time, a new entity, untouched by the lawsuit, was continuing with the infringement to the profit of the owners of both companies. As to the battlefield, the

compensation amount ranging between CNY 500,000 and CNY 1,000,000. This is also, and unfortunately, the most used of the calculation methods in patent litigation in China, which thus results in low and inadequate compensation of damages compared to Europe and the US. This shortcoming is also one of the reasons that normally keep foreign patentees away from Chinese courts. Furthermore, the lack of deterrence in low damage compensation in patent litigation is also a reason why infringement judgments cannot stop infringers from repeating or even continuing their acts of infringement unabatedly. For more information on this point, *see* U.S. Department of State Bureau of Economic and Business Affairs, 2015 Investment Climate Statement, 22 http://www.state.gov/e/eb/rls/othr/ics/2015/241518.htm (2015). *See also*: Ambassador Michael G. Froman, U.S. Trade Rep., Exec. Office of the President, 2015 Special 301 Report (2015), https://ustr.gov/sites/default/files/2015-Special-301-Report-FINAL.pdf (2015).

European company had not considered the local strength of the opponents, their involvement in the specific industry association and its capacity to rally local interests against the case of the foreign company. Eventually, the decision of the plaintiff to claim statutory damages, exposing the defendant to the risk of having to pay a monetary compensation hundreds of times lower than their illegal revenues, took wind out of the lawsuit and lacked any deterring effect on the defendant. This latest decision was unfortunately the result of having missed the fulfillment of the needed preparations in accordance with the Rules of Engagement.

Aspects related to the knowledge of the counterpart and the battlefield will be discussed in a separate paragraph, although in a mental process, no strategy can be finalized without considering these factors and their interaction. Nonetheless, there are some aspects of general strategy that a foreign company must consider in order to conceive the most effective enforcement strategy.

From the above example, we can point out a number of interesting facts concerning how the foreign company had acted when deciding to enforce its IP right. The first point that emerges is the selection of the targets. It is indeed common that a trademark or a patent may be infringed by several Chinese competitors. It is also very common for a right holder to target immediately the most dangerous and threatening of the infringers. Is this however the best course? What if the first example you want to set fails to stop the infringement like in the patent case above? How can the others then be stopped? In order to make the best choice when selecting one among several targets, the right holder must have a clear idea of his ultimate business goals. If the goal is to stop the most dangerous of the infringers at all costs because he is causing an immediate loss to the right holder's revenues, resulting in a palpable loss of market presence/shares, then it is self-evident that any enforcement plan will have to target that infringer first. However, if the goal is reducing the impact of patent or trademark infringement for a certain product line within a certain period, thus reducing the potential risk of loss of market share in the near future, then it is not a self-evidence that a successful strategy should start with a direct attack against the most dangerous and likely more difficult of the infringers. Once the goal of an action is clear, then the ancillary knowledge of the opponents and the battlefield will also support the choice of a less obvious course of action, such as attacking the smaller fish first so as to create favorable precedents with less risk and effort, to be then used to pressure the other infringers to cease and desist their illegal actions. In this way, the net is well laid when the time for dragging in the bigger fish comes. In summary, selecting the proper strategic goals to be achieved through IPR enforcement, it will help keep options open for further consideration once more knowledge of field factors is properly acquired.

The same remarks can be extended to the clear understanding of the role of legal remedies and their effective employments at a tactical level. It is most commonly heard from the right holder that purpose of the enforcement is not really money because they do not expect any large compensation from a Chinese judge. They normally want the enforcement to stop the infringement, thus setting a favorable precedent and example against other actual or potential infringers. The result of taking such words literally may be catastrophic. If you look at the above example, this is what indeed happened. The patentee was not advised to focus on damages but rather on obtaining a favorable judgment with a cease-and-desist injunction by the court. Therefore, the request of compensation was based on statutory damages which, according to the Chinese Patent Law can amount to a maximum of CNY 1,000,000 (about USD 150,000). Now you can imagine the following scene. The CEO of the infringing company receives a copy of the lawsuit with a demand of damages that could result in at most CNY 1 million in damage compensation. On the same desk, he has another sales contract concerning the infringing product for a value five or ten times larger than the claimed compensation. It is likely that the infringer will not take that lawsuit very seriously, especially if its infringement is making his company so profitable. In the specific case, it should not come as a surprise for the reader that no representatives of the infringers ever appeared in court during the judicial proceedings of first instance and appeal. Although we are now expanding the discussion to tactical aspects, the point here is that goal setting is important and must be detailed and not generic. If the strategic goals are not clear, the tactical goals and the chosen enforcement tools are also likely to be inadequate. The selection of clear goals and objectives, their timing and correlation is a critical step, and it must start as soon as an infringement is discovered. Setting the goals of an enforcement of trademark or patent rights in China is paramount due to the peculiarities of the enforcement system here and also because of the differing business strategies of a company in China compared to the one in the US or Europe. Enforcement in China must become an effective business tool that will ultimately help and support the business in China. Consider for instance the case in which patents, know-how and trademarks create a situation of strong monopoly for a certain kind of product in a key industrial sector strongly subsidized by the Chinese government. In such a case, your enforcement must also consider the after effects of a lawsuit on your market position, in your ability to do business in a conductive and unbiased market. A proper strategy would therefore consider the aftermath of an enforcement and mid-term repercussions. Also, an enforcement strategy must benefit China as well as the foreign right holders in order to be successful. Involvement of local partners and subsidiaries is therefore critical. Just as critical is the protection of parallel interests, such as consumer rights. Ideally, each foreign company should run "simulations" of enforcement strategies to set up a default profile in which conditions and goals are set a priori and then tested and adjusted upon specific cases as they come along.

In sum, goal setting is not just winning a lawsuit or cancelling a trademark. Winning a lawsuit or collecting damages are legal tools functional to something higher, like the company business goals. Goal setting has to do with the company business strategy and uses the IPR protection and exploitation, including enforcement, as a medium to support and ultimately realize the planned business strategy.[24] This means that legal achievements such as winning a lawsuit and collecting compensation are only functional to business goals. Commercial and business goals are in fact the paramount criteria for determining the enforcement strategy. Failure to set realistic and effective business goals will make it impossible for the enforcer to determine whether its action was successful or not. If after the judgment the infringer is still manufacturing

24. Alexander J. Wurzer, IP Manager, (Carl Heymanns Verlag 2009).

and selling the infringing goods then the lawsuit victory alone was not a strategy sufficient to impose on the infringer the will of the right holder and to produce the desired commercial effects. In sum, the decision to resort to judicial or administrative enforcement should always be weighed against other possible alternative tactical strategies.

However, once the decision is taken to enforce an IP right, the right holder must leave any hesitation behind and do its best to annihilate the opponent. Like in war, the opponent will be finally deterred only if the threat is subjected to present more disadvantages than risking to continue infringing.

[C] Second Rule of Engagement: Know Your Enemy (Who Are Your Trademarks' Infringers?)

Once a company has selected its goals, enforcement can enter into a tactical phase. Case peculiarities will have to be considered in order to select the appropriate and most effective tactical strategy to achieve the selected goals. One factor which is most critical, and it is unfortunately neglected in most trademark enforcement cases, is the legal, economic and human dimensions and facets of the infringer. Knowing and understanding the infringer and his motives will support the selection of appropriate enforcement strategies. An example will help clarifying this point.

A German company is entrusting an internet online monitoring provider with the search and selection of e-shops infringing its trademark rights and shut them down. In one specific instance, the online monitoring company uncovered an e-shop on an e-commerce platform, selling without authorization accessories of minor value with the counterfeit brand of the German company. After starting the take down process of the e-shop through the e-platform IPR protection processes, the alleged infringer replied to the claim and request of take down by showing a letter of the German brand owner authorizing this e-shop to sell those branded products. The German company declared that document to be a forge and the e-shop was taken down by the e-platform. The issue now was to determine whether such forged document was an isolated instance, or whether this e-shop was connected to a chain of infringers using forged documents of the brand owners to avoid take downs and continue selling counterfeits products with that German brand. Also, the involvement of the e-platform and the determination of its liabilities could depend on the investigation activities. Based on the above facts, the first impression was that the e-shop may have belonged to a larger infringers' chain. However, there were some signs indicating other possibilities, including that the infringement was the act of an individual acting alone. Answering these questions would affect the type of actions and enforcement to be taken. Initial investigations had revealed that the e-shop was registered under the name of a woman. A telephone number was provided. Preliminary investigations showed the connection of the telephone number with a trading company. Investigation of this company and tests conducted on the telephone number and investigations on newly emerging addresses showed that in reality it was a young man hiding behind all these operations. Further checks revealed his identity, personal information and data. Initially, the brand owner had suggested putting pressure against the e-commerce platform to obtain data of the infringer for possible criminal prosecution in relation to the crime of forgery in addition to trademark enforcement. However, the investigations revealed that the individual target seemed neither a professional infringer nor working for a structured criminal organization. An early move against the e-commerce platform was ruled out. A request of disclosure of the infringers' data and how he had acquired copy of the original documents of the right holder would have likely been refused, in that the e-commerce platform has no such legal obligation until at least a criminal investigation by the police is ongoing or irrefutable evidence of criminal acts of the alleged infringers had been collected. Therefore, the German company opted for the collection of evidence of a criminal conduct by the alleged infringer, which required more investigative and fact-finding activities. Based on the results of the investigations, it was ultimately decided to place a direct call to the targeted trader. Investigative instinct, an important element in a successful enforcement in China, had led the enforcement team to the right path. The infringer came on the phone and naively admitted that he had received the original authorization letter of the German company to its online monitoring service, from the e-commerce platform along with the official take down claim. He then admitted that he had downloaded and manipulated the authorization letter to serve its illegal purpose to avoid the take down decision. At that point, the right holder, together with copies of the correspondence between the infringer and the e-commerce platform including the downloadable file of the confidential original power of attorney (PoA) from the right holder, decided to drop the case against the infringer, which had already been shut down from the platform. The infringer was determined to be an occasional one, and the adopted measures were deemed sufficient to deter him from future infringements. At the same time, knowledge of the enemy had brought about facts about the processes of the e-commerce platform that needed immediate correction. This prompted the right holder to open a discussion with the e-commerce platform to make sure that the latter internal processes were quickly changed in order to avoid the repeating of such instances of sharing PoAs as public documents. Eventually, the parties reached an agreement and now changes had been adopted by the e-commerce platform preventing any future disclosure and sharing of important original PoAs or letter of authorizations with the alleged infringers subjected to a takedown action. Without need to describe the end of this matter, it is pointed out how critical the knowledge of the target and its intention is to the shaping of an effective strategy.

It can be generally stated that there are indeed many types of infringers as well as motives for infringing. Each case should be independently investigated. Case details make the difference. However, it is still possible to isolate certain types of recurring infringers and motives. Categorizing the types of infringers can indeed benefit strategic planning of enforcement especially when a company is the target of many recurring types of infringement. Smaller companies experiencing infringement of less frequency and intensity may also benefit of certain categorization in that they will facilitate the navigation of the enforcement options of a less familiar legal and business system.

[1] *Trademark Thieves* (aka Trademark Squatters, Hijackers, and Grabbers)

A Trademark thief is a person or a company that appropriates the trademarks of someone else.[25] The types of thieves are as variegates as the forms of the illicit appropriations; however, two major groups can be identified. As already pointed out in the introductory chapter, the history of trademark theft in China has highlighted the wrongdoings of local business competitors and those of professional thieves, also known as squatters, grabbers or hijackers. Both types are thieves, in that their appropriation of other trademark rights is done in bad faith and thus with illegal intent. The motives of a local Chinese competitor are mostly that of free riding the fame of someone else's trademark as much and as long as possible. This means that the free rider is normally a company or an individual in the same line of business of the original trademark's owner.[26] In such cases, trademarks were either identical as for instance in the cases of Polo Santa Barbara regarding the Burberry Haymarket trademark case of 2014,[27] the case of Michael Jordan,[28] or very similar to the Lacoste case back in 2004[29] or Kongalu v. Kelloggs in 1993.[30] In many instances, it was the Chinese name of a famous foreign brand that was grabbed by Chinese companies competing for the same market. In all these cases, the main intent was again that of free riding for as long as

25. The author does not agree with the definition of trademark piracy (squatting) as provided by WIPO. In WIPO Intellectual Property Handbook 90 (2008), trademark piracy is defined as "the registration or use of a generally well-known foreign trademark that is not registered in the country or is invalid as a result of non-use ...". This definition would be too restrictive especially in China, where squatting is no longer limited to well-known brands but to any foreign brands. What characterizes trademark squatting in China is primarily the fact that squatters register in China trademarks identical to those of their foreign targets, which the latter have neglected to register earlier, independently from the degree of notoriety of the stolen trademark.
26. The distance in the type of businesses with respect to the free-riding intent may vary depending also on the degree of notoriety of the grabbed trademark. A very famous brand can be free-ridden even by filing it in classes of goods or services completely unrelated to the original branded product. For instance, leather products using the logo of a famous mobile phone brand can still benefit of the theft because of the very high degree of recognition of the stolen brand and in spite of the sidereal differences among the businesses of the two entities in question.
27. Guanyu No. G732879 "Tuxing" Zuche Shangbiao Lianxu Sannian Tingzhi Shiyong Chexiao Shenqing de Jueding (关于第G732879号"图形"注册商标连续三年停止使用撤销申请的决定) [The Decision on the petition to revoke the No. G732879 "pattern" trademark for continual non-use for three years], November 19, 2013 (Trademark Office of The State Administration for Industry & Commerce of the People's Republic of China). *See also* http://finance.sina.com.cn/chanjing/gsnews/20131202/090417495768.shtml.
28. Maikeer Qiaodan Yu Guojia Gongshang Guanli Zongju Shangbiao Pingshen Weiyuanhui Qita Ershen Xinzheng Panjueshu (迈克尔·乔丹与国家工商行政管理总局商标评 审委员会其他二审行政判决书) [The Administrative Decision on the Second Instance Between Michael Jordan and the Trademark Review and Adjudication Board of the State Administration for Industry & Commerce of the People's Republic of China], August 17, 2015 (Higher People's Ct. of Beijing). *See also* http://www.yn.xinhuanet.com/ent/2016-04/27/c_135315431.htm.
29. Xinjiapo Eyu Guoji Jigou Siren Youxian Gongsi Su Faguo Lakesite Chenshan Gufen Youxian Gongsi (新加坡鳄鱼国际机构私人有限公司诉法国拉科斯特衬衫股份有限公司)[Crocodile International PTE Ltd v. La Chemise Lacoste] March 25, 2004 (Shanghai Interm. People's Ct.). *See also* http://www.chinanews.com/cj/2011/10-20/3403663.shtml.
30. Andrew Mertha, *supra* n. 10, at 168.

possible the notoriety of a foreign trademark.[31] In some other cases, the intent may have been also that of selling for profit the stolen trademark.[32] Aware that the trademark system was favorable to the registrant and had limited protection of well-known unregistered trademarks, trademark thieves were counting on several years of high sales, thanks to the trademark free ride. In some cases, the situation had become so untangled that the thief had even seen the possibility of increasing its gains by obtaining a final and official sanction of its ownership by filing troll lawsuits against the foreign company. In some cases, this turned into a great success and confirmed how dangerous such thieves could be to a foreign business. Good examples of successful trolls were the "Castel-Frere"[33] case in 2012[34] and more recently the "New Balance" and "IPhone" cases.[35] Some of these cases also revealed another set of motives: preventing foreign competitors from timely filing their own trademarks and thus hampering their entrance into or further penetration of the Chinese market.[36] Such a motive is probably the most prominent among those Chinese competitors grabbing trademarks of less famous foreign companies. Unlike the cases of free ride concerning famous brands, preventive and bad faith squatting of nonfamous foreign brands is characterized mostly by unfair competition intent: In these cases, a Chinese large company or SME normally files trademarks of a foreign company in the same business filed before the latter enters or expands into the Chinese market. It is evident that the preventive intent of such filing is predominant. Given the importance of brands in the penetration of new markets, depriving such brands of legal protection is an effective way to slow down or even eliminate a competitor in that market.

In spite of their different motives or the varying degree of intensity of such motives, two things are common to these types of thieves. First, they are always registered businesses, some of them rather large Chinese enterprises. The second one is that they professionally monitor the market and the trademark database and act quickly to fill in the trademark protection gaps of their foreign competitors. Also, as already pointed out, this type of IP theft is now widespread and affects any foreign company independently from the degree of notoriety. This should compel foreign companies to monitor their Chinese competitors and the Chinese trademark database.

31. Kitsurong Sangusvang, Trademark Squatting, Vol. 37, No. 1, Wisconsin International Law Journal, 259 http://hosted.law.wisc.edu/wordpress/wilj/files/2014/01/Sangsuvan_final_v2.pdf (December 2012).
32. *Ibid.*
33. Paolo Beconcini, $5M Case Highlights Risk From Chinese Trademark Trolls, Law 360, http://www.law360.com/articles/386205/5m-case-highlights-risk-from-chinese-trademark-trolls (October 17, 2012).
34. An appeal decision in 2015 reduced the amount of damages quite drastically, but the fact remain that the troll lawsuit had been successful. This case will be dealt with in more details in the following paragraphs.
35. Guangzhou Xinbailun Xieye Youxian Gongsi Su Niubalun (Zhongguo) Youxian Gongsi (广州新百伦鞋业有限公司诉纽巴伦（中国）有限公司) [Guangzhou Xinbailun Shores Company v. New Balance (China) LLC.] April 21, 2015 (Guangzhou Interm. Ct.). *See also* http://www.baidu.com/link?url=5T3_O5Yt3jKtp_hrywb271a4Lg42L68n9iSlvj7ZZi6w9WdtxTgOsbKxrH10Vuo5bkvI0Sy-ltGwekjJmdHti_&wd=&eqid=e3beaa2a0002551f000000045779d4e9.
36. Samantha D. Slotkin, Trademark Piracy in Latin America: A Case Study on Reebok, International Ltd, Vol. 18 Loyola International & Comparative Law Review, 671, 671 (1996).

Monitoring should be constant and extensive and should not only aim at finding hostile filings in the Chinese trademark database, but also focus on the products and brands of their Chinese competitors as well. In a system characterized by the first-to-file principle, foreign companies should fine-tune their trademark creation and protection pipelines so as to avoid leakages of new brands before their filing in China. Multiple-class filings, now allowed by the Chinese trademark law,[37] should be exploited in order to obtain a wide and comprehensive coverage of neighboring classes in order to avoid squatting and hostile registrations by Chinese competitors. On the defensive side, intensification of trademark use in China is the best way to obtain a sufficient degree of reputation that can be used effectively against trademark trolls.[38] Eventually, foreign company can use a number of effective preventive measures that can neutralize the ill effects of these types of trademark theft. This leads us back to monitoring systems. Monitoring is a tool commonly used by MNCs and large companies. The latter run worldwide monitoring programs that provide them with clear overall pictures of infringing trends and allow them to respond to threats in a timely fashion. Financial costs for such preventive measures are more than offset by their beneficial long-term effect of avoiding trademark theft. The case is different for SMEs. Worldwide monitoring programs are expensive and cannot be financially justified. However, monitoring is the best way to prevent trademark theft and act timely when it has already occurred. Given that China is such an important market, SMEs involved in China business should consider emplacing a monitoring system specifically for China at the very least. The business and legal costs derived by an act of trademark theft and its recovery are often much larger than those required to set up a good monitoring system at regional, if not worldwide, level.

Different is the case of trademark theft by a professional grabber. Since the database of the China Trademark Office (CTMO) went online in 2006, professional trademark grabbers have become by far the most common form of trademark thieves. No foreign business is safe from these grabbers: MNCs as well as SMEs.[39] Grabbers constantly and consistently monitor the internet to find out and list new foreign companies and their products independent of whether they are already present in the

37. Article 22.2 Trademark law provides that: "... The applicant can apply the same trademark for goods in different classes with an application."
38. Article 59.3 Trademark law provides that: "Where an identical or similar trademark has been used in connection with the same goods or similar goods by others before the registrant's application, the exclusive right holder of said registered trademark shall have no right to prohibit other people from using the aforesaid trademark from continuous use of such trademark within the original scope, but may request its users to add proper marks for distinction."
39. Office of the US Trade Representative, Small Business, http://www.ustr.gov/trade-topics/small-business/ (2012). According to the Office of the United States Trade Representative (USTR): "Small businesses are the backbone of the U.S. economy, and the primary source of jobs for Americans. Small-and medium sized enterprises (SMEs) also account for the largest group of U.S. exporters and are a major user of imported goods. In October 2009, USTR launched a new trade policy initiative to enable SMEs to grow their businesses and generate jobs through international trade. An agency-wide working group is ensuring that policymaking and enforcement better serve small-and medium-sized enterprises. USTR has also requested an investigation by the International Trade Commission on the role of small-and medium-sized exporters, to inform trade policy efforts."

Chinese market, only produce in China or have no actual relation with China. They then use the open and official internet database of the Chinese Trademark Office to see whether the targeted company and product names and logos have been registered or applied for registration as trademarks in China. If not, they will file those trademarks in the available class and even in neighboring classes to cover any suitable space. Lack of proper legislation aiming at filtering and ascertaining the good faith of trademark applicants reduce even further the possibility to prevent such form of professional squatting. As to their motivation, squatters aim principally at reselling stolen brands.[40] Professional squatters have no intention of using the stolen brands.[41] Using them would require the squatters to expose themselves to the market, and provide information they prefer to keep hidden. Using trademarks would give them away and would likely push them into legal traps. In particular, the act of openly selling or licensing the trademark could become evidence of their bad faith and could be used against them in opposition or cancellation proceedings.[42] Professional squatters just wait and see if they are approached by the victim so that they can deal with it directly.

The only way to prevent professional squatters from stealing is by filing trademarks timely. If this is what now most MNCs do, having learned how to navigate certain legal peculiarities of the Chinese trademark system, the problem remains very acute for smaller companies, which for economic reasons have less access to proper legal advice and less financial resources to build up steady monitoring businesses. The result is that once SMEs lose their trademarks, they are at the mercy of the squatters and can be easily lured into unfairly costly assignments deals or will be prevented from working their products and brands in the Chinese market.

The difference between professional squatters and competitors stealing trademarks of famous western brands are quite clear. The latter's incentives are based on free riding a famous brand to sell more of their own products. Such infringers have a business and economic structure behind them and will likely fight to keep the stolen marks until they can receive a benefit to offset their eventual loss. In such cases, the rightful brand owner must at all cost fight back and spare no efforts in winning back his rights. By doing that, he will hamper the Chinese competitor from fully enjoying the benefits derived by the stolen rights and hopefully push him to renounce to them at the prior right holder's most favorable conditions. In the case of professional squatters, the risk of troll lawsuits is extremely low, and even lower is the chance that the squatter will implement economic and financial plans to use the stolen brands on real products. A professional squatter with very active records continuously files trademarks and may hold hundreds of them at the same time. Some other operates on smaller scales. However, all of them are there hoping to see a sign of interest from the right holder.

40. Sophie Brown, Brand Wars: Battling China's trademark Squatters, CNN, http://edition.cnn.com /2014/07/17/world/asia/china-trademark-squatters-penfolds/index.html (July 18, 2014).
41. Kitsurong Sangusvang, *supra* n. 31 at 262.
42. Some Chinese case law and trademark practice recognize a presumption of bad faith in the registration of a trademark for the sole purpose of its sale. A grabber selling a trademark to a third party, even other than the right holder, is presumed to be in bad faith. This would open his flank to successful recovery actions such as a cancellation based on bad faith.

Being energetically proactive in recovering the stolen right may be actually counter-productive in that it may warn them that there will be a chance that at a certain point they may get a good economic deal out of their act of theft.

Unlike the theft of well-known trademarks by Chinese competitors, professional trademark squatting can be discouraged by reducing the chances of selling the stolen rights. In this respect, the new Chinese Trademark Law contains a number of provisions that appear to taking away those incentives that push squatters to steal trademarks of others. Among them are the norms giving legal relevance to prior use against squatters enforcing the stolen rights (i.e., against trademark trolls), the introduction of a presumptions of bad faith in case of squatters registering and selling brands without using them, making nonuse a civil defense against trolls etc. Such provisions will be reviewed in more details in the following chapter.

[2] Infringers and Counterfeiters

First, a conceptual distinction is to be made in China between Trademark infringers and trademark counterfeiters. Although the latter are also trademark infringers, they are infringers of a special type. A trademark infringer is anybody who uses a trademark of someone else without the latter's authorization. Therefore, the distinction between infringers and counterfeiters is not a legal one, but bases itself on the commercial nature of the infringer and of the infringement activities.

More commonly, we refer to a trademark infringer when a competitor is using on his products a trademark similar to that of the right holder. The generic infringer is normally a legitimate company, which mixes legit products with some others which infringe trademark rights of others. In most cases, these are stand-alone kind of infringers rather than part of an organized network. This is the typical example of a Chinese competitor copying the product and brand of the better-known foreign company to obtain an immediate economic advantage based on a free-ride effect.

Counterfeiters are normally underground organizations manufacturing and selling without authorization trademarks, products and packaging identical with those of registered trademarks' owner. In some cases, such underground operations use legally registered companies as different parts of an infringement chain (i.e., exporters, traders, part suppliers etc.).

Although there are indeed gray areas where a normally legitimate operation gets involved in counterfeiting activities within a larger organization, such distinction remains nonetheless an important one when it comes to the determination of the proper enforcement strategy. For instance, in case of a generic trademark infringement the build-up of a civil lawsuit, and therefore the use of a very strong legal deterrent are generally uncomplicated and successful, the same civil lawsuit against an underground counterfeiter may present more practical difficulties especially as to the execution of the judgment orders such as cessation of infringement and compensation, given the volatile nature of the target.

In the author's view, it is impossible to implement effective countermeasures against infringers or counterfeiters if there is no understanding and awareness of their "opportunity structures," including the relation between their motives, their actions and the consequences of their activities.[43] According to the most recent criminological studies, trademark infringers/counterfeiters can be classified based on their motives as recreational, occasional, occupational, professional and ideological.[44]

The recreational infringer is motivated by the need of amusement or entertainment. Based on the writer experience, this could be the case of the buyer of counterfeit products who knows that he/she is buying fakes and does it for his/her own pleasure or private need. In this case, the buyer and user, which for the law can be also sued for infringement, accept the legal risks of its conducts which are generally very low or merely theoretical. In such case, the personal amusement or entertainment derived by the purchase and use of counterfeits for private reasons offset the legal risk. The case of a counterfeiter involved in any of the positions of an infringement ring (manufacturing, warehousing, distribution, trading and selling etc.) appears to be different. Although even such person or entity may be to a certain extent motivated but a recreational intent, the latter will unlikely be the sole and even less the major motivational factor. Entertainment and amusement as a sole motivation would not be sufficient to offset the risks the counterfeiter is running through its direct involvement in illegal conducts that may potentially give rise to criminal liabilities.

The occasional type of infringer is the one moved to commit illegal acts of trademark infringement by opportunistic motives of a random and infrequent scale. This is the case of small and occasional trademark infringers that may combine once-in-a-lifetime illicit business with an otherwise legal employment. This is a quite recurrent type of infringer. Once caught, such infringers will normally give up illegal activities. Until caught, this infringer will repeat such experience only when a "safe" and periodic occasion presents itself. In many cases, such infringer will not be looking for opportunity, but will react and activate only if invited by third parties. This type of infringer does not derive its normal sustenance from counterfeiting. Viewed in the proper context, such kind of infringers pose only minor threats to the trademark holders. At the same time, if properly handled, they may turn into a positive investigative tool. Once caught, these infringers can be normally persuaded to disclose where they bought the infringing products from, whom they sold them, and many more information about a possible larger infringement ring in which they but played a minor but critical role, thus opening the doors to more penetrating investigative actions against professional organizations behind them. To this group belong also the trademark infringers in the traditional sense.

Occupational infringers are those that derive occasion for committing illegal acts from their professional position. Typical occupational counterfeiter is the person or entity that profits of an employment or business relation with a trademark right holder to abuse of such relation. This is for instance the case of a supplier that in infringement of its contract with the principal overproduces licensed products during after work special shifts or that of the official agent or distributor stealing the trademark of the

43. John Spink, et al., Defining the Types of Counterfeiters, Counterfeiting and Offender Organizations, 10 Crime Science, (Springer, December 1, 2013).
44. *Ibid.*

principal. A last group of occasional counterfeiters includes employees of the Chinese subsidiaries or suppliers of the right holder, acting without knowledge of their upper management. In order to maximize profits, they may decide to subcontract the manufacturing of parts and components to professional or occasional infringers depending on the scale of their counterfeiting plans. This poses an obvious and direct threat to the brand owner's supply system, as often substandard parts are officially supplied as if made by the contracted Original Equipment Manufacturer (OEM).

Professional infringers are those motivated by the fact that the crime they commit fully finance their lifestyle or sustain their daily economic needs. Typical professional infringer is the criminal organization structured purposefully to commit IP related crimes. This is the most dangerous kind of counterfeiter and the most difficult to deter from committing crimes. Their revenue model is exclusively or principally based on the acts of trademark counterfeiting, although other forms of businesses, even of legal nature, may be branched out in relation to the core counterfeiting activities. Most counterfeiting organizations have a hard core central structure made of professionals (ex. organization runs a hotel, a Karaoke club or restaurant near its factory). A professional organization is centered on professional infringers; however, it may avail itself of recreational, occasional and occupational infringers to conduct some of the relevant activities (warehousing, trading exporting etc.).

Eventually, ideological infringers are terrorists that use counterfeiting as a way to finance their ideological and subversive political plans. This latter infringer is what we would call the mastermind of a large criminal network made of professionals, occupational and occasional counterfeiters.

Depending on the motives and the related classification of the infringer, the right holder may decide to adopt different enforcement measures. A professional organization will require larger enforcement efforts in order to be deterred and precluded from further infringing the right holder's trademarks, than an occasional counterfeiter working on his own would require. However, it may be impossible and even inappropriate to expect a right holder to invest resources in combating ideological infringers, i.e., international terrorists, given the nature and scale of the involved crimes. It is sovereign States that have to find and bring to justice ideological infringers.

Most relevant to the planning of enforcement strategies in China is therefore the group of professional infringers and in particular, organizations of professional infringers. Obviously, an isolated professional infringer, well motivated and screened by internet may indeed cause some troubles to a foreign brand owner. Many such small-scale infringers are often traders making their livelihood by supplying and trading fakes online. Such type of infringer deserves to be dealt with appropriate countermeasures. At the same time, the financial resources of the right holder should not be exclusively tied down in infringement actions against such isolated targets. Counterfeiters' organizations are indeed the most dangerous trademark infringing structure for a right holder, because they can carry out large counterfeiting operations with high volumes of manufacturing and distribution of fakes, which can cause direct damages and losses to the trademark holders. A criminal organization is by definition a group of people or people and entities.[45] An organization does not need to be large to be defined as such. An organization does not need to be driven by certain loyalties but can be hold together by the fact that a number of core professional infringers decide to take common advantage of their illicit acts.[46]

Although the demand and supply of counterfeiting goods varies among different types of products, there are common structural traits characterizing the organization of counterfeiting enterprises in China, i.e., manufacturing and warehousing are mostly conducted under cover of secrecy, while trading is conducted openly. Counterfeiters can generally be distinguished based on the financial and organizational forces behind the counterfeiting activities. At one end of the spectrum, there are individuals or small-scale, often family-run types of counterfeiting ventures. These can be either legitimate businesses alternating legal to illegal manufacturing and trading activities, or small underground workshops. These entities may conceive and implement their own counterfeiting business independently or may decide to serve as one of the many manufacturing, warehousing or trading rings in a broader counterfeiting chain. In this latter case, smaller counterfeiting units will often operate without knowing or having direct contact with the masterminds of the entrusting syndicate.

Counterfeiting organizations and syndicates are economically supported and organized by financially capable entities and individuals which use a complex network of businesses to run their large-scale counterfeiting ventures, some as underground operations, and others as legitimately registered companies. The financial engines behind such counterfeiting organizations are not normally directly involved in any of the material activities required for running a counterfeiting business. They will create new structures or bring together existing ones which then take over the functions of manufacturing, labeling, trading, distributing, selling etc., often separately or unaware of each other's identity and even location. The result is that the seller, the last ring of this chain, often does not really know who has made the products he is exhibiting in its market stall or trading in the internet. In this way, a separate and extemporary intervention on any of the external manifestations of the infringing venture (shutting down domain names, and e-commerce sites, raiding of retailers, factories or warehouses as stand alones) will not be sufficient to bring down the whole organization, as each of these units are not fully integrated in and directly related to the masterminds of the counterfeiting ring and can be therefore replaced by others in short time. Such syndicates are mostly criminal organizations or local economic potentates with strong political relations in their territory.

Professional counterfeiter is a dangerous job and partakes of the typical criminal low life standards. Each person operating in a professional counterfeiting organization is aware of putting at stake in this illegal venture not only his economic interest, but also his personal safety and freedom. This explains why thugs and gangster types are

45. United Nations Convention Against Transnational Organized Crime, Article 2(a) (November 10, 2000), A/RES/55/25. http://www.un-documents.net/uncatoc.htm (accessed June 2016).
46. Jay S. Albanese, The Causes of Organized Crime: Do Criminals Organize around Opportunities for Crime or Do Opportunities Create New Criminals?, Vol. 16, Journal of Contemporary Criminal Justice, 409, 423 (2000).

normally involved in counterfeiting operations. It is evident that these psychological and sociological factors cannot be underestimated when conceiving and implementing a brand protection strategy in China. This short overview also shows how complex counterfeiting structures can be and how strong the drive of its members. Lukewarm efforts from corporate white collars sitting in sleek skyscrapers abroad will unlikely be sufficient to dissuade such highly motivated and risk-prone pirates from infringing again and again. Knowledge of these common traits of the counterfeiting organizations and the understanding of the infringer's motivating factors will be of great help to the brand owner when deciding the most appropriate enforcement strategy. At the same time, a successful anti-counterfeiting strategy must also counterbalance these human factors by having the brand owner put together a team of well-profiled and motivated workers who can emotionally engage in what can be defined without doubt as an intense psychological fight.[47]

[3] The Role of Preparatory Investigations and Case Build-Up in Trademark Litigation

Trademark enforcement in China can be successful as far as the right holder has been able to collect the most complete and extensive array of facts and evidence means in function of the planned enforcement actions and the prefixed strategic goals. Prior examples have shown how the search for evidence and the build-up of the case are strongly related to the chosen strategic goals. Also, fact finding is a component required for the selection of the appropriate legal action (tactical goals).

Investigative activities vary according to the type of infringement, the strategic and the deriving tactical goals. Generally, it is complained that in China it is difficult to find evidence of infringement and even more difficult to find evidence of illicit profit or damages. This can be partly true in that China does not avail litigants with penetrating judicial tools when it comes to civil litigation. However, this perception tends to be overstated in that there are indeed correctors and legal tools available as long as the right holder can recognize them as such and use them at the right time and the right manner. As we shall see, there is now an automatic obligation on the alleged infringer to provide accounting records related to the infringing acts of manufacturing and selling. Presumptions of authenticity of transactions can be secured prior to the lawsuit with appropriate evidence acquisition processes involving public notaries. Preliminary

47. Doing anti-counterfeiting in China is a dangerous job. There are plenty of war stories among investigators telling about suspicious mobs threatening and chasing them away. Even trying to take pictures of a stall with fake bags in a market can become dangerous and should not be practiced by inexperience neophytes. Following are examples of such cases. On November 4, 2009, counterfeiters of fake Rolex and Longines watches beat the local enforcement officials in Changchun City, Jilin Province, China in order to grab the fake watches back (*see* the link: http://news.163.com/09/1106/01/5NDBAB2700011229.html). The head of a small village in Cangnan county, Zhejiang province is the owner of an underground fake wine workshop. On December 16, 2000, when the local AIC went to the workshop to raid the infringing products, the village head instigated and led the villagers to beat the AIC officials which resulted in two official's injury (*see* the link: http://www.people.com.cn/GB/shehui/44/20010104/370087.html). More stories could be told.

injunctions, evidence and property preservations are also available to a litigant to overcome difficulties in evidence collection. All this will be considered in the section concerning evidence acquisition within a litigation procedure in China.

At this stage, fact finding is examined as a Rule of Engagement, whereby evidence collection is but a part of fact finding accompanying and completing an infringement investigation. Therefore, reference to investigation and fact finding in this section refers to the activities aiming at collecting all kinds of information about the infringer and the infringing activities, including but not exclusively focused on finding sources of judicially usable evidence. If foreign companies are partly made to believe that there are difficulties in collecting evidence, they are rarely made aware of the importance of a 360-degree approach to a trademark theft or infringement matter. Rarely a foreign company complaining of a trademark squatting will think of or be advised as to investigating in-depth and in all directions the facts of the case first. Normally, the foreign counsel or manager will contact his local lawyer or directly his Chinese correspondent and will ask him to take immediate action to recover the lost right(s). Normally the counsel will prepare a legal response with little or no further fact finding. In fact, a lawyer makes money with legal remedies and not with intense investigations and intelligence work. This is a typical legal approach dictated by the urgency of filing legal means to recover a lost trademark and eliminate obstacles. However, a strategic approach aiming at effective business solution of the problem should follow the Rule of Engagement requiring the right holder to know his enemy and the facts about his conduct. The indisputable data that will be provided in the following chapter show that most trademark opposition and a majority of trademark cancellations in China, especially when concerning not well-known foreign brands, are rejected. One of the reasons for such failure is that right holders and their counsel have used standardized legal reactions to a challenge without considering the broader picture of the case and the availability of other strategic options that may have had a better chance to succeed. The common action-standard reaction approach results in good part from the tendency of right holders and their lawyers to respond to business threats immediately and with the most direct and obvious legal tools without having as yet collected in-depth information about the infringer and its infringing activities. For instance, if a trademark opposition is timely still available, a lawyer will immediately recommend it without considering whether it will have good chances of succeeding. The lawyer will think that, given the short time window to file an opposition, it is better filing it than not. Such an approach is very common and shows the very basic legal thinking of the counsel. He will always recommend filing an opposition if still available because if he does not do that and the deadline is missed, such legal tool will be lost to the client. Therefore, such decision will derive not much from a strategic thinking process that weighs facts and business aspects of the case, but from a mere concern for missing a legal deadline and, from the lawyer perspective, the worry that this may later result in his professional liability. However, at the time the lawyer makes that suggestion, he does not know if the opposition for instance will be indeed the best way to solve the client's business problem and he cannot see that there may be better ways to provide a client with an effective legal solution that solve the business and not only the legal problem. If you ask a Chinese counsel about the chances of success of the suggested course of action, he/she will likely reply that they are 50%, which is like not answering at all. In fact, at that moment, lacking all the needed information and based on his previous experience only, the attorney cannot indeed make a reliable estimation. Once the choice of a legal tool such as trademark opposition is made, this will tie down the case for a stretch of time, preventing the use of other legal tools that, given full knowledge of facts, could have had better chances to succeed. This leads us again to the main point under discussion. A hasty decision taken without having investigated the facts about the infringement and the infringer, will likely lead to legal action with uncertain legal outcome and even with incalculable and unforeseeable business effects.

As we shall see more in details in the Chapter of this book concerned with opposition and hostile filings, it is very critical for the right holder's implementation of an effective enforcement plan to know whether the squatter or the free rider is a Chinese competitor or a professional squatter, whether he produces or sells products with the stolen trademark, whether he is working alone or within a larger organization, if he has a judicial history for IP violations, if it is a single person and individual entrepreneur or a large local company, whether it has local connections or not, whether is infringing other rights of the same person or others as well, whether it has been liquidated or he/she are dead, etc. Hostile or stolen trademarks will be normally attacked immediately by using the most obvious mean of reaction, for example opposition, without knowing the facts about the infringers and his/her intentions. The risk of neglecting such facts and building strategies based on mere legal considerations often leads to great disappointments and also explains why so many foreign brands have all and continue all to do the same mistakes. As to trademark counterfeiting, the issue is even more complex. Counterfeiting investigations are rarely conducted on a direct input from the right holder, the latter being a mere passive receiver of sightings coming by informants on the field. In such context, the risks is the incapacity of the right holder to verify whether such sightings are genuine or not, and even if they are genuine to decide whether they are indeed relevant to their ultimate business strategy. This topic will be discussed in depth in the part of the book concerning counterfeiting.

What emerges in general is the evident need for right holders to put facts first and action later, which is the opposite of what happens nowadays in relation to IP conflicts in China. Enforcement strategies and decisions are made based on scantly investigated facts. The reason for that is partly due to the difficulty of finding facts through judicial means. In Europe, a right holder will rely often on injunctions or other penetrating prelitigation tools such as evidence preservation and evidence description. In the US, discovery will lay all the facts open on the table. In China, injunctions are difficult to obtain in principle for a self-imposed conservative stance of the Chinese judges. Evidence preservation may be hampered by procedural problems which often allow infringers to hide the indicting evidence. Courts will generally grant prelitigation injunctions and preservations only if there is a solid prima facie evidence of infringement, which in turn requires the prospective plaintiff to do a lot of its evidence collection work in advance of the litigation. This obviously results in objective difficulties in finding relevant facts and evidence. Administrative burdens and inconsistent administrative practices can result in the total or partial impossibility of obtaining even company records without a court order. Even when a certain fact-finding work is conducted, this often results in ineffective work for very critical lack of strategic thinking on the part of all professionals involved. In fact, lawyers will tend to hand leadership to the field investigators and passively wait for their work's results. The investigators, if not well instructed and led will tend to go and look for the things that make sense to them or will do as little as possible to maximize his profit. However, they are not lawyers and what they find may be totally irrelevant to the case build-up. At the receiving hand, the lawyer will accept such results rather passively and come to a legal conclusion based on what the investigators have spontaneously found. The ensuing strategic planning, including the adjustment of the strategic goals may thus be based on partial and often insufficient facts, and more dangerously on partial or completely missing intelligence analysis. For example, if the investigator is not instructed to conduct thorough investigation of each single company and shareholder of a group of companies he may miss on an important party, that will result in that party being neglected as a defendant. The result could be that even a won lawsuit may not stop the infringement because that forgotten party remains untouched by the injunctions from the judgment. Also, IP lawyers will instruct investigators to look for IP relevant facts. Therefore, there will rarely be a deeper and more comprehensive strategic investigation. It is in the collection of certain facts that alternative and creative solutions may be found, as shown in the example of the canned fruit case at the beginning of the chapter, where the real blow later came from the infringer's liability of manufacturing substandard quality products! Damages are also a typically neglected field. Most lawyers will tell you that it is difficult to collect evidence of damages and so they will resort to statutory damages, which in turn weaken the importance of the case in the eye of an overworked court. This is going to be the more so now that the ceiling of statutory damages has been raised from CNY 1 million to CNY 3 million. Although this is a positive legislative development, and there are already is one case where such ceiling has been reached,[48] the risk is that Chinese lawyers and judges will not push for higher damages for a long time. This is a risky development in that damages will never in the end be apportioned on the real losses or illicit profit but on a relative perception: CNY 3 million is so much more than it used to be that we should all be happy that at least we now got as much here in China. However, this is the way it is in China and we must accept this risk factor when planning enforcement strategies (this last point belonging actually to the third Rule of Engagement: knowledge of the battlefield).

To conclude the reasoning on the relation between lawyers and investigators as critical to the implementation of the second Rule of Engagement, it is remarked that the lawyer must be the one that helps the right holder in building up the enforcement strategy and he must master the facts and "bend" them to the planned enforcement actions and arguments. Facts take a different tinge in the eyes of a lawyer. He will see them in function of its enforcement goals and plans. Investigations must therefore be "formatted" to this reconstructed, although always flexible, interpretation of the facts

48. Mengkeleier Gufen Youxian Gongsi Su Beijing Nuoyakate Fuzhuang Youxian Gongsi (蒙克雷尔股份公司诉北京诺雅卡特服装有限公司) [Monclers P.A. v. Beijing Nuoyakate Clothing Company] April 23, 2015 (Beijing I.P Ct.)(China).

by the lawyer in function of the set strategic and tactical goals. This is a mental process that has to take place before an investigator is involved in the case. Ideally, the investigator must be the operative arm of the thinking legal mind and must be given as little room of discretion as possible. At the same time, investigations must be also conducted in a broad spectrum to comb out possible relevant facts that are not known at the end of the desk investigation by the attorneys. It is a game of checks and balances in which on one hand investigators are left free to roam around and bring facts to the lawyer, to be then rained in and sent on executive tasks to obtain mean of evidence according to a plan prepared and managed by the lawyer. Normally, at the beginning of an infringement investigation, the investigator can be left free to find facts with just basic guidance. After such phase is completed, and the lawyer has acquired sufficient factual knowledge to confirm or amend its preconstructed evidence plan, then the investigator will be instructed down to the last details on which steps he will have to take next, to complete the guided fact and evidence finding actions. It is therefore very important for a right holder to build up a strong lawyer-investigators team that is used to work on these types of cases, where the lawyer has the preeminent function of planning, initiating and steering the investigative activities.

At present, fact finding about the infringers and the nature of their illegal actions are yet not in the cultural baggage of right holders and practitioners in China. However, the determination of the nature, both legal and commercial, of the infringer and its organization, along with its motives are most critical in the selection of the appropriate targets and the enforcement means, as well as the refinement of the general strategic goals. Many cases of enforcement fails because action is taken by the right holders without having knowledge or with just a superficial knowledge of the opponents, their business, business structure, appropriation models and motives. Therefore, investigations must not be confined to the phase of evidence acquisition but be a primary actuator of the enforcement strategy, encompassing all business aspects of the case and not the mere legal ones.

[i] Desk Investigations and the Challenges of China's Internet

Investigation of the facts of an infringement must focus on the identity of the infringer and all the related personal, business and legal connections. Preliminary desk work by the lawyers is critical to these searches. People and their life and relations must be carefully scrutinized. Often infringers are built in networks and organizations, and limiting investigations to the first entity appearing to be infringing may result in misplaced decisions and ultimately in the misfiring of the enforcement actions. Investigating the identity of companies and individuals is very challenging in any part of the world. In China, it is even more challenging for several reasons. Company records, as well as other company-related data in public database are often inaccessible without a court order. The problem is that desk investigations are preliminary to the filing of a lawsuit. Some administrations may allow the extraction of copies of company records only upon presentation of a notarized and legalized PoA.[49] Even when accessible, these records may not be updated and accurate. Each local administration has its own policies. At the same time, the Internet offers opportunities, while at the same time it hides insidious traps, in that information in the internet cannot always be relied upon unless after objective verifications.

Desk investigations must start from the data provided to the lawyer from his client. Even if the right holder has conducted investigations on his own, obtained credit reports on possible targets, collected some product samples etc., the external counsel, after studying these materials, must conduct his/her own searches independently and even repeat certain investigative searches already conducted by the client. The reason for this is twofold. On one hand, a fresh new search will be helpful to confirm the information already detected by the client normally through its sales staff in China or abroad. On the other hand, the search conducted by the lawyer is based on different factual and legal premises compared to the "sales" view normally informing initial searches by the client. The change of point of view will throw lights on initial facts that were not further analyzed by the client, which in turn may lead to new investigative trails. A lawyer passively accepting the facts as depicted by the client may miss on the most important facts and will build a strategy on weak or even wrong factual premises.

As indicated above, the first verifications of facts should start from the desk searches on the targets of a possible enforcement. The first basic facts to ascertain are whether the infringer is a person or an entity. In the first case, the searches will then concentrate first and foremost on details such as e-mail addresses, telephone/mobile numbers, chats and blogs. In this respect, the internet plays a most important role. For obvious regulatory reasons, it is illegal for professionals to conduct searches on most records of individuals with few exceptions. In sum, a right holder cannot ask for instance the police to tell him where the alleged infringer lives, who his wife is or whether he pays income tax regularly. On the other hand, people nowadays disseminate vital information in the internet throughout the years, and many such information is retrievable from open and public records: University affiliations, degrees, job postings, blogs on any kind of topics, QQ Chats, WeChat (Weixin) pictures etc. More traditional ways to establish connections between individuals and companies or with other individuals are telephone numbers and e-mails. Family names can also help hinting at personal relations. Only company databases are openly accessible and can show sometimes shareholding structures, thus allowing cross checks via internet. The same activities can be repeated for all the individuals involved in the targeted companies. Sales people's names in the company's web page or e-commerce platform

49. If a foreign company is the right holder, it will have to provide its Chinese agent with a power of attorney to conduct such administrative searches. In some cases, like in Guangzhou, company registry administrations require the agent to obtain a power of attorney in legalized form. Legalization is a process by which documents or evidence created abroad acquires certified authenticity in China. The legalization process varies depending on the country but it ends up always with an apostille stamped by the Chinese diplomatic authorities in that country. This process can take weeks and normally slows down proceedings unless right holders is timely advised and provide such power of attorneys to the agent along with the engagement letter.

pages always come with telephone numbers, and by cross checking telephone numbers, connections with others of individual and companies begin to emerge. In China, it is possible to conduct searches on telephone numbers that help locate the region where the number was registered or the SIM card purchased. Online chats can be surprisingly a great source of information. In many instances, it is possible to uncover the chat profile of the targeted persons and uncover precious information about their lifestyle, their business and personal relations. Also important is for right holders to keep always good records of any Chinese person and entity they have been dealing with in China. In many cases, infringers or squatters can be former business partners or employees. It is always a good practice to collect employee's data sheets including their private mail and mobile numbers, the name and data of the institutions where they acquired their education, etc. Later these data may be the one revealing that behind an infringement hides a former business relation. Such findings turn into means of proving evidence of bad faith which is a critical legal requirement in trademark oppositions, cancellations and infringement lawsuits. Generally speaking, investigation of individuals through the internet may give out results that are often more reliable than the information available in the internet about companies' business.

The same activities can be repeated for the targeted companies. For instance, job posts from companies that signal current expansion projects and whether and in which direction they are expanding. However, when it comes to the investigation of companies' data in the internet, the risk of hitting upon unreliable information is quite high. Counterfeiters operating underground will have no internet presence at all. Traders will be their mouthpieces and the only interface with the potential buyers. Other infringers may fabricate addresses and company affiliations both as a smoke screen against investigative incursions, more often to give buyers the impression that the company is part of a larger and economically solid group. In case of trademark thieves, they hide under a corporate appearance that often reveals to be a mere internet façade, behind which there are no legitimately registered businesses. In the best cases, only little information is provided on a website and parallel investigative work is paramount to find what is below this scant collection of facts.[50] If a company such as those can lie about their identity, they will also lie about their activities. Rogue websites are therefore unreliable about the provided company information. The same could be said of companies operating on e-commerce platforms. Whereby most of the company-related info in the net is of dubious authenticity, the info about the individuals operating behind them, i.e., the contact data of a sales staff or trader is normally reliable. If it was not, there would in fact be no way for this company to be contacted

50. Peter S. Sloane, Yijun Ge in their Article, Managing Trademark Investigations for Non-use in China: A Comparison with U.S. Practice, ABA Landslide Magazine http://www.americanbar.org/publications/landslide/2012_13/july_august/managing_trademark_investigations_nonuse_china_comparison_us_practice.html (July/August 2013). The authors of this article argue that: "Indeed, the online and offline worlds are less merged in China compared to the United States. Many Chinese companies thrive on centralized e-commerce platforms like Taobao as opposed to operating independent online stores like companies in the United States. Most local and small businesses do not have the need to connect with customers over the Internet. For companies that do maintain an online presence, their websites tend to be simple and do not provide sufficient business information for investigation purposes."

and do business. That is why, in many cases, intense work on the people is the fastest and most reliable way to tread back to companies. In many instances, factories or registered trading or operative companies other than the one appearing to the right holder may be uncovered by following the threads left by individuals. Just as an example:[51] an e-shop on a notorious e-commerce platform had been notified of infringing a foreign brand. It was also found that the e-shop had presented to the e-platform a PoA from the brand itself in order to avoid take down of its website. The PoA had been forged and the case turned into a criminal law matter. The brand owner was correctly advised to conduct preliminary investigation of the e-shop in order to collect sufficient evidence to file a criminal complaint against both the e-shop owners and the e-commerce platform. The e-shop trading company revealed to be inexistent. No official records of that company were found. The only remaining evidence was a woman's name and a telephone number. Further investigations revealed that the telephone number led to a company in a nearby city. This company was a legally registered one-person enterprise and its major shareholder and legal representative was located through a preliminary web search of the company public records. On-spot investigation of the company address led to a residential area where the identified man was working. Further, cross checks provided hints that this man was related by family ties to the woman originally operating the unregistered trading company behind the e-shop. Further checks were conducted on the information available on the man, and his business profile started to emerge. This allowed the specialists to classify this infringer as an occasional counterfeiter and prompted direct confrontation. Based on the collated facts and the profiling of the targets the direct contact bore immediate fruits. The man confessed he had received the original PoA the brand had issued to its online counterfeiting monitoring partner from the e-commerce platform and had modified it to look like it were instead addressed to the e-shop. He also confessed that the woman was his sister. Further pressure convinced the infringer to provide notarized evidence supporting his confession, which allowed the brand owner to prepare a strong action against the e-platform for breaching contracts and illegally providing without authorization to the infringer confidential documents of the brand owner. This is a very good example of how the three Rules of Engagement described in the book were correctly applied with successful results. Facts where thoroughly investigated, people were thoroughly checked, a correct determination of the infringer profile and its motives was conducted which revealed the most efficient course of action against the infringer. Based on the above, the legal tactical strategy was shaped correctly: Instead of pursuing the occasional infringer, he was used to build evidence against e-commerce platform, which turned to be the main target of the legal action. Without following the Rules of Engagements, the right holder would have likely concentrated all efforts against the e-shop, thus using precious resources. When later it would be likely realized that the major "business problem" lied with the e-commerce platform, his case would have run out of steam and would have required extra

51. This is a case of the author and names must remain confidential.

financing. We can imagine how stressed the in-house would have been, looking for a way to justify requesting more money from the boss or the board.

Another point that has emerged from this story is the fact that information and facts collated through the desk investigation were further checked, confirmed and expanded through fieldwork. We shall elaborate this point soon in the next paragraph. Furthermore, it is also to be remarked that e-commerce platforms are not only to be seen as a nest of infringing activities to shut down but also as a very useful investigative tool.[52] This aspect will be dealt with in more depth in the Chapter concerning anti-counterfeiting and brand protection in China.

Before concluding with these remarks on desk investigations and the complexities of navigating the internet in China, a few notes are added here on the difficulties of obtaining facts corroboration through official company records in China. In the west, official company records are normally available to any person and entity upon request to the official recorders and sometimes by payment of fees. This extends to places in Asia such as Hong Kong and Singapore. In China, the type of information openly accessible for free to the general public are limited, while for accessing the full paper records of a company, more restrictive rules apply. In particular, access to company records is regulated by the Enterprise Registration File Information Query Method (also referred to as the "Method") issued by SAIC back in the year 2000.[53] Article 5 of the provisions regulates two types of enterprise registration records: machine-readable records or e-files, and paper records. E-files are published in the website of each territorially competent company registry within the Administration for Industry and Commerce (AIC) which can be accessed freely by any person. These are official records and can be used as evidence in judicial and administrative enforcement proceedings. These records contain basic information about the company registration such as the registration number, incorporation date, name of company, registered address and capital etc. Additionally, such records may contain other information such as approval letters, Articles of association, certificate of domicile, major changes such as name and address changes, termination, liquidation etc. The paper records are the complete records of the company and contain all the documents filed by the company since its incorporation. These are most critical because they contain the financial statements and economic records of the company, major contracts, assets-related documentation, shareholders, board decisions etc. Such documents can only be accessed by the police, public prosecutors, judges, national security authorities, and inspection and supervision authorities such as tax and custom and quarantine administrations. Privates can access them only through their legally empowered lawyers within an already pending legal proceeding in which they are parties (Article 7 of the provisions). Article 7.2 of the Method further stipulates that for confidential matters in the paper or internal file, no inquiry could be made unless it got the approval from the relevant AIC. In practice,

52. Paolo Beconcini, Working With Taobao Against Fakes, The Global Legal Post, http://www.globallegalpost.com/global-view/working-with-taobao-against-fakes-27761230/#.UgyeA5IyZXt (August 15, 2013).

53. 国家工商行政管理局关于修改《企业登记档案资料查询办法》第十条的通知, Gong Shang Qi Zi [2000] No. 81 (Notice of the State Administration for Industry and Commerce on Amending the Tenth Provision of Method of Checking the Enterprise Record Information April 29, 2000).

many AICs were quite liberal in granting access and providing stamped copies to private parties not involved in legal proceedings. In 2012, AICs in major cities started applying the 2000 regulating to the letter, thus limiting again access to paper corporate filings after short-sellers used them to highlight accounting discrepancies that led to stock plunges and regulatory investigations over domestic companies listed abroad.[54] In practice, an expert investigator knows where it is possible to obtain full paper records and where it is not. However, contrary to what it is commonly believed, there are neither new national regulations nor locally written regulations limiting access to paper filings. These limits existed since the year 2000. In practice, such limits are not enforced uniformly and some AICs still provide copies of paper records to private inquirers outside the cases regulated by the law. However, it is custom that even in such cases, copies of paper records are passed along without official stamps from the local AIC. This means that these records cannot be used in court and are for mere investigative reference. It remains that everybody can at least conduct cross checks with at least the online records of a company. It is evident also that if a company is not listed in the e-files of the place of its alleged location, this alone can constitute a presumption that this company is unregistered and a mere fictitious business name.

Other accessible public records in China that can be used during desk searches and are very important in the profiling of the infringer and the fact collection preliminary to the formulation of enforcement plans are the trademark and patent official databases.[55] These are reliable information sources which are constantly updated and maintained. However, only the Chinese versions are reliable in that their English translations are not complete and slowly updated and serve only for general reference purpose. Such searches are very important in that they can reveal with high degree of reliability the type of infringer. Squatters will have large lists of many brands in their trademark portfolio. A search will show all of them and whether other brands have taken actions against such filings as well. A patent search may reveal that a company that have filed a similar trademark or has stolen the foreign brand and filed it in China as a trademark has also patented technologies that strongly compete with those of the infringed brand owner. In such case, it is evident that the trademark infringer is a serious competitor bent on attacking full front the brand owner's market shares. On the other hand, an infringer that shows no further efforts to duplicate or prevent the brand owner, may be classified as occasional infringer and may not have long standing interests in defending his hostile right takeover position for long. All these facts will help determine the best course of enforcement action in each case. The same is extended to the database of the National Administration of Copyright and in particular in respect to the catalogue for registration of copyrighted software.[56]

Other important databases that are freely accessible to the public are those concerning medical products and devices, cosmetic and disinfectants hold by the

54. Bloomberg News, China Limits Access to Company Files After Short-Seller's Bids, http://www.bloomberg.com/news/Articles/2012-06-08/china-limits-access-to-company-filings-after-short-selling-bids (2012).
55. For trademark http://sbcx.saic.gov.cn:9080/tmois/wscxsy_getIndex.xhtml, for patent http://211.157.104.77:8080/sipo_EN/search/tabSearch.do?method=init.
56. http://www.ccopyright.com.cn/filequery/apply-query.jsp.

Ministry of Health and the State Food and Drug Administration. In these databases, records can be found of whether a competitor and infringer's product has obtained the necessary licenses for being manufactured or sold in China. Such information is indeed important in that violation of such licensing regulations often provide excellent alternative actions against infringers and are mostly related to both administrative and criminal liabilities. For instance, if an opposition or cancellation is unsuccessful or very difficult and proceedings pend for long time, checks could be made of such databases to see whether the competitor is selling his competing product with all the needed licenses and registrations. The same can be extended to all kinds of chemical products which are defined as dangerous by the law. In such cases, the law requires specific labeling standards. Failure to comply gives rise to administrative liabilities that can end up in products' confiscation, heavy pecuniary fines, revocation of business licenses etc. In sum, even if the main tactical action aims is winning back a stolen trademark or stopping an infringement, parallel options cannot be discarded without the risk of missing better opportunities to achieve the final strategic goal. As long as something is good enough to deter, stop and punish an infringer, it cannot be left outside the enforcement strategy. That is why fact finding and investigations are so critical to the overall success of an enforcement strategy. Additional public records are available for other type of licensed company activities, such as those related to environmental licenses for operating certain types of businesses including those involving hazardous products.

Another research sources that could be relevant to a trademark case, especially those regarding infringement and counterfeiting, are the databases concerning the listing of product quality standards. Products that are subject to mandatory quality standards, i.e., autos, toys, home appliances, pharmaceuticals, cosmetics, food, PVC made products etc., must comply with these standards. Failure to comply with these mandatory standards results in administrative and even criminal liabilities. Consulting whether an infringer product is affected by mandatory quality standards means also that the right holder has an additional weapon against the infringer or the trademark usurper, in case investigations on the field confirm that the infringer products violate such standards. It is therefore important during investigation, to collect such information and keep this option available in case other strategies may result impossible or when additional legal pressure may be of benefit to the right holder's strategy.

Custom database can be consulted to verify if a company or individual have recorded their IP rights at Custom for Custom IPR protection.[57] This is important in defensive terms to evaluate the risk of possible use of the hostile or squatted trademark as a troll against the rightful foreign owner. In fact, such recordation will be a prelude to ex officio enforcement of the recorder trademark right by the Chinese Customs.[58]

57. http://www.haiguanbeian.com/zscq/search/jsp/vBrandSearchIndex.jsp.

58. As we shall see more in details in Chapter 4, Customs' enforcement of IP rights is either conducted upon input and request of the right holder or can be also carried out by the Chinese Customs on their own initiative when they see suspected infringing goods in entry/exit. In order for a trademark owner to enjoy the Custom spontaneous intervention, it is necessary for the former to record his/her rights with the customs. That is why the recordation of a squatted or hostile trademark is a clear sign of the intention of the competitor or the thief to use that

Furthermore, a database also kept at China Customs helps the public verify the rank of an import/export company based on their track records including violation of IP rights.[59] The General Administration of Customs (GAC) classifies importers and exporters as "Advanced Certified Enterprise" (AA in the past), "General Certified Enterprise" (A in the past), "General Credit Enterprise" (B in the past) and "enterprise needing review" (C &D in the past).[60] This classification can help investigation of counterfeiters and their distribution network and prioritize actions based on whether the exporter for instance is a company already affected by bad IP records, such as those related to prior claims or legal action related to export of counterfeit goods.

Judicial database are also available to the public. The SPC has appointed a vendor to provide such service.[61] In such database, we can search by person or entity to determine whether they have been judged in any kind of civil case. Additionally, single courts publish their judgments in internet and can be freely searched.[62] This can be useful in general trademark infringement and anti-counterfeiting cases. The fact that an infringer is repeating the same or similar illegal acts may influence also the determination process for damage compensation, in that the judge is free to consider such facts in his/her overall evaluation of the willfulness of the infringing act.[63] On other fronts, judicial records can be consulted to collect useful information about a court and a judge decision score card. For instance, how many cases a court/judge have decided involving a foreign party and IP rights. This can help rating the Court/judge "friendliness" and "IP expertise." Preliminary knowledge of a court decision trend on similar matters can be of great use to the shaping of forum shopping strategies in trademark infringement cases. In practice, this means that when a right holder has the possibility to plan and execute evidence acquisition that supports the jurisdiction of a certain court of his own choice over his/her case (forum shopping),[64] then knowledge of the work

trademark against the foreign victim. Such sign is important in that it will require immediate counter action by the right holder to prevent trolls in the form of custom seizures of OEM shipping and lawsuits.

59. http://www.customs.gov.cn/publish/portal0/tab9408/.

60. 《中华人民共和国海关企业信用管理暂行办法》已于2014年9月4日经海关总署署务会议审议通过，现予公布，自2014年12月1日起施行 (The Interim Measures of the Customs of the People's Republic of China for the Administration of Enterprise Credit, as deliberated and adopted at the executive meeting of the General Administration of Customs ("GAC") on September 4, 2014, are hereby issued and shall come into force on December 1, 2014).

61. Zhongguo Caipan Wenshuwang (中国 裁判 文书网) [Chinese Judicial Document], http://wenshu.court.gov.cn/.

62. *See* for instance www.pkulaw.com; www.openlaw.cn; www.itslaw.com.

63. Article 63 of the Trademark Law provides that if there is malicious infringement and the existence of serious circumstances, the amount may be more than one up to three times the aforesaid determined amount. These are punitive damages Chinese-style. Although not further specified, it can be argued that prior illegal conducts, infringement judgments or indictments for other IP rights infringements could be used to support the existence of malicious intention and serious circumstances.

64. As we shall see in more details in paragraphs of Chapter 3 dedicated to an overview of the Chinese litigation system, there are certain cases in which a right holder can organize its evidence acquisition in a way that supports the jurisdiction of a court rather than another one. For instance, the law generally allows the plaintiff to file a lawsuit for an IP infringement at the domicile of the defendant or that of the place where the infringement has taken place. The latter

of such court (not the assigned judge yet because this will be known only once the lawsuit has been filed!), will confirm whether the court of choice is indeed experienced on the matter at hand and has issued decision favorable to right holders in previous identical or similar cases.

Other public records are important, such as the vehicle registration records. However, record verification cannot be conducted based on license plate numbers only. The database of the police on vehicle fines and driving records can be accessed only by the Vehicle Identification Number (VIN).[65] This number is normally indicated in the front windshield area of the vehicle and it is the vehicle identity card number. Therefore, investigators must be aware that taking pictures of a license plate can only provide limited and external information, for example a database can match license plates in different cases to find that the same vehicle was used in another infringement before. However, it will not tell where the vehicle got fines, who owns and drives it etc.

Property and real estate records are not accessible by the public not even upon payment. The same applies to criminal court records. However, there is an open database that collects records about companies and individuals that have committed fraudulent business activities and have bad credit scores. These data are sourced from the Security Department of China, Safety and Supervision Bureau, China Insurance Regulatory Commission, China Banking Regulatory Commission, Office of Legislative Affairs, National Development and Reform Commission and State Administration of Industry and Commerce.[66] Another database is kept by the SPC and concerns dishonest people or entities under execution procedures.[67] It is interesting to remark how such exception to the protection of companies and peoples' privacy by the Chinese government appears also to be related to the "shame" function of individuals hurting the community by their legally as well as morally reprehensible behavior. It is indeed of Confucian heritage the shaming of morally unacceptable behaviors in China.[68] It is evident that on the other hand, infringing IP rights is considered illegal but not immoral, given that there are unfortunately no similar official records of trademark counterfeiters and infringers!

Other public records that can be freely consulted by the public are press archives in libraries and mostly in internet. Press material can be very useful in confirming peoples' identities, the date of certain facts and any possible fact or statement of an infringer against itself. For instance, a trademark infringing company may have issued a press release in which they declared the great sales figures for the allegedly infringing

can be different places, such as the place of sale or the place where the negative consequences of the infringement have occurred.

65. http://www.bjjtgl.gov.cn/ is the link for such searches in Beijing. When you type 违章 in the search engine, Baidu will provide you with the police department's link which is close to the IP address.
66. www.creditchina.gov.cn.
67. http://shixin.court.gov.cn.
68. Gordon G. Chang, The Coming Collapse of China, Random House (2001) provides examples of "shame" initiatives of Confucian memory in modern China. Also recent examples of public shaming can be found in several press articles such as Murong Xuecun's, China Tradition of Public Shaming Thrives, The New York Times, http://www.nytimes.com/2015/03/21/opinion/murong-xuecun-chinas-tradition-of-public-shaming-thrives.html?_r=0. (March 20, 2015).

product at a certain time. This could be great evidence to support a damage compensation claim in a civil lawsuit for trademark infringement.

As anticipated at the beginning of this section, investigations here have been treated as activities finalized to the understanding of relevant facts, preliminary and necessary to the build-up of a successful enforcement strategy. How this information and facts are transformed into and used as evidence in the selected enforcement plan, will be treated in the following section describing the Chinese trademark enforcement system.

[ii] Field Investigations and Evidence Acquisition

Data collected in the internet and from public records must be verified and corroborated by cross checks and other independent facts in the real world. The goal is to have one fact emerging from a piece of information corroborated by other independent facts. Certain verifications and certain facts can only be uncovered or confirmed by field work. Locations, vehicles, type of trademark use and commercial activities are to be always checked by field investigative work. Evidence of the act of infringement is also collected normally through field activities, i.e., by creating a pretentious act of sale or receiving offer for sales, uncovering a factory currently producing infringing goods or a warehouse storing them. In this section, we will provide a general overview of the investigative tools available to a right holder to confirm or uncover facts and collect evidence. Of the forms of evidence collection and the legal implications of certain formalities, we will discuss more in details in the following section regarding administrative and judicial enforcement of trademark rights.

The generic term "field investigations" encompasses all those activities that require a direct involvement of the targets, like sending e-mails, chatting online, making telephone calls under pretext with a primary or secondary target, purchasing goods via e-mail, fax, telephone or internet, surveillance of locations and targets, pretext visits to targets, pretext meetings and negotiations with targets etc.

As a matter of fact, a professional infringer, both as a one-man illegal enterprise or part of an organization, is always suspicious and cautious when interacting with new third parties, or parties that are not introduced by trusted contacts. Direct contact with a target may be more or less successful also depending on its position within a selling structure. Deciding what the opening steps of a field investigations shall be, is a most critical decision that may affect the rest of the investigation either way. A miscalculated step may uncover the pretext of the investigator and blow off his cover, and together with it, the chance of catching an infringer by surprise.

A number of factors come into play when planning and executing field investigations. Most important are secrecy and surprise. Enforcement in China will be successful if the blow can be delivered against the infringer by surprise. The greater the degree of surprise, the stronger the blow and thus the chances to send the infringer to the ground at the onset of the enforcement action. An infringer shocked on the ground will be feeling the deterring and punishing force of the enforcement action and will be less likely to recover and repeat such infringement. If an infringer is openly or indirectly warned of a possible enforcement, he will have chances to avoid the blow completely or will take actions to reduce his risks and minimize damages. Lack of surprise will reduce the deterring force of an enforcement action that will result in a chance for the infringer to keep infringing later on in a way or another. In the case of an underground counterfeiting operation, a prewarning will prompt the closure of the underground factory or warehouse, so that when the enforcers arrive for a raid, they will find nothing! In case of trademark infringement by a competitor, blowing off the preparations of a civil lawsuit, will allow the infringer to timely relocate his assets to reduce the impact of damage compensation and allow its machinery and manufacturing structure to remain in total or in part unaffected by the later enforcement. In sum, surprise is a major factor for the successful enforcement of trademark rights in China. Through the element of surprise, the initiative is left in the hand of the right holder that, under the benefit of the first surprise blow, can deliver further punches and strengthen his/her litigation position. Such necessary precondition for the success of the enforcement endeavors, must be kept at all stages of an enforcement preparation and obviously become a critical element at the moment in which the right holder approaches the infringer during the phase of field investigation with the purpose, ultimately, to collect the final needed evidence and start enforcement.

From an operative standpoint, field investigations are conducted to corroborate facts emerged during the desk investigation and collect evidence. The starting point is the complete desk investigation itself. Infringer profiling as well as a correct reconstruction of facts, will lead the field steps. There is no standard recipe for a successful field investigation. A telephone call to an infringer may be useless in many cases, but it may be the turning point in another one. Profiling of the type of infringer is the preliminary step to decide how to organize and execute the first approach to the infringer and its organization. An occasional infringer may be generally suspicious but will also be less cautious because it has never experienced trademark enforcement. Traders are the easiest to approach because they are supposed to get in contact with buyers. That is why, trademark infringements involving e-traders allow a number of covert operations that can be organized and conducted under a rather high degree of safety. Traders are always keen to respond to inquiries by phone, e-mail, e-chats etc. They provide as many contact data they have in order to facilitate anybody on the "demand" side to reach them and buy their products. It may be different in case of a trademark-squatter. A competitor that has stolen a right holder's trademark will unlikely open itself to outer inquiries; however, he wants to sell that product and patient work will open all doors. Depending on the type and the degree of awareness of the infringers, the right contact and business tools will have to be adopted to create business opportunities. One of the end goals of such investigative activities is to win the trust of the target. This will allow the investigator to uncover more relevant facts about the target and the illegal business that will affect the shaping of the underlying enforcement strategy.

One important activity during field investigation is the acquisition of samples of the infringing product. Acquisition of samples of the infringing product normally reveals a number of important information and provides critical evidence that will be the base of the enforcement action. Invoices, payment transactions including bank accounts, signed contracts, product labels and packaging, and shipment records are but some of the precious information that can be obtained through a simple purchase transaction. This information will then be acquired in specific forms to turn them into evidence that will be used against one or more people or entities that appear to be involved in the illegal transaction, such as sellers and manufacturers and among the latter, there may be different manufacturers which include for instance the parts suppliers and the assemblers of parts made by others.[69] Furthermore, the right holder will have the chance to look at the product itself, determine the use of the trademark on the product and its packaging. The process of product and packaging verification has important repercussions on the structure of the claims, including damage compensation claims and will affect the selection of the appropriate IP right to be enforced. Also, additional grounds for claims may emerge from the verification of the purchase records, i.e., unfair competition claims for infringement of proprietary rights on the decorative elements of the product, copyright claims and even design or invention patent claims, depending on the case. Also, the information acquired during the field investigation will indicate other possible claim grounds which may not be necessarily IP related. For instance, the labeling of the infringing or counterfeit product could violate relevant product quality regulations giving rise to administrative claims and liabilities against the infringer or counterfeiter. Field investigations, like the prior desk activities have therefore a double purpose. On one hand, they corroborate or uncover relevant facts that will shape the enforcement strategy, on the other, they are the moment in which evidence of such facts or those relevant to the case are collected.

Field investigations in China present challenges to the right holder, and can be indeed quite difficult. One first challenge was mentioned already. Infringers tend to be cautious. Even sales people, who normally are open to talk to and meet with potential buyers, take preventive steps to ensure such buyers are "genuine." This means that a person entering into contact with an infringer must be versed in business dealings in China. He will need to be familiar with the business jargon as well as with the product and its markets, both legal and illegal ones. Preparation of the field team before initiation of direct contact with targets is therefore necessary. Right holders must be aware that the success of a field operation will also depend on the know-how and information they can provide to their field team. Often investigators will work together with the right holder's sales staff to increase the credibility of the direct approaches to the target. Furthermore, in order to overcome cautiousness, purchase of products must be for real and sometimes more than one purchase will be necessary to convince the counterpart of the buyer's credibility. It is known that to obtain best intelligence and evidence of an infringer and its partners is to befriend its bosses, go dinner with them and share with them beloved Chinese businessmen entertainments like Karaoke, banquets and booze. Like in any business in China, success depends on building a sort

69. Article 113 Opinions on Several Issues Relating to Patent Infringement Establishment, formulated by the Beijing Higher Court in 2001. Although related to patent infringement, this provision can apply by analogy to trademark infringement. In this norm, the Beijing Higher Court listed a number of activities that are equivalent to manufacturing, such as assembling parts of a complex product or assembling the complex product itself.

of relation (guangxi) with and with the trust of the target first. This will open the doors to suppliers' factories and warehouses and will allow the right holder to increase the number of targets in the list of its planned actions. It may be objected that such information and evidence could be obtained through court investigations and injunctions. The problem materially, is that the cautiousness that cloaks the behavior of an infringer will be even more penetrable once he is sued or raided. In that moment, he will unlikely take a cooperative stance and incriminating documents may have since long disappeared, as well as leads to other rings in the infringement chain. Also, court powers are not as penetrating as those of the police. Civil courts can order an infringer to disclose names or records, but he may refuse and cannot be coerced in doing so. He may then lose the case due to his lack of defense, but will save others from the net set by the right holder. The same applies to administrative enforcement bodies such as AIC. They have no coercing powers and cannot extract information from people or their records, including digital and computerized ones. That is why it is always recommended to have the right holder's team dig as much facts and evidence as possible before entrusting any further evidence collection work to the judicial or administrative authorities. Normally, a court will be more compelled to act promptly when a request for evidence preservation or evidence acquisition is supported already by evidence. Eventually, in view of the need of considering investigations as a strategic and preparatory tool and not only as functional to evidence acquisition, it is important for right holders to invest time and resources in proper investigative activities before taking rush and likely unfruitful enforcement actions based on basic facts.

A second aspect that affects the success of an enforcement action is that of secrecy. If the party investigated gets wind of the investigation or is tipped off by someone about it, then all efforts will be in vain. One important precaution is that of having a small number of people from the company involved in China trademark infringement matter. Leaks are common within a company especially if many employees of its subsidiary are involved in the case and are not aware or reminded of the confidentiality of the information they are handling. Theoretically, certain aspects of confidentiality can be regulated in the employment agreements. However, the best practical way to reduce the risk of leaks from within is by reducing the number of heads involved in the work. Secrecy also requires that the right holder refrains from sending warning and cease-and-desist letters before having completed its investigations. Aside from the fact that such letters rarely produce any positive effect for the right holder, being in most cases ignored, they can also fire back, in that they may give the addressee the right to seek a court judgment to declare its noninfringement (i.e., negative declaratory action or Chinese Torpedo). This action, filed at the friendly home court of the infringer could stall, if not utterly ruin, the whole enforcement plan of the right holder. This issue of warning letters in China shall be examined later when describing the Chinese trademark enforcement system.

Another important aspect concerning field investigation is that of making sure they are conducted in compliance with the laws of the PRC. It is important for a right holder to work with local partners that can guarantee transparency and full compliance with the law and company's regulations. It is in fact very common, that informants and enforcing authorities will ask for money in exchange for enforcement. Right holders must ensure that none of their employees and service providers is involved in acts of bribery or corruptions during the investigative and the ensuing enforcement phases. This may be a risk in particular in counterfeiting investigations which are conducted often against criminal organizations. The integrity of local investigators is a paramount necessity and should be ensured by both contractual agreements and direct field control. Controls and verification of investigative work through intelligence analysis and by flanking investigators with trusted staff shall ensure both compliance and quality.

A serious quality and compliance issue that has recently emerged is that of the increasing number of fake sightings of counterfeiting targets and fake AIC raids reported to right holders by local Chinese informants. Informants and investigators are a peculiar trait of China anti-counterfeiting "market" as we shall later see in more details. They are key players in discovering counterfeiters and are primarily responsible for the initiation and management of administrative and police enforcement of trademarks against these counterfeiters. Therefore, their honesty and professionalism are critical requirements for the right holders to be comfortable in investing money in anti-counterfeiting field work. However, there have been, there are and there will be Informants and investigators that may be tempted into inventing a sighting to get paid fees for ghost raids, especially in a business environment characterized by high competition and small margins of profit. It must be considered that informants and investigators retain a rather tight control on the information they pass along to a right holder and are in the best position to determine the scale and relevance of infringement sightings of factories and warehouses. Brand owners have a limited capacity in filtering the information they receive from the informant and are even less capable of getting direct confirmation of the nature of a reported counterfeit sighting. If we also consider that forging documents in China is not difficult, then we can imagine how this issue may be more serious than anybody appears to admit. If a fake sighting is uncovered, there will be no case and no money will be paid to the informants and investigators. If such a case has occurred, either the right holder is not aware of it, or even if he has suspicions, he may decide not to escalate it internally for a number of opportunity reasons. The risk of such cases is not only that they result in fees paid for no real work, but also all informants will be informed of the occurrence by word of mouth and more will try to exploit that company's weakness. Also, a fake raid may become the base for an attempt at civil or criminal enforcement against the raided party which may then result in a judicial fiasco and in further loss of money and reputation.[70] Counterfeiters are business people and they know how to react to the right holder strategies. They find new ways of infringing and take all possible precautions to minimize their risks. For instance, splitting production and storage of fake products is one way to reduce

70. Kathy Chu, In the Fight Against Counterfeits, Even the Raids Can Be Fake, Wall Street Journal, http://www.wsj.com/articles/in-the-fight-against-counterfeits-even-the-raids-can-be-fake-1449171005?tesla=y (December 5, 2015). *See also*: ABB v. China United Intellectual Property Protection Center, Beijing No. 2 Intermediate People's Court (March 19, 2010). In a case involving the famous company ABB, a fake raid had been the base for an ensuing civil lawsuit. The lawsuit brought up the truth about the fake raid and the case was dismissed. ABB then sued the investigative company for damage compensation but lost the lawsuit.

enforcement efforts by right holders. Right holders have internal guidelines and budgets to be kept under control and will likely refrain from using money for administrative enforcement raids netting small quantities of fake goods, especially in industries with consumer products and fakes with low retail value (fashion and apparel). Informants in such cases will have more difficulty in convincing right holders to raid such small quantities. For an informant, a missed raid is a lost business opportunity. Informants are often unwilling to invest long time in complex investigations because larger cases are more difficult to find and require more intense investigative efforts and investments without guarantee of quick returns in economic terms. The result is that informants may prefer resorting to fake sightings to make up for lost opportunities. This is but one example of the risks posed by fake sightings and raids. More in general, right holders and their local partners in China must ensure certain standard of quality by implementing internal processes to reduce the risk that investigators may commit illegal acts, such as bribing, corruption and double plays down to fake anti-counterfeiting enforcement.

In conclusion to this section, it is again important to remark again that both desk and field investigations should be controlled by the right holder's entrusted attorney and its own legal department. By having this professional filter, the company can screen itself from wrongdoings on the field, but most of all can implement the needed measures to ensure the success of the investigation: planning by lawyers will lead execution-focused investigative actions. Proper preparation of the investigators as to the enforcement strategic and legal objectives will ensure that he will indeed concentrate on all the activities and facts that are relevant to the case, thus avoiding being uncovered and most of all wasting time on wrong investigative trails that are not relevant to the enforcement strategy. Filters and processes will also help keep secrecy and secure achievement of surprise effect. Eventually, filters and processes will reduce the risk of working with dishonest informants and field investigators, thus ensuring both compliance and achievement of the investigation's goals.

[D] Third Rules of Engagement: Know the Battlefield – An Introduction to the Trademark Protection and Enforcement System in China

Trademarks are not transnational rights and their protection scope extends only to the territory of each country in which trademark protection is sought.[71] Each country is therefore sovereign when choosing if and how to protect trademark rights. International treaties will also play an important role in the definition of the scope of protection of a trademark to a certain extent.[72] However, each country retains an exclusivity in deciding what and how is protectable as a trademark.

71. Graeme B. Dinwoodie, Trademarks and Territory: Detaching Trademark Law From the Nation-State, Vol. 41 Houston Law Review 885, 892-893 (2004).

72. International treaties relevant to China and the protection of trademarks in China are the Paris Convention for the Protection of Industrial Property, the Madrid Agreement concerning the International Registration Marks, the protocol of the Madrid Agreement, the Nice Agreement Concerning the Classification of Goods and Services for the Purpose of Registration of Marks and the Agreement on Trade related Aspects of Intellectual property Rights, known also as

Trademarks in China are protected by the Trademark Law[73] and the related implementing regulations[74] as well as by further legally binding administrative laws and regulations concerning the examination, the revision and the adjudication of trademark rights,[75] as well as several Interpretations and Provisions of the SPC concerning the enforcement of trademark rights.[76]

The present section will provide an overview of the relevant provisions concerning the protection of trademark rights and their enforcement in China. A basic knowledge of the law and procedures is fundamental for several reasons. Knowledge on the acquisition of trademark rights in China will affect the availability of protectable and enforceable legal instruments against thieves, infringers and counterfeiters. Only trademark rights that are recognized as valid in China can be duly protected and enforced. Therefore, the first part of this section will concern the registration of trademarks and the tools to eliminate obstacles to their protection and removal of hostile similar trademarks that could cause confusion among the relevant users of the

TRIPS. All these agreements are integral part of the Chinese law in force of the provision of Article 142.2 of the general principles of Civil law and are thus directly applicable in China.

73. Trademark Law of the People's Republic of China (中华人民共和国商标法) adopted at the Fourth Meeting of the Standing Committee of the 12th National People's Congress on August 30, 2013, promulgated by the "Order of the President of the People's Republic of China No. 6 (中华人民共和国主席令第6号)."

74. Implementing Regulations of the Trademark Law of the People's Republic of China promulgated under Decree of the State Council of the People's Republic of China No. 358 on August 3, 2002 and revised under Decree of the State Council of the People's Republic of China No. 651 on April 29, 2014. 中华人民共和国商标法实施条例(2014 修订) [现行有效], 根据《中华人民共和国商标法》(以下简称商标法), 制定本条例。2002 年 8 月 3 日中华人民共和国国务院令第 358 号公布 2014 年 4 月 29 日中华人民共和国国务院令第 651 号修订.

75. Trademark Examination Standards (商标审查标准) of December 31, 2005; Trademark Trial Standards (商标审理标准) of December 31, 2005; Trademark Review and Adjudication Rules (商标评审规则) of June 1, 2014; Provisions on the Identification and Protection of Well-known Trademarks (驰名商标认定和保护规定) of August 3, 2014; Measures for Registration and Administration of Collective Trademarks and Certification Trademarks (集体商标, 证明商标注册和管理办法) of June 1, 2003; Opinions of the Supreme People's Court Concerning Trial of Administrative Cases in Respect of Trademark Right Granting and Confirmation (最高人民法院关于审理商标授权确权行政案件若干问题的意见) of April 20, 2010.

76. SPC's Interpretation on Issues Concerning Jurisdiction and Application of Law (关于审理商标案件有关管辖和法律适用范围问题的解释) of January 21, 2002; SPC's Interpretation on Property Preservation Regarding Registered Trademarks (关于人民法院对注册商标权进行财产保全的解释) of January 22, 2002; SPC's Interpretation on Application of Law Concerning Stopping Trademark Infringement and Evidence Preservation Before the Trial (关于诉前停止侵犯注册商标专用权和保全证据适用法律问题的解释) of January 22, 2002; SPC's Interpretations on Several Issues concerning the Application of Law in the Trial of Civil Disputes (最高人民法院关于审理商标民事纠纷案件适用法律若干问题的解释) of October 16, 2002; SPC's Interpretations on Serval Legal Issues in Handling Criminal Cases of Intellectual Property Rights (关于办理侵犯知识产权刑事案件具体应用法律若干问题的解释) of December 22, 2004; SPC's Interpretation on the Trial of Cases of Civil Disputes over the Conflict between Registered Trademark or Enterprise Name with Prior Right of March 1, 2008; SPC's Interpretations on Several Issues Concerning the Application of Law in the Trial of Civil Dispute Cases Involving Well-Known Trademark Protection (最高人民法院关于审理涉及驰名商标保护的民事 纠纷案件应用法律若干问题的解释) of May 1, 2009.

trademarked products. The second part will focus on infringement of registered trademark rights.

The third Rule of Engagement, knowledge of the "battlefield" means therefore knowledge of the law of the country where disputes may or are already taking place. Knowledge of the battlefield, i.e., the Chinese law and legal procedures has a twofold function. On one hand this knowledge is needed as a base to conduct proper business in China by securing trademark rights and eliminate obstacles to their acquisition. In this respect, such knowledge is part of the set of information needed by a right holder to conduct business in China. On the other hand, this knowledge comes at hand when it is time to determine enforcement plans when something in the trademark business goes wrong, like in the case of theft or infringement of a trademark right. In sum, if trademark issues are business issues, all the means to prevent or remedy to the damages done by an infringement are legal matters, and knowledge of the law is key to the choice of the right legal tools to achieve the planned enforcement goals.

[1] Acquisition of Trademark Rights in China

The Trademark Law of China is conceptually designed to protect both trademark rights as private rights of ownership as well as consumers and the orderly functioning of the market.[77] This sought-after balance of interests is reflected in some relevant provisions. Articles 1 and 7 of the Trademark Law provide that a trademark owner has the obligation and is thus liable for the quality of the products in circulation in the market which bear his registered trademark in the interest of consumers. Articles 42 and 43 provide that in case of assignment or license of registered trademarks, the transferee and the licensee respectively shall guarantee the quality of the goods on which the trademarks are used. Even the determination of trademark infringement is based on the criteria that similarity is judged upon whether it is susceptible to cause confusion among the relevant users as to the origin of the disputed products.[78] Another important norm responding to the need of striking a balance among conflicting interests is the First-to-File principle governing the right of ownership of trademarks in China.[79] Unlike China, common law countries such as the US and Canada adopt a First-to-Use rule for ownership origination of trademark rights.[80] One of the reasons for adopting a First-to-File approach was that of creating a high degree of certainty for the market and the consumers as to the ownership of trademarks.

In China it is therefore the person or entity that files a trademark first, who will enjoy the related exclusive rights on the trademark. This same provision is also the primary legal reason for the existence of trademark theft.

77. Peter Ganea, Thomas Pattloch, Intellectual Property Law in China, 84 (Kluwer International 2005).
78. Article 57 Trademark Law.
79. Combination of Arts 4 and 33 Trademark Law.
80. International Trademark Association (INTA), Trademark Basics: A Guide for Businesses, http://www.inta.org/Media/Documents/2012_TMBasicsBusiness.pdf (2012).

[2] Available Rights and the Principle of Exclusivity

According to Article 8 of the Trademark Law, any sign that distinguishes the goods of a natural person, legal person or other organizations from those of others, including any word, device, letter, number, three-dimensional sign, color combination, sound[81] and combination thereof, may be registered as a trademark. Also, the law provides for the registration of "collective marks"[82] that is marks registered in the name of a group, association or any other organization and used in business activities by its members to indicate their membership, and "certification marks," that is marks which are controlled by an organization that exercises supervision over particular goods or services and are used to indicate that third-party goods or services meet certain standards pertaining to place of origin, raw materials, mode of manufacture, quality or other specific characteristics.[83] Another type of trademark is that of geographic indication of origin.[84] Eventually, the Trademark Law allows and provides for three-dimensional trademarks.[85]

Any natural person, legal person or other organizations that needs to acquire the exclusive right to use a trademark in the production and operation activities shall file an application for trademark registration with the Trademark Office.[86] This is also the legal base for the First-to-File principle and the lack of general legal relevance of prior use as to the origination of ownership over a trademark. The application for a trademark must be filed in good faith, i.e., without the malicious intent of preventing other prior right holders to register the same trademark.[87] This is a critical provision in the fight against trademark theft and will be thoroughly analyzed in the following chapter. Also, it is important to remark that an applicant can file for a trademark application directly with the Chinese trademark office (National Application) or can file for the registration of an International Trademark through the Madrid Convention and Protocol by designating China as one of the countries to which such application shall be extended.[88] Also, within six months of filing the first application for registering the same trademark for the same goods in a foreign country, the applicant may have priority in accordance with any agreement concluded by and between the PRC and the foreign country concerned, or with the international treaty to which both countries are

81. Sounds could not be trademarked before the entry into force of the actual Trademark law of 2014. An example of pending applications for sound trademarks are the music of the Intro of China Radio International in class 41 (App. No. 14503615), and interestingly the sound of a vehicle acceleration in class 9 (App. No. 15465462).
82. Examples of collective marks are for instance 绍兴黄酒 (Shaoxing rice wine) registered by the Shaoxing Rice Wine Association in class 33 (Reg. No. 1388983) and UL registered by UL LLC (Reg. No. 1219955).
83. Article 3 Trademark Law.
84. Example of Chinese Geographic indication mark is 大黄堡虾 (Da Huang Bao Shrimp) of Tianjin City Wuqing District Dahuangbao Aquiculture Association in class 31 (Reg. No. 13938194) and Scotch Whisky of the Scotch Whisky Association (Reg. No. 5915032).
85. Article 12 Trademark Law.
86. Article 4 Trademark Law.
87. Article 7 Trademark Law.
88. Article 21 Trademark Law.

parties, or on the basis of the principle of reciprocity.[89] The benefit of claiming a foreign priority is that the date of filing in China will be dated back to the date of filing of the first identical application abroad. This will help overcome all the intervening identical or similar applications from third parties between the foreign and the later Chinese filing date. It is indeed a useful tool, but it requires the owner a certain degree of skills and organization to keep track of all filings and managing them in most effective ways. This is normal for large companies, while it may be indeed a problem for small and medium enterprises. The risk of missing a priority claim is that between the original home-country filing and the extension to China within the twelve months' time window, is that a later China application may be prevented by an intervening identical or similar filing by the third party. In that case, the prior foreign application will be of no use in the recovery efforts that will have to be initiated in China. Also, failure of recovering the lost trademark will result in the impossibility of using it by our original foreign applicant in China. Knowledge of battlefield is therefore a critical Rule of Engagement and will help foreigners to make timely savvy choices when it comes to securing valid trademark rights in China.

The function of trademarks is that of distinguishing the origin of the goods or services of a company from goods or services of competitors. Therefore, the most important condition for a trademark to be registered as such is its distinctiveness. The same distinctiveness and the degrees thereof will also be the base for the determination of whether another hostile trademark can be considered similar or not. The distinctiveness of a trademark is determined by its overall shape and composition, including its visual effect, its pronunciation and meaning or lack thereof. A trademark can be composed by several of the elements indicated in Article 8. Most commonly trademarks are either made by letters and numbers compositions, by logos and the combination of logos and words/numbers. Signs which are descriptive of the quality, ingredients, functions or characteristics of the underlying products or services for which they are to be used lack distinctiveness and cannot be registered.[90] Descriptive signs can however become distinctive with their use in time.[91]

Based on the First-to-File principle, a trademark is acquired only upon registration. With the registration, the holder will enjoy exclusive name and economic rights over the trademark for the goods and services for which it has been registered.[92] Article 22 Trademark Law provides that a trademark application shall be made in accordance

89. Article 25 Trademark Law.
90. Article 11.1 Trademark Law.
91. Article 11.2 Trademark Law. An example of such instance is the trademark "Onetouch" by Johnson & Johnson (Reg. No. 3384889) in class 5 (Blood glucose monitor with the test Article). The third party Huang Yun Zhong filed nullification application with TRAB by stating the subject mark only indicates the features of the goods. In its decision Johnson & Johnson v. TRAB ([2015] Gao Xing Zhi Zhong Zi No. 1077), the Beijing Intermediate Court concluded that such mark has acquired distinctiveness through wide and continuous use by its registrant in China. Also, whether or not a descriptive sign has acquired distinctiveness depends on the cognition of the trademark by the relevant consumer's group, and there will be distinctiveness if the relevant consumers believe that the trademark is no direct indication of the goods provided (Beijing Higher Court in Panasonic Corporation v. TRAB [2010] Gao Xing Zhong Zi No. 1213).
92. Article 3 Trademark Law.

with the prescribed classification of goods/services. The designation of goods/services is the most critical feature in the determination of the scope of protection of a trademark. With a limited exception for well-known registered trademarks as we shall see later, registered trademarks extend the right of exclusive exploitation only to the goods/services of the designated classes. An application for trademark registration shall be made according to the published classification table of commodities and services.[93] Although China adopts the Nice Classification in its actual 10th edition, this "adoption" does not mean complete adherence. China in fact adopts its own classification book which is based only to a certain extent on the Nice Classification. This means that even when filing for an International Trademark designating China with goods/services based on the Nice Classification, once this application goes into the Chinese national examination phase, the "Nice goods/services" designation will be "transported" and "translated" into corresponding areas, called "subclasses" of the Chinese Classification.[94] Also, this "transition" from one classification to another will be carried out by the Chinese examiner without consultation of the applicant. The Chinese Classification book is characterized by a rigid and detailed system of subclasses. Unless otherwise determined by the same Classification book, each trademark will extend its scope of protection only to the specifically selected subclasses. For instance, if a trademark is filed for class 41, and this class contains seven subclasses, it could result that there may be seven identical or similar trademarks all coexisting in class 41 as long as each of them is applied for one of the seven different subclasses.[95] It is therefore possible that the goods of an International Trademark registration may be incorrectly translated into the wrong subclasses, thus affecting the protection of that trademark against possible hostile filings, hijacks and infringement. This is why it is strongly recommended that companies with aims at business in China focus on Chinese national applications rather than International filings. In this way, the applicant will have more chances to select the proper subclasses, thus maximizing the scope of protection of its trademark. This is more so in that for national applications, the new Trademark law provides for the possibility of a dialogue between the applicant and the examiner which can exchange clarifications on disputed points of the application, including of course the designation of the proper subclasses.[96] Ultimately, the designation of classes and subclasses will affect the possibility of enforcing the trademark against infringers and counterfeiters on one end, and to prevent, oppose or nullify hostile trademark filings and hijacked trademark applications. Knowledge is again a key factor in determining a proper business and trademark strategy. Assuming

93. Article 13 Implementing Regulations to the Trademark Law.
94. Article 39 Implementing Regulations to the Trademark Law: "Commodities or services designated in the application for the international registration of their trademarks shall not go beyond the scope of the commodities or services basically applied for or basically registered within China."
95. Dan Harris, "China Trademarks: What's Madrid Got to Do with It?" Above The Law http://abovethelaw.com/2014/04/china-trademarks-whats-madrid-got-to-do-with-it/?rf=1 (April 21, 2014)). The same can apply to all classes. For instance, in class 25, clothing under subclass 2501 is not considered as similar to footwear in subclass 2507 or headgear in subclass 2508.
96. Article 29 Trademark Law.

that an international trademark is a medicine good to cure all the malaise is wishful thinking that does not account for a country's peculiar economic and legal factors. Such knowledge is even more important if the readers consider that most international filings start from abroad, that is from attorneys that do have at most a general knowledge of Chinese law and tend to rely on local correspondence. A foreign attorney will primarily think of maximizing the use of the client resources by filing an international application with extension to China. His focus is all on getting a trademark filed in as many countries as the client requires with one application process only. Knowledge of the Chinese legal system, such a critical rule for successful IP business in China is completely neglected. China will not feature into the picture until a problem emerges, in the form of a partial or total rejection of the trademark, or, maybe worse, years later when the trademark is to be enforced but it does not possess the desired and sufficient scope of protection to guarantee a successful enforcement. Again, the Rule of Engagement is critical to the right holder and his foreign consultant, in that lack thereof will lead them to often wrong choices when it comes to structuring a trademark portfolio in China.

As to the applicant, the Trademark law does not put any limits or restrictions to his legal nature (individual and companies) and nationality (Chinese and foreigners). Restrictions apply only to the modus of filing: foreign applicants must file trademarks through a Chinese trademark agent, while Chinese nationals can apply trademarks on their own.[97] The Trademark Law provides also that applications filed and registrations obtained with fraudulent means are invalid and can be nullified.[98] In practice, there are but few or even no controls as to prevent use of fraudulent means at the time of filing. Individuals applying for trademarks are not subject to any substantive check that may help revealing their bad faith and prevent trademark theft. In particular, the only applicable norms provide that the applicant gives proof of his identity along with the application.[99] There is no further check of the applicant business or relation with the goods/services he is applying the trademark for. Also, there is no check of an applicant's criminal or trademark infringement records. This allows squatters to continuously repeat acts of theft without risk of being suspended or stopped from doing so at the time of filing.

From the moment of filing of an application, certain rights are already borne. In particular, a pending application will constitute an obstacle to the registration of a later identical and similar application for identical or similar goods/services. This also means that when planning the application for a new trademark, the applicant should

97. Article 18 Trademark Law.
98. Article 44.1 Trademark Law.
99. Article 14 of the Implementing Regulations to the Trademark Law provides that: "To apply for trademark registration, the applicant shall submit certificates that prove their identification. The name of the applicant for trademark registration shall be identical to the name on the certificates submitted." Also, on August 26, 2015, The Chinese Trademark Office issued a guideline titled "Application for goods or service trademarks" (http://sbj.saic.gov.cn/sbsq/sqzn/201404/t201 40430_144506.html), which specifies that the required documents include the identity certificate of the trademark applicant. None of the other required documents for a trademark application concerns further proof of the good faith and business of the applicant.

first verify whether an identical or similar trademark has already been applied or registered by another party in the same class of goods/services. It is through such verification that often cases of theft or free riding are uncovered. This is why availability searches for a newly planned application are a "must." These searches may not always be fully accurate, but they are nonetheless the only and most accurate way to determine trademark availability and uncover cases of trademark hijacking. As to the accuracy, it is noted here that the online database of the trademark office is not automatically updated on a 24/7 basis, and therefore even a few hours difference may be sufficient to hide a similar or identical application that was just filed. Also, trademark devices such as drawings and logos may sometimes be difficult to search thoroughly due to the required level of sophistication of the search algorithms.

The new Trademark Law allows multiple-class filings. In the past, an applicant could file only one trademark per class. This was considered one of the reasons why to a certain extent trademark squatting could not be prevented. Squatters will target the relevant class/subclass for a given trademark if available and occupy the relevant subclasses within the class designated by the right holder. If this is not possible, they will apply the hijacked trademark in neighboring classes or sometimes even in classes that are completely different and unrelated to the goods/services on which the hijacked trademark is normally used. While the latter one poses generally no concrete threat to the right holder, the former can become an obstacle to a normal and effective use of the original trademark right. For example, if a trademark is registered in class 25 for clothing, an identical or very similar one in class 18 for leather goods could turn into an obstacle to the former's holder business. In fact, consumer may be induced to buy the goods of the hijacked trademark in class 18 by the belief that this trademark is the same trademark and product of the original right holder. Trademark holders will normally tend to apply a trademark in the class and subclasses of direct interest. They may then expand the trademark scope of protection to other subclasses or to even new classes of products or services only at a later stage, when products lines and markets expand. This leaves enough space for trademark squatters to engineer hostile filings and it is therefore difficult to prevent hijacking by filing on a class-by-class basis. Multiple-class filings allow, at least in principle, to plan and execute multiclass filings that can cover since the beginning a number of connected subclasses and classes, thus creating a protective ring around the main class and subclasses. Such strategic filings will limit hijackers to subclasses and classes that will be far enough from the core filings that will result in no disturbance for the right holder and his customers. However, multiclass filings present downsides. On one end, multiple-class filing only receives one registration number and one filing/registration date, thus creating an original obstacle to squatters that find potential loopholes immediately covered by such filing. However, in case of opposition against only part of the goods/services or in case the applicant/registrant tries to assign part of the goods/services, it must involve the whole application for all the other classes as well because there is no possibility of a division of the application. A division of the application becomes possible however in case of a partial rejection of some of the designated goods/services. In this case, the applicant can choose to divide the multiclass application into one application covering the approved goods/services so as to get registration first, and one application with rejected goods/services for the purpose of filing a request for review. Another risk is nonuse cancellations. If some of the classes covered by the multiple filing have initially a defensive and blocking function only, the applicant must ensure nonetheless a concrete business use of the trademark in these classes within three years from the date of registration. Nonuse for three consecutive years could expose the trademark to cancellation actions by any third party. Multiclass filings are therefore trademark filings for mature businesses, i.e., businesses that have a clear business development plans that blends early filings with planned use within a certain period of time.

Also very important are the provisions of the law regarding division applications. This is a very useful tool that can be used in case of rejection of a trademark application and is a strategic tool that can match well with those needed to recover hijacked trademarks as we have seen for instance in the case of the canned food company example. In that case, partial rejection due to the hijacked trademark was lessened through a division application which had at least allowed the right holder to get a trademark in China for part of his goods. The law provides specifically that in case the Trademark Office rejects a trademark registration application in terms of certain designated commodities (partial rejection), the applicant may divide the partial application preliminarily approved into another application and the divided application shall keep the filing date as the original application. If the applicant needs dividing an application, he must apply with the Trademark Office for a division within 15 days upon receipt of Notice on Partial Rejection to Trademark Registration Application from the Trademark Office. Upon receipt of the division application, the Trademark Office shall divide the original application into two parts and announce the new application number formed by the divided application preliminarily approved.[100]

It is recommended practice in China to make sure that a foreign trademark or a foreign trade name is also registered in a plausible, normally transliterated Chinese version. Forgetting such precaution can cause infinite headaches.[101] Squatters have the means to find out when a Chinese brand is used but is still unregistered in China and will grab it first. As many of the examples shown in the opening chapter of this book, it is often very difficult if not impossible to win it back. If a company has not thought of a Chinese translation or transliteration of its trade name or its foreign trademark(s), then this entity should choose such Chinese translations and transliterations and file them as soon as possible with the Chinese Trademark Office before the Chinese product users will spontaneously assign one and squatters or competitors will appropriate it by filing an application first. In that case, the foreign brand owner may still try to impose a new Chinese name, but it will require very intense use in China to replace the first one that was etched in the mind of the Chinese consumers. The successful outcome of a "replacement" action will depend on how deep the Chinese name chosen spontaneously by the market or initially used by the right holder without follow-up registration has established itself among the consumers and users of the trademarked

100. Article 22 of the Implementing Regulations to the Trademark Law.
101. Guillermo Jimenez, Barbara Kolsun, Fashion Law, A Guide for Designers, Fashion Executives and Attorneys, 351 (Bloomsbury 2nd edition 2014).

product. Certain Chinese names were such good translations of the foreign name that it was no point in trying to introduce a new one, forcing thus the right holder to fight for the recovery of the stolen one, like in the case of the Chinese name of the French luxury good maker Hermes.

Eventually, once registered a trademark in China is valid for 10 years, and the validity can be extended each 10 years without time limits.

[3] Affirmative Actions

There are several situations in which a right holder may find out that someone in China has either stolen his/her trademark or has obtained a trademark that looks very similar to his own for the same goods or services.

As mentioned above, a trademark holder often finds out that there is already a pending application or registered trademark in China similar to his own, when the latter is rejected by the Trademark Office. This is a most typical case and concerns both the original foreign trademark(s) and its Chinese transliteration and is a case that mostly affects SMEs or companies that are considered large but not MNCs. Most SMEs will normally neglect registering in China till they decide to enter that market. However, it is also very common that their product already found a way and distributions in China under a Chinese name the SME did not even know it was used by the Chinese buyers. Only once the SME decides to enter the Chinese market it discovers all the unpleasantness of having been robbed of its trademarks and having been even defrauded of an appealing Chinese name, thus preventing full exploitation of an important "localization" factor for its business in China.

On the other side of the spectrum, larger companies and MNCs avail themselves of trademark monitoring services and are often able to spot hijacks or free rides through similar trademarks before these are registered. Larger companies can avail of more options for intervention in that they are often facing a trademark that is not fully registered yet, whereby SMEs will have to deal more often with registered hostile trademarks that could even be enforced against them.

Another way of noticing the theft of a trademark or the registration of a hostile similar trademark is when the foreign original right holder, his OEMs and licensees get sued by the hostile party in China for trademark infringement or their goods are blocked at the Chinese customs for trademark infringement and are then sued on the same legal ground.

What are therefore the remedies available against such acts of theft or free ride? In this section, we will provide a basic overview of the available legal tools for the recovery of lost trademark rights. A more detailed analysis of such legal tools and their strategic deployment against trademark theft will be provided in a dedicated chapter of this book. Suffices to say here that the number and efficacy of trademark protection and recovery tools vary depending on whether action is taken against a still pending hostile application or against an already registered hostile trademark.

[i] Trademark Opposition

Opposition is filed against trademark applications that have been preliminarily approved after substantive examination but are not yet fully granted.

Where any prior right owner or interested person believes that provisions of paragraphs 2 and 3 of Article 13, Article 15, paragraph 1 of Article 16, Article 30, Article 31 or Article 32 of the Law[102] have been breached or any person believes that the provisions of Article 10, Article 11 or Article 12[103] have been violated, it may raise an objection to the Trade Office against a trademark that has been published after a preliminary examination within three months from the date of announcement. The grounds for opposition under Article 32 Trademark Law are the most used to support oppositions against hijacked trademarks. This norm provides that opposition can be filed against a trademark that is identical or similar with a prior right of a person or entity. Examples of prior rights include trade names, right of name, copyright, trademarks, and event patent and design rights. As we shall see soon below, the same prior rights can be used to ground a request for invalidation of a registered trademark. In that context, we will provide some examples of recent cases in which such prior rights have been recognized as valid ground against a prior identical or similar trademark.

When no objections have been raised upon expiration of such period, the application shall be approved for registration with issuance of a certificate of trademark registration and announcement of the trademark.[104] Opposition can also be filed based on prior registrations that have been cancelled in the previous 12 months.[105] Also, opposition may be filed or awarded only for parts of the goods of the opposed trademark. This is a very important aspect when it comes to strategizing an effective use of oppositions and invalidations against hijacked or hostile trademarks.

In the event that an objection is raised against a trademark published after preliminary examination, the Trademark Office shall consider the facts and grounds submitted by both the dissenting party and the person challenged and shall decide on whether the registration is allowed within twelve months upon the expiration of announcement after investigation and verification, and notify the dissenting party and the person challenged in writing. In case of prolonging such period for certain special situations, it may be prolonged for six months after the approval of the administrative department for industry and commerce under the State Council.

102. Trademark Law Articles 13 (Well-known unregistered trademarks), 15 (Bad faith of the agent), 16 (fraudulent geographical signs), 30 (identical/similar to prior trademark), 31 (trademark registered on the same date which one used first), 32 (other prior rights and reputed unregistered brands).
103. Trademark Law Arts 10 (Absolute grounds of non-registrability), 11 (lack of distinctiveness), 12 (3D trademarks descriptive of product).
104. Article 33 Trademark Law.
105. Article 50 of China Trademark Law provides that: "If a registered trademark is revoked, nullified or subject to no renewal upon expiration of the period of validity, the Trademark Office shall not approve any application for the registration of a trademark identical with or similar to the said trademark within one year as of the day of the revocation, nullification or cancellation."

If the Trademark Office decides to approve the registration, it shall grant a certificate of trademark registration to the person challenged and publish the same. In case the dissenting party is dissatisfied, it may request to the Trademark Review and Adjudication Board for nullification of the registered trademark according to Article 44 and Article 45 hereof.

In case the Trademark Office decides not to approve the registration and the person challenged is dissatisfied, it may apply to the Trademark Review and Adjudication Board for review within 15 days upon receipt of the notice, which shall, with 12 months upon receipt of the notice, make a ruling for the review and notify the dissenting party and the person challenged in writing. In case of prolonging such period for certain special situations, it may be prolonged for six months after the approval of the administrative department for industry and commerce under the State Council. In the event that the person challenged is still dissatisfied with the ruling of such review, it may file a lawsuit before the People's Court within 30 days upon receipt of the notice. The People's Court shall notify the dissenting party of participation in the proceedings as a third party.

During the review procedure before the Trademark Review and Adjudication Board in accordance with previous provisions, where the determination of prior rights involved is based on another case that the people's court is hearing or the administrative organization is handling, such review may be suspended. After the cause for such suspension is eliminated, the review shall be resumed.[106]

Where the above-mentioned objection is rejected upon examination and thus the registration of the trademark in question is approved, the date of acquiring the exclusive right to use a trademark by the applicant shall be calculated as of the expiration of three-month announcement period of preliminary examination. From the expiry of the announcement period of the trademark till the ruling on approval of registration, there will be no retroactive effects for uses of symbols the same as or similar to the trademark or on the same or similar goods by others; however, where such hostility of users causes losses to the trademark registrant, the users shall compensate the same.[107]

[ii] Trademark Invalidations

In case an opposition is not successful before the Trademark Office or hostile/hijacked trademarks were discovered after their registration date, the only way for the holder of an identical or similar prior right is to file invalidation against such registration. As for oppositions, invalidation may be filed or awarded only for parts of the goods of the registered trademark. This is a very important aspect when it comes to strategizing an effective use of oppositions and cancellations against hijacked or hostile trademarks as well as division applications.

106. Article 35 Trademark Law.
107. Article 36 trademark Law.

One first form of invalidation of a registered trademark is based upon violation of absolute grounds for registration. In particular, the law provides that the Trademark Office upon its own initiative or upon request of any person or entity declares the nullification of a registered trademark that violates provisions of the law that are meant to protect the interest of the whole collectivity and the market. In particular, an invalidation under Article 44.1 of the Trademark Law can be filed by anybody against a trademark that is identical with or similar to China state name, national flag, national emblem, national anthem, as well as those same elements belonging to foreign countries and international organizations etc.[108] Invalidation can also be filed by anybody against registered trademarks that only bear generic names, devices, or model numbers of the goods, or simply indicates the quality, main raw materials, function, use, weight, quantity or other features of the goods, or lacks distinctive character.[109] Also, such invalidation ground can be claimed to nullify a three-dimensional trademark that merely indicates the shape inherent in the nature of the goods concerned.[110] Eventually, there is a public interest in nullifying also a trademark that is registered through fraudulent means, such as false or forged identities and filing information. This latter ground for invalidation has recently come to the practitioners' attention in that a couple of administrative decisions have used this provision to cover trademarks registered in bad faith, i.e., with knowledge of registering someone else's trademark with preventive intent. This point will be discussed at length at a later point.

As to the procedural aspects of such invalidation, the law provides that upon filing of an invalidation request, the Trademark Review and Adjudication Board must notify the relevant parties upon receipt of the application, and request them to submit arguments within a specified time. The Trademark Review and Adjudication Board shall make a ruling on maintaining or nullification of the registered trademark, and notify the party concerned of such ruling. Where the period is to be prolonged for special circumstances, it may be extended by three months after the approval of the administrative department for industry and commerce under the State Council. In the event that the party concerned is dissatisfied with the ruling of the Trademark Review and Adjudication Board, it may appeal to the People's Court within 30 days from receipt of the notice. The People's Court shall notify the counterpart of the trademark ruling procedures of participation in the proceedings as a third party.[111] It is remarked that there is no time limit for filing such invalidation. Any trademark can be invalidated anytime by anybody under the grounds provided for by Article 44.1 Trademark Law.

Unlike the invalidation described above, Article 45 Trademark Law concerns the invalidation of registered trademarks based on the interest and rights of a prior right holder. In particular this norm provides that the prior right owner or interested party can file invalidation of a registered trademark that is a reproduction, imitation or translation of a third party's well-known trademark that has not been registered in China in respect of identical or similar goods, and is likely to lead the relevant

108. Article 10 Trademark Law.
109. Article 11 Trademark Law.
110. Article 12 Trademark Law.
111. Article 44.3 Trademark law.

consumers to confusion as to the product origin.[112] Also, such invalidation can be filed in the event that an agent or a representative seeks to register the client's trademark in its own name without the authorization of the client and faces objection from the client.[113] Furthermore, invalidation can be filed against a trademark containing a geographical indication of goods misleads the public for the goods does not come from the location as stated in the indication.[114] Eventually, this type of invalidation can be used against a trademark that has been registered in spite of being identical or similar to the trademark of another person that had been already registered or preliminarily approved in respect of the same or similar goods,[115] or when the registered trademark infringes upon another party's prior existing rights, or improper means are used to register a trademark that is already in use by another party and enjoys substantial influence.[116] The latter provision is the one most commonly used to ground invalidations of trademarks registered in bad faith. The problem with this legal base is that the applicant must prove that his prior right has acquired a certain degree of reputation in China for identical or similar goods. Among the prior rights that are deemed relevant by this provision are the right of name,[117] trade name right,[118] right of portrait,

112. Article 13.3 Trademark Law.
113. Article 15 Trademark Law.
114. Article 16 Trademark Law.
115. Articles 30 and 31 Trademark Law.
116. Article 32 Trademark law.
117. Xiao Zhi Hua v. TRAB, First Intermediate Court Beijing, judgment of 2014. Xiao Zhi Hua filed a trademark "朗朗LANG LANG" with TMO in 2006, and was registered in 2010. The famous pianist 朗朗 (Lang Lang) filed invalidation application against such mark with the Trademark Reexamination and Adjudication Board by stating the mark infringes his right of name. The Trademark Reexamination and Adjudication Board cancelled the mark accordingly. Xiao filed lawsuit against the Trademark Reexamination and Adjudication Board. The court rejected Xiao's request by judging that the mark is identical with the name of famous pianist Lang Lang, and that the name "Lang Lang" has acquired high reputation before the application of the subject mark (*see*: http://www.ycwb.com/ePaper/ycwb/html/2014-11/05/content_573525.htm?div=-1[10/30/2015).
118. KOSS Corporation v. Trademark Reexamination and Adjudication Board, Beijing Higher Court [2010] Gao Xing Zhong Zi No. 841. In this case, the appellant KOSS requested to reject the registration of the hostile trademark "KOSS + Device" as the latter infringes its prior trade name. The court stated that the prior right stipulated in Article 32 of China Trademark law refers to the trade name that has a certain reputation before the application date of the hostile trademark and the designated goods of the two are identical or similar. Considering KOSS had provided evidence including registered "KOSS + Device" marks in US, sales records of KOSS earphones in 1990s in China, reports and news regarding the KOSS branded products in China, etc., the court concluded that the trade name "KOSS" had already acquired a certain reputation at the time of the application date of the hostile trademark. In a more recent case involving the tire rims from "Lexani Wheels," the Beijing First Intermediate Court rejected the trademark application for "Lexani" based on the prior trade name rights of the foreign company. What appears quite interesting is the fact that the court did set a rather low requirement to prove notoriety of the trade name Lexani in China, while acknowledging that the name "Lexani" is distinctive and original enough that it is presumed that the applicant was in bad faith about it. It thus presumed the notoriety not only by some material evidence of use but also by the degree of originality of the trade name. For more details, *see* Yang Xiaoli and Jiang Limei, Key issues: The requirements for recognizing whether a prior trade name has certain fame can be lowered under the condition that the relevant party acts in bad faith, Lexology, http://www.lexology.com/library/detail.aspx?g=98548cda-4b9a-4159-bcc5-a61db2ba6c2a&utm_source=Lexology+Daily+Newsfeed&utm_medium=HTML (November 18, 2015).

copyright,[119] trademarks, inventions and utility models, design patents,[120] geographic indications and domain names.[121] It is observed again here that these same prior rights forming ground of invalidation under Article 45 Trademark Law constitute also legal grounds for opposition under Article 32 Trademark Law.

As to the definition of "reputation" both in Articles 45 and 32 Trademark Law, it refers to a level of knowledge of the trademark among the relevant public which is of a lower degree and intensity compared to the knowledge and reputation required for the recognition of "well-known" status. However, the applicant must provide evidence that the trademark has been used for an extended period of time, and that this use has resulted in wide sales and distribution of the trademarked products so as to have been exposed to the relevant public with certain intensity. Article 18.2 of Opinions of the SPC Concerning Trial of Administrative Cases in Respect of Trademark Right Granting and Confirmation provides that a:

> trademark that has been actually used within the territory of China and is known to the relevant public shall be determined as trademark that has been used and has certain influence. Where there is evidence to prove that the preliminary trademark has been used for continuous period in certain territory by referring to sales volume, advertising or publicity of the trademarked commodities, such trademark could be determined as having a certain reputation (...).

As to the procedure, the law provides that within five years upon the registration date of such trademark, the prior right holder or interested party must apply to the Trademark Review and Adjudication Board for nullifying the same. In the event of malicious registration, owners of "well-known" trademarks are exempted from the aforesaid five-year limitation period.

The law requires that the Trademark Review and Adjudication Board issues a decision within 12 months upon receipt of such application on maintaining or nullification of registered trademark, and notify the parties concerned of such ruling in writing. In case more time is needed for certain special situations, like for instance when there is complex evidence to review and it takes time to collect it, the procedure may be prolonged for six months. The party dissatisfied with the ruling of the Trademark Review and Adjudication Board can appeal to the People's Court within 30 days from receipt of the notice. The People's Court will notify the counterpart of the

119. Groupe Auchan v. Trademark Reexamination and Adjudication Board, Beijing First Intermediate Court [2008] Yi Zhong Xing Chu Zi No. 1299. Auchan filed opposition against the hostile trademark "ADO + Device" by stating such mark infringe its prior copyright (device of a bird). Both TMO and TRAB rejected the opposition. GROUPE filed lawsuit against TRAB to request to cancel the TRAB's decision.

120. Shaoxing Rice Wine Group v. Trademark Reexamination, Beijing Higher Court [2015] Gao Xing Zhi Zhong Zi No. 110, and Adjudication Board.

121. Xuefang Huang, China Court recognizes merchandising rights in Kung Fu Panda case, Lexology, http://www.lexology.com/library/detail.aspx?g=ff5e0240-ac79-4816-bd5d-5da094b579c4&utm_source=Lexology+Daily+Newsfeed&utm_medium=HTML (November 17, 2015). In this case, the Beijing Higher Court ruled that merchandise rights over the exploitation of economic rights of a movie title, a movie that has acquired a certain reputation, can also be considered as prior rights in the sense of Article 32 Trademark law.

trademark ruling procedures and of the right of participation in the proceedings as a third party. If, during the review of invalidation by the Trademark Review and Adjudication Board in accordance with previous provisions, the determination of prior rights referred to is based on another case that the people's court is hearing or the administrative authority is handling, the review may be suspended. After the cause for such suspension is eliminated, the review is resumed.[122] In case none of the parties concerned applies for review against the decision of invalidation of the registered trademark by the Trademark Office or files any lawsuit with respect to maintaining or invalidation of the registered trademark by the Trademark Review and Adjudication Board before the People's Court, this decision shall come into force.

The registered trademark declared as invalid according to Article 44 and Article 45 is deemed as inexistent *ab initio*. The decision or adjudication of invalidating a registered trademark has no retroactive effect upon trademark infringement verdicts, adjudications or mediation agreements made by the People's Court that have been already enforced, trademark infringement decisions made by the administrative department for industry and commerce that have been made and enforced or trademark assignment or license contracts which have been performed; provided, however, that in case the hostility of the trademark registrant causes losses to others, the trademark registrant shall compensate the same. When the trademark infringement damages, assignment fee and trademark royalties will not be returned according to previous regulations, which is obviously contrary to fairness, the trademark infringement damages, assignment fee and trademark royalties will have to be returned in whole or part.[123]

Eventually, the Trademark law provides for the cancellation of a trademark that has not been used for three consecutive years by the registrant or its licensee(s) without any proper reason.[124] Anyone applying for cancelling a registered trademark by claiming such trademark has been stopped for use for three consecutive years without any justification shall make such cancellation application after expiration of three years as of the announcement date of the registration of the trademark concerned. The law provides that the burden to prove the trademark use is upon the registrant. After acceptance of the application for nonuse cancellation, the Trademark Office shall in fact notify the trademark registrant and order him to submit, within two months upon receipt of the notice, the relevant material evidence to prove the use of the trademark before the cancellation application is filed or to state the justifications for not using the trademark. If it fails to submit any "material evidence" as proof within the time limit, or the said evidence is inadmissible or irrelevant, or the right holder has no other justifiable reasons for the nonuse, the registered trademark is canceled.[125] The term "material evidence" includes the materials proving a trademark registrant's use of the registered trademark and materials proving a registrant has licensed other persons to use the said registered trademark. However, there must be also proof of the material

122. Article 45 Trademark Law.
123. Article 47 Trademark Law.
124. Article 49 Trademark Law.
125. Article 66 Implementing Regulations to the Trademark Law.

and effective use of the trademark by the licensee. Eventually, "proper reasons" for justifying nonuse and avoid thus cancellation are force majeure, policy limitations set by the government, bankruptcy liquidation and other justifiable reasons that can make the trademark registrant free from liability. More details on the evidence of use will be discussed in the chapter concerning trademark theft and nonuse cancellation strategies.

[4] Infringement of Trademark Rights and Cause of Actions

The registrant of a Chinese trademark has an exclusive right to use the registered trademark. The exclusive use of trademarks refers to such activities as using trademarks on goods, goods packaging or containers and goods transaction documents, or using trademarks in advertising, exhibits and other commercial events so as to identify the sources thereof. Also, the right of exclusivity extends to the revenues and monetarization from the economic exploitation in the above-described forms of use. A legally relevant use of the Trademark, i.e., a use that produces legal effects, as well as its economic exploitation of the right of exclusivity are limited to the goods and services for which the trademark has been approved. It is therefore very important for a trademark applicant to select the proper classes and subclasses of goods and service at the time of filing. The chosen classes and subclasses will determine the boundaries of the economic exploitation rights and by reflection, the scope of legal protection of the trademark right against use of the same by third parties.

Based on the definition of distinctiveness and exclusive use provided before, it can be safely stated that the owner of a registered trademark in China may not prohibit others from the rightful use of either different trademarks on the same goods or identical/similar trademarks on different goods. Also, the exclusive right holder cannot prohibit third parties to use generic names, models or designs of the goods, or direct reference to the quality, main raw materials, function, use, weight, quantity or other features of the goods, or geographical names as included in the registered trademark. Also, the exclusive right owner of a registered trademark of 3D symbols may not prohibit others from rightful use of the shapes generated from the nature of the goods in respect of which the trademark is used, or shapes of the goods to realize certain technical effects, or shapes to provide the goods with substantive values.[126]

If a third party violates the right of exclusivity of the trademark owner, the former commits an act of trademark infringement. The Trademark Law provides an open list of acts that are to be considered as trademark infringements. In particular, Article 57 of the Trademark law stipulates that the following acts constitute trademark infringement: (1) using a trademark that is identical with a registered trademark on the same goods without the consent of the trademark registrant; (2) using a trademark that is similar to a registered trademark on the same goods, or using a trademark that is identical with or similar to a registered trademark on similar goods, which may be easily confusing, without the consent of the trademark registrant; (3) selling goods that

126. Article 59 Trademark Law.

violate the exclusive right to use a registered trademark; (4) counterfeiting or arbitrarily forging others' registered trademark, or selling the counterfeited or arbitrarily forged trademarks; (5) altering the trademark registrant's registered trademark without authorization of the same and selling goods bearing such altered trademark; (6) providing convenience for or even help others to infringe the exclusive right to use a registered trademark on purpose; and (7) other conducts causing prejudice to others' exclusive right to use its registered trademark.

The provisions under Article 57.1, 57.2 define the general grounds of enforcement of trademark rights against infringers. Article 57.1 concerns the typical case in which a competitor uses an identical trademark on similar goods to free ride on the right holder brand's reputation. This is also the ground of action that could be invoked against acts of trademark counterfeiting. In such case, due to the identity of trademarks and goods, the law presumes that consumers will be automatically confused by the use of the identical trademarks. In case of trademark similarity, Article 57.2 requires instead that the right holder proves that the relevant public is confused by the hostile trademark's use on identical or similar goods. This is indeed a major difference, and it is dictated by the need of limiting the protection of trademark's exclusivity to clear infringement cases, thus reducing the risk of an overextension of the trademark's scope of protection that could indeed hamper fair business and competition to the ultimate detriment of consumers. As to the definition of use, it includes the use on goods, goods packaging or containers and goods transaction documents, or using trademarks in advertising, exhibits etc. Article 57.3 provides specifically for the liability of the seller independently from that of the manufacturer. Article 60 however, provides for an exemption to the seller's liability if the latter can prove that he was not knowingly selling commodities infringing a trademark. In this case, the seller must prove that the commodities were obtained legitimately and identify the provider. If the seller can meet this burden of proof, he will only be ordered to stop the sale of infringing goods but will not be liable of damage compensation. Furthermore, the infringing goods will be exempted from confiscation or the destruction. In practical terms, once the infringer provides a regularly paid purchase order, a contract or an invoice[127] and the name of the retailer/manufacturer, the infringer will not need to pay any damage compensation and the infringing goods will remain in circulation in the market if already resold. Such provision creates indeed a number of problems. First, such infringing commodities may be dangerous to consumer safety because of their poor quality compared to those bearing the original trademark. We can think here of any kind of counterfeit product with safety relevant features. In this case, the buyer of the infringing goods may not be sufficiently protected by the law. In fact, if the goods could be confiscated and destroyed, he could receive at least a refund from the seller and would no longer be in contact with a potentially dangerous substandard product. Also, this norm could be put to good use by the counterfeiters. They may create a small chain of traders that will legitimately transfer to each other the infringing commodities, thus escaping direct liability. In fact, each trader could be naming the one before him who sold him the

127. Article 79 Implementing Regulations to the Trademark Law.

product without need of naming the manufacturer and counterfeiting mastermind. The trader would not be liable of damages, the goods would escape confiscation and the manufacturer would remain hidden and shielded from enforcement. Surely, this norm should be revised or its application strongly restricted to avoid all these sets of problems especially in the field of counterfeiting.

Article 57.6 codifies for the first time the illegal conduct of those abetting and supporting someone else's acts of trademark infringement. A much disputed issue in the past is now solved in favor of punishing also ancillary conducts that favor a trademark infringement, giving thus effective relief to the trademark owner. Circumstances of providing convenience as specified in Item 6 of Article 57 of the Trademark Law include intentionally facilitating an infringement by another person or party of an exclusive right to use a registered trademark through providing storage, transportation, posting, printing, concealment, business place, network commodity trading platform and similar.[128] Such norm is particularly important in case of counterfeiting in that it establishes the liability of markets and stalls for hosting infringing activities.

Another important provision providing for a possible legal base for enforcement action is that of Article 57.7. It is an open clause that should help fitting in borderline cases that would not otherwise find legal base for civil or administrative enforcement. This clause was present in the previous trademark law and its meaning had been explained in the 2002 Interpretation of the SPC as including: the use of the words that are identical or similar to the registered trademark of any other person as the name of one's enterprise on identical or similar commodities so that the relevant public are liable to be misled; copying, imitating or translating the registered well-known trademark of another person or the major part thereof on nonidentical or dissimilar commodities as a trademark for the purpose of misleading the general public so that the interests of the registrant of the well-known trademark may be damaged; registering the words or characters identical or similar to the registered trademark of another person as a domain name and engaging in the electronic commerce of relevant commodities via the domain name so that the relevant general public are liable to be misled.[129]

[i] Similarity of Trademarks and Trademark Goods and Services

Two trademarks are "identical" when there are basically no differences in visual perception between the trademark that is charged of infringement and the registered

128. Xiangnaier Gufen Youxian Gongsi Su Wen Daxiang, Guangzhou Kaixuan Dajiudian Youxiangongsi Huameida Dajiudian, and Guangzhou Kaixuan Dajiudian Youxian Gongsi (香奈儿股份有限公司诉文大香、广州凯旋大酒店有限公司华美达大酒店、广州凯旋大酒店有限公司) [Chanel Company Limited by Shares v. Wen Daxiang, Huameida Grand Hotel of the Guangzhou Kaixuan Grand Hotel Ltd., and Guangzhou Kaixuan Grand Hotel Ltd.] May 4, 2015 (Guangzhou IP Ct.) (China). *See also* Luyiweideng Malidi Su Wuxi Zhaoshangcheng Youxian Gongsi Deng (路易威登马利蒂诉无锡招商城有限公司等) [Louis Vuitton Malletier v. Wuxi Zhaoshangcheng Ltd. Company et al.] April 10, 2015 (Wuxi Interm. Ct.) (China).
129. Article 1 of the SPC Interpretations of the Supreme People's Court Concerning the Application of Laws in the Trial of Cases of Civil Disputes Arising from Trademarks, adopted by the Judicial Committee of the Supreme People's Court on October 12, 2002, Docket No. 32 [2002].

trademark of the plaintiff.[130] The term "similar trademarks" as provided in Article 57.2 of the Trademark Law refers to that the trademark charged of infringement and the registered trademark of the plaintiff are similar in the font style, pronunciation, meaning of the words, or in the composition and color of the pictures, or in the overall structure of all the elements combined, or in the cubic form or combination of colors, so that the relevant general public may be confused about the origin of the commodity or believe that there exist certain connections between the origin and the commodity which is represented by the registered trademark of the plaintiff.[131] The people's courts involved in a trademark infringement case, when determining whether two trademarks are similar, will have to take the general attention of the relevant general public as the standard test, and compare not only the whole structure of the trademark but also the major parts of the trademarks involved. The comparison shall be made in a situation where the objects are isolated from each other, while taking the notability and reputation of the registered trademark that is pleaded for protection.[132]

"Similar goods" as provided in Article 57 of the Trademark Law refers to those commodities that are identical in respect to functions, purposes of use, producers, marketing channels, target consumers, etc. or that the relevant public usually believe that there exist certain connections between them so that confusion may result. "Similar services" are those that are identical in respect of the purpose, content, manner, object, etc. of services, or that the relevant general public usually believes that there are certain connections between them so that confusion may result. The similarity between a commodity and a service refers to that there exist certain connections between a commodity and a service so that confusion may result.[133] When determining whether a commodity or service is similar, the people's court must take into comprehensive consideration the general understanding of the relevant public about the commodity or service. The Classification Table of Commodities and Services for the International Registration of Trademarks and the Classification Table of Similar Commodities and Services may be referred to in judging whether a commodity or service is similar.[134]

[ii] Likelihood of Confusion

A court required to determine the likelihood of confusion for an infringement based on claims of trademark similarity, will have to evaluate both trademark similarity and goods/services proximity. The standard for such evaluations is the "relevant public" or "relevant consumer." For the SPC, "relevant public" or "relevant consumer" is the consumer relating to a certain type of commodities or services covered by the trademark and other business operators that are closely connected with the marketing

130. *Supra* n. 130, Article 9.1.
131. *Supra* n. 130, Article 9.2.
132. *Supra* n. 130, Article 10.
133. *Supra* n. 130, Article 11.
134. *Supra* n. 130, Article 12.

of the aforesaid commodities or services.[135] The relevant consumer is an abstract legal concept and embodies an ideal person with an average attention to details.

In legal terms, the determination of goods/service similarity is based on two major types of comparisons. One is an objective comparison, based on the above-listed criteria of production, marketing, sales channels etc. This comparison is conducted among goods against goods and services against services.[136] The other determination is based on the more subjective determination of confusion of the relevant public. Based on the latter, more subjective method of evaluation of similarity, even a good and a service may be considered to be similar. This could be the case of repair shop showing that they service products of a certain brand and the products sold by the same shop. In that case, the user of that repair service will buy also spare parts or repair parts believing they are part of the brand under whose name the repair service is provided without the parts themselves being branded at all.[137] More in general, consumers may perceive a certain association between products that formally belong to different classes of goods. For instance, what about a car and a fashion item such as a t-shirt or a cap? In the case of a well-known brand, its notoriety will influence the determination of goods and services' similarity by nearing classes that may be not so directly related. The higher the degree of notoriety, the less will differences in distribution, materials, sales channels, etc. influence the overall impression of similarity. Therefore, marks in apparently distant classes will still be held similar if the registered one is well known. For instance, a Rolex watch against a Rolex piece of furniture. A Roll Royce car against a Rolls Royce TV set. For all the other brands that are not well known, there still is the possibility of establishing a similarity between goods/services based on common sense and associations based on the average knowledge of the normal consumer. For instance, every car user knows that nowadays car companies sell merchandise as well. This common knowledge can indeed create a certain mental association between the

135. *Supra* n. 130, Article 8.

136. Yu Hui, Preliminary Research on the Judicial Judgment of Similar Goods in Trademark Infringement Cases, 14 IP China Intellectual Property Magazine, http://www.chinaipmagazine.com/en/journal-show.asp?id = 207 (October 2006). While explaining the objective criteria, Yu Hui interestingly points out that "(...) objective criterion also varies along with social development. The specific contents of function, use, production department, marketing channels and target consumers are different in different cases. Judgment shall be made by the presence of particular goods. For example, different conclusions will be drawn in the comparison between ordinary motorcycles and economy cars, and the comparison between motorcycles and trucks. Ordinary motorcycles and economy cars are both transportation devices. Their target consumers are those requiring riding instead of walking. The production departments and marketing channels are basically the same. Therefore they are deemed as similar goods. However, the comparison between high grade motorcycles and ordinary cars is different. The price of a 'Harley' motorcycles is far higher than that of economy cars. Their target consumers are totally different. Therefore they are not similar goods. The value in using trucks does not lie in 'riding instead of walking', but in 'transporting'. From the objective rule, trucks and motorcycles will certainly not become similar goods. But the similarity comparison between top grade motorcycles and high grade cars, which are popular among the same targeted consumers, is not so easy and direct. Other factors shall also be put into consideration."

137. *Ibid.*

car brands and fashion items and apparel. The same is the relation between merchandise products and a movie production company and so on.[138] Other factors to be considered are price and size of goods and, as we said before, the level of reputation of a brand in the market. The more a brand is known (not necessarily well known), the farther will the associative connections stretch out and connect the original products with not immediately similar classes of goods/services. Examples can be referred to a case in which an unregistered trademark in China with a certain reputation (but not well known) that is used on watches has been deemed to extend protection to swimwear bearing the same unauthorized trademark.[139]

[iii] Infringing Conducts

As to the commercial activities that are considered to be infringing upon the trademark's exclusive rights, they include the acts of manufacturing, selling, offering for sale, importing and exporting the goods, use on goods packaging, use on transaction documents etc. Evidence of such activities will be the object of the investigation and evidence acquisition, which in turn will influence the choice of jurisdiction, the selection and involvement of different infringers, and the structuring of damage compensation claims.

[5] Trademark Enforcement: Administrative Enforcement

The feature that most characterized the trademark enforcement system in China is its rather peculiar 'duality'. This means that a trademark right holder has a choice between civil and administrative enforcement of its trademark rights.[140]

138. Yu Hui *supra* n. 136: "(...) Under this rule, function, use, production department, sales channel and target consumers of goods are not as important, but we cannot forget these factors in our study of the similarity issue related to goods. When we see a 'Montagut' trademark on a bicycle, we will naturally associate it with that trademark name on shirts. Can we reach a judgment that shirts and bicycles are similar goods? With the slightest thought, no one will think that a shirt factory produces bicycles. The two goods are totally different. Such an association by the public is caused by the popularity of the 'Montagut' trademark. This text will not discuss this issue because it is under the protection for renowned trademarks. In the above example, more consideration should be given to the comparison between top grade motorcycles and high grade cars, and to the consumption habits of this particular group of consumers and to such factors as price, service, quality or just the brand name in making their purchase. Generally speaking, 'special association' refers to the practical and essential association, not in abstract imagination. For instance, vehicle and vehicle repair have an association between products and services, and ordinary motorcycles and economy cars have the following common points: they are operated by a motor, and the quality of the motor determines the performance of vehicle. But for a 'Montagut' shirt and a 'Montagut' bicycle, their association only comes from the fame of the shirt brand, without any essential association between the products."
139. King Wood & Mallesons, Five recent typical trademark cases in China, Mondaq http://www.mondaq.com/x/283840/Trademark/Five+recent+typical+trademark+cases+in+China (January 3, 2014).
140. Article 60.1 Trademark Law: *"In the event of infringement of the registered trademark as specified in Article 57 hereof that leads to disputes, the parties concerned shall settle such*

Administrative enforcement of trademarks can be demanded from a number of administrative bodies, often with overlapping functions and competing interests. Mostly, trademarks are enforced by territorially competent branches of the State Administration of Industry and Commerce (SAIC), China Customs, Public Security Bureau (PSB), and Technical Supervision Bureau (TSB) on behalf of the Administration for Quality Supervision, Inspection and Quarantine.[141] Civil enforcement is exercised by the People's Court territorially and functionally competent to hear trademark and more generally, IPR infringement claims.

The legal competence of the AIC is derived by the Trademark Law. In particular, it is therein provided that the AIC has the power to inflict administrative punishment in the form of monetary fines to the infringer. At the same time, the same provisions expressly exclude the power of the AIC to determine and liquidate damage compensation claims.[142] Damage compensation claims and their liquidation can only and exclusively be heard and awarded by a civil court. This is one of the many differences between administrative and judicial enforcement. Also, AICs do not have legal authority to issue prelitigation remedies such as injunctions, as well as evidence and property preservations. Also, AIC trademark enforcement can be initiated only at the place where the infringer is domiciled, which is also the place where he is normally committing the infringement by act of manufacturing and selling (*locus commissii delicti*). On the other hand, the Civil Procedure Law and relevant Interpretations by the SPC allow for forum shopping in civil litigation, so that lawsuits can be filed against different parties, which in turn allows the plaintiff to engineer and choose a court at any of their different domiciles or that at the place where the tort/infringement has occurred. At the same time, AIC enforcement is normally less expensive than civil

disputes through negotiations; where no negotiation is prospective or fails, the trademark registrant or any interested party may file a lawsuit before the People's Court or request the administrative department for industry and commerce for handling."

141. Aside from the most active and most involved administrative bodies listed in the text, there are however many more bodies in China that list IPR enforcement among their institutional functions: State Food and Drug Administration, State Tobacco Monopoly Administration, Ministry of Agriculture, National Copyright Administration of China, General Administration of Press and Publication, Ministry of Culture, State Administration of Radio, Film and Television, Anti = Pornography and Anti-Piracy Office and the Ministry of Health, to cite some others.

142. Article 60.2 and 60.3 Trademark Law provides that: "Where the foresaid infringement is confirmed, the administrative department for industry and commerce shall order the infringer to cease such infringement, confiscate and destroy the infringing goods and tools used in producing such goods or forging logos of the registered trademark. In the event of illegal business revenue of over CNY 50,000 a fine up to five times of the revenue may be imposed; in the event of no illegal business revenue or illegal business revenue of less than CNY 50,000, a fine up to CNY 250,000 may be imposed; in the event of trademark infringement of more than two times within five years or other serious circumstances, a heavier punishment shall be given (...) Where there is dispute concerning the amount of compensation for infringing the exclusive right to use the trademark, the party concerned may request the administrative department for industry and commerce for mediation or file a lawsuit before the People's Court pursuant to the Civil Procedure Law of the People's Republic of China; In case of absence of agreements or nonperformance of mediation agreement upon effectiveness after the mediation by the administrative department for industry and commerce, any party concerned may file a lawsuit before the People's Court pursuant to the Civil Procedure Law of the People's Republic of China."

proceedings, it requires lesser formalities as to evidence acquisition and admissibility and most of all, it enables right holders to obtain swift surprise enforcement actions against infringers in the form of administrative raids "*inaudita altera parte*" (without prior notification to the infringer).

AIC raids are mostly employed in anti-counterfeiting operations. Specifically, brand owners can resort to such swift and less expensive enforcement tool to carry out several enforcement actions whose overall cost would unlikely be sufficient to cover more than two civil lawsuits in one year. However, the low deterring force of AIC raids results in the very high degree of repetition of infringement, especially among professional infringers. Another relevant factor for a right holder to determine the most appropriate enforcement path for its case is that administrative AIC enforcement is carried out at a very local level and often involves AIC offices which are small and not infrequently influenced by local economic, social and political factors. AIC are not legally and morally bound to the rule of law in deciding cases as much as courts are. Administrative bodies enjoy larger discretion which allow them to arbitrarily choose when to enforce and when not. This discretion is primarily founded on the very general nature of IP laws in China which normally provide principles' enunciations, which leave to field practice and internal regulations space for practical application.[143] Targets which are for economic and political reasons important to the local economy may enjoy AIC protection, and any attempt at raiding them could repeatedly be rejected without excuses or with flimsy justifications.

Once a choice between civil and administrative enforcement is made, there is no way to stop the ongoing proceeding and switch to the other one. Also, once justice is obtained before a civil court, there is no right to refile the same claim against the administrative authority., Once an AIC enforcement has been completed, the trademark holder still has the right to file a civil lawsuit for the determination of damage compensation.[144] However, the civil court cannot hear claims other than compensation, and no further sanctions or punishments can be later imposed by a civil court.[145]

As mentioned above, administrative AIC action can be taken upon petition of any party or ex officio. The petition by a third party must be submitted to the AIC office at the place of domicile or location of the infringer (if the latter is an underground unregistered entity), supported by evidence of the target, the infringing act and the supporting trademark rights. Additionally, the petitioner must commit to provide to the AIC technical expertise to recognize original trademarked products from the fakes. Overall, the decision of whether to choose administrative or court enforcement is indeed a strategic one and must be the conclusion of a fact finding and analytical process as described in the preceding sections of this chapter. At present, the goal is just to provide general information about the functioning of the enforcement system

143. Randall Peerembоom, China Long March Toward Rule of Law, 16 ff (Cambridge University Press 2002).
144. Article 60.3 Trademark Law.
145. *Supra* n. 130, Article 21.2 provides that: "... Where the administrative department for industry and commerce has already imposed administrative punishments to a same act of infringing upon the exclusive right of the registered trademark, the people's court shall not give any more civil sanctions."

and further strategic considerations will be left to the Chapter concerning anti-counterfeiting in China.

Customs, PSB and TSB are also important players in the trademark enforcement arena. Customs are entrusted by the law with the protection of IP rights in force of Articles 44 and 91 of the Custom Law of the PRC. These norms provide that Customs may carry out protection of IPR, which are related to import and export of goods according to laws and regulations. In particular, in case of acts of imports or exports goods constituting infringement on the IPR under protection by laws and administrative regulations of the PRC, the infringing goods shall be confiscated by Customs and a fine shall be imposed thereof; where the case constitutes a crime, the person or persons concerned shall be investigated for criminal liability according to law. It is remarkable to notice that till now China Customs are among the few Customs in the world that are actively involved in seizing trademark counterfeits in exit, whereby most customs focus exclusively on inbound fakes.

PSB derives its IPR enforcement jurisdiction from the Trademark Law[146] which refers to the 1997 Criminal Law and the related interpretations of the SPC of 1998 and 2004. According to the Criminal Law,[147] whoever, person or company uses a trademark identical with another person's registered trademark on the same kind of goods without permission from the owner of the registered trademark and if the circumstances are serious, must be sentenced to a fixed-term imprisonment of not more than three years or criminal detention, and concurrently or independently be sentenced to a fine.[148] If the circumstances are especially serious, the offender must be sentenced to fixed-term imprisonment of not less than three years and not more than seven years, and concurrently be sentenced to a fine. The Criminal Law adds that those knowingly selling goods bearing counterfeited registered trademarks and under the condition that their revenue from sale to be relatively high, must be sentenced to fixed-term imprisonment of not more than three years or criminal detention, and concurrently or

146. Article 67 Trademark Law provides that: "Any person who, without the permission of trademark registrants, uses a trademark identical with the registrant's trademark for the same goods, where the case constitutes a crime, shall be prosecuted according to the law for its criminal liabilities, in addition to compensation of the losses suffered by the infringed (...)".

147. Article 213 Criminal Law.

148. Article 1 of the Interpretation by the Supreme People's Court and the Supreme People's Procuratorate of Several Issues Relating to Specific Application of Law to the Treatment of Criminal Cases of Intellectual Property Infringement (Promulgated by the Supreme People's Court and the Supreme People's Procuratorate on December 8, 2004 and going into force on December 22, 2004), provides that: "(...) (1) the illegal business turnover is more than CNY 50,000 yuan, or the illegal profit is more than CNY 30,000 yuan; (2) two or more registered trademarks are counterfeited, with the illegal business turnover being more than CNY 30,000 yuan or the illegal profit more than CNY 20,000 yuan; and (3) there are other serious circumstances. Whoever has done an act with one of the following circumstances has, he/it has done an act with the 'especially serious circumstances' provided for in Article 213 of the Criminal Law, and shall be sentenced to a fixed-term imprisonment of not less than three years but not more than seven years or criminal detention, and shall also be fined for the crime of counterfeiting registered trademarks: (4) the illegal business turnover is more than CNY 250,000 yuan, or the illegal profit is more than CNY 150,000 yuan; (5) two or more registered trademarks are counterfeited, with the illegal business turnover being more than CNY 150,000 yuan or illegal profit more than CNY 100,000 yuan; and (6) there are other serious circumstances."

independently be sentenced to a fine.[149] If the sum obtained through sale is very high, the offender shall be sentenced to fixed-term imprisonment of not less than three years and not more than seven years, and concurrently be sentenced to a fine.[150] This second provision however, must be read in light of Article 60 Trademark Law exempting sellers that can prove that acquisition of a trademark infringing commodity was done legally, from damage compensation. Even if the form of acquiring the trademark infringing goods is done through legal channels, the criminal liability still exists for the seller if he knew the goods were counterfeits.[151]

Administrative enforcement of trademarks will be examined again in the Chapter concerning trademark counterfeiting. In this section, we will instead focus on a presentation of the general outline of the court system of China and the judicial enforcement of trademark rights.

[6] Trademark Enforcement: Judicial Enforcement

A trademark right holder can file a civil lawsuit against acts of infringement of its registered trademark. Judicial remedies are also available to stop an infringement before filing a lawsuit. Civil judges of the Chinese People's Courts have jurisdiction over infringement of trademark rights.

[i] Degrees of Civil Recourses

People's Courts are entrusted by the law to hear IP cases. There are three degrees of jurisdiction in Chinese civil litigation: The first instance, the appeal and the retrial. The

149. Article 214 Criminal Law.
150. Article 2 of the Interpretation by the Supreme People's Court and the Supreme People's Procuratorate of Several Issues Relating to Specific Application of Law to the Treatment of Criminal Cases of Intellectual Property Infringement of 2004 provides that: "Whoever knowingly sells goods bearing counterfeit registered trademarks shall, with the amount of sales amounting to more than CNY 500,000 yuan, he/it has done an act with the 'relatively large amount' provided for in Article 214 of the Criminal Law, and shall be sentenced to fixed-term imprisonment of not more than three years or criminal detention, and shall also, or shall only, be fined for the crime of selling goods bearing a counterfeit trademark. If one's amount of sales exceeds CNY 250,000 yuan, which is a 'huge amount of sales' provided for in Article 214 of the Criminal Law, he shall be sentenced to a fixed-term imprisonment of not less than three years but not more than seven years, and shall be fined for the a crime of selling goods bearing a counterfeit registered trademark."
151. According to the SPC interpretation in the preceding notes, knowledge of the illegal nature of the trademark is presumed when: the infringer knows that the trademark on his goods have been altered, changed or covered; the infringer has been punished by administrative authority or pursued with civil liability due to selling infringing goods, yet selling the same goods again; the infringer received notice or warning before hand, yet refused to correct his behavior; the infringer intentionally choose illegal way to purchase goods and the purchase price is apparently much lower than the original goods; forge invoice, accounts; sell/distribute large quantity of infringing goods; transfer, destroy the evidence after the case happened, provide false proof or statement; forge, alter the right holder's authorization documents or knows these documents have been forged or altered; and other circumstances that the suspect knows or should know that the goods are infringing goods.

first instance is usually heard by a panel of three judges,[152] but in simple cases, there may be only one judge in session. The decision of the first instance court is collegial[153] and must be eventually ratified by the President of the court. The president is always a member of the Communist Party.[154] The court president has the final say and may always disagree with the panel and negotiate changes in the panel's final decision. Appeal is filed with the court of first instance that will then transfer the case to the Appeal Court. This transfer should take place within few days, but the deadline is not peremptory and delays are common, sometimes stretching for several weeks or even months. The appeal panel is composed of three to five judges,[155] and decisions are taken by majority. The appeal instance is not a new case and focuses only on the review of the facts and the law of the first instance case. After hearing an appellate case, the people's court of second instance can: (1) reject the appeal and sustain the first instance judgment if the facts were clearly found and the law was correctly applied in the original judgment; (2) amend the judgment if the law was incorrectly applied in the original judgment; (3) overrule the first instance judgment and send the case back to the court of first instance for retrial if in the original judgment the facts were incorrectly found or were not clearly found and the evidence was inconclusive. The people's court of second instance may also decide to amend the judgment itself after investigating and clarifying the facts; (4) overrule the first instance judgment and send the case back for retrial if in the original judgment there were violations of the prescribed procedure that may have affected its correctness.[156] A judgment of appeal is immediately effective and enforceable. Both in the first as in the second instance, and in case of special circumstances of the case (i.e., case involving an important person, complex matter, etc.) a case can be entrusted to a special decision-making body referred to as Judicial Committee. This is however extremely rare in trademark litigation cases. Eventually, it is still possible for any party in the procedure to apply with the SPC or the Court of higher instance for the retrial of the case. Retrial is possible only under special circumstances categorically provided by the Civil Procedure[157] and the invested court has a clear discretion in determining such circumstances and the acceptance of a request for retrial.

[ii] Courts and Jurisdiction

Courts in China can hear a case based on territorial and subject matter jurisdiction. Territorial jurisdiction define which among the courts with abstract subject matter

152. Article 40 Civil Procedure.
153. Article 43 Civil Procedure.
154. Article 16 of China Judges' Law provides that the court's president and presiding judge could review the judgment made by the collegiate bench but could not change the conclusion of the collegiate bench. Although the China Judges' Law does not specify that the president should be a "member of the communist party," Article 9.4 of China Judge's Law provides that the judge shall have good political characters, which practically is always presumed to exist when the candidate president is a member of the Party.
155. Article 41 Civil Procedure.
156. Article 153 Civil Procedure.
157. Article 179 Civil Procedure.

jurisdiction over a case, is physically related to such case. The second defines the jurisdiction of the territorially competent court depending on the court degree, function and specialization as regulated by the law.

Territorial jurisdiction of a court is determined upon the circumstances of the case. The law provides that a civil action instituted on the ground that the exclusive right to use a registered trademark has been infringed upon is subject to the jurisdiction of the people's court where the infringing act is carried out (*locus commissii delicti*), where the infringing commodities are stored or sealed up and detained, or where the defendant has its domicile.[158]

As to subject matter jurisdiction, basic courts in China have jurisdiction over trademark cases involving Chinese parties or whose dispute value is rather low. Basic courts have no jurisdiction over trademark disputes involving foreign elements.[159] Intermediate People's Courts are in charge of trademark infringement cases involving a foreign right holder.[160] In 2013, the Third Plenum of the Communist Party of China's 18th Central Committee adopted the Decision on Major Issues Concerning Comprehensively Deepening Reforms[161] which set up three specialized IP courts in Beijing, Shanghai and Guangzhou. The Beijing IP Court was already operative in November 2013.[162] Nowadays, when an infringement case is within the territorial competence of these courts, IP lawsuits involving any parties, Chinese or foreigner alike, will fall under the subject matter jurisdiction of these three IP courts respectively. For the lawsuits filed before courts other than those three mentioned above, Intermediate Courts and basic courts will have subject matter jurisdiction as it was before.

The fact that there are several possible places where a trademark lawsuit can be filed, the selection of a convenient jurisdiction can be thus engineered, at least to a certain extent. This is what legal experts call "Forum Shopping," i.e., shopping for the judge the plaintiff thinks the best to hear his case impartially. Such option is indeed important, especially in a country like China where local factors play such an important role. Ideally, trademark infringement litigation should be filed away from the court of the domicile of the defendants. Litigating away from the court of the domicile of the

158. Article 6 Interpretations of the Supreme People's Court Concerning the Application of Laws in the Trial of Cases of Civil Disputes Arising from Trademarks (Adopted at the 1246th Session of the Judicial Committee of the Supreme People's Court on October 12, 2002. Docket No. 32 [2002] of Legal Interpretations).

159. These are referred to as *Shewai*, foreign matters. According to Opinions on the Application of the Civil Procedure Law of PRC Article 304 such matters are those where: (1) one or more parties are a foreign natural or legal person or organization; or (2) the legal relationship between the parties establishes, changes, suspends or occurs outside the territory of China; or (3) the location of the object of litigation is outside the territory of China.

160. Article 19 Civil Procedure.

161. It was adopted at the Third Plenary Session of the 18th Central Committee of the Communist Party of China on November 12, 2013 (*See*: http://www.china.org.cn/china/third_plenary_session/2014-01/16/content_31212602.htm for an English version). This provision mirrors the general provision of Article 29 Civil Procedure for tort law claims.

162. The Beijing IP court counts about 30 judges. The Court is exclusively competent for all IP cases filed in Beijing after November 2013, while the Intermediate Courts retain jurisdiction over the old pending cases.

defendant is indeed always a good idea. In case the infringer is a large and well-developed competitor, the plaintiff can reduce the possibility for the defendant to try to exercise undue to influence over the court as it would if it were before its hometown judges. It also reduces the risk of the local court being affected by "local" factors such as social and political considerations (i.e., whether punishing a local infringer may cost jobs and having negative fallout on the local economy for instance). Even in cases in which the defendant is evidently without "political weight," filing litigation away from his home court will force him to find a lawyer outside his comfort zone, or choose his local lawyer which is not familiar with the court in charge of the case. Also, it will make them travel and spend money, which are all issues that can influence the defensive stamina and determination of the infringer and in the end can influence the outcome of a judicial case.

Forum shopping can be engineered through evidence acquisition. In a trademark infringement case, the prospective plaintiff can set up the purchase of the trademark infringing product from a trader located for instance in the territory of an experienced court such as Beijing, Guangzhou or Shanghai and away from the place of manufacture of the infringing product and domicile of the infringer. In that way, the prospective plaintiff has the right to file the lawsuit in the place of the sale as the place where the act of infringement was committed (*locus commissii delicti*). The evidence in this case plays an important role in that it supplies the object of the infringement as well as the legal base for preselecting a suitable court for an impartial and more professional hearing of the case. The situation may be more complicated in case of purchase made directly from the infringer or through the internet. In cases where the purchase and the infringement of a trademark is committed online, i.e., offer for sale is online and the purchase is made online, the law would not offer any help in determining whether the court at the place of domicile of the buyer or at that of the plaintiff could have jurisdiction over the case. Until 2013, there was no clear rule on this and the jurisdiction had to be that of the domicile of the defendant.[163] Since January 1, 2013, a new SPC regulation is in force and provides a general frame to determine jurisdiction in all internet-related matters.[164] According to this regulation, jurisdiction in civil infringement cases in network dissemination rights disputes is in the court of the place where the infringement occurred or the court in the place of the residence of the defendant. The place where the infringement occurred includes the place where the

163. *See* Shenzhen Yuan Hang Technology Co Ltd v. Shenzhen Tencent Computer System Co Ltd, Tencent Technology Co Ltd. (Shenzhen), and Shenzhen Tencent Computer System Co Ltd, (Xi'an Branch), Civil Ruling (2007) Xi Min Si Chu No 23 issued by the Xi'an Intermediary People's Court on March 5, 2007. In this case, the Court had applied by analogy the provisions of the SPC Judicial Interpretation on Several Issues Concerning the Application of Law in the Trial of Cases Involving Copyright Disputes relating to Computer Networks Copyright (last amended in 2006) to trademark infringement to support that the place where the server was located was the place where the tort is committed. The decision was then overruled by the Higher Court arguing that such provisions are only applicable to copyright disputes. For more analysis on this case, *see* Brian Fitzgerald, Sampsung Xiaoxiang Shi, Civil Jurisdiction, Intellectual Property and the Internet, Sydney University Press 389 (2008).

164. Regulations on Several Issues on Application of the Law in Civil Cases Concerning the Right of Network Dissemination of Information, of November 26, 2012.

network server or computer terminal conducting the infringement is located. When the place where the infringement occurred and the residence of the defendant are difficult to determine or in foreign countries, the place of the computer where the plaintiff discovered the infringement can be taken as the place where the infringement occurred. In this way, the court at the place of domicile of the defendant could still be avoided if the server or the terminal where the infringement is committed is located in a place different from the domicile of the defendant. If such place cannot be exactly located or it is located abroad, then jurisdiction can be established with the court of the place where the prospective plaintiff discovered the infringement, i.e., the place of his computer from which he carried out the online purchase. In case of direct purchase by order to the manufacturer, the court of the place where the act of manufacturing takes place will determine the jurisdiction. For this reason, a direct purchase should be avoided unless the prospective plaintiff is comfortable with the jurisdiction of the court at the place of manufacturing.

Eventually, forum shopping is not available in case a lawsuit follows up a custom seizure, an AIC or PSB raid and punishment. In all these cases, civil claims for damage compensation will have to be filed with the court of the place where the preceding administrative enforcement took place, the only alternative being the place of domicile of the defendant, if different from the location of the administrative enforcement action, which is not normally a recommended choice anyway.

[iii] Claims and Remedies

Cessation of infringement and damage compensation are the most common claims in a trademark civil lawsuit. Cessation of infringement is also the first remedy sought by a right holder, while damage compensation is a critical claim that will affect the deterring force of a judicial action aside from, when possible at all, remedy to the suffered economic losses. Although not directly provided by any Chinese law, noninfringement declaratory claims and judgments are nonetheless allowed, based on a decision of the SPC in 2002.[165] In the case law, and by analogy with the Interpretation of the SPC of 2009,[166] one of the conditions for creating a right to file a negative-declaratory action is the reiterated issuance of warning letters to competitors and clients that can disrupt the business of the accused but only alleged infringer. Such abuse gives right to the alleged infringer to file a noninfringement declaratory lawsuit with the court of his domicile to prove that he is not committing the infringements of which he is accused and to re-establish his reputation. The filing of such action, will

165. Suzhou Longbao Shengwu Gongcheng Shiye Gongsi Su Suzhou Langlifu Baojianpin Gongsi (苏州龙宝生物工程实业公司诉苏州郎力福保健品有限公司) [Suzhou Longbao Bio-engineering Company v. Shuzhou Langlifu Healthy Food Ltd. Compay] July 12, 2002 (Supreme People's Ct., China).

166. Zuigao Renmin Fayuan Guanyu Shenli Qinfan Zhuanliquan Jiufen Anjian Yingyong Falv Ruogan Wenti de Jieshi (最高人民法院关于审理侵犯专利权纠纷案件应用法律若干问题的解释) [Interpretations of the Supreme People's Court Concerning Certain Issues on the Application of Law for the Trial of Cases on Disputes over Infringement on Patent Rights] January 1, 2010 (Fa Shi 2009 No. 21).

prevent the establishment of jurisdiction by the court of a later infringement lawsuit, in that the mentioned jurisprudence of the SPC clearly indicates that the object of the noninfringement action is the same of the opposite lawsuit by the right holder and there cannot be two courts deciding on the same right and facts (*ne bis in idem* principle). This means that sending out warning letters without having planned and timed an immediate follow-up lawsuit, risk giving to the alleged infringer the opportunity to strike the first blow by filing a nondeclaratory action before his home court. This will prevent the trademark holder from filing his infringement lawsuit elsewhere, thus disrupting any possible forum-shopping plan and prejudicing his chances to successfully enforce his trademark right.

Warning letters in China are not enforceable by courts and in most cases are ignored by the infringer, while giving away the plans of the enforcer along with the element of surprise that is a winning factor in the planning and execution of successful judicial enforcement. A prewarned defendant will be on guard and expect the lawsuit. He will adjust his internal records and evidence to meet evidence burdens and reduce his risks and exposure to legal liabilities. In some cases, it may allow him to monitor its selling networks so that he will be warned of unusual attempts to purchase his products that will betray the right holder attempts to acquire the infringing product in his jurisdiction of choice.

Cessation of Infringement

The remedy of cessation of infringement is provided through a court injunction contained in the main judgment, in which the defendants are intimated to stop and cease from their infringing activities, i.e., manufacturing, selling, offering for sale, exporting, importing, abetting others' acts of infringement etc. In case a defendant defies this court injunction and continues with its acts of infringement, and in case of serious circumstances, its legal representative may be sentenced to not more than three years of fixed-term imprisonment, criminal detention or be fined.[167] According to an internal regulation issued by the SPC on investigation on crimes of refusing execution of judgments "serious circumstances" include the case of a person who must execute judgment or order concealing, transferring, damaging or assigning property which has been used as security with the court; the guarantor or the person who must execute the judgment hide, transfer, sell or deliberately destroy the property which has been provided as guarantee to the people's court, which can hamper or impede the execution of the judgment or the ruling; the person, who has the obligation to assist the implementation of a judgment or ruling, refuses to assist after receiving a notice for request of assistance by the people's court, which causes the judgment or the ruling to be no longer enforceable; the person in charge of the execution, the guarantor or the person, who has the obligation to assist the implementation of a judgment or ruling, colludes with the state organ personnel, disrupt the enforcement by taking advantage

167. It is regulated in Article 313 of China Criminal law that "Whoever has the ability to execute the judgment or order made by a People's Court but refuses to do so, if the circumstances are serious, shall be sentenced to not more than three years of fixed-term imprisonment, criminal detention or be fined."

of the state organ personnel's position, which causes the judgment or the ruling to become unenforceable; other serious circumstances in which the person has the ability to execute but refuses to do so.[168]

Damage Compensation

Article 63 of the Trademark Law provides that the amount of compensation for infringing the exclusive right to use the trademark shall be determined based on one of the following methods: The right owner's actual losses due to infringement or the infringer's actual interests obtained due to the same if the actual losses are hard to be determined, or may be determined based on times of the royalties of the registered trademark when both the losses or the infringer's actual interests obtained are hard to be determined. The law provides therefore for a mandatory sequence of calculation methods. Until the implementation of the new Trademark Law of 2014 and its Implementing Regulations, the loss suffered by the trademark owner, was to be calculated as the decreased amount in sales during the infringement period multiplied by the unit profit of the trademark owner's branded products.[169] Currently the calculation appears more complex due to a larger number of parameters the Court has to consider when determining illegal profit.[170] The income obtained by the infringer from the infringement can be then determined by multiplying the quantity of the infringing products sold by the unit profit; if the unit profit is difficult to ascertain, the trademark owner's own unit profit in the goods in questions can be used.[171] Reasonable expenses and costs incurred by the right holder to enforce his right shall also be compensated, including attorney fees.[172] The same must be compensated to the defendant in case of noninfringement.

For seriously malicious infringement, the amount of compensation may be one time - three times of the aforesaid amount determined in light of the foregoing regulations. The amount of compensation shall include reasonable expenses of the right owner to prevent the infringement. This part of the damage calculation is defined also as "punitive damages." Punitive damages aim at punishing the malicious behavior of the infringer and should constitute reinforcement to the deterring function of damage compensation.

168. Article 1 of the Notice on Conducting Serious Investigation on Crimes of Refusing to Execute Judgment or Order and Violent Resistance to Execution of the Court jointly issued by Supreme People's Court (SPC), Supreme People's Procuratorate (SPP) and Ministry of Public Security (MPS) (Fa Fa [2007] No. 29).
169. Article 15 of the Interpretation on Issues Regarding the Application of Law in Civil Cases Involving Trademark Disputes, Issued by the Supreme People's Court in October 2002.
170. Article 78 of the Regulation on the Implementation of the Trademark Law of the People's Republic of China (2014 Revision), 中华人民共和国商标法实施条例(2014修订). This norms provides the following parameters for the judge's consideration: (1) The sales price of infringing goods. (2) The marked price of unsold infringing goods. (3) The actual average sales price of verified infringing goods. (4) The median market price of genuine goods. (5) The infringer's business revenues resulting from the infringement. (6) Other factors enabling the reasonable calculation of the value of infringing goods.
171. *Supra* n. 169, Article 14.
172. *Supra* n. 169, Article 17.

Another important provision introduced by the new trademark law to facilitate right holders' burden of proof in relation to damages is that providing that for the purpose of determining the amount of compensation, where the account books and information regarding the infringement are held by the infringer while the right owner has put to the proof as practical as possible, the People's Court may order the infringer submit such account books and information; in case the infringer refuses to submit the account books and information or submit a false version thereof, the People's Court may determine the amount of compensation with reference to the right owner's claim and proof.

Eventually, when it is very difficult for the right holder to prove and for the court to determine the right owner's actual losses due to infringement, the infringer's actual interests obtained due to the same or the royalties of the registered trademark, the People's Court, can determine damages based on the actual circumstance of infringement and up to CNY 3 million (approximately USD 450,000). This form of compensation is also commonly referred to as "statutory damages," and it is nowadays the most used base for damage calculation in civil litigation in China.[173]

Other Remedies: Confiscation and Destruction of Infringing Tools and Public Apology

Other remedies which are critical for reducing the risk of continuation or repetition of the infringement are those concerning the confiscation and destruction of manufacturing tools. Unlike administrative enforcement, where the law provides expressly and clearly as to the power of the enforcing body to confiscate and destroy the goods and tools used in producing such goods or forging logos of the registered trademark, such a provision of the Trademark Law is not available to civil judges.

However, the legal base for determining available judicial remedies is to be found in Article 134 of the General Principles of Civil Law. In accordance with such provision, judges can order the infringer to bear the liability of ceasing the infringement, removal of obstacles, elimination of dangers, compensation for losses and elimination of all ill effects. It also has the discretion to impose a fine, detain infringing goods, confiscate infringing trademark reproductions and materials as well as the tools and equipment used in the production of the infringing goods.[174] Unlike the norm concerning administrative enforcement, the one for civil judges does not mention the word "destroy." However, in practice in both administrative and judicial enforcement, confiscation and destruction is often limited to tools and goods "exclusively" used to produce the infringing products. For instance, the court may order the confiscation and destruction of the mold with the embossed trademark, but will not confiscate and destroy the whole injection machine. Nonetheless, this remedy is indeed the most sought after next to damage compensation because it is the one that appears to be more effective as a deterrent, in that it causes economic losses to the infringer. Molds with embossed trademarks can in fact costs tens of thousands of dollars depending on their complexity! The costs of the confiscation are on the infringer. One downside of

173. *Supra* n. 48.
174. *Supra* n. 169, Article 21.

confiscation by administrative authorities is that the latter may sell the counterfeits after stripping them of the trademark, rather than destroy them.[175] This provision however does not apply to judicial enforcement.

[iv] Evidence: Burden of Proof

According to Article 64 Civil Procedure, it is he who alleges a fact who has the burden to prove it. Therefore, burden of proving that a trademark has been infringed is on the trademark holder once he becomes a complainant with a civil court. The defendant will have the burden to prove the facts that he alleges to its defense. This general rule explains also why evidence acquisition is so critical for the success of an enforcement strategy. The right holder has the burden to collect all the evidence to support his claims with little to help him in the law to alleviate such burden of proof. The burden is heavier in that there are formal requirements for evidence to be admitted in civil proceedings in China.

As to the first aspect, the law provides that under certain circumstances, the claimant can request the support of the court in collecting evidence. In such cases, it will be the court to acquire the evidence or, at least in one instance, the law will shift the burden of proof onto the defendant. In particular, court investigation of evidence is possible only when: the evidence under the application for investigation and collection belongs to the documentary materials that shall be kept by the relevant authority of the state and must be transferred by the people's court ex officio; the evidence belonging to the materials concerning state secrets, commercial secrets, or individual privacy; the evidence regarding other materials that cannot be collected by the party concerned and his agent *ad litem* themselves due to impersonal cause. The first two causes of evidence acquisition by court intervention refer to public documents that are in the possession of other administrative bodies of the State. In this case, if a party wants certain tax records or custom records or Company registry records of the other party, it may ask the court to order the corresponding administrations to provide such documents. Only the third one is concerned with the objective situation of impossibility for the requesting party to obtain a piece of evidence. This was typically the case of internal documents of the defendant, especially accounting records on point of proof of economic damage. However, exactly on this very point the new trademark law has intervened by switching the burden of proof to the defendant. In particular, the already cited Article 63 Trademark Law provides that the court can order the defendant to disclose the relevant data and figures in its accounting books; in case he refuses to submit the accounting books and information or submit a false version thereof, the People's Court may determine the amount of compensation with reference to the right owner's claim and proof. This seems therefore to limit the relevance of court investigations to the first two points cited above. Also, when requesting the court intervention, the applicant must describe with precision the type of evidence he is looking for and must file such request seven days before the expiration of the deadline imposed on

175. SAIC Circular 254/2002.

him by the court for filing evidence,[176] normally no less than 30 days after the plaintiff receives notice of acceptance of the lawsuit.[177]

Another remedy that a court can adopt is evidence preservation. Evidence preservation is regulated by Article 66 of the Trademark Law as a pretrial remedy to acquire evidence before a lawsuit is filed in order to avoid the loss or destruction of evidence due to the passing of time (*periculum in mora*). It has been questioned if such remedy is also available once a lawsuit is already pending. Before 2012, there was no specific provision in the Trademark Law or the Civil Procedure to answer this question with certainty. Now, Article 81 of the Civil Procedure in the 2012 amendment provides for the right to request evidence preservation within an already pending lawsuit. In that case, the court must decide within 48 hours whether to adopt the preservation measure. The court may require a security deposit from the applicant as guarantee in case the other party is damaged by the act of preservation. This guarantee is determined by the court at its discretion, but practice shows that it averages normally 5% of the damage compensation demand. The guarantee is paid either by bank transfer to the court special account, or by bank guarantee. This will depend from the amount of the deposit. Measures to implement the preservation can include audio and video recording, notes taking, sealing and confiscation of documents and objects, copying and even expert opinion. The court may in fact appoint experts for the review of the preserved materials when necessary, i.e., auditors for accounting books. Preserved evidence may be sealed and remain not accessible to the plaintiff till the trial or till an expert report is filed with the court that analyzes the evidence. Evidence preservation may be indeed helpful in obtaining documental evidence from the plaintiff as well as evidence of the infringing goods. However, a request for evidence preservation in the already pending lawsuit will have to be based on the prima facie evidence already collected by the plaintiff during the prelawsuit evidence acquisition phase. This means that even in cases where the court would be willing to intervene directly in an act of evidence acquisition, such intervention is not easy to obtain, unless the plaintiff can prove that he has made sincere and concrete efforts to obtain evidence upon his own initiative.

In sum, evidence acquisition is a primary objective for the prospective litigant. The strength of a lawsuit, its chances to shock the counterpart frozen and obtain a successful and enforceable decision rely on the preparatory work of the right holder during the initial investigative part of the case and evidence collection phase.

Related to evidence preservation is the issue of evidence spoliation. In western legal systems such as the US, the spoliation of evidence is the intentional, reckless, or negligent withholding, hiding, altering, fabricating, or destroying of evidence relevant to a legal proceeding, that can result in a criminal liability. Article 111.1 of the 2012 Civil Procedure in China provides that if a participant in an action or another person forges or destroys important evidence, thereby obstructing the trial of the case, the people's court may fine him or detain him according to the seriousness of the case. If the act constitutes a criminal offense, the person shall be prosecuted in accordance

176. *Supra* n. 175, Article 19.
177. *Supra* n. 175, Article 33.

with the law. This is a very important tool in litigation. Unfortunately, the erratic and inconsistent interpretation and application of the law, especially by the police in the initial stages of a criminal proceeding, have deprived right holders of the practical benefit of such legal tool. It is in fact very uncommon to see such actions filed within IP litigation cases in China, even when it is evident that the defendants are hiding and tampering evidence. Judges will tend to regard such conducts as detrimental to the defendant's case in respect with burden of proof, but will rarely sanction them. This lack of moral restraint among Chinese infringers finds therefore no effective boundaries in the criminal law, thus making evidence tampering a common occurrence in Chinese litigation.

[v] Evidence: Formalities

As to the formalities for evidence admissibility in civil proceedings, the law provides that it must be filed in original or copy equivalent to original. If it is not in the Chinese language, it must be translated into Chinese by a licensed translator. Evidence acquired outside China must be notarized and legalized according to the processes in place on the country where the evidence is taken[178] in order to be admissible in court in China. Eventually, evidence must be obtained legally.

A most critical issue with evidence in Chinese litigation is authenticity. On one hand, evidence forgery is common in China. A defendant will tend to create documents in which he declares he was the first user of a right, or he had an authorization from a right holder to do that, etc. Also, believing evidence only once authenticated by a government body is also a very peculiar trait of evidence admissibility in China. For instance, an official company stamp, issued by the AIC at the time of incorporation is in China the only valid and legally binding signature, whereby in Europe or the US that would be the hand signature of the company's legal representative. Considering the above, it is normal for Chinese to think that an evidence produced by a party without any official mark of authentication is to be doubted as original. For instance: A business license can be filed as evidence without any further formalities, because the original can be verified by anybody by accessing official online company records. However, a print out of a web page of an alleged infringer will not be presumed as being authentic until it is either supported by other objective and authenticated evidence, or itself, it is acquired through a formal process that ensures at least a basic presumption of authenticity. The same can be said of a contract, an invoice or any other private document. Therefore, special regulations have emerged in China that allow any party to a legal dispute to acquire evidence through a given notarial process, which will ensure that a private document will assume a certain degree of public relevance and

178. Article 11 of the Supreme People's Court Interpretation on Several Issues Regarding the Evidence in Civil Actions, adopted on December 6, 2001, provides: "If the evidence provided by a party concerned is created out of the territory of the P.R. China, such evidence shall be testified by the notarial organ of the host country, be authenticated by the embassy in this country of the P.R. China, or the proving formalities shall be gone through as specified in the relevant treaty concluded by the P.R. China with this country."

authenticity, until evidence to the contrary with at least the same degree of authenticity is provided by the other party. This system is to a good extent unique to China and finds no immediate relatives in the Western hemisphere.

The process of notarization of the evidence acquisition processes (and their legalization in case of evidence acquired outside China) is borne out of the need to provide a formal guarantee about the authenticity of the origin and/or formation of a certain document or act. As to evidence collected in China, the best way for a party to authenticate its origin and formation process is by involving a paragovernmental body into the evidence acquisition process. This is the figure of the Chinese notary. Notary offices (公证处) are an agent of the Ministry of Justice.[179] Notarization means that a government-authorized agent proves the authenticity, truthfulness and legality of documents and facts requested by a private party.[180] Notarization of evidence is the best way to create a presumption of authenticity and shift the burden to prove the contrary on to the other party. The notarized civil legal act, fact and document of legal significance must in fact be taken as the basis for ascertaining a fact except those that can be overturned by counter-evidence.[181] According to the law, notaries act upon request of a person or entity and perform a number of activities including acquisition and preservation of evidence as well as authentication of signatures, seals and dates as indicated in a document, duplicate or photocopy of a document conforming to the original document.[182] Furthermore, notaries have investigative functions and powers, in handling evidence preservation.[183] They can act undercover without disclosing their identities during purchase transactions and meetings with trademark infringers. In this way, the infringer will not know that his correspondence, deliveries and payment's processes are tracked down by a notary office. Notaries are also employed in the certification of the content of web pages and domain names related to the infringement. These are the functions of a notary that are most relevant to a right holder collecting evidence of an infringement. Generally, once the right holder discovers an act of infringement, notary offices will be involved from the very beginning in the evidence -collection process. The web page or e-shop pages of the infringers will be notarized as proof of an offer for sale and advertising of the infringing product. This evidence not only certifies the infringing act of offering for sale, but it will also be useful to support claims for damage compensation. Purchase transactions including bank transfers will be also notarized. This means that e-mail, mobile massages, telephone calls between infringer and undercover buyers will be notarized. In order to have all these documents notarized, such purchase and communication activities must be conducted, at least at the very beginning at the notary office, using authentication software owned by the notary. In case of web-based information, the download of the requested information should be conducted through the notary's computer in order to authenticate not only

179. Article 4 of the Notarization Law of the People's Republic of China, adopted at the 17th meeting of the Standing Committee of the National People's Congress of the People's Republic of China on August 28, 2005.
180. Article 2 of the Notarization Law of the People's Republic of China.
181. Article 36 of the Notarization Law of the People's Republic of China.
182. Article 11 of the Notarization Law of the People's Republic of China.
183. Article 12 of the Notarization Law of the People's Republic of China.

the downloaded information but their source as well.[184] This formality is important in that a web-based information, electronic data downloaded from a party's computer will lead to a notarization that ascertain that the notary downloaded certain given data but it will not confirm their origin and authenticity. In those first meetings, the notary will also identify and certify the identity of the undercover buyers and their e-mail and telephone numbers. In this way, the following correspondences and messages will not need to be sent or received at the notary office. They can be later brought to the notary for their incorporation in the final deed. An important moment requiring the presence of the notary is that of the delivery of the purchased infringing product. Notary should be present at the time of delivery to confirm that the transacted purchase and the delivery are indeed related to each other. All these activities are most critical to the construction of a solid and unchallengeable chain of evidence. These activities required handling by experienced counsel. Further difficulties are also brought about the inconsistent practice of notarial offices as to what they can and they cannot do. There are indeed large differences among regions in China. Notaries in the south, especially in the counterfeits-ridden Guangdong province are very strict as to formalities and action limits. For instance, they are often reluctant to notarize the purchase of a trademark-infringing product, if there is no full certainty that the infringed trademark is offered for sale. This is the most critical case in that many infringers offer for sale a product identical in shape to the one of the right holder but without showing the trademark, so as to divert suspects and avoid committing an open infringement in internet. However, without explicit request by the buyer they will sell that same product with the counterfeited trademark later on. If notarization of such purchase is not possible, then it may be very difficult, if not impossible, to sue the infringer. Also, in case of delivery, many Guangzhou notaries would refuse notarization if delivery is not carried out by a registered courier service. This practice is not founded in the law and gives rise to many critics. However, the reasoning behind it is that in the past Guangzhou notaries had notarized fake deliveries, either knowingly or not. This prompted the notarial association in that locality to tighten up internal requirements to avoid the repetition of such cases.

Such differences among notarial offices in the same city and those in different regions must be considered by the right holder when preparing an enforcement strategy, in that they will shape the plans to conduct an effective purchase test. It will be thus important to consider in advance what is to be notarized and where it would be better to have it notarized, in order to avoid problems due to local practices that often have no real legal base, but virtually affect the way an evidence acquisition will be shaped. This is more important if we consider that evidence acquisition, and in particular acquisition of the evidence of the infringing conduct, is strictly related to the selection of a suitable court jurisdiction.

---

184. NuCom Online (Beijing) Information Technology Co., Ltd. v. China Network Communications Corporation Limited, Zigong Branch, judgment of the Supreme People's Court (2008) Min Shen Zi No. 926.

[vi] Court Hearing and Evidence Cross-Examination and Evaluation

A lawsuit in China can be made of a number of hearings. Generally, in normal trademark cases, one hearing could be sufficient to have all evidence cross-examined. In more complex cases, where preliminary questions of law or jurisdiction are raised, where experts may be appointed, the court will need more hearings to complete the trial of the case. Court hearing is open to the public unless the case involves trade or State secrets. The hearing normally starts with opening statements by the parties, evidence cross-examination, witness and expert testimony, debate, closing statements of the parties, offer of court mediation. At the end of a hearing, the court will ask the parties whether they intend to settle the case. Court mediation is a very common way for parties to settle matters. Court mediation in particular, can be a useful tool for the trademark holder in a strong trial position. Courts have high persuasive powers and are appreciative of plaintiffs that do agree to settle. In such cases, the court may often pressurize the defendants to settle at conditions most favorable to the right holder. The opposite is true if the plaintiff case does not rest on strong grounds.

Cross-examination of evidence is conducted before the court. China has not adopted a discovery system like in the US (no deposition or interrogatory procedures, and even no early disclosure of documents); therefore, evidence will be cross-examined during court hearings or in a pretrial hearing organized specifically for the exchange of evidence.[185] During this hearing, parties exchange evidence and provide an outline of their pleadings. The court uses such hearings to get a flavor of the case and identify the major controversial issues. However, there is no cross-examination at this hearing. The main purpose of such pretrial hearing is twofold: give the court a head up on the case before the formal hearing, reduce the risk of trial by ambush, i.e., reduce the chances of new evidence filed at the last minute at the formal hearing, which would likely and does indeed in most cases require a new hearing for further cross-examination, with a fallout on the court trial schedule. The risk of trial by ambush in China is a reality. The time limit to submit evidence is at least 30 days from the filing of the lawsuit, or the filing of the defensive pleadings respectively. Witnesses should be named even earlier, i.e., 10 days before the 30 days deadline elapses. If evidence is not submitted in due time, it cannot be admitted to the proceedings. However, judges tend to be very large when determining exceptions to these terms, thus allowing filing of evidence at the first hearing. In some cases, courts allow the filing of evidence without respect of evidence assumption's formalities, as long as the party can cure these formal flaws at the hearing. All this slows down the proceedings and makes the time between the filing of the lawsuit and the first hearing rather unremarkable, if not utterly a waste of time, in that nothing much happens and little is known of the other party's case and defensive strategy.

185. *Supra* n. 178, Article 37.

[vii] *Prelawsuit Remedies and Measures*

Prior to the filing of a lawsuit, a right holder may suffer prejudices of different kinds depending on the passing of time for the filing and running of a civil lawsuit. In China as in most Western countries, there are three major prelawsuit legal tools: Interim injunctions, evidence preservations and property preservation. Preliminary injunctions can only be requested before the filing of a civil lawsuit for trademark infringement, while requests for evidence and property preservation can be accepted by a civil court even after a civil complaint has been filed. In this context, we will focus only on injunctions and evidence preservations that are most commonly used in trademark litigation compared to property preservation.

Interim Injunctions and Property Preservation

Under Article 65 of the new trademark law provides for a form of interim injunction prior to litigation in case of an impending or already started infringement that could cause an irreparable damage if not stopped immediately. In particular, if a trademark registrant or any interested party submits evidence proving that another party is engaged in or will soon engage in actions that infringe upon the former's exclusive right to use its registered trademark and that, unless they are stopped promptly, will cause irreparable injury to its legitimate rights and interests, the registrant may, before filing a lawsuit, apply to the civil court territorially competent for the future lawsuit for the granting of an injunction prohibiting the actions and protecting its assets.[186] As to the definition of interested party, the Interpretation of the SPC of 2001 provides that this can only be the licensee and the legitimate heir of the deceased person or legal successor of an entity.[187] Entitled to file a preliminary injunction is also the legal heir or successor of trademark property rights, and the sole licensee - if the trademark registrant does not promptly apply. The application must be filed to the People's Court having jurisdiction over the trademark dispute, be in written form and contain the introduction of the parties, the specific contents and scope of the application, and the grounds of the application - including, more importantly, the evidence demonstrating the irreparable harm caused to the right holder which is likely to happen if the requested injunction is not acted by the judge.

Furthermore, the trademark registration certificate must necessarily be submitted in the application together with a sample of the accused infringing products - or, in general, other evidence showing that the respondent is infringing or about to infringe the trademark rights.

186. Article 65 Trademark Law. While an injunction will stop the manufacturing and selling activities of the infringer, the property preservation aims at preventing the loss of assets of the defendant that may later prevent the plaintiff from recovering the liquidated damages.
187. Article 4 Interpretation by the Supreme People's Court of Several Issues Relating to Application of Law to Trial of Cases of Civil Disputes over Trademarks (Adopted at the 1246th Meeting of the Adjudication Committee of the Supreme People's Court on October 12, 2002 and entering into force on October 16, 2002).

If the applicant is not the proprietor but the licensee of the infringed mark, he shall also provide the trademark license agreement and recordation documents, and even the evidence that the trademark registrant is not willing to file an application for the prelawsuit preliminary injunction.

The injunctive order of the People's Court cannot exceed the limits of the application filed by the applicant. A bond – in the form of cash, guarantee, mortgage or other valid forms accepted by the People's Court – must be provided by the applicant of the presuit preliminary injunction, failing which the application will be rejected. The Court is empowered to order the applicant the issue of a higher bond, if the one provided is likely to be insufficient to cover the probable damages to the respondent during the execution of the preliminary injunction. If the payment of such higher bond is refused by the applicant, the Court may cease the procedures for enforcing the preliminary injunction.

The People's Court decision will take place in no longer than 48 hours after the acceptance of the case. If the Court orders a preliminary injunction, such order is to be immediately executed, and notified to the respondent within five days. The order can be appealed by the affected party within 10 days, but the appeal does not stop the order.

A prelitigation injunction order is valid for 30 days, and the missed filing of the substantive complaint by the applicant by the end of the 30th day causes the automatic vacation of the interim order. Unlike patent infringement cases, injunctions are more frequent in trademark matters, because a court has fewer challenges in determining a trademark rather than a patent infringement. However, a serious obstacle in the obtainment of such an injunction is the required level of evidence to prove the "irreparable harm." Also, the fact of having to place a bond, which in practice could be a very high arbitrary amount, can create an insurmountable obstacle, especially for a smaller company with tight enforcement budgets. If we consider that a right holder has the possibility to resort to administrative raids to enforce a trademark, it is much less risky and easier to obtain first an administrative enforcement to stop the infringement, and then filing a civil lawsuit for the determination of damage compensation than requesting an injunction. Such alternative way is particularly suitable if the infringing trademark is identical or very similar to the registered one.

Evidence Preservation

Where the evidence is likely to be destroyed, or in case it might be difficult to obtain the proof of the infringement in future, the trademark owner is entitled to apply to the People's Court for an order of preservation of evidence. Chinese courts, if the evidence submitted is able to convince them that the evidence is effectively in the infringer's hands and it is likely to be destroyed, can grant the request.

Foreign companies often use investigators to obtain relevant information, but the investigator's report is not sufficient to make the court approve the reservation request: such report has indeed to be signed and sealed by a company which is authorized to do that kind of business in China.

In practice, evidence preservation is a very good litigation tool that should be used along with a lawsuit. If well timed, the preservation should be served upon the counterpart contextually along with the lawsuit. The defendant will therefore receive them together and will have to open his doors to the court officials and let them carry the preservation action without having even had the time to read the lawsuit! Such a well-timed attack not only enjoys the element of surprise and prevent evidence tampering and spoliation, but also provide a considerable psychologic advantage to the plaintiff, which can thus send the defendant to the ground with a rapid one-two knock out. This is also one of the best moments for settling a dispute, in that the knock out will force the other party to accept more unfavorable conditions, than if it were after receiving only the lawsuit notification or once the case is ongoing already.

Considering that in many cases evidence preservation concerns accounting books, it may well be that such a tool has lost some of its relevance following the introduction of the new provision of Article 63 Trademark Law regarding burden of proof and accounting books. Specifically, Article 63 Trademark Law provides that for the purpose of determining the amount of damages, where the account books and information related to the infringement are held by the infringer, and where the rights owner has presented as much proof of its claims as is practically possible, a People's Court may order the infringer to submit such account books and information. If the infringer refuses to submit such account books and information, or submits a false version thereof, a People's Court may determine the amount of damages with reference to the right owner's claims and proof.

In practice, this new provision does not completely eliminate the need for evidence preservation of accounting books for a number of reasons. The first reason is that there is a risk that such books may indeed be tampered if the defendant is given sufficient time to do so. Second, it is the plaintiff/right holder that has then to prove that the filed books were tampered, which is also a very difficult task. Third, it is not easy for a plaintiff to find evidence supporting a specific damage compensation demand, and that is why accounting books are so important! This means that a defendant who knows that his accounting books contain very high figures that could support large damage compensation, may have interest not producing these books and let the court decide based on the claims of the plaintiff that are supported by solid and irrefutable evidence. It may well be that such claimed figures are largely inferior to those hidden in the books or, even worse, the claims of the plaintiff contain no specific figures. In the latter case, the court would decide based on statutory damages, its highest amount being CNY 3,000,000 (around USD 450,000).

If we consider the above reasons and we sum to them the psychologic effect of evidence preservation on a defendant, it is evident that such legal tool maintains fully its importance in the planning of a successful enforcement strategy.

Chapter 3

Trademark Protection: Hostile Trademarks and Trademark Theft

Trademarks are the legal embodiment of brands. They are assets and important business vehicles in today's global market. There is no company today who is not aware of the importance of investing resources to build up brand value and protect it. However, this awareness does not necessarily combine with the appropriate legal knowledge. This leads to misperceptions and prejudices about the Chinese legal system and the protection of trademark rights.

Most foreign brand owners perceive the Chinese trademark system as unjust, and the trademark law inadequate to protect their brands – all to the advantage of aggressive Chinese competitors and criminal organizations. There are indeed reasons for such a negative perception of the trademark law and, more in general, the legal and enforcement systems of China.[188] In particular, foreign companies view trademark filing in China as too expensive when compared with the low rate of success in winning hijacked trademarks back from the Chinese trademark grabbers. The first-to-file principle that characterizes the Chinese trademark system – a system that gives little or no legal value to pre-use, save for few exceptions such as well-known trademarks – has indeed contributed to the proliferation of hostile trademark filings and theft by Chinese individuals and competing enterprises. At the same time, remedies have only occasionally been effective, while they are always expensive and time consuming. For

188. Turgut Guvenlu, Rajib Sanyal, Perception and management of legal issues in China by US firms, Vol. 32, Issue 2 The Journal of Socio-Economics, 161-181 (May 2003): "A survey of senior managers of American-owned firms in China about their experience with China's legal system and with intellectual property rights violations indicates that none of them found the system efficient and few found it fair. Chinese business ethical standards were perceived to be lower than in the US. Certain types of firms and business strategies were more prone to product piracy and patent violations. A variety of methods were used to address them. Foreign managers with experience in China have insights into the functioning of the legal system and are more satisfied with it than less experienced managers." *See* more recently EU Chamber of Commerce in China, European Business in China–Position Paper 2014/2015 http://www.europeanchamber.com.cn/en/publications-position-paper (2014).

instance, lack of clear laws on bad faith and preventive registrations coupled with inconsistent jurisprudence by smaller provincial courts in trademark infringement cases, have contributed to the skepticism on the real possibility of protecting IP rights in China. This often creates in foreigners the impression that there must have been a political will behind the insufficient protection of foreign trademarks and more in general, IP rights in China, prompting for instance the US to file legal actions against China at World Trade Organization (WTO) level.[189]

However, not all the perceived disadvantages are attributable to malicious political will, as many foreigners seem to believe. Lack of knowledge of the Chinese legal system, but more importantly of the Chinese way of doing trademark business is one of the main reasons why foreign brands come to China committing always the same mistakes. It cannot be all blamed on China. It would be absurd to blame the Chinese legal system for having chosen a "First-to-File" trademark system, or that foreign right holders usually neglect the existence of such rule when structuring their worldwide trademark portfolio. Unbiased knowledge of a legal system is a basic must for any foreign trademark lawyer or manager who serves foreign enterprises in China. Trademark portfolio and strategies encompassing China must therefore be based on solid knowledge of its legal system as it is and not as they would like it to be. Reliance of local Chinese partners has in many cases revealed insufficient to bridge this knowledge gap. It is not just a language, but fore and foremost a cultural issue. A foreigner does not understand China, but Chinese often cannot explain China to foreigners so that the latter can understand it. This knowledge gap must be filled up. Considering the importance of China for any company IP portfolio, foreign lawyers and trademark practitioners must be helped to gain more in-depth knowledge about the Chinese law, the Chinese business and the way to combine them according to the Chinese way, in order to obtain maximized business and legal solutions to their China trademark challenges. This is why books like this are still worth being read.

Another factor to be considered as a contributor to western misperceptions of the efficacy of the Chinese trademark system is the swift evolution of commercial practices due to the ever expanding use of the Internet, which have often put the Chinese legislative and judicial system under the urgent need for quick adaptation to continuous and rapid changes. In this respect, it must be acknowledged that, since 2001 – the year of China's accession to the WTO – the IP field in China has seen one of the largest proliferations of new legislations, and has rapidly adapted its laws and legal practices to such changes. China has taken its WTO/TRIPS obligations seriously and has begun enacting laws and regulations which comply with the required international standards for trademark legal protection. At the same time, IP-specialized courts have been created in major cities and have set up their own websites where their jurisprudence is publicly available. Judges have joined in educational activities and information

189. In August 2007, the Government of the United States filed a request for World Trade Organization (WTO) dispute settlement consultations with the People's Republic of China over deficiencies in China's legal regime for protecting and enforcing copyrights and trademarks on a wide range of products (Case Dispute DS362) in http://www.wto.org/english/tratop_e/dispu_e/cases_e/1pagesum_e/ds362sum_e.pdf.

exchanges with the public, and exchanged experience with other judges from foreign jurisdictions within several cooperation programs.[190] This allows the SPC to collect knowledge and experience, and issue interpretations and opinions each year addressing disputed legal issues, thus allowing courts to interpret and adapt the trademark law in a more consistent fashion.[191] In most cases, the result is that amendments to the law have been somewhat anticipated by judicial practice. Though some gray areas remain – inasmuch as real life business practices and technology normally outpace the law – the Chinese legal system now has the instruments and the cultural means to adapt the written law to the evolving forms of infringement and enforcement.

Blaming the Chinese legal system for failing to protect their trademarks in China is only part of the story, and often becomes an excuse for managers to divert attention from their own responsibilities. A review of many trademark cases that have gained notoriety abroad shows how unprepared the foreign company actually was, and how ill-considered its actions in China. If there is indeed reason to put some blame on China's real political will to protect foreign companies' IP rights, there is as much reason to criticize foreign companies for their poor performance.

The new Trademark Law of China in force since May 1, 2014, and the most recent jurisprudence of the SPC have introduced a series of provisions and interpretations of the law which seem to finally provide more preventive tools and even more effective remedies against the plague of trademark grabbing, especially for all the trademarks that are not famous or have but little or no reputation in China. Strategic planning can now avail of more tactical choices. If the planning is done correctly and in accordance with the Rules of Engagements presented here, the chances to succeed will surely increase compared to the past. Failure is still possible, but there will be fewer chances to blame it on China.

In the present Chapter, the author will explore the issue of trademark theft and trademark free riding and will try to apply the strategic approach presented in the first Chapter and summarized in the Rules of Engagement to real cases and instances, to show that even in difficult cases, the right approach can bring good results no matter what the law says and courts do! The key to a successful protection of trademark rights lies thus in the preparation work of the right holder, the adoption of sound strategic goals and the correct use of the legal tools as concretely provided by the Chinese law, not as those wished for, to each case.

§3.01 LESSONS FROM A TYPICAL CASE OF TRADEMARK HIJACKING

Trademark thieves are like buccaneers: ragged and sometimes colorful adventurers roaming the vast Chinese business seas in search of unaware and undermanned

190. *Supra* n. 7.

191. *See* Summary of the Annual Report of the Supreme People's Court on Intellectual Property Cases (2015) http://www.pkulaw.cn/CLI.3.269028; *see also* Summary of the Annual Report of the Supreme People's Court on Intellectual Property Cases (2014) http://www.pkulaw.cn/CLI.3.247219; *see also* Summary of the Annual Report of the Supreme People's Court on Intellectual Property Cases (2013) http://www.pkulaw.cn/CLI.3.223958.

galleons from the far away West. Buccaneers sail on light and very fast ships, have full knowledge of their backyard waters, they quickly hit and disguise themselves. When the western galleon is in need to anchor to patch the damages it finds itself in foreign waters and among unfriendly indigenous tribes, or worse at Tortuga, the island of the lawless. As picturesque and evocative this might sound, the reality is bitter and upsetting for the victims, as it emerges from the pirate story below.

On an August day of 2012, a US company informed his foreign lawyer in China that few of his trademark applications in the Middle Kingdom had just been rejected due to prior identical registration by an unknown third party. In fact, identical trademarks had been applied earlier by a company from the Sultanate of Brunei, since 2010! The US company's trademarks were first created in 1971 and had since then been registered as such in the US. Also, it was learned that the client had been doing business in China since the early nineties, when it had appointed a Chinese individual as its local distributor. Since 2010, the client had started losing money in China. Orders were down, millions of dollars in revenues quickly vanished. The distributor was suspected of wrong dealings and was fired after over 15 years of business relation. However, in August 2012, there was no hard evidence that the Chinese distributor had applied those trademarks in 2010, and that he had diverted business away from the US principal. The latter was upset and clueless as how to fix the problem of losing orders and money. Eventually, intense searches revealed that the former distributor had set up a bunch of Chinese companies using the principal's name and presenting themselves to the market as the principal itself. The principal started slowly to realize for the first time that there was a direct relation between these uncovered facts and their steady losses in China since 2010. It took another month or so of investigations to bring first evidence of a large infringement scheme orchestrated by the former distributor with the collusion of his close family. Experience and investigating instinct quickly brought the attorney on the right trail: a relation between the Chinese distributor and the Brunei's company was suspected. More facts were investigated, collected and analyzed so that the suspicions turned into strong hints. Trademark searches revealed that the Brunei enterprise owned over 150 of the principal's trademarks in China and Taiwan and many had been already registered back in 1994. This led the investigations to further trademark searches till a direct evidence of the relation between the distributor and the Brunei's entity was found. Once all the available facts were lined up, it emerged that the former distributor had been actually the first to apply the principal's trademarks in China in his own name without the principal's authorization since 1994. He had then begun assigning such older trademarks to the Brunei entity in 2009. Most important, evidence revealed that he had signed the trademark assignment agreements of 2009 both on his own behalf as the assignor as well as on behalf of the Brunei entity, the assignee! That was the smoking gun. From then on, all the later applications and registrations since 2009 were made directly in the name of this Brunei entity. Further investigations of other subcontractors had revealed important hints of the parallel business the former distributor had created during the 15 years of his work with the American principal.

Once the infringement had been reconstructed and evidence collected, legal actions were promptly taken. Hundreds of invalidations for registration by the agent in bad faith and oppositions on the latter ground were filed against the most recent trademarks (since 2008), while nonuse cancellations had to be filed for the older trademarks from the nineties because the limitation period for the cancellation of bad faith registrations expired after five years from the date of registration of the targeted trademarks. Eventually, evidence as to the shareholding structure of the infringer was obtained through a legal trap set forth by the attorneys of the US right holder in the nonuse cancellation procedures, that were supplied as evidence of bad faith in the other set of bad faith invalidations and oppositions. A complex case reconstruction was therefore followed by a massive legal action. Meanwhile, the infringer had turned his stolen trademarks into trolls by filing an infringement lawsuit in Wuhan, China against the principal and his local distributors. This in turn forced the principal to suspend the use of his old trademarks and launch a new brand in China and Taiwan and protect it by new trademark filings. Eventually, after four years of battle, decisions favorable to the US right holder in the nonuse cancellations as well as the agent bad faith registration begun to pour in, and the market has recognized that the usurper is not the legal entity entitled to use the stolen brand.

In spite of the good news after over four years of battles, still partly ongoing with some appeals pending, the damage inflicted to the US right holder will take a long time to be fully absorbed. In the flurrying of legal actions, the market has been confused for long stretches of time. Buyers were no longer able to discern between who is who. Trademark hijacking had cost million in lost orders and a hundred thousands of dollars in lawyers' fees. At the same time, if the US entity had duly registered its trademarks back since 1994, when they started an official distribution relation in China, it all would have cost a few thousand US dollars and this case would have never occurred.

Keeping in mind the basic facts described above, which are all but a little portion of the whole story, a number of relevant issues emerge which are worthy of remarks. The right holder, not well counseled and misled in thinking that prior use and a registration in the US could cover his rights in China, set about doing business in China from the mid-nineties with an individual person without taking steps to register his trademarks in China until 2012! Business developed quickly and profitably for over 10 years. Nobody at the US headquarter was even remotely concerned about trademarks in China, and no independent checks were ever conducted on the distributor, so that the US entity completely missed any sign of the distributor build up. Only after the company started losing money and dismissed the distributor in 2012, it started questioning its business model in China. Why had they let one single individual manage many dozens of millions of US dollars worth of business in China without any trademark protection and control? Why did not they ever check his trademark portfolio? How could they have failed in detecting the distributor companies shadowing the principal's identity in China?

The most crucial factor and the initiator of the whole matter was the failure of the principal to timely secure its trademark rights in China. China's trademark protection is based on formal registration rather than prior use as in the US and to a certain extent Europe. The protection model for trademarks in China is based on the "First to File" principle. The first person or entity applying for a brand registration as trademark in China will be granted a 10 years exclusive right over that trademark, which is renewable for further 10 years *ad infinitum*.

This first-to-file has been the major legal con-cause of the proliferation of trademark theft and the emergence of a lucrative trademark hijacking economy.[192] Individuals, alone or organized in gangs of serial trademark hijackers have exploited this provision of the Chinese trademark system to trade on stolen trademarks. In addition to the first-to-file rule, implementing regulations do not impose on individual applicants to prove they are conducting legitimate businesses. While this has been surely a serious problem for the many famous brands, and in some cases an utter nightmare, it has always been a real tragedy for small- and medium-sized companies from the West. For many, trademark hijacking meant the appalling perspective of being prevented from entering the Chinese market or paying absurd ransoms to recover their trademarks. At the same time, exploiting deregulation in the trademark agents market, myriads of small consulting companies have turned themselves into filing agents and many of them have soon realized that there was more profit in trademark thieving than prosecution in spite of regulations prohibiting such filings.[193] In some cases, agents slyly avoid professional liability by having their owners or employees filing stolen trademarks in their own personal names. In sum, the trademark filing system in China does not have any preventive filter or checks to reduce the risk of hijacking. The result is simple and clear: a trademark holder must move quickly to secure its trademark rights by filing them in China before others may do that.

Blaming the infringers or the law cannot eliminate the fact that such problems would not emerge if foreign brand owners were aware of such rules and acted consequently, by timely planning their portfolio filings in China and worldwide. In sum, we cannot make a principle of law such as first-to-file the sole responsible for trademark hijacking in China. On a scale, the negligent ignorance of the Chinese law by foreign brand owners and their legal consultants should bear thus more weight and responsibility for the continuous raise of trademark theft. It is evident that lacking knowledge of China business practices and Chinese law are one of the major reasons for the failures of western companies in the China IP arena. Evidence to this is the simple fact that in the last 20 years, scores of western companies have been affected by exactly the same problem and have all committed the same mistake! How can the repeating of the same mistake, devilish to a certain extent, be justified by just blaming it on the Chinese law? Ignorance is the answer. And this ignorance is not just limited to the first-to-file principle or to other basic law concepts. It is a deeper cultural issue, whereby foreign companies plan China IP business while wearing the lenses of their own countries' business and law practices. For example, China does not recognize

192. *Supra* n. 31, 264.
193. Article 32 Trademark Law.

explicit protection to trade dress. Therefore, signs, patterns and three-dimensional designs or marks must be registered either as trademarks (if distinctive and functioning to identify a product's origins), design (if their esthetic value is the object of protection) or both. Ultimately, if a work of high and original intellectual value, they could be protected by copyright as well. Also, such forms of protections can be cumulative. However, in case none of the above forms of protection is available, it will be difficult for a right holder to claim protection under trade dress for the lack of specific regulations. The fact that trade dress is protectable in other legal systems should not mislead the right holder when seeking protection in China. It cannot surely be blamed on China to have chosen a first-to-file rule for IP protection in the first place or for not having clear regulations on trade dress, when the former is also adopted in western countries for other IP rights (the US for instance), and the latter is not even available in some more modern western legal systems. Basing a strategy on wrong assumptions, without knowledge of the way the law and business work concretely in China can have far-reaching consequences. For instance, securing a trademark right but not a design for a certain shape or pattern may, in some cases, results in a flawed scope of protection. Ultimately, a misplaced right, i.e., a pattern registered as a trademark but used as a design right, may even lead to the loss of the trademark for nonuse, as it happened to the Haymarket trademark of Burberry.[194]

Also, a good portion of the debate on trademark theft has concentrated on the cases involving famous western brands, such as those we listed in the opening chapter to this book. Little thought has so far been given of how much deeper wounds can trademark theft cause to companies other than MNCs. Many attorneys still suggest that right holders should file their trademarks in China in as many classes as they can, if not all 45 of them, to prevent the risk of trademark hijacking.[195] In case of theft, it is often and blindly recommended to try all available legal means to obtain the trademark back through the law. These recipes may work for MNCs with deep pockets (likely it will not work for them either); surely they do not work for the overwhelming vast majority of western companies. Even the premises of these debates and consulting focus merely on MNCs business problems. For instance, a number of stolen trademarks are often applied in classes which are not of direct interest for the targeted brand. This happens when a trademark is well known, and therefore has an attractive added value even when it is not related to the goods with which it is normally associated. It is in fact possible to find hijackers who apply the Italian famous fashion brand PRADA in class 1 in association with industrial resins. In spite of the apparent remoteness among the goods in question, the presence of such trademark may indeed pose a problem to a well-known brand, in that its use may contribute to the dilution of the former

194. Paolo Beconcini, Protection of Pattern Trademarks from Non-Use Cancellation in China, https://hk.lexiscn.com/topic/legal.php?tps = pg_ls&act = detail&id = 120044&newstype = 3&is English = Y (February 28, 2014).
195. Such recommendations are also not sound from other legal point of views. In fact, filing trademarks in all 45 classes without using them for the respective goods or services, may lead to a cancellation for nonuse and cause useless costs to the right holders.

exclusivity and association only with luxury goods. On the other hand, SMEs are not threatened of brand dilution in the first place, but to their immediate commercial survival in the Chinese market, if not abroad. If a western brand is not famous, at least in China, then hostile filings of the same brand by trademark thieves in totally unrelated classes will unlikely occur and even when it happens, it constitutes no case of hijack. In fact, the scope of protection of a normal trademark will be limited to the classes and subclasses of goods and services for which such trademarks should have been registered or has been registered. Its lacking of notoriety also delimits the boundaries of its protection to exactly those designated goods and services. If an identical or similar trademark is filed in a class of goods other than the designated one by the original trademark, it is evident that lack of the latter's notoriety will also mark the lack of any commercial proximity and risk of confusion among the relevant public. This explains why in case of normal trademarks, unlike that of well-known brands, trademark theft concerns the hijacking of the original trademark in the originally designated classes or in classes similar to the designated ones by the original brand. This is what hurts SMEs and proportionally, it hurts more than the issue of brand dilution suffered by MNCs, at least in the short term. Being prevented from using its own trademark in China, may result in the foreign SMEs' economical demise or market share downsizing in a very short period of time. Trademark grabbers or Chinese competitors want to make money or gain direct and immediate business advantages by the act of theft, and none of them would invest money on stealing a "nonfamous brand" in classes irrelevant to the original brand of the right holder. Which SME would in fact buy or request the return of a trademark identical or similar to their own unless it was registered by the usurper in the exact class covering the product and services of the brand of the original foreign holder? Trademark hijacking affecting the vast majority of brands focuses on exactly the classes of goods and services related to the stolen trademark. This hurts them a lot and in a very short time! That is why trademark theft is even more pernicious for SMEs than MNCs.

In this respect, the right holder could have always prevented the act of theft by the grabbers if he had duly registered his trademark in the relevant classes.

The same reasoning pattern can apply also to remedies for the recovery of a stolen trademark. Well-known brands have more tools and remedies available that can be put to good use, but are not available to SMEs. For example, opposition proceedings must be filed within a short time window of three months from the preliminary approval of the stole trademark application. While MNCs and well-known brands have monitoring systems in place to warn them timely of a potential case of trademark hijack, thus giving them the option to timely oppose the hostile application, small to medium enterprises do not normally possess a trademark monitoring system. They are thus rarely informed in a timely fashion of the possibility to file an opposition. In most cases, hijacked trademarks of SMEs and large enterprises will be registered without opposition. This leaves such companies, representing the majority of the world trademarks, not only with less available remedies (i.e., opposition is mostly unavailable for time reasons), but also exposed to the risk of trademark trolls, i.e., trademark infringement lawsuits filed by the hijacker based on the stolen and now registered trademarks. Even for those that can file timely oppositions, thus preventing the risk of trademark trolls, opposition procedures used to stretch for years and the percentage of successful outcomes for the opponents has never been very high,[196] due to the difficulty of supporting with objective evidence the defenses such as "certain reputation" and "bad faith." There is therefore a disparity of treatment between MNCs and the rest of the business world when it comes to trademark protection in China. Although part of the differences are perfectly legitimate and justifiable by the fact that MNCs have better resources and lawyers, SMEs and large enterprises could benefit and reduce their business risks and exposure to trademark theft if they could access better information about China business and legal culture. So instead of blaming China and thinking how things should be, it is better for most foreigners to learn how indeed things are here in China, so that they can better manage their expectations and plan better and more effective business and IP strategies.

§3.02 TRADEMARK THEFT AND TRADEMARK TROLLS: CHALLENGES TO THE BUILD-UP OF BRANDS IN CHINA

Trademark thieves are Chinese entities or individuals who actively follow a strategy of registering IPR in China that arguably belong to their foreign competitors. Aware of the very strict First-to-File rule, they identify, apply and register trademarks belonging to others who have not yet taken steps to register them. Trademark trolls are lawsuits by which trademark thieves attempt to extort money and business advantages through judicial blackmailing. Trademark thieves can be moved by different aims and purposes. Therefore, not all trademark hijacks will result automatically in a trademark troll lawsuit. There are occasional trademark thieves who act based on opportunistic motives. They will normally try seeking a return of their investment in a very short term and will thus not contemplate civil litigation as a viable option to achieve their goals. Also, they are often unaware of certain legal risks and may in fact commit errors such as openly offering for sale the stolen trademark without having used it. As we shall see, such inconsistent and random trading behavior may be regarded by the law as a presumption of bad faith intent in the registration. Others are professional trademark squatters, also referred to as thieves or grabbers. These are people or entities engaging in systematical searches of unprotected foreign brands with the goal of applying them for registration in China. As outlined at the beginning of the book, professional squatters were born with the launch of the official trademark database in the Net and the fast spreading accessibility to internet in China, which allows professional grabbers to scout foreign companies before deciding whether to target them with a preventive trademark filing. Their goal is also economic. Unlike the

196. Mr Zang Bao Qing, http://www.aiweibang.com/yuedu/66882752.html (2013). Mr. Zang, director of legal affairs department of TRAB, reported that the total of fully or partially rejected oppositions from 2010 to 2013 amounted to 80%.

occasional infringers, professional grabbers act more systematically and are more careful when seeking to close deals on the stolen trademarks and register them with the main purpose of selling them back to the legitimate owners or any other interested party. In some cases, they may act as hired hitmen on behalf of legitimate competitors (including foreign ones) of the targeted foreign company. However, all grabbers act based on a business plan and must manage resources. If they see that there is no easy money to be made on a hijacked trademark, they will move on more profitable ones. In sum, a trademark thief will set time and priorities, will consider the right holder reactions in order to determine whether he still has a sellable item at hand or whether he should neglect it and focus on others in its portfolio. This also means that grabbers are rarely involved in economic activities using the hijacked trademarks. Different is the case in which the thief is a person or company competing in the same market of the foreign brand owner. In such case, there is indeed an obvious risk of a trademark troll lawsuit. A company hijacking a competitor's trademark has a clear intention: disadvantage the competitor in the Chinese market, thus gaining an unjust profit from the stolen right. Professional grabbers and competitors represent two clear distinctive constellations of trademark infringers that require different strategic approaches. Knowledge of the enemy is therefore critical and strictly functional to the goal setting as well as to the concrete planning of the trademark recovery actions. Investigations started since the very inception of the dispute are critical and will reveal the nature and intents of the infringer, thus helping the right holder to set up its rescue plan.

Particularly sensitive to trademark theft and trolls are the often neglected Chinese transliterations of foreign brands. Chinese consumers are indeed used to refer to foreign brands with their Chinese name. This is something a foreign company may not sufficiently be aware of. This tendency to create a Chinese version of a brand or product name is such that even in case a foreign company has not yet decided to use a Chinese name for its products, the Chinese consumers of that product will likely create one or more on their one. The name(s) will then spread to others through the internet, and one of them may quickly establish itself as the official Chinese name of that brand or product name, even without the right holder's knowledge. In such circumstances, failure to create and immediately register a Chinese name or to register the one coined and adopted by the relevant consumers, will likely result in others registering it as a trademark. Below is an example of this kind of trademark hijack.

Castel Group is one of the world leaders in wines, beers and soft drinks. An internationally recognized name, it has a wide range of brands and a presence worldwide. Castel Frères SAS entered the Chinese market first when it set up a filling center in China in 1998. In 2001, Castel started cooperation with Changyu, the largest wine maker in China, under the name "Ka Si Te – Changyu Chateau" and with a product for the Chinese market whose name was "Changyu Ka Si Te" (张裕卡斯特). Sales were going very well and the brand "Ka Si Te" gained more and more reputation amongst Chinese consumers. Bent on making profits and expand its market share, Ka Si Te – Changyu Chateau, did grossly neglect to file its trade as well as product name as a trademark with the Chinese Trademark Office. This did not go unnoticed. On

March 7, 2000, the name "Ka Si Te" in Chinese characters (卡斯特) had been registered as a Chinese trademark in class 33 by a company called Wenzhou Wujin Jiaodian Huagong Group. In 2002, it was then transferred to a certain Mr Li Dao Zhi, allegedly a Spanish-Chinese winemaker. It was only in 2005, almost 10 years after having started marketing the name "Ka Si Te" in the Chinese market, that Castel became aware of the hostile trademark "Ka Si Te" of Mr Li's. Castel had belatedly realized the need to protect its now established brand as a trademark in China. Only when its application was rejected, Castel had realized that its brand "Ka Si Te" had since long been hijacked by third parties. A battle for the recovery of the brand ensued. On July 8, 2005, Castel filed with the Trademark Office a request to cancel Mr Li's hostile trademark"Kai Si Te" for nonuse for three consecutive years.[197] This cancellation dispute lasted for six years and the final ruling came from China's SPC on December 17, 2011 rejecting the request for cancellation.

Meanwhile, in 2008, almost eight years after the original trademark registration, Mr Li established Shanghai Ka Si Te Wine Co. Ltd which imported into China French wines with the trademark "Ka Si Te." In October 2009, parallel to the cancellation action cited above, Mr Li together with Shanghai Banti Wine Company filed a trademark infringement lawsuit against Castel and Shenzhen Castel (its Chinese dealer) with the Wenzhou Intermediate People's court. In the civil complaint, Mr Li claimed compensation for CNY 40,000,000 (at that time over USD 6.3 million) by alleging that Castel and its dealers had illegally earned such an amount of profit by their unauthorized use of his trademark "Ka Si Te" from January 2007 to October 2009, including using the brand on wine products, advertisements and packaging.[198] This lawsuit is a perfect example of what we call a trademark troll.

The Wenzhou Intermediate People's court held three hearings, during which Castel argued that its use of the trademark "Ka Si Te" was in good faith as "Ka Si Te" is long known to be the official translation of the Latin name "Castel" and has served as a graphic illustration of the trademark "Castel," rather than being an indication of the origin of the wine sold in China. Castel also argued that it is their Shenzhen dealer who labels the imported wine with the trademark "Castel" together with the Chinese characters "Ka Si Te" (卡斯特) and therefore the dealer should be the only defendant in this case. The Wenzhou Intermediate People's court rejected Castel's arguments and judged that Castel had always had knowledge of the registered Chinese trademark "Ka Si Te" (卡斯特), and that the wine Castel produced in France would have been labeled with the infringing mark "Castel Ka Si Te" once arrived in China. Therefore, Castel and Shenzhen Castel were to be seen as joint infringers.

On April 10, 2012, the Wenzhou Intermediate Court issued the first instance judgment regarding the trademark infringement lawsuit between Li Dao Zhi and Castel

197. "Ka Si Te" Decision on cancellation [2010], Intellectual Administrative Decision No. 55 issued by SPC on December 17, 2011.

198. Another famous case, this time a patent troll, had been judged in 2009 and awarded a Chinese troll the equivalent of USD 50 million in damage compensation. This case was later settled by the parties for less than half that amount. *See* Harry Yang, Chint v. Schneider on Patent Infringement, http://www.chinaipmagazine.com/en/journal-show.asp?id = 258 (2008).

& Shenzhen Ka Si Te Wine. The Court judged that the conduct of the two defendants infringed upon the trademark rights of Mr Li and condemned the defendants to pay damage compensation for CNY 33,734,546.26 (more than USD 5 million). To date, this is one of the largest damage compensations for an IP infringement cases in China.

Mr Li and his company also started enforcing their registered trademark "Ka Si Te" against Castel and its distributors, wholesalers and retailers in China, by a number of collateral legal actions, like a lawsuit against Beijing Yansha Youyi Mall, Carrefour and Wal-Mart for selling fake "Ka Si Te" wines. In the litigation against Beijing Yansha Youyi Mall No. 2, the Beijing Higher People's court ordered Beijing Yansha Youyi Mall to stop selling 14 types of wines bearing the "counterfeit" Chinese trademark "Ka Si Te" (卡斯特).[199] Eventually, on April 23, 2012, Shanghai Ka Si Te sued four companies selling wine bearing with the "fake" Chinese trademark "Ka Si Te" (卡斯特) in three courts in Shanghai and had been coordinating with other relevant enforcement departments to raid and penalizes the infringers. At the end of 2015, the Appeal Court overruled the judgment of the lower court by reducing the damage compensation from CNY 136 million to something more than half million CNY.[200] Although this judgment constituted a mitigating factor for Castel, it still provides little redress for the lost brand. At the end of many years of legal battles, in which Castel suffered economic damages from lost business, damages to name and reputation, damages to its supply chain, economic hardship due to the costs of defending its rights in several legal proceedings, Mr Li is still the lawful owner of the trademark. Castel can no longer lawfully use it and cannot ripe the economic benefit of an exclusive IP right that really should have belonged to Castel, following years of investment in building up that brand in China. In sum, with the cooperation of local trademark enforcing administrations, Mr Li has been able to raid Castel wines in 50 cities in China.

In this case, it was clear since the year 2000, when Mr Li registered "Ka Si Te," that the same name had been used sufficiently by Castel to become famous in China. The word "Castel" sounds similar with the Chinese word "Ka Si Te" (卡斯特), and rarely will Chinese consumers be able to tell the difference between the two, since Chinese consumers are more pronunciation-oriented and would thus tend to deem the two trademarks as having an almost identical sound. Although Castel set up its own business in China early in 1998, and cooperated with one of the top three Chinese wine makers, Changyu (张裕), to produce wine bearing with the brand "Changyu Ka Si Te" (张裕卡斯特), it still failed to apply the Chinese name "Ka Si Te" (卡斯特) for trademark registration in class 33 immediately before or upon starting the joint

199. Li Daozhi V. Beijing Yansha Youyi Mall ([2009] Gao Min Zhong Zi No. 5383) dated February 11, 2010.

200. At the end of 2015, the Appeal Court overruled the judgment of the lower court by reducing the damage compensation from CNY 136 million to something more than CNY half million. Although Castel Frere has suffered economic damages since the year 2000, the appeal decision seems nonetheless to mitigate the economic consequences of the infringer and sends also a positive signal against squatters. For more details, *see* Cassie Lam, "Things are different in China," Alleged Trademark Squatter Claims after Court Win, World Trademark Review, http://www.worldtrademarkreview.com/Blog/detail.aspx?g=9e669097-ac3c-47de-b571-444a29144681 (2016).

marketing of the brand "Ka Si Te" and "Castel" in the Chinese market. Recognizing this mistake, Mr Li appreciated the opportunity and exploited it to his advantage. Unlike many trademark grabbers, who register trademarks of others without intention of using it, in this case it was registered with the intention of preventing a competitor's brand gaining lawful access to the Chinese market.

This case exemplifies all the things that can go wrong with trademark theft and trademark trolls. It shows also what a company should not do, namely forget to file its own trademarks for registration in China timely. The fundamental lesson any company, big or small should learn is that there is no better cure here than prevention, and that the only way to prevent such occurrences is by timely filing for trademark protection in China. More generally, considering that no foreign company big or small can ignore the central role played by China in the international economy, either as a market, world factory or both, China trademark filings should be on top of the priority list of any trademark department or agent outside China when planning its client's or company's portfolio filings. Also, it emerges clearly that the need of timely filing concerns not only the original foreign trademarks, but their Chinese transliteration as well. This requires brand owners not only to think one, but also to think it as soon as possible, so that once filed as a trademark it will be available for registration. Another important tip about the Chinese transliteration of a foreign trademark: Once selected and applied for registration as a trademark in China, the Chinese name should be used and not left alone and neglected. Why? Because if not used, the Chinese market will likely find and get used to a Chinese name anyway and in most cases it will not be the same as the one selected and protected. In such case, the registered but unused Chinese name will be a useless asset, while the one imposed by the market will acquire great economic value, but will be at the mercy of any grabber.

Even if a brand is not meant for commercialization in China, failing to secure it as a trademark in this country may have further dire consequences. The most obvious would be the lack of a strong direct weapon against counterfeiters. In fact, without a trademark in China, the right holder could not raid and shut down the infringer's factories and original sources here on the spot. Even if enforcement could still take place in Europe or the US via custom protection, precluding the possibility of a direct enforcement in China for lack of registered trademark and design rights will not help stemming counterfeits and will speed up the dilution of the trademark's economic value. In fact, EU and US customs seize but a small percentage of all fake goods arriving from China and judicial enforcement may hit at most traders and shut down websites, but will not stop the fakes from finding their way into these markets, unless the counterfeiters are shut down here in China and sent to jail and made to pay for damage compensation and lose their manufacturing assets and capabilities. We shall learn more about this in the part of this book dedicated to brand protection. Another negative consequence of losing a trademark to a hijacker, can negatively affect the official Chinese suppliers and retailers of the trademarked products. If the brand is not trademarked in China, the grabber could enforce it against the factory making the product[201] or by seizing the trademarked goods at the port of exit through the Chinese Customs.[202]

In sum, trademark theft, with or without the risk of ensuing trademark trolls, is a very bad thing for a company's business. The only preventive remedy is a careful trademark portfolio planning and timely registrations in China.

§3.03 TRADEMARK THEFT AND TRADEMARK TROLLS: CHALLENGES TO THE BUILD-UP OF BRANDS IN CHINA

If timely filing is the only way to prevent the theft of trademarks, what are the remedies in case a theft could not be prevented? From a procedural point of view, a right holder finding that his trademark has been applied without his authorization has two remedies. If the application has not been granted, he can file opposition within three months from the preliminary approval of the hostile application.[203] If the hostile trademark has been already granted, the right holder can file a request for invalidation within five years from the date if registration.[204] Only if his nonregistered trademark was famous at the time of the filing of the hostile application, then there is no limitation for filing an invalidation action.[205]

Both opposition and invalidation are based on specific grounds. Both oppositions and invalidations can be filed on grounds of bad faith of the applicant, but with clear delimitations, as we shall see below. Oppositions and invalidations can also be grounded on the fact that the stolen trademark was well known or had gained a certain

201. Simon Speeks, China Supreme Court Decision: OEM Production Does Not Infringe Trademark Rights – But This is Not the End of the Story, http://www.marks-clerk.com/Home/Knowledge-News/Articles/Clarification-around-OEM-production-in-China.aspx (2016). A recent decision of the Supreme People's Court in Focker Security International v. Zhejiang Yahuan Lockset, provided that OEM manufacturing of a product with a registered trademark of others in China does not amount to infringement of that trademark if the products are meant for export only and the trademark in question is not marketed in China by either the OEM or the original foreign principal. This jurisprudence is still controversial, in that in other recent cases, courts found that the OEM was infringing by manufacturing for export only, based on the fact that the trademark in question had a certain reputation in China. *See also* Jung Mei Chu, Trademark Infringement of Original Equipment Manufacture (OEM) For Export in China, http://www.ipo.org/wp-content/uploads/2015/03/Trademark-Infringement-of-Original-Equipment-Manufacture-OEM-For-Export-in-China.pdf (2015). The author in this article provides a review of judgments providing conflicting definitions of usage by OEM. In particular, the authors points out that: "For example, the courts of Shanghai area consider that the determination of trademark usage shall be based on the function of identification. If the usage has the function of identifying the source, such usage constitutes trademark usage. If not, such usage does not constitute trademark usage. The court of Zhejiang holds the opinion that any usage that meets the provisions of 'Using a trademark that is identical or similar with a registered trademark in connection with the same goods or similar goods without the authorization of the owner of the registered trademark' constitutes trademark infringement."

202. Article 14 of the Implementing Measures of the General Administration of Customs Concerning the Regulations of the People's Republic of China on Customs Protections for Intellectual Property Rights (中华人民共和国海关关于《中华人民共和国知识产权海关保护条例》的实施办法).

203. Article 33 Trademark Law.

204. Article 44 Trademark Law.

205. Article 45 Trademark Law.

reputation in China at the time of filing, thus constituting a prior and enforceable right.[206] Additionally, a trademark can be cancelled in case the hostile identical trademark has not been used for three consecutive years.[207]

In cases of trademark theft, and to a certain degree in the case of hostile similar trademarks[208] as we shall see, the major legal ground for opposition or cancellation is indeed that based on bad faith. However, bad faith has not been apparently provided as a "catch-all" norm that covers any kind of fraudulent intent of the registrant, but has been scantly defined as a general principle to be applied in very specific circumstances, such as for instance in case of registration of the trademark of the principal by the agent without the former's consent, or when forging documents or providing false identity information at the time of the application. This leaves courts and the trademark administrative bodies the burden to adapt the given definition of bad faith to ever emerging forms of trademark hijacking. The result of this situation has been a stream of inconsistent decisions by the Trademark authorities and civil courts. Most oppositions and invalidations grounded on a general bad faith arguments are likely to be rejected unless there is clear evidence that the right holder's unregistered trademark was well known in China at the time of the theft. In practice, this leaves few chances for an effective recovery of the hijacked trademarks of SMEs.

There is at present no legislation in China that may really prevent with efficacy the risk of trademark grabbing and trolls. The "first-to-file" system on one side and the objective difficulty of finding preventive legal tools which would tackle trademark hijacking without reducing or even hampering the access to trademarks by the whole business community, makes prevention an almost impossible task. The battle against trademark hijacking and trolls moves therefore from the field of prevention to that of recovery and deterrence. However, some of the most criticized provisions and practices based on the old trademark law, seems however to have been at least partly corrected by the new Trademark Law of May 1, 2014 and by a very recent stream of decisions that are trying to find plausible legal grounds for a broader and more open application of the general principle of bad faith as a stand-alone ground for opposition against and invalidation of hijacked trademarks. Also, and aside from the definition of an independent ground of opposition and invalidation based on bad faith by the jurisprudence, other normative changes have been introduced by the new Trademark law that could reinforce the efficacy of the available legal remedies and make them effective for all brands, and not only for the well-known ones as it has been till now

As to trademark trolls, the new Trademark Law in force since May 1, 2014, has introduced quite effective new deterrents, thus reducing the risk of such unfair

206. Article 32 Trademark Law provides specifically that: "No trademark application shall infringe upon another party's existing prior rights. Nor shall an applicant rush to register in an unfair manner a mark that is already in use by another party and enjoys substantial influence."
207. Article 49 Trademark Law and Article 66 Implementing Regulations to the Trademark law.
208. The author distinguishes between hijacked trademarks and hostile trademarks. The former are identical trademarks in the same or similar class of goods or services. The latter are similar trademarks filed in the same or similar class. In the case of hostile trademark, we do not talk of hijack but rather of free riding others' trademarks by slight visual, and wording associations: STARBECKs v. STARBUCKS, ADIDOES v. ADIDAS, and BTENETON v. BENETTON etc.

lawsuits. This has been achieved by recognizing legal effect to prior use of a trademark in China, thus breaking the monopoly of the "first to file" rule over claims of trademark ownership. The standard behind this law provides that if someone has used a mark identical or similar to a registered trademark, in respect to identical or similar goods, before the date of filing of the trademark by others, and under the condition that the prior unregistered mark has meanwhile obtained a certain degree of reputation in China due to its use, the trademark registrant has no right to prevent the prior user from further employing such mark within the original scope of its use. At most, the trademark registrant may impose to the prior user the addition of an indication of distinction to the prior mark.[209] This standard aims at deterring bad faith applicants from grabbing trademarks and using them as trolls against the original owner so as to obtain unfair advantages and illegal profit. The standard set forth by the new law should deprive the grabbers of their most powerful blackmailing tool, which is the threat of filing a trademark infringement lawsuit to force the rightful owner to settle at unjust terms. This is indeed a most welcomed improvement.

In addition to this, the new trademark law contains another troll-deterring provision. The victims of a troll lawsuit can now claim the cancellation of the grabbed trademark for nonuse as a defense. Considering that many grabbers do not really use the stolen trademarks for real business purposes, such provision may indeed have a further deterring effect on trademark hijacking and trolls. In particular, it may deter from trolls, in that the attacker will have to take into account the possibility of losing the case and the hijacked trademark at the same time due to nonuse. It is more difficult to predict whether such provision will deter hijacking. Through some basic checks on the right holder's use of the unregistered trademark in China through desk searches, a hijacker could determine to a certain extent whether the targeted trademark is worth being stolen. Hopefully, this should deter filings on unregistered foreign trademarks that show some degree of use in China. However, the goal of the hijacker may never have been that of filing a troll. He may just want to possess the trademark and benefit from the "blackmailing" effect that this possession alone may have on the legitimate owner, thus preventing the latter from using it in China to expand its business, and forcing him ultimately to give in and buy the stolen trademark out of mere exasperation. A grabber may think of selling the hijacked trademark to others unrelated to the owner as well as his principal business motive, thus making the troll prevention tool less effective as a theft prevention one. In sum, an infringer may have reasons to grab a trademark and may not be necessarily deterred by the legal tools provided in the new trademark law against trolls. The new provision will surely be of great help to the victims of trademark troll lawsuits, while it may not be much of a deterrent to trademark hijacking for purposes different from that of attacking a foreign right holder with a troll.

Generally, it appears difficult for the Chinese legislator to take at present more drastic preventive measures against trademark theft. The reason is that the First-to-File system is believed to strike a fair balance between the interests of brand owners to have

209. Article 59.3 Trademark Law.

a certain degree of certainty about trademark origin and the need to grant access to the trademark system to any possible business player. The right holder is given thus the chance to come first to register his rights and secure exclusivity. If he does not do that, he may not be able to recover them because the system will also need to protect the person and entity that have come first to file that same sign or name as a trademark. The Chinese trademark law and the Chinese government are of course aware that the system is not watertight and that First-to-File favors trademark hijacking. However, corrective measures belong only to recovering remedies and not to prevention, in order not to upset the above-mentioned balance of interests. Therefore, when a foreign company is on the losing side of the scale, the only way to tip it back is that of convincing the Chinese trademark authorities that the actions of the counterpart violated its right and are therefore not meritorious of protection. Legal remedies are therefore the only tool left to tip the balance of interest back in favor of the original right holder.

In this respect, the element of "bad faith" plays a central role. It is the intent of a filing in fact that separates those who file without knowing that the trademark belongs to someone else, and those who do actually know and have an illicit, unjust intent when applying for that trademark. In this respect, the Chinese trademark system is in line with international standards and no specific criticism could be moved to the choice of seeking balance of interests through the adoption of recovery remedies based on the bad faith intent of the applicant. The problem in China is that neither the Trademark Law nor the jurisprudence has provided a coherent and effective definition of "bad faith," which results in a high degree of uncertainty that favors intentionally fraudulent trademark applications which so much characterize the Chinese trademark system. It is this flawed definition and application of the principle of bad faith that, together with the principle of First-to-File, are the main con-causes for the systematic proliferation of trademark thefts in China to endemic levels.

Under the trademark law in force till April 30, 2014, there was no direct enunciation of the principle of good/bad faith in trademark matters. Bad faith was neither a guiding principle to filing and using trademarks, nor a legal ground of opposition and invalidation against stolen trademarks. Jurisprudence had elaborated some indirect ways to give some legal weight to bad faith, but case law was inconsistent and most decisions recognizing bad faith intent upon application were hinged on the well-known status or high reputation of the hijacked trademarks. In spite of a growing awareness among the Chinese trademark authorities and courts of the shortcoming of the trademark system at that time, decisions till 2013 continued recognizing bad faith as fraudulent filing intent only when related to well-known unregistered trademark or prior rights with a certain reputation in China.[210] The problem with this limited use of bad faith and the clear denial of a stand-alone bad faith

210. An example of such decisions is a judgment in "GAP vs Xin Heng Li", issued by Supreme People's Court; Zaishen (2012) xingtizidi 10 (再审 （2012）行提字第10号). For more examples of such decisions prior to the entry into force of the new Trademark Law, *see* King & Wood Mallesons, Five recent typical trademark cases in China http://www.mondaq.com/x/283840/Trademark/Five+recent+typical+trademark+cases+in+China (2014).

ground for opposition or invalidation left the largest majority of brands (those that are not known or have not achieved a high degree of reputation in China) without any protection against trademark squatting. Eventually, the mounting pressure on China to do something against trademark squatting, brought about a rather strong formal change, heralded by the New Trademark Law that entered into force on May 1, 2014.

Article 7 of the new Trademark Law of 2014 now expressly provides that the application for registration and use of a trademark shall be based on the principle of good faith. The change is important if we consider that before the entry into force of the new Trademark Law in 2014, there was no certainty about the existence of such a legal ground. However, it is still disputed whether upon its direct enunciation by the law, the bad faith of Article 7 is indeed a valid stand-alone cause of action in trademark oppositions and invalidations. The doubt is still unresolved because opposition and invalidation decisions seem all to refer to the bad faith of Article 7 as an ancillary enunciation, subordinated to the conditions set forth by Article 32 Trademark Law, which set forth the grounds for opposition based on an identical prior right with a certain reputation in China and those of Article 15 Trademark Law regarding unauthorized registration by an agent of the right holder.[211] The problem with such legal constructions is that they hinge the scope of application of the principle of bad faith to the presumption of knowledge of the unregistered trademark proportional to its level of reputation among the relevant Chinese consumers/users (Article 32). If a brand is indeed well known or has reputation in China or if it is well known in Europe or in the US and the grabber is a competitor in the same field of business in China, then the notoriety, united with the fact of the identity of the trademarks, create a presumption of knowledge by the applicant in China and therefore a bad faith intent. In the case of the unauthorized registration by an agent, the bad faith is hinged on the knowledge of the prior right derived by existence of a legal relation between the thief and the right holder. Although the jurisprudence before 2014 had already extended protection to indirect forms of commercial relation beyond the general case of the agency relation,[212] and the new trademark law has codified such indirect forms of agency relation, it remains a bad faith related to the existence of a certain degree of business relation between the involved parties. Trademark squatting affects trademarks that are not known due to the thieves by their intense use in China, but simply because trademark squatters systematically search them through the internet with the illegal intent of

211. *See* for instance the administrative judgment "TRAB vs Guangzhou Baitian Information Technology Co., Ltd" issued by Beijing Higher People's Court; (2015) Gaoxingzhizhongzidi 30 (二审 （2015）高行（知）终字第301号). In this case, the court found that the trademark "Aoxingla" was not only distinctive but also possessed a certain influence among the relevant public. The grabber here was qualified as a competitor in the same industry, and that given the notoriety of the trademark, should have known the name of this product. However, the court concluded that the grabber registered also series of trademarks related to the same product, and this behavior was aimed to unfair competition and attempt to obtain illegal benefits by bad faith.

212. Xianggang Leibo Youxian Gongsi v. Shangbiao Pinshen Weiyuanhui and Jiayuan Gongsi 雷博公司诉商标评审委员会、家园公司 and Lehmanbrown Limited v. Trademark Review and Adjudication Board and Jiayuan Ltd. Company, http://www.pkulaw.cn/Case/pfnl_1970324841412887.html.

hijacking them to obtain illicit economic benefits, independently from their level of reputation in China. The knowledge in the squatting phenomena is not that derived by intense use in the market but is a short term, finalistic knowledge. In this context, the bad faith enunciation of Article 7 would bring no practical relief for the plague of trademark squatting. This restrictive interpretation would render the enunciation of Article 7 virtually superfluous and practically useless. In particular, the lack of notoriety of a trademark and/or the absence of commercial relations among the right holder and the thief would be sufficient to take away the minimum degree of connection needed to support a legal presumption of bad faith. The vast majority of foreign brands that are not famous or have not achieved reputation in China (i.e., they are not used in China) and those famous in their own country but grabbed by a professional squatter in China rather than a competitor, will remain, as before, without protection.

If Article 7 of the Trademark Law currently in force is nothing but an empty enunciation without practical use, what is the point of having it at all? This is an issue that has been debated for almost two years after the entry into force of the new amendment to the Trademark Law, and has given rise to a surge of conflicting decisions and an array of proposed solutions. One thing must be kept in mind. If a law states a provision, such provision should be always interpreted as having a concrete meaning in the overall frame of the law. It would be contrary to the law itself to interpret a norm to an extent that makes the norm virtually abolish itself. So far no legal papers have really tried to make sense of the provisions of the Trademark Law in this light and the recent interpretations and trends have been confusing so that foreign brand owners in particular are currently without guidance as to how to react to squatting when their hijacked brand is not famous. Ultimately, it will be shown how a trend is emerging which appears to be indeed the most sensitive and logic: Article 7 Trademark Law is indeed an independent ground for opposition and invalidation of hijacked trademarks.

The Trademark Law expressly provides a number of cases in which trademark application/registration is considered to be done with bad faith intent. Bad faith, according to Article 15 of the Trademark Law, is presumed when there is a registration by an entity or individual that has or had business dealings or a contractual relationship with the legitimate trademark owner. Primarily, this is the case of the agent registering the trademark of the principal without the latter's consent, as in the example at the opening of this chapter. The new Trademark Law has then extended such presumption of bad faith of the applicant to all the cases in which the applicant applies for registration with respect to the same or similar goods is the same as or similar to an unregistered trademark that has been used by others, and there is contractual, business or any other relation between the applicant and others. The existence of a contractual relation or a business relation of any form may imply the existence of bad faith. In the example cited at the beginning of the Chapter, the TRAB determined that the company in Brunei was the agent of the US principal in that the Principal's former distributor was one of the shareholders of the Brunei entity. In this case, we could say that the TRAB found that there was a relation of second degree between the trademark thief (the Brunei entity) and the principal. However, relations even of more distant nature can also been deemed to be in violation of this provision of the Trademark Law as long as an uninterrupted and sequential relation between people and actions can be established according to recent interpretations of the SPC.[213] A number of judicial decisions have further provided content to Article 15 Trademark Law.[214] In this respect, the degree of notoriety of the stolen trademark will play an important role. The higher the degree of notoriety of the trademark, the more it will be possible to establish a certain connection between the thief and the applicant/principal and its business. However, in case of no business relation whatsoever, for instance in the case of a grabber, such provision cannot find useful application. If the bad faith is related only to the brand notoriety, then we are applying Article 32 of the Trademark Law and not Article 15. In sum, this provision is indeed very useful especially because it was not so broadly defined from the prior Trademark Law. However, it still does not help covering the many cases of trademark hijacking: unknown trademarks, or known trademarks taken by professional grabbers rather than competitors.

Another ground of opposition and invalidation is the already-mentioned Article 32 Trademark Law: someone rushes to register a trademark which is already used by another party by improper means and has certain influence/reputation.[215] In this

213. Article 12 of Opinions of the Supreme People's Court Concerning Trial of Administrative Cases in Respect of Trademark Right Granting and Confirmation, extends the application of the provisions of Article 15 to the case of contractual distribution. In particular it stipulates that: "If the trademark of the principal or of the one represented, without authorization, is registered in the name of trademark agents, representatives or other agents and representatives based on sales and agency relationship such as distribution and agency, the people's court shall deem it to be the preemptive registration of trademark of the principal or of the one represented by the agents or representatives. In judicial practice, if the preemptive registration occurs during the negotiation stage of the agency or representative relation, that is, the preemptive registration is before the agency or representative relation, the preemptive registration shall be deemed as the action of the attorney or representative. The trademark registrant that colludes or conspires with the abovementioned attorney or representative on the preemptive registration may be deemed as an attorney or a representative. The collusive or conspired registration shall be presumed based on the special relation between trademark registrant and the abovementioned attorney or representative." Furthermore, Article 11 of Provisions of the Supreme People's Court on Several Issues concerning the Trial of Administrative Cases Involving the Granting and Determination of Trademark Rights (Draft for Comments) further extend the concept of distribution by stipulating that: "Where a trademark registrant has a specific identity relation or other specific connection with the agent or representative as provided in Paragraph 1 of Article 15 of the Trademark Law and it can be presumed that the trademark registration is the act of the registrant by colluding and conspiring with such agent or representative, the people's court shall apply the provisions in Paragraph 1 of Article 15 of the Trademark Law for trial. (The second opinion: where a trademark registrant has a specific identity relation or other specific connection with the agent or representative as provided in Paragraph 1 of Article 15 of the Trademark Law and it can be presumed that the registrant knows the existence of the person so represented or the trademark thereof, the people's court shall apply the provisions in Paragraph 2 of Article 15 of the Trademark Law for trial)."

214. In Xindongyang Enterprise (Group) Co., Ltd. v. Xindongyang Stock Co., Ltd. & TRAB (SPC [2013] Zhi Xing Zi No. 97), the Supreme People's Court stated that Article 12 of Opinions of the Supreme People's Court Concerning Trial of Administrative Cases in Respect of Trademark Right Granting and Confirmation is applicable in this case. In particular, it found that the legal representative of Xindongyang Entreprise Mai Shi used to be the deputy CEO of Xindongyang Stock from 1978 to 1993 and is now one of the directors of Xindongyang Stock. Thus, Xindongyang Enterprise fulfilled the "agency" condition of Article 15.1 of the Trademark Law.

215. *Supra* n. 207.

context, improper means refers to unfair or illegal means adopted by the applicant, including but not limited to taking advantage of the peer relationship with another party, of the cooperation experience with another party, of the knowledge of inside information, etc. Through these improper means, the applicant in his own name applies for the registration of a trademark which is used by another party but has not been registered. Again as stated several times before, this provision benefits only those trademarks that have acquired a certain degree of reputation in China, or at most are well known in the EU or the US and have been registered by a Chinese competitor in the same business. It therefore leaves out all the trademarks that do not have such reputation in China or even if they are well known abroad, have not been taken by a competitor but by any other person or entity unrelated to the business for which these trademarks have been used. In practice, more and more administrative decisions seem to soften and lower the evidence threshold of recognition of a certain reputation, so as to widen the protection umbrella of Article 32 Trademark Law against squatters. This is indeed a positive development, but it has a clear legal limit. The concept of reputation and the evidence to prove it cannot be emptied to a point of defying the literal meaning of the law. For this reason, and in spite of a more generous application of this norm, it will not alone be enough to solve the squatting problem.

Another embodiment of the bad faith principle is that of Article 19 Trademark Law regarding the registration by trademark agents. It is evident here the presumption of knowledge of the agent and therefore his bad faith. This constellation had already been tackled by the jurisprudence shortly before the entry into force of the new amendment of the Trademark Law in 2014. In the matter of Hangzhou Jun Bo IP Agency (Jun Bo) v. Hangzhou Cui Qin Zhai Halal Food Co., Ltd. (Cui Qin Zhai) it was disputed about the hijacking of the Trademark "Cui Qin Zhai."[216] Cui Qin Zhai filed a cancellation against the trademark "Cui Qin Zhai" registered by Jun Bo. In the final instance of the cancellation procedure, the Beijing Higher Court ruled that, as a professional IP agency, Jun Bo violated the principle of good faith and Article 4 of China Trademark Law (it will be Article 7 of the new Trademark Law), by filing the same trademark as that of a third party that has been using it and had thus gained a certain reputation on similar goods. In particular, the court pointed out that, according to the evidence, after the trademark registration, Jun Bo had not used the same, while trying to gain profit by selling it. The court pointed out that such an act of selling or attempting to sell, was proof that the trademark registration had been applied for in bad faith. What appears of interest in this decision, it is not the fact that the grabber was liable in light of its position as a trademark agent in the position of knowing the injured trademark. This stems from the express provision of the law. More interesting is the fact that the court felt compelled to add that such behavior violates a general principle of good faith in trademark dealings, and gets down listing a number of facts and behaviors that are evidence to bad faith intent of a squatter: nonuse of the hijacked

216. Hangzhou Junbo Zhishi Chanquan Daili Youxian Gongsi Su Hangzhou Cuixinzai Qinzhen Shipin Youxian Gongsi (杭州均博知识产权代理有限公司诉杭州翠沁斋清真食品有限公司)[of Hangzhou Jun Bo IP Agency v. Hangzhou Cui Qin Zhai Halal Food Co., Ltd] February 20, 2014 (Beijing Higher People's Ct. Gao Xing Zhong Zi No. 130).

trademark, but for attempting to sell it to the best bidder. Interestingly, these are elements that will be present in more recent decisions as "symptoms" and test of trademark squatting and bad faith intent. They will be important, as we shall see to give substance to the general enunciation of Article 7. On the other hand, this instance of bad faith only covers a very specific case constellation and cannot benefit the majority of cases of trademark hijack.

Eventually, an instance of bad faith expressly regulated by the trademark law is that of a trademark registered by use of fraudulent means, as provided by Article 44.1 Trademark Law. This norm refers expressly to the use of fraud in the production of information and documents at the time of filing and maintaining trademark applications. The norm clearly provides that a trademark registered through fraudulent means is invalid and can be nullified by any interested person or entity within five years from the date of registration. Although it may be true that in many cases fraudulent means derive from a fraudulent intent, trademark squatting is generally conducted with fraudulent intent but not necessarily by fraudulent means. Some authors and a few recent TRAB decisions have nonetheless attempted using this provision against trademark squatting. In particular, it has been suggested that this provision can be used to give practical application to the bad faith of Article 7, so that there would be no need for the applicant in an invalidation proceedings to prove neither the reputation of the stolen brand, nor the thief's knowledge of the brand, in that they operated in the same business. More specifically, there have been three decisions from TRAB based on Article 44.1[217] (in one case it was more specifically Article 41.1 of the older trademark law[218]), in 2015 concerning foreign unregistered trademarks neither used nor well known in China, and where the grabbers were professional squatters and not competitors filing for preventive purposes. In all these three cases, it was found that the Chinese applicants had violated Article 44 in that their registration constituted registration by "fraudulent means." TRAB argued that the illicit means were fulfilled in that the identity of the applied trademarks with the names in question, are either the name of foreign people or fantasy words with high originality. TRAB deemed in all three cases that identity of the applications with these names and words was not coincidental, but a symptom of bad faith intent. Also, the fact that the squatters had not used the trademarks in business transactions and had also applied many other trademarks which were identical to other brand names from the west, some of them with a certain reputation, made TRAB presume bad faith intent. If this interpretation of Article 44.1 were indeed legally founded, we could have eventually found the norm that allows bad faith to be used as a general clause to attack any kind of trademark hijacking. However, this does not appear to be the case. The reasons why TRAB decided to define the "symptoms" of bad faith as "fraudulent means" under Article 44.1 escapes the author's comprehension, and probably that of any sound jurist. Once identified the symptoms

217. The invalidations decisions concern the registered trademarks Carla Fracci and Naj Oleari in class 3 were handed down by TRAB based on Article 44.1 (old Article 41.1). For more information about these cases, *see* Xiaonan Zhang, Combating Pre-emption in China, No. 55, World Trademark Review, 59-60 (June/July 2015).

218. TRAB v. Guangzhou Baitian Information Technology Co., Ltd; issued by Beijing Higher People's Court; (2015) Gaoxingzhizhongzidi30 (二审 （2015）高行（知）终字第301号).

of a bad faith intent, the next logic step would have seemed that of finding a violation of Article 7 Trademark Law. Why TRAB refrained from that conclusion? It is possible that the cultural mindset of trademark officers in China and the jurisprudential rigidity of the Chinese legal system, conjured that TRAB needed to find a house to those symptoms of bad faith other than Article 7. Clear is that TRAB's decision to choose a legal cover in Article 44.1 is legally wrong for many reasons and even defies logic and creates legal disparities between opposition and invalidation not foreseen by the Trademark Law. Eventually, further supporting such type of reasoning would just distract from supporting Article 7 as an independent cause of action against squatters, as the only logical and useful interpretation of the Trademark Law that could reduce if not end trademark squatting as it is known today. The first and gravest flaw of such an approach is that Article 44.1 literal interpretation suffices to make it clear that this provision refers to "illicit means" and not illicit intent. In sum, the bad faith does not concern here the act of theft, but the act of hiding the applicant's real identity. In this respect, most correct has been the interpretation given to Article 44.1 (although referred to the same norm in the previous version of the Trademark Law) by the Beijing Higher Court in the Michael Jordan case: "acquired by fraud or any other improper means refers to the improper means instead of improper purpose."[219] Therefore, the interpretation by TRAB lacks of legal ground and is incompatible with the literal interpretation of the law. This reason alone is sufficient to discredit this line of recent decisions. However, there are additional reasons for not further supporting this TRAB jurisprudence. Ground for opposition based on application/registration of others prior rights, such as in the cited cases, can be requested only by the prior right holder or its exclusive license (i.e., interested person). So it is provided by Article 33 Trademark Law. This is because, this ground of opposition is provided solely to protect the rights of a private individuals and entities (like the case of prior rights of Article 32 Trademark Law). Article 33 provides that anybody and any entity can file opposition against trademarks that violate public interests, such as the case of trademarks violating Articles 10, 11 and 12 Trademark Law. Therefore, an opposition for a bad faith registration of a prior right would be filed by the prior right holder only. Now, in the cited cases, TRAB was reviewing two invalidation decisions. It is important here now to keep in mind the distinction we have just made about the types of oppositions and how the law determines who is entitled to file which one. This is because the same distinction applies to invalidations of registered trademarks. In fact Article 44.1 deals with invalidation of registered trademarks. However, Article 44 specifically concerns

219. The Michael Jordan case is made by a number of judgments. Here we cites the second instance judgments of the Beijing Higher Court: 二审 （2015）高行（知）终字第1037号, (2015) Gaoxingzhizhongzidi 1037; 二审 （2015）高行（知）终字第1051号(2015) Gaoxingzhizhongzidi 1051; （2015）高行（知）终字第1052号, (2015) Gaoxingzhizhongzidi 1052; （2015）高行（知）终字第1576号, (2015) Gaoxingzhizhongzidi 1576; 二审 （2015）高行（知）终字第1572号, (2015) Gaoxingzhizhongzidi 1572; （2015）高行（知）终字第1064号, (2015) Gaoxingzhizhongzidi 1064; （2015）高行（知）终字第1577号, (2015) Gaoxingzhizhongzidi 1577; 二审 （2015）高行（知）终字第1575号, (2015) Gaoxingzhizhongzidi 1575; （2015）高行（知）终字第965号, (2015) Gaoxingzhizhongzidi 965; （2015）高行（知）终字第975号, (2015) Gaoxingzhizhongzidi 975; （2015）高行（知）终字第972号, (2015) Gaoxingzhizhongzidi 972.

invalidations of those trademarks that violate public interests; in particular those violating Articles 10, 11 and 12 Trademark Law. In order to invalidate a registered trademark for violation of another's prior right, such as in the case of trademark hijacking, the provision to be used is that of Article 45 of the Trademark Law! That provision, mirroring the one regarding oppositions, gives the right to act only to the holder of the prior right and his licensee to file invalidation. It is evident that TRAB, in front of invalidation based on the theft of a prior right should have applied Article 45, and not Article 44.1. By doing this, TRAB has interpreted and applied the law incorrectly.

Further misinterpretation and wrong application of the law would also create a different treatment between oppositions and invalidations, whereby as just see, such procedures are regulated by norms mirroring each other. Opponents will not be able to claim bad faith because Article 44.1 is available only for invalidations. Such outcome is neither legally founded nor desirable.

More important, such jurisprudence would distract us all away from what it is really important: founding a concrete and independent use of the bad faith principle in Article 7 of the Trademark Law. The TRAB cases, to a certain extent are very useful because they confirm that there is now a consistent agreement among officials, judges and practitioners about the existence of a number of concrete facts that can be presumed as symptoms of a bad faith intent when applying a trademark: identity of the trademarks when the stolen one shows a certain degree of originality (pay attention: originality, not fame); the grabber is in the same business field of the foreign right holder; the grabber has applied many other trademarks of other companies; the grabber has no business at all with the goods using the stolen trademark; the grabber's main efforts are in trying to sell the trademark. All the decisions under examination show that the presence of at least two of these symptoms can be sufficient to ground bad faith intent.[220] This is a very important achievement. The existence of an agreement on the "symptoms" opens the way to the following step: to use these symptoms to give body and content to the general enunciation of Article 7 Trademark Law and make it an independent cause of action against trademark grabbing.

In a recent case of opposition concerning a European trademark covering goods in class 20, the Trademark Office concluded that the principle of good faith of Article 7 Trademark Law applies to the whole process of trademark application, registration and use. Authors commented that this fully reflects the efforts of the Trademark Office in trying to avoid trademark confusion from the initial stage of trademarks registration and highlights the Trademark Office's aim and principle of shielding consumers from confusion.[221] This is to the author's knowledge the first and only pointing to the right direction so far. It is nonetheless a pointer and should be followed by more similar

220. Lin Dong Liang v. Juqing Guangdong Machinery Co., Ltd; Supreme People's Court, Zaishen (2015) Mintizidi 49 (再审 （2015）民提字第49号. In this recent judgment, the Supreme People's Court recognized that a trademark must be used in good faith and that registering a trademark and then licensing it is evidence of bad faith.

221. The case is reported in Lanny Li, Overview of the changes in the practice of trademark examination by CMTO, Lexology, http://www.lexology.com/library/detail.aspx?g=397e9c5c-553d-45ec-9ca3-edf6bdba44aa (July 30, 2015).

decisions. More important appears a decision of the SPC in 2014. In this decision, the court hints at bad faith in itself as a cause of action. However, the case specifically refers to bad faith as a ground to reject a lawsuit based on a stolen trademark, thus deny protection to such a type of trademark. Although it is not automatically extendable to a case of opposition or invalidation, it seems already a major opening towards a more direct recognition of Article 7 as a stand-alone cause of action.[222]

Although there is no other jurisprudence at present supporting Article 7 as a stand-alone cause of action in oppositions and invalidations of stolen trademarks, it is the right way to go in the future. It is the duty of the practitioners to believe in this line of argumentation and to present it to the trademark administrative offices and to judges in opposition and invalidation procedures and to be persuasive about it. Changes are to be expected in the near future and the achievement of this one, will most than many others benefit trademark holders against squatters. Emancipation of Article 7 is now mature, and it is recommended that foreign right holders will not refrain from such new creative approach and use it with conviction so as to create more favorable case law that will automatically lead to the establishment of a new practice and rule that will benefit all, but the squatters.

§3.04 THE FREE RIDE OF TRADEMARKS AND PROCEDURAL STRATEGIES FOR THE RECOVERY OF STOLEN BRANDS

One of the negative consequences of trademark filing proliferation in a first-to-file legal system of an emerging economy is an increase of conflicts among similar trademarks, conflicts which become an acute problem, if we consider not only the phenomena of trademark grabbing, but also the even more common form of free riding, i.e., the filing of hostile similar trademarks in the same or similar classes. In this context, the expression "hostile trademarks" or "hostile applications" will therefore refer to trademark filings containing wording, pictorial elements or both, that look similar but not identical to an already-registered trademark or to an unregistered trademark. Trademarks that evoke and attempt to exploit the reputation of an already-registered foreign brand are continuously filed by unknown Chinese parties. What is more disturbing here is that such filings are often successful, forcing foreign right holders to invest money in attempting the removal of such hostile applications and registrations, thus preventing or reducing the risk of consumer's confusion and by relation, brand dilution.

The reasons for the high numbers of granted hostile trademarks and hijacked trademarks may depend on several concurring factors. One factor is the very structured and rigid system of classes and subclasses of the Chinese Classification of Goods and Services, which allows the co-existence of similar trademarks in the same class as long

222. Basic Rules from Supreme Court's Selected Cases in 2015, http://www.lexology.com/library/detail.aspx?g = 86e1996e-92f6-4dcf-89e5-0048babf2029&utm_source = Lexology + Daily + Newsfeed&utm_medium = HTML + email + - + Body + - + General + section&utm_campaign = Lexology + subscriber + daily + feed&utm_content = Lexology + Daily + Newsfeed + 2016-07-05&utm_term = (July 2016).

as they are registered in different subclasses. Another factor may be the scarce knowledge of foreign languages, e.g., English, among the Chinese examiners, which can lead to inconsistent decisions as to trademark similarity. Another negative cause may be the not always efficient way in which work is distributed among examiners, which may hamper consistency. Manpower shortages at the Trademark Office in front of steadily growing filings leaves examiners with little time for each file with a fallout on quality decision making. Ultimately, and specifically for the case of trademark theft, foreign brands which are not well known, will not ring any bell to the examiner which will surely not conduct any trademark search to determine their use.

In front of acts of trademark hijack or hostile filings, the affected foreign companies and individuals face the critical decision of what remedies to use in order for them to eliminate the threat or repossess the lost trademarks. Often, such decisions are to be taken in a short time and a wrong choice may cost years of legal entanglements and monetary exposure. Trademark opposition has always been the first and foremost response to such aggressions, as long as the right holder was timely informed before the expiration of the three-month opposition deadline, though, whether opposition is the most effective solution for every case is questionable. Changes to the opposition system may now compel foreign brand owners to revisit their opposition strategies and consider alternative avenues and solutions.

§3.05 INVALIDATION OF A TRADEMARK LACKING REGISTRATION REQUIREMENTS (ARTICLE 44 TRADEMARK LAW)

This form of invalidation aims at avoiding registration of trademarks which are not embodying the substantive requirements for trademark protection. This includes trademarks which are identical or similar to state names, national flags or emblems, governmental symbols, anthems, military songs of China and of other countries or international organizations, names of regions or cities worldwide, those deceptive trademarks which are likely to mislead the public to misidentify the quality or other characteristics or place of origin of the goods. This type of invalidation can also be used against trademarks which are descriptive of the goods or service itself or describe the characteristics or raw materials, function, use and other features of the goods in respect of which the trademark is used. More generally, this type of invalidation can be used against trademarks which are not distinctive. Aside from these groups of registrations, the present procedure can also be used against trademarks registered by fraud or any other unfair means. Although this wording may give the impression that unfair means could include the case of registration of nonfamous or reputed stolen trademarks in bad faith, it is however not the case. As amply clarified in the preceding paragraphs, the letter of the law refers to means and not to the motives and intent. Therefore, the norm is only applicable to cases in which the application conceals or forges information or data about the applicant's identity or business. For instance, if a company is set up only for the purpose of holding a squatted trademark, this could not be a case of registration that can be invalidated under this norm. It appears therefore difficult to understand why the TRAB has used such provision against cases that are clearly re-conducible to bad faith intent in the sense of Article 7 of the Trademark Law. The reasons for criticizing such decisions have been discussed already and will not be repeated here.

In practice, such form of invalidation, whose procedure presents slight differences with that based on registration of prior right of others or preventive registration in Article 45 Trademark Law, is not applicable to the bad faith registration under Article 7 or any other ground of bad faith registration of prior rights (i.e., Articles 15 and 32 in particular). In spite of recent attempts to extend its use beyond its clear legal meaning, this norm should be irrelevant to our trademark theft cases. It may be relevant only in that the use of illicit means to obtain the registration can be proved, such as the case in which a registrant uses a fake identity or make false declarations about its business activities when applying for a trademark. In some cases, it is possible that illicit means and intents are mixed together, such as when the registrant provides false information about its identity to conceal his intent of stealing another person's trademark, or uses a conniving third party to register and hold the trademark on its behalf. However, in many cases the bad faith intent is not coupled with the use of fraudulent means at the time of application or while maintaining the registration. In most cases, a grabber will not conceal his real name. In such cases, Article 44.1 cannot be of use to the rightful trademark holder.

§3.06 TRADEMARK INVALIDATION ON GROUNDS OF EXISTING PRIOR RIGHTS (ARTICLE 45 TRADEMARK LAW)

As clarified in the prior paragraphs, the law provides prior rights holders with tools to recover the lost trademark or to avoid the registration of a hostile application. In the first case, the action is brought against an already-registered trademark and is called "invalidation." The outcome of such procedure will be the deletion of the hostile registered trademark and a prohibition for the registrant as well as any other party to file it again for one year.[223] This invalidation procedure can be initiated to invalidate registered trademarks which are identical or similar to prior trademarks in the same or similar class,[224] to prior well-known unregistered trademarks,[225] to unregistered trademarks with a certain reputation or any prior rights (i.e., a prior copyright or a design with a similar content as the trademark; trade names etc.),[226] to trademarks registered in bad faith by the agent of the right holder[227] and eventually to the geographical sign of the designated goods which do not originate from the place where the geographical sign indicates and is likely to mislead the public.[228]

Invalidation on these grounds can be filed by any interested party. Interested party is the legitimate owner of the trademark and the licensee of the same right.[229] This means that not every person can file invalidation unless it shows to have direct

223. *Supra* n. 105.
224. Article 30 Trademark Law.
225. Article 13 Trademark Law.
226. Article 32 Trademark Law.
227. Article 15 Trademark Law.
228. Article 16 Trademark Law.
229. *Supra* n. 187.

economic interest in and receives an economic damage from the registered identical/similar trademark. Invalidation must be filed with the Trademark Review and Adjudication Board within five years from the registration date of the said trademark. In the case of a well-known trademark, the applicant shall not be subjected to the five-year time limit. The TRAB shall make a decision either to maintain or to declare such registered trademark invalid.

During the examination procedure of the declaration of invalidity, where the affirmation of the prior right involved is subject to the result of another ongoing trial of the people's court or another ongoing case handled by the administrative agencies, the TRAB may suspend the examination procedure. However, the TRAB shall restore the examination procedure once the cause for suspension no longer exists. This last provision is very important in that it allows a suspension of the procedure to wait for a decision on the affirmed right, and it is an important defensive weapon for the party under threat of invalidation.

In case of invalidation, a public announcement shall be made by the Trademark Office, and the exclusive right to use such registered trademark shall be deemed as nonexistent from the very beginning. The invalidation decision will have no retroactive effects on any judgment, adjudication or mediation agreement entered and enforced before the said declaration of invalidity. However, if the ascertained bad faith of the trademark registrant has caused damages to any other party, the registrant is liable to pay compensation. The damaged party will have to file a civil lawsuit to obtain such compensation. Also, a refund of trademark assignment fees or of the trademark royalties should be made if the conduct of the registrant violated the principle of fairness.

This type of invalidation focuses on prior rights, both registered and unregistered. The main argument used to support the request for invalidation in these cases is the existence of a prior trademark or other IP right (i.e., trade name, copyright, a design etc.). In particular, this is the form of invalidation that is commonly used to protect unregistered well-known or well-reputed trademarks, but often the only one available to SMEs against the hijack of trademarks that are neither famous nor reputed in China. As explained above, this provision is the most founded one from a legal point of view to invalidate a trademark in case of bad faith registration. However, due to the fact that the norm does not expressly list Article 7 as a stand-alone ground for invalidation, both TRAB and courts have been reluctant to invalidate squatted trademarks outside the cases of bad faith provided for by Article 15 (registration by agent without consent) and Article 32 (prior well-known or reputable right). Again, this has left the vast majority of stolen foreign trademarks without concrete protection against hijacks.

At the same time, such situation of practical injustice has not passed unobserved to the Chinese trademark authorities. Bad faith as a stand-alone cause of invalidation (and opposition) may soon start to take hold against concrete-strong formal tenants about Article 7 and Article 45 of the Trademark Law. In practice, recent cases have shown that the enforcing bodies are trying indeed to find some correctors to the strictly formal interpretation of Article 45, so as to let the general principle of good/bad faith set forth in Article 7 to become itself a ground of invalidation and thus extending the benefit of invalidation ground to all hijacked trademarks, including those not so famous or not famous at all. The most common corrector has been that of loosening the requirements for the application of Article 32, i.e., reducing the threshold for establishing "certain reputation." More and more invalidation decisions seem to recognize "certain reputation" as long as the prior right holder can prove that he has used its trademark in China aside from mere symbolic use.[230] By lowering the threshold for the determination of "certain reputation," many more foreign stolen trademarks can and will find protection. This seems also a better solution than TRABS attempts to apply against trademark squatters the provisions of Article 44.1 which are clearly limited to absolute grounds of nonregistrability of a trademark as explained above.

The above legal considerations are very important to understand the strategic value of such form of invalidation. In fact, as already stated, the combination of Articles 32 and 45 Trademark Law is the most common form of invalidation filed against trademark squatters. However, limiting the employment of such legal tool to such tactical function would be limiting the potentials of such provision. Aside from the more typical employment of the invalidation under Article 45 Trademark Law in combination with a stolen prior right under Article 32 Trademark law, this invalidation tool presents other forms of employment with an important strategic value. For instance, this ground of invalidation includes the case of the registration of the trademark of a principal by his agent without the former's consent (Article 15 Trademark Law). This form of invalidation is very useful in that the letter of the new Trademark law does not limit its application to the existence of a strictly legal agency relationship. If the prior right holder can prove that there was a certain connection between him and the usurper of the trademark, even in the absence of a direct agency relationship, such norm is applicable. Under the old trademark law and not until recently, the law and the jurisprudence interpreted the concept of agency in a very legalistic sense.[231] The prior right holder should have proved a strict legal connection such as a direct sales contract or a distribution agreement with the trademark usurper.

---

230. Fu Yanan Su Shangbiao Pingshen Weiyuanhui (付亚楠诉商标评审委员会) [Fu Yanan v. The Trademark Review and Adjudication Board] March 25, 2011 (Beijing Higher People's Ct. Gao Xing Zhong Zi No. 264). Most important is the Supreme People's Court Decision in 成超诉商标评审委员会（2015）知行字第181号, in which the Court stated that in determining whether a trademark has been in use, the court should consider whether the registrant has the real intention of use and use acts. Symbolistic use just for maintaining the registration such as use in an advertising agreement or in a license agreement without actual implementation does not amount to actual use of the mark. For a summary of this decision, *see* http://www.lexology.com/library/detail.aspx?g = 86e1996e-92f6-4dcf-89e5-0048babf2029&utm_source = lexology + daily + newsfeed&utm_medium = html + email + - + body + - + general + section&utm_campaign = lexology + subscriber + daily + feed&utm_content = lexology + daily + newsfeed + 2016-07-0h (July 2016).

231. Paul Jones, China: Bad Faith Registrations by Distributors, IBA Legal Practice Division, International Franchising Committee Newsletter, http://www.jonesco-law.ca/89/files/pdfs/PIP - China bad faith TM registration by distributors.pdf (June 2008). *See also* the case Chongqing Zhengtang Pharmaceutical Ltd. v. Trademark Review and Adjudication Board and, Sichuan Animal Pharmaceutical Ltd (Supreme People's Court, File No. 2, August 31, 2007 available online in Chinese). In this case, the parties had been connected by a sales agreement of the trademarked products. The Beijing Higher Court had excluded the applicability of Article 15 Trademark Law because there had been no strict principal-agent relationship between the parties, but a mere commercial or contractual relation.

The new trademark law provides that an agency relation can be established also when there is no direct contractual or business relation between the registrant and the prior right holder. The law does not actually provide a limit to the degree of the relationship either. This means that the focus is moved from a strict legal concept, the agency, to the evidence of a whatsoever business connection. To succeed in such action, the evidence will have to prove the existence of a business relation in a univocal manner and form a logic and uninterrupted chain that can connect the principal to the usurper. As stated in a preceding chapter, there may be even a certain distance between the prior right holder and the thief. As long as evidence is provided that the latter had a business contact with the former at a certain point, and this evidence is solid and clear, bad faith under this provision can be established. On the other hand, bad evidence or partial evidence that leaves space to speculation as to the links between the interested parties will not be sufficient to support a bad faith under this provision even if the parties are very close. For instance, in a case the author had handled as second counsel, the registrant of a prior trademark of his client was a subcontractor of the client's supplier, The evidence the client and his original counsel had provided was a contract between the principal and the supplier, and a bunch of e-mails in which the subcontractor was copied in relation to the manufacturing of a batch of the products of the principal. The invalidation was rejected. According to the TRAB, this evidence could not prove that the registrant had any business with the principal. E-mails exchanges, unless written before a notary, will unlikely be admitted as authentic evidence. There are too many uncertainties about their origin, and manipulations are abstractly possible. Also, even admitting their authenticity, they could not prove that that employment of the subcontractor was acting in a legally binding way on behalf of his company and also that the correspondence is linked to the use of the trademark or to a concrete transaction involving the trademarked products. In sum, such type of evidence is an example of how it should not be done. The author, who intervened as a second counsel, applied to the case the Rules of Engagement and consequently investigated facts and discovered that the legal representatives of both supplier and subcontractor was the same person. This was a more objective evidence of an agency relation between the supplier and the subcontractor and indirectly provided a wholesome evidence of a relation between the principal and the third party contracted by the supplier. As shown in the examples, this type of invalidation ground should always be investigated and considered as one of the most effective tools for obtaining the elimination of a hostile trademark. It can be here concluded that the invalidation under the ground provided for by the new Article 15 Trademark Law appears to partly overlap with that of Article 32. It is undeniable that the degree of notoriety of the stolen trademark will also contribute to the determination of an agency relation, especially when such relation stretches to more indirect form of business connections. Using both grounds in the same invalidation is therefore a possibility and in many cases will enhance the strategic value of this form of invalidation. A lawyer handling such case, should therefore be open minded and follow first of all the Rules of Engagement in order to collect a clear knowledge of all the relevant factors and facts so as to make the appropriate decision as to the employment of the available form of invalidation of an hostile squatted trademark.

This last remark brings us to a last group of remarks about this form of invalidation and its strategic employment. It is often stated by practitioners that invalidations have less chances to succeed than oppositions. Statistics however are lacking and cannot support such statement. This statement is based mostly on a typical Chinese perception: it is more difficult for TRAB to overrule the decision of the Trademark Office than for the latter to reject a trademark application, because both offices belong to the same administration. This skepticism about the efficacy of invalidations under Article 45 in China is based on the "cultural and political" perception of the relation among administrative bodies by which government bodies support each other's decision under a nonwritten code of conduct and honor/respect, which implies also the administrative mistrust on the good faith of any "private" complainant's arguments. There surely is some truth in this perception, and such a cultural and political factor must be taken into consideration when deciding on a trademark recovery strategy in China. However, it would be erroneous to make strategic decisions only based on such external assumptions. In the last years, TRAB has shown in many decisions a growing and very high degree of independence from this presumed comradeship with the Trademark Office, and overruling of the latter's decisions is simply a common knowledge among practitioners. It really all comes down to the specific case's facts and history, as well as to the strength and the completeness of the selected facts and the supporting evidence.

Invalidations are actually the only options to recover a stolen trademark when a deadline for opposition has expired. Therefore, knowledge of the available grounds and forms of invalidation is critical to selecting the right one. Again, this is not a mere legal choice, but the result of a more strategic thinking process. Following safe rules of engagement will provide a clearer view of the possible tactical tools and their employment, their advantages and disadvantages and will allow the construction of more articulated strategies which will allow alternative courses should one become precluded or fail. It is very common in China to see foreign brand owners decide about the filing of invalidation only based on the legal evaluation of similarity and the state of reputation upon Article 32 Trademark Law. Article 32 is the one supporting invalidation when a prior unregistered right is famous or has gained a certain reputation. Often all energies and efforts are concentrated on this point, and most efforts will be on the right holder to determine, select and provide the supporting evidence to the normally very passive external counsel. It seems strange, but it is rare to see a lawyer proposing to the client a thorough investigation of the facts before making such a strategic decision. The Rules of Engagement we have presented in this book will help the right holder and their counsel to gain the needed awareness of the strategic importance of all the collated facts and the tactical value of each available invalidation tool and cause of action. For example, as exemplified above, Article 15 Trademark Law offers indeed a very good ground for claiming bad faith in substitution or in addition to the ground of invalidation provided by Article 32. However, it is rarely seen that efforts are made by the right holders and their counsel to take time and invest resources in building such an argument. Normally, if a prima facie check reveals no direct connection with the trademark thief, such ground is immediately abandoned, without considering that the law provides in fact much more playroom, if only facts were scrutinized and investigated more thoroughly. If it is considered that the notoriety of a trademark is also very critical in the determination of the "enlarged" definition of agency, the link between grounds under Articles 32 and 15 of the Trademark Law should be sought and built together. The supporting facts and evidence for one cause of action would thus support those for the other one, and it would make for a much stronger and refined argument before the trademark authority. One last remark can also help explain why in many cases foreign companies are not guided through the strategic standards set forth by the Rules of Engagement, but are rather driven by a legal service market conditioned by low prices and low quality. In the last years in China, legal service providers have been increasing in numbers and have forced each other into lowering prices to keep their market shares. If this is a good thing for foreign right holders, it becomes quickly a bad one if quality is sacrificed to price. An inexpensive invalidation, in spite of its factual and legal complexity, may reveal in fact an unsuccessful one. The attorney will not engage in it with the same motivation and will not dedicate to it the same efforts as if it were paid for the real time spent on it. The result is a lot of standardized, assembly-line style pleadings and defenses, which have somewhat driven the quality of the decision making of the trademark bodies in a downward spiral. Only high-quality work can be reflected in high-quality decisions. We cannot expect the Trademark office or TRAB to be excellent in their job if the parties are not excellent either!

A last remark on strategic importance of this form of invalidation and its effective tactical use: invalidations under Article 45 Trademark Law are a very important ancillary tool to support the chances of success of reexamination proceedings against rejection decisions by the Trademark Office. If a right holder receives a rejection decision for his trademark application, he should not only focus on whether he has argument to dispute on identity/similarity with the cited trademarks, but also should initiate a fact-finding action to determine if there are accompanying grounds for invalidating or cancelling one or more of the cited marks. If such grounds can be found, then invalidation proceedings should be initiated. TRAB practice allows the applicant for a revision to request the suspension of the reexamination procedure pending invalidations or nonuse cancellations.[232] The removal of a cited mark is a more effective way to obtain a trademark registration than arguing on lack of similarity with the prior, often purposefully stolen cited trademark.

§3.07 CANCELLATION FOR NONUSE

If Article 7 of the Trademark law has to be interpreted restrictively, i.e., it cannot constitute on its own a legal base for invalidation, then the owners of stolen trademarks other than those protectable under the invalidation grounds listed by Article 45

232. Article 31 of Trademark Review and Adjudication Rules (Revised in 2014): "Where the hearing results of cases of priority rights are needed in accordance with Paragraph 4 of Article 35 and Paragraph 3 of Article 45 of the Trademark Law and Item 5 of Article 11 of the Implementing Regulations, the Trademark Review and Adjudication Board may decide to suspend such case of trademark review and adjudication."

trademark law analyzed above, have no recourse of invalidation for bad faith registrations. This may not be the case in the future, if and when the jurisprudence will expand on the interpretation of the law and include a new ground for invalidation based on Article 7. However, without such jurisprudential consolidation, nonfamous brand's reliance on Article 7 or even Article 32 Trademark Law to invalidate stolen trademarks may still be shaky. For small and middle enterprises, such restrictive use of the invalidation grounds of Articles 44 and 45 of the Trademark Law seem to leave no room for protection against hijacked trademarks but for "nonuse cancellation."

According to Article 49 of the Trademark Law, any entity or individual may file an application with the Trademark Office for the revocation of a registered trademark that has not been used for three consecutive years without proper reason. The Trademark Office must make a decision within nine months from the date of receipt of such revocation application. Under certain particular circumstances, the time limit could be extended for three months upon the approval of the administrative department for industry and commerce under the State Council.

Although cancellation for nonuse may appear a meager option for the many owners of stolen trademarks, it is likely the most efficient and for a number of specific reasons, the most cost-effective form of invalidation against trademark grabbers.

The burden to prove the use of the trademark is not on the applicant but on the trademark owner. This alone is a "big" incentive that drives costs and risks down. Although the regulations of the trademark office require the applicant to provide a prima facie claim of nonuse for three consecutive years, such burden can normally be fulfilled by providing evidence from desk or basic and inexpensive field investigations. Second, the evidence of use provided by the trademark owner must be of a concrete use. In practice, just licensing a trademark without concrete use by the licensee or selling a few symbolic units of the trademarked product are not legally relevant forms of use and cannot interrupt the three-year period countdown. On the other hand, the use of the trademark by the licensee is a legally relevant use in the sense of Article 49 of the Trademark Law, as long as it is not merely symbolic.[233] Also, according to a principle stated by the SPC in the Castel judgment we cited above, a use in the sense of Article 49 of the Trademark law must be a legitimate use according to the trademark law.[234] This is where things become favorable to the victim of trademark theft. The use in bad faith, like the one in the Castel case or the use in bad faith as in the examples provided at the very beginning of this chapter, i.e., the use of a stolen trademark, should not be a legally "relevant use" in the sense of Article 49 Trademark Law, as long as the applicant for cancellation can prove the bad faith of the registrant. This will be easy to prove in all the cases of professional trademark thieves that have no direct

233. Article 66 Implementing Regulations of the Trademark Law.
234. 中华人民共和国最高人民法院 - 行政裁定书 - (2010)知行字第55号. 法国卡斯 特兄弟股份有限公司与 中华人民共和国国家工商行政管理总局商标评审委员会、李道之商标 撤销复审行政 纠纷申请再审案 (The second instance of the dispute of the Trademark Cancellation Administration Re-examination between Castel Freres Sas and the Trademark Review and Adjudication Board and Li Daozi, December 17, 2011 (The Supreme People's Ct. (2010) Zhi Xing Zi No. 55).

business relation to the stolen brand and are serial grabbers of many other foreign brands.

Furthermore, trademark grabbers rarely use trademarks and will unlikely be in a position or even interested in fighting against a nonuse cancellation. Grabbers will not likely use the stolen trademarks. They will file way too many, and they do not have any intention of using them. Their filings are finalized to a quick money return, and they know that this return must come within three years from the registration. Once this does not happen, they will go on filing new ones and so on. This means in practice that the chances of a trademark thief to respond and provide evidence of use may be extremely low, and even if they used the trademark to interrupt the three years nonuse deadline, a bogus licensing, a symbolic or an illegitimate use (use in bad faith) will not be relevant kinds of use and should not prevent the cancellation.

One downside of this type of cancellation is that a right holder must wait for at least three years from the time of registration of the hostile mark before taking action. The risk here is that at any time in the three years' time span, a thief could start indeed using the trademark legally or transfer it to someone that starts using it legally, thus preventing nonuse cancellation. Such risk is practically nonexistent in case of professional grabbers with serial applications. Such grabbers will unlikely take part into the procedure and fulfill their obligation to prove the trademark's use. The choice of such invalidation tool is more critical when the grabber is a competitor that hijacked the foreign trademark with preventive intention. In that case, nonuse cancellation may not be an option if the competitor is indeed using the stolen trademark. In practice, a decision will be depending on proper fact finding and on the evaluation of the motivations and conduct of the competitor. If evidence is collected that the competitor is not using the stolen trademark and such evidence is solid and at least three years from the registration have passed or are soon to pass, then a nonuse cancellation can still be an alternative to an invalidation under Article 45 Trademark Law. A choice is done case by case and based on solid and thorough facts and economic evaluations, aimed at finding the best and fastest commercial solution for the theft's victim.

Also, the norm under examination provides a defense against nonuse accusations. In particular, the law stipulates that nonuse due to "justifiable reasons" save the right holder's registered right from cancellation. Article 49 of the Trademark Law provides that "justifiable reasons" include force majeure, policy limitations set by the government, bankruptcy liquidation and other justifiable reasons that can make the trademark registrant free from liability.[235] In practice, such defenses have no impact on cases of trademark theft because this rule is based on the assumption of a normally legitimate use which is interrupted due to certain exceptional circumstances. In most of our cases, there will never be a use since the registration of the trademark, or if any, such use will be an illegitimate one.

In conclusion, owners of unregistered well-known trademarks and of unregistered trademarks with a certain reputation in China can enjoy both nonuse cancellation and prior right/bad faith invalidation procedures against both stolen trademark

235. Article 67 of Implementing Regulations of the Trademark Law.

(identical trademarks in the same or similar classes) and more generally hostile trademarks (i.e., similar trademarks in the same or similar classes). SMEs who forgot or neglected filing their trademark in China and a third party stole it and registered it in its own name (trademark theft), will only have the possibility with a nonuse cancellation procedure. Generally, nonuse cancellation is a most effective tool against trademark thieves because the procedure is fast (about nine months), inexpensive (burden of proof of legitimate use is on the registrant) and has a high rate of success in that trademark thieves mostly do not use trademarks.

In spite of the many tactical benefits, nonuse cancellation has also some negative downsides. It is thus important to make some practical remarks as to how it really works with nonuse cancellation. If the procedure is filed against professional and serial trademark thieves, the chances of success of a nonuse cancellation are very high, for the simple reason that the registrants will not show up in the proceeding and will fail to comply with is burden of proving use. nonuse cancellation becomes more complicated if the registrant decides to file some evidence of use. The first problem is that the Trademark Office is very generous in admitting "use" evidence. In the author's experience, the Trademark Office tends to admit and refer to any piece of paper whatsoever as sufficient evidence of use. For the reasons already presented above, the Trademark Office examiners have little time for in-depth evaluations and tend to work on a rather superficial level. The other problem is that the filed evidence of use will not be accessible to the applicant of the procedure and no rebuttal is admitted. To see the evidence and rebut it, the applicant must file first a revision appeal. It is the author experience that rejection decision by the Trademark Office can be successfully overruled by the TRAB in many cases for being hinged on insufficient or completely irrelevant evidence of "use." The overruling percentage by TRAB of "use" decisions by the Trademark Office is surely higher than the one regarding invalidation or trademark rejection decisions. For instance, evidence of symbolic use, i.e., sales or few units of a trademarked product in the three-year period under cancellation, is often accepted by the Trademark office but it is always rejected by the TRAB. It is very common that fake or tampered invoices are filed as proof of use and are accepted by the Trademark Office as evidence of "use." In all such cases, an overruling by TRAB is almost guaranteed. In the end the tool is still effective but the procedure, originally inexpensive and fast, is slowed down and forces right holders to take on further costs to correct mistakes of the Trademark Office examiners that could have honestly been easily avoided. In this respect, the author blames China trademark system and its regulations. If changes are not adopted in the organization of the examination system overall, the costs of the current inefficiencies will have to be unjustly borne by the right holders. Speeding up processes at the Trademark office level only pushes the bottlenecks further down the line of recourses, without benefit for anybody.

§3.08 TRADEMARK OPPOSITION

With the introduction of trademark monitoring systems, foreign companies have come to realize how widespread trademark theft and free ride trademark applications are in

China. On one hand, language differences, the parallel existence of English and Chinese versions of a trademark, the sheer numbers of applications, have all led to a high rate of provisional granting of what may be indeed similar trademarks in the same or similar classes. The system became clogged and the work of trademark officials went sloppier, while the timing for such cases started stretching on and on.[236] Also, given the absence of clear filters as to who could file opposition and upon what legal grounds, the result was that proliferation of procedures that has led to a system misuse allowing bad faith oppositions[237] while issuing bad quality decisions often to the detriment of well-founded actions by foreign victims of hostile free rides and trademark theft.[238] In general, the opposition system in China is perceived as being less cost-effective because of the poor quality of the decisions and its lack of consistency. Another problem is timely accessibility to the tool itself. Only large foreign companies with trademark departments and resources can afford a worldwide or regional monitoring system that can timely identify hostile trademarks within the peremptory three months period. For the majority of small and middles sized companies, finding a hostile trademark published in China still within the three months opposition window is far more difficult and less frequent.

Opposition can be filed only before a trademark application is fully granted. Specifically, an opposition can be filed after a trademark application has undergone substantive examination and has been preliminarily approved and published. Unlike invalidation, which eliminates a trademark retroactively from the date of its publication, an opposition will aim at a rejection of the trademark application, so that in case of its success, that application will never become a trademark. Opposition is an effective tool in that it prevents hostile trademarks to come into existence. This does not mean Opposition does not have dark sides.

The amendment to the trademark law which has been in force since May 1, 2014, has brought about some relevant changes to the system of trademark opposition in China. As stated above, these changes appear to reduce the scope of use of trademark opposition. Although such new provisions may at first sight be unfavorable to the opposing parties, especially against stole and hostile trademarks filed by unauthorized third parties, of a restrictive nature, in reality they rationalize the use of opposition, thus making it stronger when it is indeed the best recourse available, thus increasing the chances of success, and leaving room for more effective alternative solutions that would be prevented by the pending of an opposition.

236. During an interview dated April 29, 2014, the director of Administration for Industry and Commerce (SAIC) Zhang Mao stated the newly amended trademark law SAIC is now taking effective measures to simplify the opposition procedure and shorten the examination period (*See* the link: http://jjckb.xinhuanet.com/2014-04/29/content_502595.htm).

237. *See* the Article of Mr. Wei "新《商标法》设立审查审理期限的意义", http://www.unitalen.com.cn/html/unitalen/report/46525-1.htm (2014).

238. Paul F. Kilmer, The Value Equation of Trademark Oppositions: A Multinational Comparison of Costs and Perceived Benefits, Vol. 68 INTA Bulletin, 5, http://www.inta.org/INTABulletin/Pages/TheValueEquationofTrademarkOppositionsAMultinationalComparisonofCostsandPerceivedBenefits.aspx (March 2013).

[A] Limiting Access to the Opposition Process

One of the goals of the new trademark law is that of reducing the amount of unfounded oppositions by entitling only to a restricted number of individuals or entities, the right to file trademark oppositions. The official reason for introducing such filter is to reduce the amount of bogus oppositions, and offer relief to the overworked trademark examiners. By limiting the right of action by restricting the right to a smaller number of entitled complainants, the norm will likely prevent the filing of many bogus and bad faith oppositions, which have often been filed by Chinese companies only as dilatory tactical actions against foreign competitors. As to the ensuing improvements to the examiner's work flow, the norm is expected to enhance the quality of its decisions by reducing the number of docketed cases. Some authors criticize the fact that the short deadlines for opposition decisions introduced by the law (i.e., 12 months from date of filing) will lead to very superficial examinations.[239] However, it can be safely stated that it was not better before when the examination procedures had no preset time limits. In fact, an unfocused examiner may be often sloppier than an examiner under pressure. In practice, it is true that examiners at the Trademark Office are overworked and have objectively very few minutes per case in average due to the shear volumes of filings and pending procedures and the limited human resources available.

Article 33 of the new Trademark Law provides that, where any prior right owner or interested person believes that provisions of paragraphs 2 and 3 of Article 13, Article 15, paragraph 1 of Article 16, Article 30, Article 31 or Article 32 of the Law have been breached, it may raise an objection to the Trademark Office against a trademark that has been published after a preliminary examination within three months from the date of announcement. In such case, where rights on a prior trademark or other IP right are at stake, only the right holders or any interested parties can file opposition on "relative" grounds (i.e., unregistered well-known trademarks, trademarks filed by the agent without the consent of the principal, similar or identical prior registrations, infringement of prior's existing rights, etc.). In this case, the right of opposition would serve only private business interests. Therefore, the law limits access to this recourse only to those parties with a direct and immediate relation to the protected economic interest. Furthermore, according to the legal practice and the jurisprudence, interested parties are only the exclusive licensees. Article 4 of Several Questions on the Application of Law in Trial of Trademark Civil Dispute Cases Interpretation (Fa Shi [22002] No. 32) defines it as "*licensees under trademark licensing contracts for registered trademarks, lawful successors to registered trademark property rights (...).*"[240]

The case in which a trademark application violates the provisions of Article 10, Article 11 or Article 12 of the Trademark Law appears to be different. Same as under the old Trademark Law, any person can file opposition based on "absolute" grounds (i.e.,

239. Qiang Ma, Jessica Chumen Ju, Lessons for Trademark Owners, China Law and Practice, http://www.chinalawandpractice.com/Article/3399222/Search/Lessons-for-trademark-owners.html?Keywords=filing (November 2014).
240. *See also* TRAB v. Appellee Huazhou City Meijiang Wine Factory ([2010] Gao Xing Zhong Zi No. 747, http://www.110.com/panli/panli_26633894.html.

trademarks reproducing symbols of State, nondistinctive and descriptive trademarks and 3D marks). In this case, the grounds for opposition aim at protecting general public interest, and there is, indeed, no reason to limit access to such a legal tool to specific groups of right holders.

[B] Simplification of the Procedure for Trademark Opposition

Article 35 of the new Trademark Law provides that in the event an objection is raised against a trademark published after preliminary examination, the Trademark Office shall consider the facts and grounds submitted by both the dissenting party and the person challenged, shall decide whether the registration is allowed within 12 months upon the expiration of announcement after investigation and verification, and shall notify the dissenting party and the person challenged in writing. Where the Trademark Office decides to approve the opposed trademark registration (i.e., rejection of the opposition), it shall grant a certificate of trademark registration to the person challenged and publish the same. The dissenting party may then file a cancellation action before the Trademark Review and Adjudication Board according to Articles 44 and 45 of the Trademark Law.

This means that, if the opponent loses, the opposed trademark gets registered and the opposition procedure is concluded. This may be a good thing if a foreign brand owner is the victim of a bogus opposition. However, when we apply this preclusion of recourses to the case of stolen and hostile similar trademarks, where the opponent is always the foreign company, and upon considering the chances that such trademarks may be indeed confirmed in spite of an opposition, the employment of such tool as a default to recover stolen trademarks becomes even more questionable. In fact, in this context, an opposition appears no longer the always-good-for-everything tool that many believe it to be. An opposition may turn into a wasted year or more and in misplaced financial resources which may prevent or preclude alternative recovery strategies with better chances to succeed and bring about a real business benefit to the usurped right holder.

The inadequacy of the opposition to play the all-round IP tool to solve trademark conflicts was evident already under the prior Trademark Law. The new Trademark Law seems to be sanctioning this as an undisputable fact. By introducing such a cut-off, it forces the alleged prior right holder to make a more strategic decision in order not to waste time and resources on a case with little foundation. The new provisions seem to understand that in many cases oppositions were not well planned and were misused. With the new limitations, opposition gets a finer definition from a strategic point of view. This change should not be read in a negative way by the foreign victims of theft. It gives them opportunity to think deeper and better whether opposition is indeed the best way to go in their case. Such strategic approach should have been the appropriate one even in the past, but that is not how western companies used to deal with trademark challenges in China. Opposition should have not and should not be now selected passively as the only way to recover stolen trademarks, as it were a default decision. It is in the best interest of the usurped right holder to determine if and how to file opposition only after having completed all the fact finding and strategic analysis as suggested by our Rules of Engagement. In that context, it can be safely assumed that an opposition is used as a proper tactical tool. Filing oppositions blindly, without even knowing against whom we file them, without having considered other business downsides (like for instance prolonging thus the launch of a new product pending an opposition which may have low success chances, whether the infringer is an agent or is somewhat related to the brand supply chain or is a foreign company with good moral standing) will preclude the right holder from considering other alternative or also parallel options. This should have been recognized in the past as well, so that many companies would not have wasted valuable resources and time in pointless legal actions. The new Trademark Law, with its barring preclusion to further recourse for failed opposition requests, will force foreign companies to consider and earnestly evaluate the chances of success of an opposition, and limit its use to those cases in which such chances are objectively high or when it is the only tool to secure some tactical leverage before an unavoidable negotiation or to win time for a change of the overall branding strategy.

[C] Grounds for Opposition: A Further Restriction

Like in the case of the cancellation right provided by Article 45 of the Trademark Law, Article 33 of the Trademark Law also seem to introduce a restrictive list of grounds for opposition. Importantly, there is no mention of Article 7 as a ground for opposition. It is questionable whether an opposition can be filed only upon ground of bad faith under Article 7. We will need to see concrete decisions to understand whether Article 7 has indeed created an autonomous ground for opposition as we already mentioned above. For now, it does not seem to be the case. In such situation, the victims of a trademark theft will be left unprotected in case the stolen trademark is neither famous nor well reputed in China and precludes them from utilizing opposition based only on such ground, in that their chances to succeed only upon Article 7 will be extremely low. In such case, the legitimate right holder will have to wait for the hostile filing to go through granting and then, after at least three years from the granting, file a nonuse cancellation.

[D] Critical Review of the Use of Opposition Normally Made by Foreign Companies against Trademark Thieves and Free Riders

Although specific statistics are not publicly available, it is safe to assume that the success rate of trademark oppositions in China is not higher than 50%–60% for all the reasons indicated in the preceding paragraphs. Overworked examiners are now under greater pressure to deliver quick decisions while flooded with never ending amounts of recourses. The result is that oppositions will more and more be used by parties in bad faith to stretch disputes for lengthy period of times, prevent their foreign competitors' business expansions.

Filing opposition has always been the first recommendation of a trademark attorney to a client. Often the client's in-house counsel are IP attorneys and trained trademark specialists. It is natural for them to resort immediately and without much hesitation to a ready legal tool such as opposition to counter a hostile act of trademark filing. Also, there may be a perception that trademark opposition in China works as it does in Europe or the US. This is understandable from the point of view of a trademark practitioner; maybe it appears less understandable from a business perspective. The IP manager should not be acritical when structuring a trademark enforcement strategy. He should consider first the business strategies and goals of his company, the role of each trademark in his overall business strategy, collect solid facts about the infringer and the act of theft and only then consider the available and appropriate legal tools to protect his trademarks and consequently its business strategy in China. In sum, the brand manager should always look at a trademark challenge not just from a mere legal point of view, but also as a business matter overall by applying these Rules of Engagement.

Rushing into an opposition in China may not in fact be the best solution for all cases of trademark theft or hostile similar trademark filing. Pursuing opposition as the only way to solve such problems may even lead to paradoxical occurrences and surely to economic and time losses. An example: An opposition is filed against a hostile trademark in a case of disputable similarity. No investigations of the opposed party are conducted, as it is normally the case. What if the owner of the hostile trademark has been liquidated before the date of filing of the opposition? What if the trademark was transferred to another entity with different business and interests from the first applicant? Or what if the applicant was just a trademark grabber who would never have had the will and resources to use such trademark? The opposition could be lost and time and resources wasted away, whereby alternative solutions were available? For instance, if the right holder had timely discovered the intervened liquidation or death of the hostile applicant, he could have saved the risk of losing against a no longer existing counterpart, by simply waiting for the maturation of the conditions of nonuse cancellation or could have applied one year later for the revocation of the trademark for liquidation of the owner without transfer of the trademark right to a legitimate successor.[241]

An assessment of the trademark value to the owner and a background investigation of the hostile party could provide information and grounds for alternatives not only in relation to oppositions but also to revisions of trademark rejections due to the presence of a prior hostile trademark or due to successful opposition by third parties. Companies with shallow pockets and SMEs could for instance drop some of the available revisions or oppositions after determining which trademarks are more important to their business, so as to concentrate on them their limited resources. For instance a company making sweets faced with a rejection or an opposition in class 25 (clothing/merchandising) and class 30 (sweets), may decide to drop class 25 at present and concentrate on class 30. Such decision is simply based on the determination of the

241. *Supra* n. 234.

company strategic goals and knowledge of its own business strengths and weaknesses. Another example: it is not disputable that most trademark grabbers will never file a troll due to lack of sufficient resources for infringement actions, but most of all due to the fact that trolls are not their main and direct goal. If a trademark cannot be sold quickly, they will move on others. This in turn affects the decision of whether filing an opposition or not. In such a case, an opposition may even be re-awakening the grabber's awareness of the importance of such trademark and may persuade him to defend its case, make it difficult for the original right holder so as to force the latter down to a costly settlement. If we also consider that the new trademark law recognizes a certain legal relevance to preuse as a defense against trolls, there are indeed some good arguments here to counsel the usurped party to renounce to the opposition, and opt for cheaper and less risky forms of protection, which will also come into effect at a time not far removed from that required for an opposition. In case of a professional grabber, alternative actions could be waiting for a three-year nonuse cancellation which in case of a professional grabber will have a very high chance of success. As stated above, a grabber, after three years from the registration, and in the complete silence of the legitimate right holder, will have already abandoned and forgotten that trademark. Alternatively, if the hostile applicant is a nonChinese company but not a competitor, why not negotiating a trademark coexistence agreement instead of filing opposition? In the new jurisprudence and according to the latest draft of court regulations by the SPC on trademark administrative disputes, it is expressly mentioned that a court shall allow these agreements to produce legal effect.[242] Furthermore, other circumstances emerging from an investigation of the case may help shape more effective strategies alternative or together with the filing of an opposition. If for instance the hostile filing entity exports products with the hostile trademark abroad, why not consider custom protection or a civil lawsuit in the destination country while filing opposition in China, thus increasing the chances of convincing the counterpart to settle for a trademark transfer or abandonment of the hostile mark? What if, aside from filing a hostile similar trademark, the Chinese grabber also uses the foreign company brand on his products in China? A civil lawsuit would help not only stop an act of infringement, but also persuade the infringer to transfer or abandon the hostile trademark filing. Given that, there are many variables of a case each may suggest different and various solutions.

Some may object that opposition deadlines are tight, and that maybe there is no time for making such investigations or taking such decisions, and that not missing the opposition deadline becomes the highest priority. Well, this may be true especially if a company does not have a good trademark monitoring systems in place; surely, it is no longer true for large companies and MNCs. Also, SMEs should consider some sort of monitoring in at least in a few key countries such as China, in order to reduce the risk

242. Shangbiao Pingshen Weiyuanhui and Beijing Tailian Liangzi Baojian Jishu Youxian Gongsi Su Shandong Liangzi Ziran Jianshen Yanjiuyuan Youxian Gongsi (商标评审 委员会 、 北京台联良子保健技术有限公司诉山东自然健身研究院有限公司) [Trademark Review and Adjudication Board and Beijing Tailian Liangzi Health Technology Ltd. Company v. Shandong Natural Health Institution Ltd. Company] November 15, 2011, (Supreme People's Ct. (201) Zhi Xing Zi No. 50).

of receiving warning of a hostile filing hours before expiration of the opposition deadline.

In general, investigating case backgrounds reveals information which allows companies to make better business decisions. This applies to all kinds of business activities, especially in difficult countries such as China, in light of its peculiar business habits and legal system. Blind filing of oppositions as the only tool available against hostile trademark filings has often backfired on the opponents by wasting his time and money. Determining the chances of success based on Chinese law and the factual background of a hostile filing should be a must when deciding whether to file a trademark opposition. Deciding to file an opposition as a default matter to slow things down, especially in cases where the chances of success are 50% or lower, may backfire on the opposing party as described above.

The legislator has somewhat given a legal nobility to the author's vision of the real function of trademark opposition by restricting its access to specific groups of claimants and by barring the opposing party from further recourse in case of a rejection of the opposition request. In this way, the opponent may be motivated to focus early on in evaluating not only the formal collision among trademarks and the level of similarity, but also in investigating the commercial and factual background of the case of hostile filing, and choose the most suitable legal and commercial tools to solve such trademark disputes, which may indeed be alternative and more efficient than filing a one-shot opposition according to the new Trademark Law.

§3.09 TRADEMARK THEFT: A BAD CASE BUT A GOOD EXAMPLE: HOW TRADEMARK THEFT AFFECTS OTHER IP RIGHTS

In 2013, the news that Burberry, the world-famous UK fashion brand, had lost its trademark rights over its signature tartan pattern (hereafter also referred to as the Haymarket Check or Tartan trademark) in China was welcomed in the western hemisphere as yet again another example of the unfairness and unreliability of the Chinese trademark system.[243] However, reports of this serious legal debacle in Europe and the US have been scant and have blamed the bad faith of the Chinese "rider" and the Chinese legal system. The issue is however far more complex than it was reported and shows that Burberry could also be blamed for this debacle. In fact blaming it all on China would not render a service to all those foreign enterprises with trademark rights in China. It is rather more useful to take a more factual stance if lessons can be drowned from this case that could help preventing such cases in the future. We may surely talk about the bad faith of the Chinese party filing the cancellation here. In many cases, the first mistakes here in China are committed by the foreign entity and only afterwards exploited by Chinese competitors or professional grabbers in bad faith. They know the laws very well and can exploit their gray areas and understand their application better than Westerners do. If a foreign company were very familiar with the local uses and

243. http://www.abc.net.au/news/2013-12-13/an-burberry-defends-distinctive-27check27-trademark-in-chines/5155118.

laws before deciding what steps to take in the Chinese market, it would help a lot reducing risks and preventing downfalls. Ignorance of the market and its laws lead to serious mistakes. However, foreign brand owners are more likely to blame the Chinese law than recognizing and understanding their mistakes. Although the Chinese legal system is far from perfect, this cannot become the scapegoat for all the times foreign companies repeat the same mistakes, like forgetting to timely register their trademarks in China. In sum, foreign companies should stop thinking about how the law should be and rather focus on how it is and use it efficiently in their best interest! It is like when you play a game. You will be explained the rules, and then you decide whether to play or not. Once you decide to do business with China, you should know already the rules of the game, then plan and act accordingly. Complaining and blaming the law of China and its legal system will not bring any benefit to foreign companies. Again, another case study can show that even large companies and famous brands are not immune from very basic mistakes when it comes to protecting their IP rights in China.

On November 21, 2013, a Chinese manufacturer called Foshan Polo Santa Roberta Leather Products Co. Ltd. ("Polo Santa Roberta"), and unknown to western and even to Chinese consumers, held a press conference to announce that it had successfully obtained the revocation of the international Haymarket Trademark G732879 of Burberry in class 18 for leather goods such as suitcases, bags and wallets, based on ground of nonuse for three consecutive years. Polo Santa Roberta is a Chinese bag manufacturer who likes to keep a very low profile. It does not even possess an official website! It is indeed very common of such Chinese companies to act under the radars and exploit bad errors of foreign brand with their portfolio management. In its statement, Polo Santa Roberta accused Burberry of having unjustly attacked and harassed her with multiple trademark infringement lawsuits in Hong Kong, Taiwan and mainland China since 2004. According to the same press statements, the successful revocation of the tartan trademark was only the beginning of a counteraction by Polo Santa Roberta to protect its trademark rights. In particular, Polo Santa Roberta declared its intention to claim damages from Burberry for about CNY 500 million (about USD 83 million) as compensation for the commercial losses suffered by Polo Santa Roberta during the nine years long enforcement by the UK brand. Also, Polo Santa Roberta invited other companies which had suffered losses due to the enforcement of the now revoked trademark to join Polo Santa Roberta in a class action against Burberry.

The above-mentioned press conference had immediately drawn the attention of the Chinese media which had covered the matter with interest and proChinese feelings which showed in titles such as "*Burberry has lost its tartan trademark*" or by coverage defining the revocation as the first Waterloo battle for luxury brand in the IP field in China. Obviously, those journalists have very limited knowledge about the trademark cancellation procedure in China: the ruling from CTMO is only the first step of a complete revocation, and far from final. In fact, Burberry filed a request for review of the ruling with the Trademark Review and Adjudication Board (TRAB) on November 18, 2013. Against the TRAB decision, any party who is not satisfied with the ruling of review can file an administrative lawsuit against the review, which in turn is still appealable. The whole procedure may still last years before a final and executive decision on revocation is issued.

Although the CNY 500 million damage lawsuit threatened by Polo Santa Roberta may be actually a bluff or a mere psychological weapon in this long fought war with Burberry, and in spite of the attempts from Burberry to downplay and minimize the case, the revocation is actually a serious setback for the English brand and opens questions about its portfolio management in China. An analysis of the possible legal grounds which may have led to the revocation decision by the Chinese Trademark Office as well as other precedents in China, suggest us to be cautious and wait till the final decision before any conclusive remark is made. However, some general and preliminary remarks about the already-known facts can be made for the benefit of the readers and some practical suggestions to companies in situations similar to that experienced by Burberry.

We have already mentioned in several instances that opposition is not always the most effective weapon against trademark theft. Although the detailed facts of the oppositions filed by Burberry against Polo Santa Barbara are not known to the author, few facts emerge which can be considered. One is the fact that Burberry had taken multiple actions in different countries against the thief. It is in fact always very important to connect cross-border actions to achieve a higher level of pressure against the trademark thief. In this respect, there was nothing wrong in acting across-borders. Also, we know that litigation against Polo Santa Barbara had been pending for almost 10 years before the cancellation decision in 2013. This is a typical example of the length of opposition procedures. Burberry had been entangled in such procedure for long time which had precluded other possible legal actions, such as filing themselves a nonuse cancellation. The paradox is that by holding on to the opposition, which in this case appeared to be rather complicated as shall see Burberry had given precious time to Polo Santa Barbara to prepare a counterattack. Instead of Burberry being successful in cancelling for nonuse, the stolen trademark (a likely occurrence in that Polo Santa Barbara may have discontinued its use considering that the company does not seem to be involved in any real business with that brand), they fell victim of a nonuse cancellation. What maybe learned here is that, if you have a complex legal issue at hand, related for instance to the use of your brand, or whether similarity is somewhat disputable, then you should consider whether opposition is really the best way to go. Fortunately, the new Trademark Law seems to help us in such decision. By cutting the procedure short to the first degree in case of confirmation of the opposed trademark, it forces the victim of the theft to look for other ways to recover its stolen trademark at the earliest possible stage and decide for opposition only when the chances to succeed in it are very high. One alternative to opposition is that of filing nonuse cancellation. Nonuse cancellation, the most effective of all against IP thieves, requires patience and good knowledge of the infringer, its activities and motivations. Patience is needed because the usurped right holder has to wait for at least three years from the date of registration before filing for such cancellation. However, this is not as bad as it seems. In fact, an opposition can also last for over one year, and it may last longer than three years in case the opponent wins but the opposed files appeal. Second, you must make sure that the thief will not use the brand and will not enforce it against you. As stated above, most trademark thieves are not really after manufacturing and selling. They rather want to make quick bucks by blackmailing the right holder and induce him to buy the stolen trademark from them at a high price. Once the blackmail effects vanish (i.e., in case nobody shows interest in the stolen brand), they will forget that brand and focus on new ones. A good investigation of the background facts will help assess these risks and select the most effective strategy. With the advantage of hindsight, we could say that a brand, knowing the risks of the legal complexities behind an opposition action, and thus its possible length, may have instead decided to investigate facts and determined that a no-use cancellation, rather than an opposition would have best served its purposes. In the case of Burberry, the never-ending oppositions provided Polo Santa Barbara with time to assess weaknesses and use them against Burberry and most of all with the knowledge that they now could effectively blackmail Burberry into a deal.

In sum, foreign brands should first concentrate in collecting facts. Knowledge of facts will help making the right decisions. Using opposition as a default defense against thieves has often turned into a boomerang such as in the Burberry case.

The Burberry case offers also another interesting learning opportunity regarding the determination as to what can be considered relevant "use" evidence in a nonuse cancellation dispute. According to the Trademark Law of China in force at the time of the Burberry decision, as well as for the new trademark law in force since May 1, 2014, a trademark can be cancelled if it has not been used for three consecutive years. This was the provision used by Polo Santa Roberta to demand and obtain the revocation of the tartan trademark in relation to leather goods of class 18 of the Chinese Classification System. This request was the only defense Polo Santa Roberta could use to obtain a decision of "not infringement" in the main opposition and civil proceedings instituted by Burberry. If the tartan trademark of Burberry was void at the time of the alleged infringing act, Polo Santa Roberta was no longer infringing and the Burberry opposition was groundless.

The Chinese Trademark Law also provides that it is the trademark owner that has to bring evidence of the use of the trademark. According to the law, evidence of "use" is rather free and it is not preordained in its form. In practice, proving trademark "use" may be a rather complex task. Evidence must be clear and show an effective use in a proven time frame. Often, pieces of evidence which are perceived to be good for the task are indeed unclear about many of the facts to be proved. We can take an invoice as a typical example. Although a sales invoice is an authoritative document with a defined date and self-explanatory of an act of sale, which is indeed a form of effective use, it may not contain the trademark or the goods name and cannot be therefore connected to the registered trademark and the goods in the dispute. In sum, such evidence alone would completely miss the point of proving that the referred use through sales concerns indeed the trademark under risk of cancellation. Another example of use is advertising. However, what if advertising is conducted in the name of a retailer or carried in the name of other third parties? For instance, promotion in China is not conducted only by the trademark owner. If the third party doing promotion and advertising does not possess a lawful and registered license, can this type of use be referred to the trademark owner? The risk of revocation remains. The same can be extended to the retail and distribution system. If the use cannot be referred directly or by license back to the trademark owner, use by third parties is not relevant and will not avoid cancellation.

Given that the authors are not familiar with the evidence filed by Burberry in this case, the above notes are made for general information and to explain the practical difficulties of a brand owner defending against nonuse cancellations. For the same purpose of providing guidance to other companies, let us assume that Burberry may have indeed offered evidence of use. Considering the reputation of the company and the diffusion of its products, it is not hard to imagine that its own bags with tartan patterns may be a good evidence of use. This seems to be the most logic evidence when such branded products are so famous. However, is this evidence of use in the sense of the Trademark Law? Even if the brand owner could prove that it has used the pattern such as the tartan pattern on its bags and accessories of class 18 and 25, the legal question will be whether the use of that pattern fulfils the function of a trademark or instead only that of a design patent (pattern used for aesthetic reasons v. recognition of origin). According to the Chinese law, designs and trademarks have very clear and delimited functions. The former protect the aesthetic value of an industrial product giving thus recognition to a certain creative effort and an added commercial value related to the ornamental parts of the product. The latter identify the origin of a product and connect the product to a specific manufacturer/seller. Using a pattern on the inner or outer side of the bag such as in Burberry bags appears to be first and utmost fulfilling the conditions for design protection. At the same time, the intensive use of the Haymarket pattern for an aesthetic function made it very famous, so that the leather products bearing it were immediately identifiable as belonging to Burberry. Is therefore such a pattern used as a decoration on a bag also a use of the pattern as a trademark? It is indeed a disputable issue and the boundaries between design and trademark protection may become blurry especially in case of design patters that become famous to the point of going beyond the mere aesthetic value and becoming a sign of recognition of the product origins. In practice, the functions remain a decorative and aesthetic one. Chinese law protect such functions with design patents and more recently, as trade dress, in case a design patent for such decorative element has not been obtained or has expired.[244] However, from a strict literal interpretation of the law, it can be explained how evidence of use of a pattern as a design on bags, may not fulfill the requirement of use for trademarks. If the pattern becomes very famous, it may acquire decorative value and become protectable as trade dress. Trade dress protection is not offered under the trademark law, but rather under the law against unfair competition.[245] It seems therefore that an examiner may have indeed formal grounds to reject the proof of such borderline use of a pattern as trademark use under Article 49 of the Trademark Law.

244. Article 5 of the Anti-Unfair Competition Law, Promulgated by SCNPC on September 2, 1993 and effective as of December 1, 1993 with 33 articles stipulating the protection of fair competition; 中华人民共和国反不正当竞争法， 由全国人大会常委会于1993年9月2日发布，自1993年12月1日起施行。共33条.

245. *Ibid.*

A company finding itself in dire straits such as Burberry, risks losing its trademark. Losing a trademark registration is obviously a very bad occurrence for brand owners, especially considering that in force of the "first to file" rule the exclusive rights on a trademark in China only come to existence once the trademark is registered with the Chinese Trademark Office. Unregistered trademarks enjoy protection only if they are well known or have a certain reputation in China. Without that trademark in its exclusive ownership, a company could not prevent any third parties from using it on the goods in question. That trademark would become the pray of anyone willing to use it. However, things can get worse, since the loss of the trademark right may influence actions against design patent grabbers. In the Examination Guideline for Patent 2010 version, trademark rights were added as one prior right to invalidate a design patent. As to the scope of the trademark, from the wording of Guideline and China Trademark Law, generally speaking, it means registered trademarks in China. An example of such an important use for trademarks was that made by Louis Vuitton in an older case.[246] In this case Wang Jun, a Chinese individual had registered quite some design patents with LV logo on bag, fabric, etc. The prior registered trademarks of LV were the key evidence for the court to judge that Wang Jun's designs were lacking novelty and were registered in breach of registered prior IP rights.

In conclusion to this case study, it may be worth recounting some more facts about the long going battle between Polo Santa Roberta and Burberry. Although in some unofficial public websites, Foshan Polo Santa Roberta claims its brand Polo Santa Roberta originated from the UK, in fact, the trademark is registered in the name of City POLO Cosmetic Co., Ltd. ("Guangzhou POLO") in Guangzhou, China. Interestingly, the legal representative of Guangzhou POLO, Mr Zhang Ke Ming, seems like a big fan of design patents containing Burberry elements as well. One of Mr Zhang Ke Ming's patent identified with registration number 200430001158.8 was granted on October 27, 2004. On March 1, 2010, Burberry filed a cancellation against this design patent based on a prior design patent under No. 03316733.8 which is registered also by another Chinese individual with the name of Lin Cang. The Patent Reexamination Board (PRB) issued No. 15611 Decision on November 12, 2010, ruling that the design patent of Mr Zhang was void because similar to that owned by Mr Lin. Mr Zhang filed an administrative lawsuit against the No. 15611 Decision, and the Beijing First Intermediate Court judged that the involved design patent was not similar to that of Mr Lin and the case went in appeal. The first instance judgment was sustained by the Beijing Higher People's Court in the appeal in 2012. The No. 200430001158.8 patent was then void since February 5, 2012 because Mr Zhang Ke Ming did not pay the annual fee.

If the above design patent were still valid, we can imagine that Burberry may have used against it its trademark in class 18 as well. However, in case of revocation this could not have been possible any longer.

In spite of its setback against Mr Lin, Mr Zhang registered more design patents with the tartan pattern. For instance, Patent No. 200830250293.4, titled as fabric was

246. Luyi Weiding Malidi Gufen Youxian Gongsi Su Wang Jun (路易威登马 利蒂股份有限公司诉王军)[Louis Vuitton Malletier SA v. Wang Jun] April 10, 2007, (Beijing No. 1 Interm. People's Ct.).

granted on January 13, 2010. According to available public information, it was cancelled in December 10, 2010 for failure to pay annual fees. Mr Zhang also owns design Patent No. 201030653050.2 titled "handbag," which was granted on June 8, 2011. According to the public information, it appears to be still valid.

It is interesting to notice that Burberry had not been able to secure design patents for its patterns in China. In the worst case scenario, i.e., Burberry eventually loses all its tartan trademarks, the English brand will not only lose its exclusive trademark rights over the pattern in class 18, but would also allow someone like Mr Zhang, strong of a valid design patent to attack undisturbed the patterns on Burberry's leather products for design patent infringement without the risk of being checked with a valid registered trademark. The only defense left to Burberry would be that of proving the lack of novelty of the design patents in question, forcing the English brand in an embarrassing defensive position.

Although our reflections may not be all exactly applicable to the Burberry case, lacking the author the full knowledge of the case facts, such reflections overall are valid as a general warning and reminder of risks related to the management of an IP portfolio in China. Brand owners are warned to be very cautious of the type of usages of their rights to fulfill the requirements of the law and avoid risks of nonuse cancellation. Also, use of trademark should be always well coordinated with the design patents portfolio in order to be able to optimize the scope of protection of the various elements of a successful product line.

§3.10 CONCLUSIONS TO CHAPTER 3

Trademark theft and trademark grabbing could be paralleled to mop up operations in enemy territory, where the enemy is impalpable but effective thanks to his hidden position and knowledge of the territory. Operating in a new environment with different rules and uses compel brand owners to invest first in knowledge of the territory and the behavior of the infringers. Rush actions may lead to ambushes.

Following the Rules of Engagement presented in the Second Chapter of this book and as exemplified in many examples in this Chapter, will help foreign brands and entities to prevent the mistakes typically committed by their western competitors in China and reduce the risk inherent to the Chinese trademark system. In particular, the setting up of clear strategic goals and guidelines, the collection of reliable information about the local laws and practices, as well knowledge of the infringers and their businesses can help anticipate risks and to take the right decisions to avoid them or reduce their negative impacts at the earliest possible stage.

If all this sounded obvious, the horror stories presented till here show that it was not. Excuses rather than lessons were sought out. Scapegoating exercises have created wrong impressions about the IP environment in China and have given rise to legends and to the overestimations of obstacles and underestimation of possibilities. Metropolitan legends about trademark enforcement in China have been built on wrong interpretations of defeats. Only lack of proper knowledge of the Chinese law or a knowledge built up on now well-consolidated "metropolitan legends" could explain how scores of foreign companies in China have committed the same mistakes about their IP protection years after years. It could not be explained otherwise. Again, we are not here to justify IP criminals or to condone China for lax regulations, poor organization and sometimes lack of real political will. However, reducing the whole discussion to this, would not justify doing business in China anymore. There are indeed rules and ways how to do things here in China that are beneficial to foreign brand owners. These foreign right holders just need to know this and make the right use of it. If foreign brand owners can make this learning effort and adapt their mindset to the local conditions, there will be less horror stories in the future, because they will be able to prevent many such cases.

CHAPTER 4

Against All Odds: Brand Protection in China

In spite of rampant trademark enforcement in China, counterfeiting seems to be increasing and prospering. For companies, intense trademark enforcement in China has become a source of frustration that finds no satisfactorily solutions. In front of such a publicized phenomenon, some extreme reactions of foreign brands are witnessed: Some get into a paroxysm of enforcement work, mostly characterized by myriads of small administrative actions in the vain attempt to "terminate" counterfeiting. Others, resigned to the inevitability of being infringed, prefer to save the money in what they perceive to be useless battles against a hydra with infinite new heads. If we just read the media, the stories about counterfeiting, about western companies blaming China to do too little and too bad, about external political pressure to make China become "civilized," we then surely gain the impression that it is the exclusive fault of China. Like for trademark theft and trolls, the truth is far more complex and those who blame China can be blamed in turn for a number of good reasons. Again, this is not a justification of China's political will and legal system at all costs. The administrative enforcement system of IP rights, with its chaotic involvement of agencies of different levels, and overlapping functions as well as conflicting parochial interests, the lack of legal disincentives for both infringers and corrupted government enforcers, plays a massive, critical role in this game of cat and mouse between right holders and infringing organizations. However, that alone would not be sufficient to describe and explain why in spite of intensive field enforcement, infringers continue to pop up, factories that were shut down reemerge a few days later in a different building a block away from the one sealed by the police. There are a number of factors that must be known and understood before making an objective evaluation of the available tactical options to protect trademarks in China. Again, following the Rules of Engagement introduced earlier will help making more precise and realistic assessments of the situation and lead to the adoption of more effective short and mid-term strategies.

The perceived failure of the administrative enforcement of trademarks, the most commonly used mean of trademark enforcement in China against counterfeiters, is founded on many reasons.

Macroreasons for the failure of anti-counterfeiting strategies of foreign brands in China are often perceived to be the lack of the political will in the Chinese government and its localized enforcement authorities to protect foreign IP rights, in favor of a young Chinese economy still on a build-up phase. This lack of will seems to reflect first of all in the insufficient or substandard regulations at local level, and the lack of transparency and consistency in their applications by local enforcement agencies. In particular, the protectionism of local interests by enforcement authorities, the mixing-up of public and private interests at local level, corruption and illegal relations ("guangxi"[247]) appear as the concrete manifestations of the macroreasons described above. The blaming game can continue by listing many more of such reasons, all legitimate, till they become "metropolitan legends" for Western political reasons and excuses for not well-conceived enforcement practices. Again, it is a matter of knowledge on one side and of conceptualization on the other. The way things are seen and perceived by foreign brand owners may be also affected by the conceptual categories they use to interpret the counterfeiting landscape in China and to set up their important strategic goals. Trademark enforcement initiated by brand owners has been often tasked with the eradication of counterfeiting in China. Taken literally, this can lead companies to pursue any and every infringement irrespective of its economic values as well as its relevance to the company overall business strategy. Measuring the success of a counterfeiting strategy on whether it can eliminate counterfeiting of a given company's brands, will ultimately end in a failure because eradication of counterfeiting is not an economic or business goal, but rather a political one. This goes without considering that companies' brand protection budgets are always insufficient compared to the tasks assigned by the board to the in-house legal or brand protection team.

Microfactors are those influencing the conception and implementation of anti-counterfeiting/brand protection strategies in China by foreign brand owners. Some of these important factors are for instance, the correct categorization of the different types of brands and their functions, the identification of common traits of counterfeiting manifestation and motivational structure, the Chinese trademark and IPR enforcement system, and the awareness and collocation of brand protection issues within the management structure of the brand owner's company.

This Chapter will focus on the machinery revolving around anti-counterfeiting. It will start with a general introduction of counterfeiting in China and its manifestations both online and in the field. It will then provide an overview of the legal recourses available and will then introduce and discuss some critical topics such as the

247. Fang Yang, The Importance of Guangxi to Multinational Companies in China, Vol. 7, No. 7, Asian Social Science, 163, 163-164 (July 2011). Guangxi can be roughly translated as relationship. In practice, it is a key element of doing business in China. It is based on the creation of a network of mutually beneficial relationships to be used for personal and business purposes.

downsides of actual anti-counterfeiting strategies, the role of investigators and informants and that of local administrative bodies in charge of enforcement. Eventually, it will provide some alternative concepts and ideas for a possible change of direction in the trademark holders' strategies.

§4.01 INTRODUCTION TO TRADEMARK COUNTERFEITING IN CHINA

Brands and their legal embodiments (i.e., trademarks, trade dress and designs) are valuable economic assets of any company in today's globalized economy. Brands embody corporate values and stand for the quality and reputation of the related products. This is particularly so for brands associated to luxury and high quality goods. Companies owning such brands are especially sensitive to the issue of counterfeiting and brand protection in China.

China is the world's factory and the country where most counterfeited brands and goods are made and come from.[248] This explains the need for brand owners to conceive and invest in brand protection polices for the Chinese market. Such need has become even greater now since the surge of consumerism as a driving economic philosophy and policy in China along with the rapid development of an internal demand for foreign goods.[249]

Counterfeiting can be generally defined as the manufacturing of the faithful reproduction of a product and its original markings, product which is then sold in the market as an original but at a far lower price.[250] Counterfeiting pervades the very

248. Statistics of the U.S. Department of Homeland Security show that 63% of seized counterfeit goods at the US borders in 2014 were coming directly from China. However, another 25% of the seized goods were coming from Hong Kong. Considering that Hong Kong is but a transition station to overseas market for fakes coming from China, and especially southern China, the total percentage of fakes made in China seized in the US rises to 88%. For a total value of almost USD 1 billion (https://www.cbp.gov/sites/default/files/documents/2014%20IPR%20Stats.pdf), *see also* the provisional report of the Chinese State Administration for Industry and Commerce (SAIC) on anti-counterfeiting activities in the first half of 2012 in http://money.163.com/12/0802/17/87TTGG2N00253B0H.html. *See also* Report on EU Custom Enforcement of Intellectual property Rights of 2011 (http://ec.europa.eu/taxation_customs/customs/customs_controls/counterfeit_piracy/statistics/).

249. Jessica Lin, Fake Stuff, Ruthledge 2011, pages 2-7; Lisa Carducci, Behind the China New Consumerism January 11, 2012: http://www.china.org.cn/opinion/2012-01/11/content_24376660.htm; Some authors are pointing out the tendency of the Chinese consumers to take distance from foreign luxury goods. It is speculated that these recent trends, which have been object of academic studies, may have been induced by government policies, ethnocentrism and improvement of Chinese made products. For contribution on this topic regarding development of Chinese consumerism, *see also*: Lianxi Zhou, Michael K. Hui Symbolic Value of Foreign Products in the People's Republic of China Journal of International Marketing, Vol. 11, No. 2, Special Issue on Marketing in Transitional Economies 36-58 (2003).

250. Daniel C. K. Chow, Counterfeiting in the People's Republic of China, Vol. 78, No. 1 Washington University Law Quarterly, 9, 10 (2000), which observes that there is no legal definition of counterfeiting in Chinese Law. Daniel C. K. Chow, Anti-Counterfeiting Strategies of Multi-National Companies in China: How a Flawed Approach is Making Counterfeiting Worse, Vol. 41, No. 4, Georgetown Journal of International Law, 750 (2010) maintains that however, the definition can be extrapolated from the wording of Article 52 of the Chinese Trademark Law (now Article 57 of the 2014 Trademark Law) in the terms defined above. Counterfeiting must not be confused with piracy. Counterfeiting is a form of piracy. However, piracy more broadly

industrial infrastructure of the Chinese economy and encompasses fashion products as well as automotive products, toys, household products, electronics, machinery, chemicals, pharmaceuticals and high-tech goods of all sorts. The wealth of entire industrial regions of China is somewhat related to counterfeiting and the subsidiary economy revolving around it. However, not all counterfeiting hubs concentrate in the richest regions of China.[251] The geography of counterfeiting is indeed very complex. On one hand, certain regions with a tradition in a certain industrial field may be also those harvesting the largest counterfeiting rings: see for instance the fashion and textile industries in Guangdong province, or the thriving shoe counterfeiting in Fujian province. This is because such regions already had "legal" infrastructures that helped support a rapid expand of the counterfeiting industries. For instance, the regions mentioned above are those where most foreign brands have been manufacturing their respective products first. It would be odd to find an apparel counterfeiter in the northwest or northeast of China, which are regions historically, focused on heavy industries and manufactured industrial products. However, you may find large fashion counterfeits and wholesalers in regions that have no tradition in fashion's manufacture, because of their convenient location near large markets or harbors (e.g., Yiwu and Ningbo in Zhejiang province near Shanghai). On the other hand "counterfeiters' migrations" have been observed in some industrial fields in more recent times due to radical changes to the economic infrastructure of a certain province. For instance, the triangle of Rui'an, Wenzhou, Taizhou cities in Zhejiang province has been for decades the center of automotive spare parts counterfeiting. Zhejiang is also one of the richest provinces of China with ever-growing local high-tech businesses. Growing legal industries and the emerging role of local legit Chinese automakers have created a legal part business which is affected by counterfeiting as much as the foreign brands. This has pushed the local authorities to step up enforcement, thus forcing some counterfeiters to move to outlying areas in neighboring regions such as Anhui province. The latter are more than willing to receive much-needed economic boost, given their

encompass all forms of unauthorized imitation of products or services that are legally protected under intellectual property rights and/or unauthorized use of IP-protected work. Yang, Fryxell, and Sie, Anti-Piracy Effectiveness and Managerial Confidence: Insights from Multinationals in China, Vol. 43, Journal of World Business, 321 (2008). Also counterfeiting must be kept distinct from copyright piracy, which is also a form of piracy but concentrates on the copying of the content of media, such as films, musical records, books and computer software. According to Daniel C. K. Chow, Vol. 78, No. 1 Counterfeiting in the People's Republic of China Washington University Law Quarterly, 9 (2000): "In the case of copyright piracy there is not necessarily any attempt to convince the consumer that the pirated product was produced and distributed by the original copyright owner." For further definitions of counterfeiting and piracy, *see also* Organization for the Economic Cooperation and Development (OECD), Economic Impact of Counterfeiting and Piracy – Executive Summary (2007), http://www.oecd.org/industry/industryandglobalisation/38707619.pdf (2007).

251. These are the provinces of Fujian, Jiangsu and Zhejiang in the south east and Guangdong in the south. Guangdong and Jiangsu are the provinces with the highest GDP according to official statistics in 2011. For a reference, *see* Zhang Junmian, Top 10 Largest Economies in China, http://www.china.org.cn/top10/2012-03/20/content_24929040.htm (March 2012). *See also* Kevin Biggs, Protecting against Counterfeits, http://www.amcham-shanghai.org/amchamportal/mcms/presentation/publication/insight/InsightDetail.aspx?Guid=%7BAA1C601B-A330-4E49-901A-CBF89057E992%7D (October 2010).

current more depressed local economies. However, manufacturing over capacity, and sluggish internal growth are pushing for renewed heights of counterfeiting activities also in the traditional Zhejiang triangle. All these considerations have not as yet touched upon other critical factors such as the corruption of government officials and the dirty games played by local investigators and informants as an intermediary between brands and corrupted enforcement authorities. All these factors and their incidence on the way anti-counterfeiting work is conducted in China will be dealt with at a later stage.

Particularly hit by counterfeiting are foreign brands. However, counterfeiting does not hit all brands in the same way. While the continuous infringement of fashion brands result mostly in their dilution and the loss of investments and market share,[252] counterfeiting of brands of products such as for instance cosmetics, electric and electronic products and home appliances, cars, pharmaceuticals etc. and their components or spare parts respectively, not only may cause loss of market shares and dilution by erosion,[253] but could also lead to erosion and direct economic damages related to potential warranty and product liability claims,[254] administrative product recalls[255] or

252. Recent market studies and investigations have shown that fake clothing can also cause damages to health as well. According to a report of Europol in 2012, poison in children's clothing is the latest risk emerging from counterfeiters. A recent investigation found formaldehyde in woolen and cotton clothes which was 500 times higher than safe levels should be. The chemical is used to give a permanent press effect to clothes but high levels (20 parts per million) can cause eye, skin and nasal irritation, respiratory problems, asthma and skin cancer. For a reference, *see* https://www.europol.europa.eu/sites/default/files/publications/counterfeitproducts.pdf (2013).

253. In 2012, Ubiquiti Networks Inc. reported market share losses due to increasing market of counterfeits of its products. For a reference, *see* http://www.marketwatch.com/story/ubiquiti-plunges-on-struggles-with-fake-products-2012-08-10 (August 2010).

254. A man in Guangzhou, China, was killed when his cell phone blew up and severed an artery in his neck. For a reference, *see* http://www.newser.com/story/49739/exploding-cell-phone-kills-man.html (2009). More recent fake phone parts related deaths in China were also reported, *see* https://www.youtube.com/watch?v=s4nf-2BYBps (2014). Half the deaths in traffic accidents in Saudi Arabia are caused by fake car parts – including brakes and tires – that are imported to the Kingdom, according to Judge Ahmad Bin Dhaifallah Al-Ghamdi, chairman of the 11th Administrative Circuit at the Administration Court in Jeddah. He said that incidents caused by the counterfeit parts result in 3,000 out of the Kingdom's 6,000 annual traffic fatalities and noted the Saudi Authorities seized 8 million fake products in the first half of 2010. For a reference, *see* http://www.saudigazette.com.sa/index.cfm?home.con&contentid=2010101285143 (2010). According to a report in the Indian press in 2007, fake automotive parts were responsible for 66,330 accidents even as long back as 1997-1998, according to a study conducted at the time by Acma. These accidents caused 13,180 deaths and injured 65,550 people. At the time, Indians bought 3.8 million vehicles a year, compared with more than 10 million now. There has been no study on the accidents caused by fake parts since, but the association says the number could only have increased. For a reference, *see* http://www.livemint.com/Companies/YrbpLFkdIbdg6joFcmKy8I/Fake-auto-parts-take-toll-of-lives-deprive-govt-industry-o.html (December 2007). As to fake pharmaceutical products, *see also* the case cited in the article of Michelle Wein, The True Cost of the Global trade in Illicit Goods, Georgetown Public Policy review, http://gppreview.com/2012/08/06/the-devil-wears-counterfeit-prada-and-sells-fake-glycerin/ (August 6, 2012).

255. Most recent was the case of Aston Martin in China. In February 2014, China's product quality and Safety watchdog AQSIQ ordered Aston Martin to recall almost 18,000 vehicles for defective brake arms. Aston Martin found that Shenzhen Kexiang Mould Tool Co Limited, a Chinese

voluntary service measures[256] related to the inherent quality and safety risks posed by counterfeits to consumers. The brand owner may often be able to reject warranty claims or defend its case before civil courts or product quality authorities, but there are not only risks of not being able of succeeding in it. Also, while in the process of proving that the defective part which caused death or injuries was not an original one, there is always the problem of aggressive press and skeptical public opinion. Often, legal or administrative procedures last long time and when the lawsuit is won or the administrative procedure is closed in favor of the brand owner, the public will not care anymore and will only tend to remember the bad headlines at the beginning of the case. Such considerations are important for a strategic and effective approach to anti-counterfeiting in China, especially when considering the limited resources brands often allocate to anti-counterfeiting work in the Chinese market. It is evident that for products suffering direct economic damages from brand dilution and customer disaffection, intervention should be focused on hitting certain channels of distributions, such as online retailing of fake fashion goods, rather than street markets, and to privilege targets with larger quantities of fakes in store. For products which are more "safety-sensitive," enforcement should not be bound by quantities if a part is critical to the user safety (i.e., a fake airbag, a fake medicine pill etc.), whereby even one single safety-related fake product, component or spare part, that enters the market, may cause severe legal fallouts, aside from the obvious brand dilution and loss of market share.[257]

Brand owners have engaged with varying degrees of intensity in battling counterfeiting directly on the field in China. Some multinationals or famous brands have been involved for well over a decade in intensive trademark enforcement and political lobbying in China. However, mid-sized foreign enterprises have at best made sporadic attempts to stop counterfeiters directly in China.[258] As to the most active foreign brands, experts have witnessed an almost frenzied and random increase of IPR enforcement actions especially in the form of administrative raids[259] and seizures of counterfeits based on trademark rights for a number of years, which has then led to an

subcontractor that molds the affected accelerator pedal arms, was using counterfeit DuPont plastic material. For reference, *see* http://www.cnbc.com/id/101393220 (February 2014).

256. In the summer of 2013, prompted by several death accidents related to fake IPhone battery rechargers, Apple started a service campaign offering replacement of fake rechargers with genuine ones for a discounted price (http://www.bbc.com/news/technology-23585898).

257. For more information on the studied impacts of counterfeiting, reference is made to Organisation for Economic Co-operation and Development (OECD), *supra* n. 249.

258. For many enterprises, especially medium- and small-sized ones, the first problem in tackling counterfeiting in China was and it is still nowadays the lack of proper IPR portfolios. This problem has been amplified by the corresponding emergence of the phenomenon of IPR grabbing by both Chinese legally operating competitors and counterfeiters. In reality, the phenomenon of IPR grabbing has not spared both large and multinational enterprises. The reasons for such situation are multiple and can be summed up in two main categories. The first group of reasons is related to the lack of knowledge of both Chinese legal system and culture. The second group of reasons can be related to economic and legal factors. In any case, the result is that counterfeiting cannot be stopped unless and until the brand owner will have recovered its stolen IP rights, which is in practice a very difficult and frustrating enterprise. More details on this issue are in Chapter 2 of this book.

259. Martin k. Dimitrov, *Supra* n. 22.

ever growing frustration among foreign enterprises as to their ability to effectively and durably enforce IP rights in China. In spite of enforcement, counterfeiting is stronger than before, while financial resources appear to be invested in a hopeless enterprise, hopeless to the point of giving rise to very critical voices from the corporate world, claiming that IPR enforcement against counterfeiters in China is useless and even counterproductive. Some of the most critical ones have started investing their resources in other forms of enforcement such as suing importers and e-traders in the US or in custom protection in the US and the EU.[260] All these negative experiences have also influenced the behavior of smaller foreign companies. In front of the failure of their better compatriots, they perceived investing their smaller resources in anti-counterfeiting in China as frustratingly useless.

A phase of reconsideration of the brands commitment to anti-counterfeiting actions against trademark infringers in China, especially after the emergence of internet as the major counterfeit market is ongoing. Administrative raids conducted without prior notification of the counterfeiting targets, once the most popular and cheapest form of trademark enforcement in China, is nowadays under heavy critic and has become less attractive, to the point that even the Chinese legislator has tried to revamp it by reforming relevant provisions of the Trademark Law concerning administrative enforcement of trademarks as we shall see ahead. Online enforcement strategy have also been oscillating between direct conflict with e-commerce platforms such as Alibaba, Taobao and JD.com and cooperation in their take-down systems, and the attempt of finding a third way such as attacking single e-shop owners with civil litigation.[261] The reasons of the frustration of foreign brands, mostly pointed towards the Chinese legal and enforcement system, have partly concealed to them the shortcomings of their strategic planning. There can be no doubts that the Chinese system is not perfect, and it surely will never be, in that "perfection" from the point of view of a brand owner is in itself a mere subjective parameter. Taking some distance from daily enforcement activities and the acquisition of a deeper knowledge of the inner operation of the Chinese anti-counterfeiting and enforcement machine may assist companies and their service providers in identifying efficient and effective anti-counterfeiting strategies.

Upon considering that a trademark is an immaterial and intellectual right, while at the same time an asset and a marketing and selling tool, brand protection strategies

260. For an example, *see* Hannah Elliott, Louis Vuitton and Burberry win millions in landmark Canadian counterfeit suit in Forbes.com, http://news.yahoo.com/louis-vuitton-burberry-win-millions-landmark-canadian-counterfeit-151451343.html (July 6, 2011): "In a decision dated June 27, the Federal Court of Canada awarded a total of $2.5 million (CAD) in damages, including $1.4 million for Vuitton and $1.1 million for co-plaintiffs Burberry Limited and Burberry Canada Ltd. The fashion houses had filed suit last year against Singga Enterprises Inc., and Carnation Fashion Company... and the respective owners and operators, importers, distributors and online sellers of each company". Also *see* Erin Coe, Tory Burch Awarded $164M in Counterfeiting Case, Law 360, http://www.law360.com/articles/250748/tory-burch-awarded-164m-in-counterfeiting-case (June 7, 2011).

261. Instead of suing Taobao, Louis Vuitton went after three Taobao e-shops seeking damage compensation for their alleged trademark infringement. For reference, *see* http://www.vogue.co.uk/news/2016/01/12/louis-vuitton-sues-taobao-alibaba-counterfeit-users,(January 2016).

should be the result of a comprehensive and interdisciplinary IP management decision process. In such process, financial, commercial and legal considerations can all be summed up into a trademark enforcement plan aiming at the most effective trademark exploitation in function of the overall business strategy of the enterprise.[262] The consequence of such approach is that both the conception of a brand protection strategy in China and the parameters to determine its success will likely be different for each enterprise and functionally adapted to its specific business strategy. Although foreign brands in China all share the common final strategic goal of reducing the impact of counterfeiting on their trademarks and businesses, success of an enforcement strategy is only measurable in terms of whether and how much it contributes to the achievement of each company's strategic business goals.

Such approach looks at brand protection as part of a company's IP management. Brand protection and anti-counterfeiting work does not generate money; however, it can save losses many times bigger than its costs. This strategic rethinking of brand protection should help brand owners avoid extreme strategies such as reducing or even abandoning trademark enforcement in China on one end, and enforcement at all costs against everything and everybody on the other. These extremes are the result of the functional erosion of abused and improperly used enforcement tools and the related psychological frustration and chronological mistrust induced in the brand owner by misplaced enforcement goals. Rethinking consolidated strategies for trademark enforcement against counterfeiters in China will also help finding and set forth achievable and realistic goals upon which successes of a durable and concrete kind, can be achieved and demonstrated. For instance, quantities of seized goods have been the only or the most important parameter to measure the success of a brand protection strategy in China. However, such goal setting is based on a conceptual contradiction. If a brand protection strategy is to be deemed successful based on seized quantities of fake goods, then such strategy achieved success only when the seizure figures will show a downward spiraling trend within a short period of time. If each year the seized quantities increase together with the budget and this for many years, it can also mean that the work of each previous year may have indeed failed to achieve its goals! So either the tools employed are wrong, or the strategic goals are wrong, misplaced or misinterpreted.

Conceptually, rethinking brand protection as an overall strategic and business issue, rather than a mere legal one or a matter of corporate security, will likely prevent errors in the goal setting and during the strategic planning and execution phases. This, in turn will benefit the field work and facilitate the achievement of a sustainable balance between budgets and successes. Also, very important, is that such strategic planning shall consider also relevant factors such as corruptibility of government officials in the equation, so as to prepare needed antidotes to minimize the related risks. Once all these factors are taken in, understood and correctly used, goals can be set and realistically achieved to the benefit of the company and its management.

262. *Supra* n. 24.

In the following pages, the book will explore some of the major factors influencing the conception and implementation of anti-counterfeiting/brand protection strategies in China by foreign brand owners. The goal is to demonstrate that the conception of a brand protection strategy must be guided by a comprehensive, interdisciplinary approach which is able to consider and synthetize all the relevant economic and legal factors peculiar to the Chinese market and legal systems. Some of these important factors, like for instance the correct categorization of the different types of brands and their functions, the identification of common traits of counterfeiting manifestation (*see also* Chapter 2), including online counterfeiting, the legal and political aspects of the Chinese trademark and IPR enforcement system, and the role of local investigators, will be separately considered and analyzed.

A second part of this chapter will analyze more in details the administrative trademark enforcement, the most common form of IPR enforcement strategy in China in light of the above factors, and the new Trademark Law in force since May 1, 2014. In particular, it will highlight the shortcomings of administrative trademark enforcement in China in its present manifestations and suggest corrections and improvements to enforcement strategies by foreign brands, with a special eye to those smaller or emerging brands which have even tighter budgetary constraints than multinationals.

§4.02 THE ROLE OF BRANDS IN ANTI-COUNTERFEITING

For a foreign brand owner, manufacturing and selling consumer products or luxury products[263] in China, the conception and implementation of an anti-counterfeiting strategy should be founded on a comprehensive and intercompany IP management process, whereby a multiplicity of internal and external factors are considered, evaluated and synthesized in a trademark exploitation model functionally adapted to the company's business goals. With respect to brand protection, this translates first of all into the process of identification of how a brand works in the Chinese market, how it is understood and appreciated by the consumers in and outside China, how it is understood and unlawfully exploited by counterfeiters and competitors, how it is protected by the local law and how the deriving IP rights can be concretely exploited (enforcement being one form of exploitation) with the ultimate goal of using IP exploitation to support and realize the company business strategy.

One first factor which a brand owner should consider when determining an anti-counterfeiting strategy is the relation between the brand and the related products, and how the brand influences the behavior of consumers and the selling of these products. Although all consumer products rely on strong brands, the latter will have a different degree of importance in the consumer's decision to buy a certain product. This

263. There is no legal definition of luxury products. A legal term and definition with a proximity to luxury brands may be that of "well-known" trademarks. However, a luxury brand and product may not necessarily be related to a well-known trademark. For a definition in marketing terminology refers to Wiedmann, Hennigs, Siebels, Measuring Consumers' Luxury Value Perception: A Cross-Cultural Framework, Vol. 2007, No. 7, Academy of Marketing Science Review, http://www.amsreview.org/Articles/wiedmann07-2007.pdf (2007).

will in turn affect how those same branded products will be counterfeited and the degree of awareness a consumer has of their counterfeited nature when buying them. Online shopping further blurs the boundaries between fake and genuine products, increasing the safety risks fakes pose for consumers. Through this process of evaluation, the brand owner will acquire the information he needs to decide in which way he can legally protect his brand and its related products in China from counterfeiters.

While a brand may be the only value a consumer is after when buying fashion or accessories, this may not be the same when purchasing pharmaceuticals, cosmetic products, a high-tech home appliance or spare parts for a car. For pharmaceuticals and industrial products, additional concurring factors aside from the brand dilution and the erosion of the product's outer design may come into consideration.[264] Understanding the function of the brand and the relevant IP rights with respect to the underlying goods as well as their market, will assist brand owners in conceiving and implementing effective brand protection strategies in China.

Brands, and luxury brands in particular, confer to their goods a symbolic value, and it is this symbolic value that consumers seek in many cases.[265] The possession of a branded bag or a luxury car confers to the owner a "privileged" social status. However, the purchasing behavior and priorities of consumers vary depending on whether they are buying a car's spare parts, an electronic gadget or a branded leather bag. Correspondingly, the behavior of the counterfeiters varies as well. Counterfeiters act and perceive themselves as businessmen and to a certain extent they will act and think according to the same market rules of the brand owners.[266] For instance, while part of counterfeit luxury fashion products (e.g., most of those sold on street market) are purchased by people who understand that they are buying the fake version of a product they often cannot afford to buy, fake spare parts of a car instead are sold to people who already bought the original wholesome product. In the case of fake fashion items, consumers are often fully aware they are purchasing and using a fake product,[267]

264. In particular, fake pharmaceuticals, as well as fake car spare parts will directly or indirectly threaten the health of their users with all related legal risks such as civil and criminal liabilities, as well as administrative investigations and recalls, until the brand owner proves the incriminated products are not his own. For examples in the pharmaceutical industry, we refer to Bronshtein, Counterfeit Pharmaceuticals in China: Could Changes Bring Stronger Protection for Intellectual Property Rights and Human Health? Vol. 17, No. 2 Pacific Rim Law & Policy Journal Association, 439-466 (March 2008).

265. Delener, Nejdet, International Counterfeit Marketing: Success without Risk, Vol. 21, No. 1 Review of Business, (St. John's University March 2000) and Jessica Lin, Fake Stuff, (Ruthledge 2011).

266. *Ibid.* Delener, Nejdet: "A product counterfeiter looks for projects to pursue the same as MNEs, but the rules of the game are different. When a MNC does a feasibility study, it takes into account many cost factors, such as marketing and R&D. After the cost factors are analyzed, the potential profitability of a project can be assessed. Counterfeiters, on the other hand, are not constrained by overhead costs. They find established products and decide whether they can copy them at a minimal cost. Since there is no overhead other than production, human resources and transportation, counterfeiters can undercut the MNEs that spend millions on marketing and R&D." *See also* Organization for the Economic Cooperation and Development (OECD) *supra* n. 249 at 9.

267. Delener, Nejdet, *supra* n. 267: "Prestige, brand image and fashion are important to purchasers of premium brands. Buyers of counterfeit replicas also value image characteristics, and they are trying to gain the image benefits at a bargain price. Several researchers have suggested that

while in the case of industrial or household products consumers may often not be aware of it.[268] The facts above, in turn, influence the channel through which both fake and genuine goods are sold. Counterfeit of goods whose brand is the major reason and motivation for the purchase and for which there is an immediately recognizable difference between the price of the original and that of the fake, will be likely found in open street markets, while their original counterparts are to be found in high-street shops. In these cases, consumers will normally be aware or, at least, can become aware of this difference and can willingly decide where to go to buy the genuine or the fake product.[269] Industrial or household products, electronic or mechanical parts and components are always available at official shops. However, genuine parts also enter the market through other channels and can be available elsewhere (nonauthorized shops, wholesalers and shopping malls stores), thus mixing with fake ones in a nebulous entanglement. Furthermore, in the case of technical components and parts where the technical content is predominant compared to the design component, both the real and the fake products will not be traded directly among consumers. When consumers have a home appliance or a car repaired or maintained, they will not often directly see the parts and components that are changed during the technical service. Furthermore, many original industrial parts find their way into the market only through specific distribution channels operated by professionals and the same is true for their fake counterparts. This is the case for instance of certain "function-specific" parts for cars, bikes, yachts or private jets. In this case counterfeiting will not spread to open markets, but will likely be limited to targeted infiltrations of the official supply chain. These differences are important and must be weighted by the right holder against the background facts of an act of infringement, in order to determine the most effective enforcement measures.

Internet adds further complexities to such determinations. Unlike those sold on street market, fashion items sold in internet can deceive the buyer and affect his level of awareness. In fact online shops provide large amounts of fake information as well, with false statements about the products, by stealing copyrighted pictures, by manipulating prices and thus reduce margins of difference with the original ones. In such

individuals buying counterfeits have the tastes of a snob with low-price acceptability. Thus, price is a salient attribute for individuals choosing a counterfeit product Consumers who knowingly choose counterfeits see themselves as less well off financially and less confident than other consumers. If financial reasons motivate the purchase of counterfeits, these same reasons might be used to encourage consumers not to buy the counterfeits."

268. *Ibid.* Delener, Nejdet: "To further compound the problem, especially in the case of industrial products, consumers do not realize that they purchased a counterfeit They send the product back to the company whose 'name' is on it for a replacement. In the interest of customer service, the company may replace the part or the product. They might not publicly announce that they received a counterfeit for fear of bad publicity (...)." *See also* Organization for the Economic Cooperation and Development (OECD) *supra* n. 249 at 10.

269. Daniel C. K. Chow, *supra* n. 250, at 10: "In certain instances the consumer is aware that the goods he purchased are counterfeit. This tends to occur in cases of clothing, shoes, handbags and other accessories, where product quality is either not of major importance to the product, or where there are not significant differences between the quality of the counterfeit and the genuine product and it is the prestige associated with a certain trademark that the consumer wants...".

circumstances, a buyer may be seriously thinking to buy a second hand original or an outlet original good rather than a fake. The same applies to spare parts for different kinds of industrial and household products. This is alone a good reason for right holders to consider online protection as part of their anti-counterfeiting strategies. At the same time, brand owners must not give in to the temptation of investing huge amount of money in online shops take-downs alone, due to the fact that such actions alone will unlikely benefit the right holders in the mid and long terms for a number of obvious reasons. In spite of self-regulating provisions by the e-commerce platforms banning repeating infringers from their online market, infringers are clever enough to know that once taken down they can set up a new account very quickly and reappear online within hours from the take down action. Also, take-downs require product verification work and provision of some basic evidence of the infringement by the right holder, which in turn demands a certain time and economic effort which may not match up all the time to the effective benefit of such enforcement actions. Eventually, take-downs may just warn an infringer and allow him to improve its distribution structure and bring it out of reach of field enforcement for a longer time. It all comes down again to strategic considerations. There is little denial that a lot of the frenzy around online take-down programs is the result of the "partisan" interests of a group of private online businesses with their in-house proprietary software, which have an obvious interest in magnifying and emphasizing the importance of online-counterfeiting to win business and make money. Online anti-counterfeiting has indeed created a new business as counterfeiting created the business of IP investigative companies a couple of decades ago. It is therefore important to brand owners to be careful and not to buy in full the messages issued by such online anti-counterfeiting service providers. They do not have any magic potions or solutions. A strategic approach should then help right holders determining if and to what extent such take-down services are needed, and how to coordinate them with the parallel field work of other service providers like lawyers and investigators. Knowledge of how the brand works, also online, and how infringers behave, will help right holders find the right formula to combine online take-downs, filed enforcement and legal actions, so as to maximize their budget and achieve realistically set goals.

Another factor to consider when determining the best enforcement strategies is the degree of importance a brand has in the consumer choice of a product. In the perception of modern consumers worldwide, it is the brand that is the most important feature of a fashion item rather than the quality of the product itself. Luxury products such as fashion and accessories, jewels, watches etc. are characterized mostly by their forms and design. They are largely sold based on their outer appearance and look. In this case, the consumer will not be aware of the technical complexity behind the creation of such products. For such products, the added value for the consumer will be therefore represented mostly, and in many cases exclusively, by the brand and the product's outer design. If the brand becomes a value independent from the quality of the product, the result is that consumers will willingly buy counterfeits of these types of luxury products, because for them it will be more important to acquire the "symbolism" of the brand than the quality of the product itself. Considering that luxury products are meant to be sold to a "selected" group of people, counterfeiters simply go there to occupy an empty space in the fashion market.[270] This also leads to that apparent paradox that a brand is not famous until is counterfeited![271] It also explains why most foreign tourists coming to China, surely more aware and culturally prepared to recognize fakes than their Asians counterparts, will dedicate at least one day to scurrying around fake product markets to buy loads of branded items to bring back home.

The same is only partly true for other consumer goods in which not only the aesthetic element but also their underlying technical complexity is perceptible or openly visible to consumers. In this type of cases, the brand will be more intensely associated with the technical reliability and good performance of the product and not only with its aesthetic and symbolic value.[272] This point is important to understand both the purchasing behavior and the sale organization of such products as well as the corresponding behavior of their counterfeiters. In particular, this will reflect on the kind of products the counterfeiters will decide to target and those they will decide to exclude, and the sales channels they will select. For example, unlike designer fashion products, not all consumer products of a high technical complexity are counterfeit in mass. For example, although it is true that in China there have been attempts at copying the design of entire Mercedes-Benz or BMW vehicles by Chinese car manufacturers and some case have made it to court[273] or have created some media uproar,[274] these were not cases of counterfeiting strictly speaking. These were cases of design

270. In an interview to Bloomberg TV in May 2012 the CEO of Prada, Mr Fabrizio Bertelli stated: "Fake goods aren't totally bad at least it created jobs at some counterfeit factories. We don't want to be a brand that nobody wants to copy." *See*: http://lawoffashion.com/blog/story/05/26/2012/135 (2012).
271. Renee Richardson Gosline, Counterfeit Labels: Good For Luxury Brands?, Forbes Magazine http://www.forbes.com/2010/02/11/luxury-goods-counterfeit-fakes-chanel-gucci-cmo-network-renee-richardson-gosline.html (December 2012). The author of this Article agrees with the fact that brands in luxury products have a high symbolic value that transcends the quality of the products itself, to the point that middle-class ladies in the US, some of whom could hypothetically afford to buy original designer bags, prefer buying fakes because they will give them the brand without spending a lot of money, thus being willing to buying fakes at apparently respectable "purse parties."
272. To a certain extent, this could be true also for fashion items. By fashion products, the first impulse of a buyer will be that of buying the brand added value rather than the product quality. It may be in a later moment, after the fake products has started showing its poor quality, that the consumer becomes more aware of the "technical complexity" behind such types of products as well. However, the consumer of these products often knows and accepts the risk that he is investing money on a product with lower quality than the original one. This perception again seems to be relatable to a misperception of the technical complexity behind the manufacturing of fashion products.
273. Neoplan v. Zonda ([2006] Yi Zhong Min Chu Zi No. 12804) dated January 14, 2009 by Beijing First Intermediate People's court; Fiat v. Great Wall Motor ([2008] Ji Min San Zhong Zi No. 84) dated December 15, 2008 by Higher People's court of Hebei Province; Honda v. Shijiazhuang Shuanghuan ([2004] Yi Zhong Min Chu Zi No. 9897) dated September 16, 2009 by Beijing First Intermediate People's court.
274. Mercedes-Benz published statement that the "Nobel" manufactured by Shijiazhuang Shuanghuan is just a duplication of Mercedes-Benz Smart; GM claimed damages from Chery (one of biggest Chinese auto manufacturers) by proving Chery QQ pirates the exact design of GM Spark (however, the Chinese court granted compensation on basis of unfair competition); Apple also issued statements by claiming HTC and other electronic communication manufacturers pirate their designs.

patent infringements by Chinese competitors. Counterfeiting of entire cars or boats or airplanes, unlike sports shoes or designer bags, may be technically impossible for the counterfeiter. Counterfeit of whole cars, for instance, would require huge investments and manufacturing plants which are not available to counterfeiters often operating from underground, unregistered and technically unsuitable factories. Their production would be visible and easy to target and this contradicts the basic principle of counterfeiting ventures, their secrecy. In sum, there is no such thing as counterfeit of whole cars or whole airplanes at industrial scale as there is for fashion items or electronic products.

In the case of consumer goods with high and complex technological content, counterfeiting will occur only as to their spare parts or components. As already stated above, a person buying a car or motorbike will not only consider the "brand" added value, or its design and aesthetic elements, but also the product's mechanical reliability and safety. The same can be said for other types of products such as home appliances, yachts, private airplanes and, to a lesser extent, electronic communication devices. This is because of the inherent nature and usage of these types of products.

Among spare and replacement parts, a clear distinction must be drawn in order to understand the behavior of the counterfeiters. On one side, there are spare parts or components of cars, bikes, boats, plains or home appliances in which the aesthetic value prevails over the technical one. In those cases, the consumer's purchase will be motivated by this aesthetic value rather than by safety or performance considerations. Tire rims in cars are a typical example. Tire rims have a high volume market, because these are easily changeable car parts, with a strong impact on the overall visual effect of the vehicle. There is therefore a strong incentive for the counterfeiters to manufacture these products in large quantities for a continuous output, considering also the relatively smaller amount of technical knowledge required to copy tire rims. In this case, the buyer may be aware that the product is not genuine, but he is not concerned with safety because he perceives that this is not a safety-related part.[275] In this respect, the brand and the design or often the design alone, will constitute the added value of the product, as in the case of a pair of designer shoes or bags.

On the other hand, there are spare parts and technical components of industrial consumer products which have technical functions and relate to the proper performance of the product and the safety of its users, such as mechanical or electronic spare parts for all kinds of transportation means (cars, busses, motorbikes, bikes, airplanes, boats etc.), for home appliances, and even some parts of mobile phones and other media devices for consumers use (i.e., batteries and rechargers). In these cases, the buyer will not be driven to the purchase only by the "brand" value of the product, but also by performance and performance/price related values. The writer's experience with the counterfeiting of spare parts of industrial consumer products has shown that when buying function-related spare parts, consumers will indeed understand that the part they need to replace is indeed technically related to the performance of the

275. This Perception may be however wrong. For instance, tire rims are also a safety related part. Cracks in their alloy or plastic parts may lead also to break downs with possible consequences on the tire itself and the stability of the vehicle drive.

product. This understanding may in turn lead to different purchasing behavior when the consumer is given the choice between genuine and fake. In practice, the misperception of the technical function of a spare part can lead to different types of behavior. In some cases, the economic and monetary factor will prevail over technical considerations and saving money will be the major motivation for the consumer to consciously buy a fake part. In other cases, the uncertainty about the technical risks related to buying fake parts may push the same buyer to prefer safety and performance over saving money and then to purchase the more expensive genuine part.[276] Also, in this category of products, there are many cases in which a consumer believes that he is buying indeed a genuine product, while in reality the product is a counterfeit. This is often the case for spare parts or product components with middle to low technical content.

It can also be observed that for instance, counterfeiting of auto spare parts affects equally all car makers and OEM. Only the quantities of fake may be different, in that it will be proportional to the number of vehicles sold in a certain market. Also, price differences vary depending on the margin of profit of the infringer. For simpler replacement parts, fakes are generally much cheaper than the originals, given that the margin of the counterfeiter's profit is driven by quantities. For other more technically complex parts, the price difference may be lower due to the fact that the numbers of required fakes are not very high and are mostly produced upon specific orders. Generally, all car manufacturers and spare parts OEM are affected in a similar way by counterfeiting. Interestingly, in the fashion market, there may be relevant differences among different brand tiers. Counterfeiters appear more and more inclined to attack younger, emerging and not yet famous fashion brands because the latter are less likely to enforce due to budget constraints. Proportionally, counterfeiting can erode their emerging brand faster than tier-one world-famous fashion names. This should compel these minor fashion brands to be more active in the anti-counterfeiting arena, while at the same time savvier as to the use of resources that are comparably inferior to those of tier-one brands with decades of experience in the China brand protection arena.

276. The awareness concerning product quality is also present in the buyer of fashion products. The buyer knows that he is buying a product of likely inferior quality. By many it is even suggested that a buyer of fake products will likely change his behavior and will not buy fake anymore, and will rather develop a bond to the original and if affordable will next time buy the latter rather than the former. However, the difference remains that by fashion products, the issue of performance is in most cases outweighed by that of possessing the brand, because the risk of buying low quality products is offset by the fact or the perception of saving money. In sum, a consumer could likely spend two times EUR 30 to buy two fakes, but may never plan to spend EUR 300 only one time to buy the corresponding original. Again, many of those who buy fake designer bags are unlikely able to buy the original ones, while by luxury industrial products the problem of counterfeit does not directly concern the product when purchased but its components and spare parts once these are needed for replacement. This makes counterfeiting a more serious economic threat to this second group of cases by being likely to cause more direct economic damages. An example: If you buy a fake designer bag and its handle breaks down after a few days, you will not go to the official shop to claim a warranty. You will maybe decide to buy another fake one. However, if a fake spark plug causes the luxury car to go on fire, the manufacturer will surely have to face a warranty claim or a product quality/liability claim and will have to decide whether to accept it or not without often knowing that the replaced spark plug was a fake part not covered by warranty.

The correct understanding of these distinctions will be most helpful to the brand owner when confronted with the task of setting up a strategy to fight back counterfeiting in China. However, this is not the only set of information a brand owner should possess in order to conceive and implement suitable and effective brand protection strategies in China. Once awareness of these factors is acquired, they will have to be considered in light of other important factors specific to the Chinese market and legal system, before coming to the final decision as to which IP rights to acquire and enforce to maximize brand protection.

Formerly, traditional counterfeiting was directed to exports towards Europe and the US. Driven by the rapid and steady growth of an inland market, due also to the economic crisis in the Western hemisphere, counterfeit products have now found their way into China, impacting for the first time Chinese brands as well. Protecting a brand against counterfeiting coming from China requires foreign brand owners to understand the continuously changing economic, social and technological landscape of China. At the same time, brand owners must develop enforcement strategies with the aim of maximizing the economic value of their trademark assets in support of the company's overall business strategy.

In sum, brand owners are well advised to acquire and analyze field experience as to how counterfeiters operate in the same market environment, using the conceptual methodology discussed above.

§4.03 COMMON TRAITS TO COUNTERFEITING ORGANIZATIONS IN CHINA

This topic has already been treated in some depth in Chapter 2. In this section, we will have a brief recap and add some additional notes, especially in relation to online counterfeiting.

Although the demand and supply of counterfeiting goods varies among different types of products, there are common structural traits characterizing the organization of counterfeiting enterprises in China, i.e., manufacturing and warehousing are mostly conducted under cover of secrecy, while trading is conducted in the open. Counterfeiters can generally be distinguished by the financial and organizational forces that support and feed them. At one end of the spectrum are the individuals or small-scale counterfeiting ventures. These can be either legitimate businesses alternating legal to illegal manufacturing, traders, and small underground workshops. These entities may conceive and implement their own counterfeiting business independently or may decide to serve as one of the many manufacturing, warehousing or trading rings in a broader counterfeiting chain. In this latter case, these smaller counterfeiting units will often operate without knowing or having direct contact with the masterminds of the leading syndicate.

Distinct from these small-time infringers are counterfeiting organizations and syndicates. This type of infringers is economically supported and organized by financially capable entities and individuals which use a complex network of businesses to run their large-scale counterfeiting ventures, some as underground operations, others as legitimately registered companies. The financial engines behind such counterfeiting organizations do not normally involve in any direct manner any of the material activities required for running a counterfeiting business. They will create new structures or bring together existing ones which then take over the functions of manufacturing, labeling, trading, distributing, selling etc., often separately or unaware one of the identity and location of the others. The result is that traders, including online e-shops, are the last ring of this chain and often do not really know who has manufactured the products they are offering for sales. In this way, a separate and extemporary intervention on any of the external manifestations of the infringing venture (taking down a bunch of domain names, raiding a retailer, or even a factory outside a larger and more complex operation) will not be sufficient to take down the whole organization, as each of these units are not fully integrated in and directly related to the masterminds of the counterfeiting ring and can be therefore replaced by others in short time. Actions against single targets should ideally be coordinated within a broader plan in which enforcement actions are not just an isolated episode but a step in a broader investigation and enforcement action. The role of each target should be carefully considered, as well as the type of brands and products he is faking and the way he is faking them, as described in the preceding paragraph. A raid action even against a "small fish" trader, may be a critical step if the goal is for instance to press the weaker link to give away information on the stronger one which gives him instructions. It will depend on the outcome of the investigations, the strategic evaluation of the collected facts and the investigative instinct of the right holder and his consultants whether such a target is indeed weak and can provide the desired information for escalating the investigations and the enforcement against heavier targets in the organization ring. In the same way, a right holder may decide to suspend enforcing by an administrative or police raid of a large target such as a wholesaler's warehouse with a lot of fake products in store, if making business with that target instead of raiding it immediately, may be a good way to uncover the related factories. Such an approach is not cheap, but it is also the only one that makes economic sense in the long term, because spending even little money in isolated or uncoordinated enforcement actions is a much worse way to invest a right holder's budget.

Another group of counterfeiters includes OEMs or employees of OEMs without knowledge of their upper management. In order to maximize profits they may decide to subcontract the manufacturing of parts and components to illegal ventures. This poses an obvious and direct threat to the brand owner's supply system, as often substandard parts are officially sold and assembled as if they were made by the officially contracted OEM. This is a risky group of infringers and requires special attention and continuous undercover checks of their activities by the foreign principal. Overproduction is but the most evident form of infringement by these companies. The market will then see products which are materially identical to the originals (because made by the same official OEM), bearing the same brand but sold at a lower price. They damage the right holder in that their overproductions drive down the price of the originals as well and cause a shrinking of the right holder's margin of profit. Another problem may be that OEMs subcontract the production of some parts components they are supposed to make to unauthorized third parties. The safety implications of such illicit action (normally in breach of the supply agreements) are very severe, if we imagine that a subcontractor, outside the quality control system of the brand owner may produce substandard parts that will be sold as legitimate parts in the market by the brand owner who receives them from his OEM in force of their normal contractual obligations. A most famous such case was the one involving a Chinese OEM of Aston Martin, which had illegally subcontracted the manufacturing of some parts components to an unauthorized factory and had allowed the impression on those parts of the trademark of the official supplier of the part, DuPont in this case.[277] Lastly, OEM may produce goods identical to those of the principal but without using the trademark. The quality of these products and their lower prices will in most cases constitute a breach of the supply agreement and in most cases a violation of the principal's design rights or copyrights. It is surprising to hear important figures such as Alibaba's Mr Ma justifying and even praising these behaviors, especially when he is at the helm of an IP relevant company such as Alibaba.[278]

Resources should be allocated by the brand owner in uncovering, punishing and thus deterring syndicates from targeting the right holder's brand. Such syndicates are often related to criminal organizations or to local economic potentates with strong political relations at local level.

Eventually, it is noted that each counterfeiter puts his personal life and safety in danger and, therefore, has not only a high economic interest in the venture, but also put his personal freedom at stake. This explains why often thugs and gangster types are involved in counterfeiting operations. It is evident that these psychological and sociological factors cannot be underestimated when conceiving and implementing a brand protection strategy in China. A successful anti-counterfeiting strategy must counterbalance these human factors by having the brand owner put together a team of high profile and motivated workers who can emotionally engage in what can be defined without doubt, as an intense psychological warfare.[279] Again, for more details on this point we refer to the more detailed descriptions in Chapter 2.

Knowledge of these common traits of the counterfeiting organizations and a human understanding of the infringer's motivating factors will surely be of help to the brand owner when deciding the most appropriate enforcement strategy.

§4.04 ONLINE COUNTERFEITING: A NEW FACE FOR AN OLD PROBLEM

In the last few years, online counterfeiting has taken center stage. Once were the street markets to fill the news, with famous cases such as the administrative raids of the

---

277. *Supra* n. 244.
278. During a speech at his Alibaba's HQ in Hangzhou, China, Mr Ma was quoted as stating that "The problem is the fake products today are of better quality and better price than the real names. They are exactly the [same] factories, exactly the same raw materials but they do not use the names ...". For reference, *see* http://www.independent.co.uk/news/business/news/alibaba-chief-jack-ma-says-fakes-are-better-quality-than-authentic-luxury-goods-a7083236.html (June 2016).
279. *Supra* n. 47.

Beijing Ya Shao and Silk Road markets.[280] Nowadays it is Mr Ma and his Alibaba group that are the center of legal and political battles for the protection of IP rights. In this section, legal notions concerning the legal frame for the protection of trademark rights in the internet in China will be introduced along with some reflections and strategic tips for more efficient enforcement approaches to this phenomenon.

[A] The Dangers and Risks Posed by Online Counterfeiting

After conquering Western countries as a quicker, more effective and convenient way of shopping, e-commerce has landed in China where it is undergoing an overwhelming development. Indeed, thanks to the continuing improvements in online credibility, payment services, express delivery and to the efforts promoted by the 12th Five-Year Plan aimed at increasing the contribution of e-commerce to the national economy,[281] e-commerce is definitely becoming a key-player in enabling more and more transactions and purchases of goods to happen in the Chinese market. However, the growth of e-commerce is mirrored by a parallel growth in counterfeiting activities on-line: in fact, along with it comes a renewed and sophisticated way for counterfeiters to enlarge their businesses. From small shops selling fake goods in local markets to well-organized and branched companies carrying on counterfeiting activities worldwide: these are the new actors who distribute counterfeit goods through all the main online retailers despite the various provisions that, in China like in other countries, follow one another in the attempt to crack down one of the most problematic issues affecting fair trade. A recent example is given by the company Xiang Peng Heng.[282] Active on many online retailer markets, from JuMei to Jingdong, from Amazon to Gome online, this company would provide the Chinese market with counterfeit luxury goods, claimed to originate from overseas famous brands, like Armani, Burberry, Prada and others, by forging authenticity statements, making fake goods available online at quite low prices and pretending to offer after-sale customers service.

The referred case may be regarded as a piece of evidence showing the intensified dangers online counterfeiting can cause. In fact, counterfeiters may now be able to access a far wider market being their goods purchasable by any consumer using the internet and clicking the relevant link, which would both expose consumers to frequent risks of coming across poor-quality products, and exacerbate the violation of the rights of the actual owners of brands. Moreover, it would enhance to problem of successfully identifying counterfeiters, who could have their headquarters and factories scattered anywhere and whose localization would be thus more difficult to determine. Therefore, the Xiang Peng Heng case cannot but invite to reflect on the available means and

280. For references to the Silk Market case in Beijing in 2005, *see* http://yaleglobal.yale.edu/content/european-luxury-brands-challenge-chinese-pirates (2005).

281. Yu Hong, Reading the Twelfth Five-Year Plan: China's Communication-Driven Mode of Economic Restructuring, Vol. 5, International Journal of Communication, 1045-1057, 1047 (University of Southern California 2011).

282. Frank Tong, A Chinese E-Retailer Steps UP its Fight against the Sale of Counterfeit Goods, https://www.internetretailer.com/2014/12/19/chinese-e-retailer-steps-its-fight-against-counterfeits (December 2014).

the desirable strategies to resort to in order to react to the known, much discussed, but still present and persistent phenomenon of counterfeiting.

Counterfeiting immediately recalls violations of the trademark rights of brand owners. However, brand owners are not the only ones affected by counterfeiting, which, indeed, impairs also the interests of consumers and, with specific regards to online counterfeiting, of online retailers themselves.

Brand owners are the direct victims of the commerce of fake goods. Indeed, when counterfeit products are made to circulate in the market, the rights of brand owners to exclusively exploit the reputation of their brands and the gained loyalty of consumers are violated. This would not only limit the opportunities of right holders to expand and increase their businesses, but it would possibly affect their reputation as well, being, usually, fake goods of a lower and poorer quality. Consequently, not only sales of the original and actual goods may diminish, but also rightful owners might be exposed to lawsuits because of products' malfunctioning.

Although at first sight fake products could appear tempting and attractive especially since they tend to be sold at lower and thus more affordable prices, in the long run counterfeit goods may damage consumers. And in fact, low-price items generally correspond to poor-quality products, which may not simply mean that the purchased good would last for only a short period of time and then perish, but could also lead to dangers suffered from deficiencies in its manufacturing. In this regard, consumers would be certainly interested in making sure that the product they purchase is concretely the desired one.

Notwithstanding the rumors about online retailers taking advantage of and profiting from sales of fake goods on their platforms, counterfeiting is, on the contrary, to be regarded as a practice negatively impacting on their business. In fact, on the one hand, online service providers are to respect legal obligations with regards to the need to monitor sellers accessing their platforms and to the related need to remove any identified counterfeiter. Consequently, online retailers could be held liable were they found not to have successfully complied with the said rules and, hence, may have to respond to complaints and lawsuits both of brand owners (for not respecting their IPRs), and of consumers (for not adequately verifying the quality of the goods made available). On the other hand, online retailers would also want to fight counterfeiters for the obvious reason that being considered a "hub" of infringers would impair their ability to attract further clients, as well as investors and retail partners. Therefore, online retailers would be likely willing to contrast counterfeiters both for diminishing the risk of lawsuits, and for strengthening their attractiveness and thus expanding their business. This is also the reason for many e-commerce platforms in China for adopting internal regulations for the protection of IPRs in spite of lacking legal obligations and for their attempts at promoting their efforts to brand owners and consumers alike.

The above list of individuals who are deemed to suffer from the trade of fake goods aims at providing some evidence of the fact that many are the interests involved and to be protected when cases of counterfeiting occur. Opposing counterfeiting may not only mean protecting the private rights of brand owners, but it may also include ensuring an adequate protection of consumers, usually considered as the weaker party in commercial transactions, as well as providing solid and fair basis for the business of online retailers to develop and grow.

[B] Evolution of a Bad Relation: Alibaba versus The Brands

Owners have to protect their brands. This includes online and in international marketplaces available on the Web. As an example, Taobao is a Chinese language website for online shopping founded by Alibaba Group in 2003, which has become, by far, the largest e- commerce platform in the world, and thus a very appetizing market for counterfeiters. Similar to eBay, already in 2014, before the US IPO of its mother company Alibaba, Taobao had more than 127 million visitors daily, 306 million online shoppers in China alone and had a Consumer-to-Consumer (C2C) turnover of over USD 177 billion.[283] As a consequence, it has become the object of attack for foreign brand owners who are fighting an ongoing battle with counterfeiters and who have invested heavily in attempts to curb the illegal transactions of counterfeits on websites such as Taobao.

Strategies to tackle the challenges of online counterfeiting on e-commerce platforms have been at the center of heated disputes between brand owners and e-commerce giants such as the Alibaba group and its Chinese ramification, Taobao. The relation between these two groups representing apparently conflicting interests, have oscillated between direct confrontation and external political pressure, to forced cooperation and attempts at finding common grounds and processes to efficiently enable e-commerce platforms to take upon themselves more preventive IPR protection work. Each of these approaches to online counterfeiting is meritorious of a quick review and analysis.

[1] Confrontational Approach and Its Legal Basis

When the phenomenon of counterfeiting is analyzed from the perspective of either brand owners or consumers, the profile which may stand out more strongly is that of granting to the damaged subject an adequate compensation and to have the e-commerce platform held partly accountable for such acts of infringement. It thus follows that the provisions scattered in various laws and other regulatory acts in China could be seen as positively achieving this goal. Indeed, they provide brand owners and consumers with the theoretical possibility to claim their rights not only before the actual counterfeiters, who could be difficult to identify, but also against the online retailers whose platforms have been used by the counterfeiters.

According to Article 36 of China's Tort Law,[284] internet service providers may be held jointly and severally liable were they informed by the victim or were they already

283. http://venturebeat.com/2014/06/16/worlds-biggest-ecommerce-player-alibaba-reveals-sales-figures-in-new-ipo-filing/ (2014).
284. Article 36 Tort Law provides that: "A network user or network service provider who infringes upon the civil right or interest of another person through network shall assume the tort liability. Where a network user commits a tort through the network services, the victim of the tort shall

aware that a user would use their platform to infringe the civil rights or interests of another party, and were they to fail to take adequate remedial measures. The present provision is then further enriched by a series of regulations subsequently issued either by the Ministry of Commerce (i.e., MOFCOM Announcements 21 and 18), or by the State Administration of Industry and Commerce (i.e., SAIC Order 49), or yet by the China E-Commerce Association (i.e., OTPS Standards).[285] More lately, the 2014 Trademark Law has also codified the liability of third parties abetting and facilitating acts of trademark infringements by others and specifically of online commodity trading platforms providing space for counterfeiters.[286] The limit of the latter provision is that the right holder must prove the intention of the e-platform. In this respect, a claim based on the Tort Law may be more suitable in that negligence would be likely easier to prove than intention.

The above-mentioned rules would reiterate a few standards with which internet service providers, and thus online retailers, are to comply, standards which essentially aim at ensuring the greatest transparency of information of vendors operating through e-commerce platforms. Indeed, online retailers not only are required to implement a real name registration system and to authenticate the provided information for verification, but they are also deemed to actually examine the identity and status of online commodity vendors to check the legitimacy of their businesses as well as to establish an internal regulatory system to deal with complaints regarding IPRs infringements and counterfeiting. Were they unable to disclose complete contact information of vendors and were they not active in taking the necessary remedial measures, they could be held liable and thus they themselves may have to compensate the victims.

---

be entitled to notify the network service provider to take such necessary measures as deletion, block or disconnection. If, after being notified, the network service provider fails to take necessary measures in a timely manner, it shall be jointly and severally liable for any additional harm with the network user. Where a network service provider knows that a network user is infringing upon a civil right or interest of another person through its network services, and fails to take necessary measures, it shall be jointly and severally liable for any additional harm with the network user."

285. 第三方电子商务交易平台服务规范/Third Party E-commerce Transaction Platform Service Specification, MOFCOM Announcements 18 issued by the Ministry of Commerce, http://www.mofcom.gov.cn/aarticle/b/c/201104/20110407516456.html (July 2016). 网络商品交 易及有关服务行为管理暂行办法/Interim Management Measures on Online Commodity Trading and Relevant Service Behaviors, SAIC Order 49 issued by the State Administration of Industry and Commerce (link: http://www.gov.cn/gongbao/content/2010/content_1724815.htm). 网络交易服务平台服务规范/Standards for Online Transaction Platform Services/OTPS standards, http://www.100ec.cn/detail--4608966.html (July 2016).

286. Article 57(6) Trademark Law: "Any of the following constitutes an infringement of the exclusive right to use a registered trademark:...(6) Help any others to infringe the exclusive right to use its registered trademark with intention to provide convenience for infringing the exclusive right to use its registered trademark." More specifically, Article 75 of the Implementing Regulations to the Trademark Law provides that: "The provision of storage, transportation, mailing, or printing service, a concealment or business place, or an online commodity trading platform for the purpose of infringement upon another party's right to exclusively use a registered trademark shall be within the meaning of providing facilitation as mentioned in Article 57 (6) of the Trademark Law."

In light of the above, subjects damaged by counterfeiting could try to seek compensation by taking action against the online retailers whose platforms have been used for realizing the illegal activities. Similar actions could prove to be successful given also the stricter conditions that China's judicial practice appears to require in order to exempt internet service providers from liability. This is a kind of strategy brand owners had looked at quite favorably a few years ago: on the one hand, victims of counterfeiting would have a clear and known defendant (namely the online retailer), and their rights may not be frustrated by the impossibility of identifying and localizing the actual counterfeiter; on the other hand, also the execution of an obtained favorable decision may be more likely to happen since online retailers would be both more willing to comply with the judgment (so to be able to continue their business), and concretely able to pay the compensatory damages (possessing the needed resources) and to remove the infringing content (being the masters of the platforms).

However, online retailers' liability is still very disputable under Chinese law and many lawsuits filed by brand owners against e-commerce platforms have often resolved in watered settlements or even very soft judgments with low deterrence for the e-commerce traders, if not in utter defeat for the manufacturers. If the costs of such actions are added to the mix, such approach is rarely justifiable from an economic and strategic point of view.[287] Aside from the difficulty of proving the intent of the e-commerce platform as required by the Trademark Law or the negligence of the Tort Law, none of these laws provide effective remedies in case of victory that could be of real deterrence for further infringements.

As to prevention, as we shall see in the next paragraph, the law only requires e-commerce to adopt internal IPR protection systems without providing more detailed regulatory frame, thus leaving it up to the e-commerce platforms how to implement such obligation. The choice of the Chinese legislator can be explained by the fact that it cannot be realistic to impose an obligation to prevent infringement online on e-commerce platforms because they are not objectively in the position to determine when a post on their platform concerns fake products. The law seems to privilege a more cooperative model, where e-commerce implements internal IPR protection system focused on the removal of fakes from their platform, and brand owners provide basic evidence of an infringement to trigger a take-down of a suspicious e-shop from the platform.

Therefore, the confrontational approach characterized by filing civil lawsuits against e-commerce platforms has been abandoned by most brands, with few exceptions. Even those brands that have not given up on trying to held e-commerce legally liable of trademark infringer or for its abetting, are now trying their judicial chances outside China, especially against Alibaba since it went IPO in the US in 2014.[288]

287. E LAND v. Alibaba and DU Guo Fa ([2011]Hu Yi Zhong Min Wu (Zhi) Zhong Zi No. 40) (link: http://www.china.com.cn/guoqing/zwxx/2012-03/23/content_24970937.htm (July 2016) This is the first trademark infringement case in which Alibaba was ordered to bear joint trademark infringement liability.

288. Kering sued Alibaba in 2014 in the US accusing Alibaba of knowingly encourage, assist and profit from the sale of counterfeits on their online platforms. The lawsuit was withdrawn after out of court discussions among the parties. However, a few months later, in 2015, Kering sued

Even if there were case law in China imposing an obligation on Alibaba and Co. to prevent trademark infringement, the technical feasibility of such a legal obligation would remain unresolved: How could an e-commerce platform determine whether an e-shop is offering for sale a fake without the cooperation and help from the brand owners? Also, such direct approach against the e-commerce platforms appear to present another problematic challenge: how can it really prevent and affect the real counterfeiters? It is evident that it may not alone eradicate counterfeiting since sellers of fake goods might be able to continue their activity elsewhere or under different names on any of the myriads of platforms popping up every day in the World Wide Web.

[2] Cooperation and Self-Regulation: The Take-Down System

The relation between brands and e-commerce has then moved away from direct judicial confrontation to a more silent battle focused on forcing Alibaba and other e-commerce traders to adopt effective internal regulations to protect trademark rights. For instance, Alibaba and its subsidiary Taobao have been confronted by brands accusing the former of not implementing effective regulations to protect their IPs. Such systems centers on the adoption of an efficient procedure to manage the requests of right holders to take down e-shops offering for sale counterfeit products. Heart of any such procedure is the request by the e-commerce platform to the claimant to provide evidence of the counterfeit nature of the products offered for sale on their platform. It is on the issue of verification that most heated battles have been fought by the concerned parties. The first such system was implemented by Alibaba in 2008. This system went through a phase of trials and errors punctuated by some heated disputes with brand owners and critics in the western business community at large and the media.[289] Alibaba has thus continued improving its IP protection system through the introduction of Aliprotect and TaoProtect[290] in 2013 and their further improvement in 2015 with the introduction of an express procedure for the handling of take down

---

Alibaba again for the same legal grounds. This lawsuit was under mediation but it is still pending. For references to this latest case, *see*: http://money.cnn.com/2015/05/17/investing/alibaba-lawsuit-fakes/ and http://www.reuters.com/Article/us-alibaba-kering-counterfeit-lawsuit-idUSKCN0T121T20151113. Actually, this lawsuit was not focused on the take down system but on the failure of Alibaba to prevent counterfeiting (*See*: http://www.chinalawblog.com/2015/06/alibaba-takedowns-and-a-lawsuit.html).

289. *See* for example the news about a lawsuit in 2001 filed by three Swiss watch brands against Taobao in Beijing, http://www.china.org.cn/business/2011-07/22/content_23046304.htm (July 2011). Also *see* Carlos Tejada, U.S. Warns Alibaba Again About Selling Counterfeit Goods, WSJ, http://www.wsj.com/articles/u-s-warns-alibaba-again-about-selling-counterfeit-goods-1450406612, (December 2015).

290. Aliprotect and TaoProtect work online, and complaints are managed more efficiently than in the past. A point deduction system was also introduced to ensure that repeating offenders will be barred from using the platforms. *See*: the WIPO Advisory Committee Report for the Ninth Session of March 3-4, 2014 "Intellectual Property Protection Practices of Alibaba Group Under the Internet Platform-Based Business Model" prepared by Ni Liang, Senior Director, Security Department, Alibaba Group, China (WIPO/ACE/9/24).

requests of well-known brands.[291] Alibaba has also been actively cooperating with Chinese enforcement agencies in order to train their officials and improve enforcement of trademark rights in administrative actions related to online counterfeiting. This type of protection systems allows rights holders and brand owners to register all their trademarks, patents and copyrights in the platform. After proving the entitlement to the claimed trademark right, the right holder or his lawful agent can then file complaints against suspected infringing links in order to have them removed from the platform. In the Alibaba system for instance, if the infringing party does not respond to the complaint within three working days of receiving the complaint, Alibaba will delete the infringing link. The consequence for the infringer will be the prohibition of posting the same content on Alibaba again. On the other hand, if the infringing party files a cross-complaint, Alibaba will have to deal with this dispute within a few working days. In the author's experience, most counterfeiters will not even bother to file a defense, and will rather let the link be removed. This is for them not without consequences. Take downs come along with punishment in the form of prohibition to the same user to post in Alibaba if caught reiterating the infringement. It may have even some deeper personal consequences, such as a bad credit record with banks and the ability of single individuals to access credits and loans in the future.[292] Take-down action can be also initiated through specialized online take down service providers in force of a PoA from the right holder. Such private online anti-counterfeiting service providers have become a lucrative business. Many develop proprietary software to filter and identify counterfeiters on online platforms and provide take-down services. Larger brands operate their online anti-counterfeiting protection programs through such companies. SMEs may not have access to such services which are in most cases very expensive.

The fact that such systems have been improved has resulted in massive actions of removal. However, brands still make pressure on Alibaba and different lobbying groups, and institutions are seeking more dialogue and cooperation to further improve such systems. Among such projects, there are some known to the author that aim at providing Alibaba with sufficient technology and IT know-how from groups of brands so as to enable Alibaba itself to filter and prevent the posting of counterfeit offers for sale. This would be the ultimate frontier of the cooperation. In such a scheme, Alibaba would eventually take over more work and responsibility on the preventive side, thus even anticipating and making take-down procedures a secondary protection too. This is also what the Kering lawsuit against Alibaba in the US is dealing with. It remains to be seen if such lobbying efforts will succeed and in what measure. It is evident that for such a concept to work, brand owners will have to provide Alibaba with sufficient know-how. Also, monitoring and comanagement structures should be built to keep Alibaba under objective control so as to ensure that the system works. There are indeed reasons to be optimistic. However, even such approach has clear downsides which

291. *See* for a reference to these provisions: http://www.youripinsider.eu/alibaba-revises-taobao-ipr-enforcement-system/ and also: https://rule.alibaba.com/rule/detail/2049.htm.

292. Mr Shen Chang Yu (president of National Intellectual Property Bureau) stated that the National Intellectual Property Bureau will focus on establishing Intellectual Property Protection and include the infringement behaviors into the social credit records on April 9, 2016, http://www.sipo.gov.cn/wqyz/gndt/201604/t20160422_1264267.html (July 2016).

may prejudice its real efficacy. On one hand, brand owners may not want to share with Alibaba know-how without making sure that other brands will also access it, or Alibaba employees will misuse it. On the other hand, even if controls and cooperation systems where mixed Alibaba and brand teams work together to secure each other's backs are foreseeable, they will be very expensive. In front of such difficulties, solutions may result in compromises that may sacrifice the effective efficacy of anything coming out from such negotiating efforts.

More in general, the attitude of brands, especially luxury brands towards Alibaba is at least conflictual. Attempts at cooperation are often frustrated by the practical stance of Alibaba that seems to be unwilling to give in to this external pressure. If there had been opening to Alibaba by the international business community, such as the removal of the company from several lobby and governmental black lists in Europe and the US, these have been offset by very recent events at the time of writing this book. On May 2016, the International Anti-Counterfeiting Coalition (IACC) suspended the recent new member Alibaba, after the angered decision of some more traditional members like Tiffany, Gucci and Michael Kors to leave the coalition in protest to Alibaba's admission.[293] Furthermore, the recent statements of Alibaba Mr Ma sparked further controversy about the real will of Alibaba to tackle fakes. Mr Ma, after reaffirming the commitment of Alibaba against counterfeiting, could not help observing that "*The problem is that the fake products today, they make better quality, better prices than the real names (...) The exact factories, the exact same materials, but they do not use their names.*"[294] The game is still on.

[C] Finding Enforcement Strategies That Work

Aside from the strategic and political issues concerning the brand lobbying efforts to cooperate with Alibaba, it is important to consider whether the actual take-down systems and the use brands made of it are effective given the involved costs and allocated resources.

Hundreds of Taobao shops handling counterfeit goods are closed daily through the platform selfregulating IP protection system, but it is an apparently lost battle. Each time one link is shut down, more pop up to take over the business. The perception among IP owners is that monitoring these sites and shutting down their counterfeit shops is a necessary evil without having a clear perception of its real benefit. On one hand, refraining from taking down infringing e-shops will not provide any restraint to the trading of counterfeits online. Taking down however, costs a lot of money and only multinationals can afford it, and even when they can pay for it, the results seem disappointing. It is difficult for a brand owner to actually assess if any damage at all has been done to an infringer by taking down its online shop and the real impact and benefit of each take-down on the company's overall brand image. Frustration is the inevitable outcome together with resignation and a sense of inevitability. It begs the

293. http://www.vogue.co.uk/news/2016/05/16/iacc-suspends-alibaba-following-mass-objection.
294. http://www.bbc.com/news/world-asia-china-36535728.

question of whether the actions IP owners take with respect to shutting these operations down are really working in the long term to achieve their IP management goals.

For instance, the frustration of IP owners towards e-commerce like Alibaba and its Chinese company Taobao leads often to a misperception. Alibaba and Taobao have been often accused by foreign brands of illegal handling and intentionally profiting from counterfeit business. If this was true for the initial phase of the take down systems back in the period 2008 to 2012, it may no longer be that true today, when the take down process at Alibaba lasts in most cases just on few working days! In spite of these improvements and the increasing numbers of take downs, online counterfeiting seems unstoppable. Not only Alibaba is one of the e-commerce available worldwide but also in the Chinese market. Infringers can in fact use other platforms when one becomes too difficult to deal with. Although improvements in the take-down system are continuously made through cooperation work with foreign brands, the results are not as good as expected. Is therefore e-commerce to be solely blamed for such failure? Have brand concentrated their effort on the right legal tools to fight online counterfeiting? More specifically, are massive take-down programs with the related investment of large financial resources really the best way to move forward for foreign brands?

In order to answer this question, brand owners need to put online counterfeiting into context and in function of a larger, strategic view of anti-counterfeiting work. Most of the shops on e-commerce platforms are traders, who in turn are often individuals that are only thinly connected to the other parts of the infringement chain. Other times these individuals are used by criminal organization to net in the demand for fakes coming from the world market. More rarely, underground factories will offer fakes directly on online e-commerce platforms. Occasional infringers may actually do that even when they are a factory. In practice, e-commerce platforms are a huge worldwide market where products are offered on sale mostly by traders. From a business point of view, such traders are the same as those shops on the street, or in street markets. They are there to sell goods. There are of course very important differences, and from the point of view of counterfeiting, internet traders are more difficult to identify and to catch, and they can operate on a world scale, thus increasing the volumes of traded fakes, compared to localized street markets. However, they are mostly just traders. As we shall see below, large brands have since long reduced their investments in raiding street markets, shops and small distributors for a number of reasons. As we shall see later on in this chapter, a most important reason for this was the realization that administrative enforcement against shops and small targets was draining resources while it was not deterring infringers from repeating their illegal acts or abandoning their criminal intents. Thus resources were allocated to longer and more complex investigations targeting factories rather than traders, on actions in which traders were netted-in at a later stage while bringing down a whole criminal organization. With internet, it should not be any different. Traders in internet will not be deterred by a take-down. Investing on blind take-down actions will therefore have very low deterrence and as we know, will not stop the same traders to be online somewhere else or under a new identity in the same platform just few hours later. If considered under this light, take-downs, a necessary evil, should become more strategic and not just like a spray of bullets in the dark. Eventually, the investments on take-downs may shadow the other possibilities offered by the web to help specialists in investigating larger infringing networks.

In practice, shutting down e-shops may, at most, lead to a very temporary slowdown of infringing activities. The shutdown almost certainly will not be a deterrent to infringers to stop counterfeiting nor will it result in a direct hit at the core structure of the counterfeit organization. For instance, if we rank trademark enforcement activities based on the deterrent value they have on an infringing ring, shutting down a web-based trader shop does not rank among the first and most incisive actions. If the success and effectiveness of the online enforcement action is not realistically measured according to these factors, it is evident that a brand owner will be easily and quickly frustrated, in that increasing take down figures will not likely result in a corresponding effect on the infringing chain, while budgets are drained up!

Using an IP management program that consists of isolated enforcement activity will lead to frustration, misperceptions, and, ultimately, to ineffective enforcement and improper use of the possibilities offered by online e-commerce in the fight against counterfeiting. Websites such as Alibaba and Taobao should not be seen only as an enforcement target, but also as a very effective investigative tool. The availability of e-commerce to cooperate with brands and authorities should not be used only to shut down e-shops, but to collect more information, evidence of infringement and general intelligence collection. It can provide important information about counterfeiting, distribution channel control, and even act as a test for checking the popularity of certain brands over others, thus helping manage supply chain and marketing. Although specialized take down companies will claim to be also doing this intelligence work while taking down, the reality does not match their claims. Online anti-counterfeiting services will mostly focus on the web data and metadata they can collect from their take down activities. However, they will not conduct any field work, which is not only old but also the best way to dig out an infringement ring. If sites such as Taobao are seen more as an investigative tool and a source of information rather than as infringers, new brand protection strategies can be planned to exploit this tools. Information collected on these sites could be the perfect start to investigations aimed at finding not only the trader behind the e-shop, but also the factories and syndicate behind the trader.

Without denying the importance of take downs in the overall economy of anti-counterfeiting and without downplaying the importance of online anti-counterfeiting software and services, it is questionable if such services can take over the whole budget of a company for online anti-counterfeiting work and become the center of solid anti-counterfeiting strategies. Take-down strategies should be subjected to more selective parameters dictated by the overall company enforcement strategy. It is observed that there is still a serious lack of coordination between online anti-counterfeiting work and the enforcement fieldwork. Service providers of the brand acting on field investigations and enforcing the trademarks before the Chinese authorities have often no knowledge of what their online counterparts are doing. There is in particular little exchange of information. Even when an in-house filters such information, this may not have sufficient knowledge of China to make the right decisions as to what information to pass along to the relevant actors. Such coordination is of critical importance for the success of an anti-counterfeiting strategy in China.

When, for instance, traders handling high volumes of fakes are found, the IP holder should refrain from asking the site owner to delete that e-shop. Rather, the owner should subject the target to further investigation and IPR enforcement by raids or civil lawsuit. By routinely shutting down the page (and this is what normally happens), the brand owner deprives himself of the chance to hit a larger counterfeiting organization. In a comprehensive brand protection management strategy, such action would be an obvious mistake.

Generally, a brand should not target any given e-shop allegedly offering fakes for sale without distinction. The same brand would not do the same if it were any street shop. In this respect, there is no difference between the two of them. Also, investigating e-shops rather than taking them down immediately as they pop up on the online software monitoring radar does not mean they will never be taken down. After the investigation has uncovered the factories and other infringement rings related to the online trader, the right holder may include the take down of the trader online shop within the selected enforcement measures.

The decision of which types of e-shops shall be taken down immediately and which not, is a strategic decision and will be founded on the same Rules of Engagement presented in this book and applied so far to any strategic approach of trademark challenges in China. Parameters will have to be set up to preliminary investigate the targeted online shop, such as for instance the determination of what minimum quantities will no longer trigger a take-down, or if geographical information may stop a take-down and prompt deeper investigation (example if the shop is located near an already raided infringer!) and so on and so forth.

In conclusion, any online anti-counterfeiting strategy must strike a balance of interests among different necessities and must ultimately support the overall company's business strategy. A major coordination between service providers, the exchange of their different set of know-how and experience should be also an important goal for any in-house brand protection manager. Success will depend on the balance of the different needs and the coordination of the work of online and field teams. So far, most companies have not achieved either of those goals.

§4.05 ANTI-COUNTERFEITING ENFORCEMENT IN A COMPLEX ENVIRONMENT

Trademark enforcement against counterfeiters in China can be a very frustrating enterprise, both for the brand owners and for the professionals assisting them by sighting infringements and selecting the most effective enforcement strategy. It has also been frustrating for officials of the EU and US governments trying to pressurize China to take concrete and effective steps in implementing tighter and more efficient enforcement standards and increase administrative transparency and accountability. Both foreign firms and governments have since then been greatly baffled by the unique and complex structure of the Chinese administrative apparatus dealing with IPR enforcement. For government officials from abroad, this translated into the rather frustrating result that any major commitment and legislative changes that China undertook internationally, did not automatically translate into a contextual improvement of the situation on the field. This in turn has reduced foreign brand owners to a rather passive role in a game of whack-a-mole that does not automatically translate into successful results and it rarely justifies the money invested in it. In this section, the trademark administrative enforcement apparatus available to foreign brand owners will be introduced with the goal of providing foreign brands in particular, with an insight into how the trademark protection machines in China really works beyond the letter of the law.

As we already described in Chapter 2, enforcement of IPR in China can be both judicial and administrative. It is the right holder who can choose which way to go. The judicial enforcement system is normally used against competitors or in case of infringement by similar trademarks. The judicial enforcement system is in fact suitable when the major goal of the right holder is obtaining damage compensation. Also, a judicial injunction order of cessation of the infringement carries a heavy weight in that it can be forcefully enforced in case of repetition of the infringement and carries along additional criminal liabilities for the infringer who can be held in contempt of the court judgment in case he ignores the order of cessation of the infringement. For this reason, judicial enforcement before a People's Court is most suitable against lawfully registered legal entities, whose assets can be attacked and used to deter the counterpart from further infringements.

Typically, anti-counterfeiting enforcement in China takes the form of administrative enforcement. This is because administrative enforcement focuses on the swift cessation of the infringing activities rather than damage compensation. Administrative enforcement of trademark takes normally the form of a raid by administrative officials without prior notification to the infringer, within few days from the complaint filed by the right holder. These features of administrative enforcement explain why it is most suitable against fluid targets such as counterfeiters, who operate on a quick manufacture & deliver schedule, and are often underground operations with no legal registration or attackable assets.

This dual enforcement structure is quite peculiar to China and has no parallels in the enforcement systems in the US and the EU. Even more peculiar is then the structure of the IPR enforcement system at the administrative level and the major role "politics" and "local interests" play within the system affecting its decision-making processes. Before entering into a description of the concrete functioning of the administrative enforcement apparatus, the book will try to convey some impressions on the complexity of this system and the challenges that such complexity poses at local level in the concrete enforcement actions.

§4.06 A BRIEF INTRODUCTION TO THE CHINESE ENFORCEMENT APPARATUS AND OTHER RELEVANT PLAYERS

The administrative enforcement system of trademark and other IP rights in China is characterized by complex legal and political relations among different administrative agencies with overlapping functions at both a horizontal level. Furthermore, each agency presents peculiarities in its pyramidal structure. The result of such complexity is not lack of enforcement, because China has likely the highest volumes of trademark enforcement worldwide, but rather its lack of quality and concrete efficacy on reducing counterfeiting in the long term.[295]

[A] The Horizontal Structure of the Trademark Enforcement System in China

Enforcement of trademark rights in China is characterized by the overlapping and even competing jurisdiction among administrative agencies belonging to different Ministries, each moving according to their own political agenda and jealous of their prerogatives and privileges. Such fragmentation affects both the formation of clear IPR protection policies[296] and affects the concrete functioning of the enforcement apparatus, and be reflection, the strategies of foreign brand owners as well as their inability to control the concrete implementation of such strategies on the field for lack of consistency and legal predictability. Important academics have identified two factors in particular that can explain the existence of a hiatus between China's international commitments and promises and their concrete implementation: distribution of authorities and the structure of incentives.[297] The fragmentation of authorities both territorially and functionally is such that the formulation of policies and objectives in relation to trademark and more in general IPR protection, is fragmentary and the result of conflicting interests. In practice, many authorities of different administrations have their own trademark enforcement mandate from their hierarchical superior, thus

295. In his exceptionally documented book "Piracy and the State, The Politics of Intellectual Property in China" Dimitrov provides evidence to the statements above. According to Dimitrov, administrative IPR enforcement in China has so far failed to make an impact on counterfeiting because of its lack of quality, rather than lack of intervention by the State. However, western governments have failed to recognize this and continue to focus their political pressure on requesting more China to provide enforcement. It is evidently the result with a clear misconception and understanding about the political complexity of the government machinery in China. *See* Martin K. Dimitrov *supra* n. 22 at 33 ff.

296. Kenneth Liebenthal, Michel Oksenberg, Policy Making in China: Leaders, Structures and Processes, Princeton University Press (Princeton, 1988). The authors in this book correctly identify the existence of a hiatus between commitments to policies and promises at international level and their implementation and identify two important factors affecting this underachieving performance of the administrative bodies: distribution of authorities and the structure of incentives.

297. Kenneth Liebenthal, China's Governing System and its impact on Environmental Policy Implementation, 1st Series China Environmental Series, 3 (Wilson Center's Asia Program First Series, 1995), https://www.wilsoncenter.org/sites/default/files/CES%201%20Part%202.pdf (2012).

creating an issue of coordination among them. The possible conflicting policies and interests among different administration create different incentives that lead administrations to seek fulfillment of their partisan interests against the objective need of coordination. In practice, this can result in these authorities hand picking the cases they wish to enforce in fulfillment of their policies and agendas and in response to the interests of the involved enforcement body locally involved in each case.[298] A strong tradition of administrative discretion enhances the fragmentation and quality of administrative trademark enforcement. The result of all this is inefficiency. Although there are forms of control of such discretion and regulations to coordinate activities among different branches with overlapping functions these are of difficult implementation and find seldom concrete application. In the horizontal relation, a particular problem is posed by the ranking of the various administrative agencies. Only an agency with a leading relationship can issue binding orders to a subordinate agency. If the relation between two agencies is only of professional nature, then they cannot issue binding orders to each other.[299] Adding this to the fact that agencies compete for cases as they are for them a good source of income, this explains why we seldom encounter cases of interagency joint actions or cases in which an AIC or the Customs transfer a matter to the PSB in spite of existing regulations providing for such case transfer. By transferring the case to a parallel authority, an administrative agency will lose the fine imposable upon the infringer. Also, transfers require a lot of work and a very good relation among the two agencies at the specific local level. Given that they compete for the same provincial government funds and budgets, they tend to keep good cases in spite of the fact that the thresholds for criminal liability and the preconditions for transfer to the criminal authorities are met.

At a central level, the main agencies involved in the enforcement of trademarks are the State Administration for Industry and Commerce (SAIC), The Ministry of Public Security (PSB), the Administration of Quality, Supervision, Inspection and Quarantine (AQSIQ), the Chinese Customs, the State Food and Drug Administration, the Ministry of Health and the State Tobacco Monopoly Administration (STMA). State Intellectual Property Office (SIPO) has also a theoretical overseeing power over trademark enforcement; however, its function is theoretical due to the strong decentralization of trademark enforcement in the vertical sense. In practice, the most important authorities in the daily enforcement of trademark rights against counterfeiters are the territorial agencies at provincial level of three agencies: The PSB (Ministry of Public Security), the Administrations for Industry and Commerce (SAIC) and the Chinese Customs. The territorial agencies of AQSIQ also play some marginal role in the enforcement of trademark rights especially when aspects of consumer safety and substandard dangerous products are involved. All these players have with each other professional relations, and none can give order to the other or take leadership over the other (save in case of joint campaigns). Conflicting interests result in inefficient enforcement. In particular, an agency may decide to refuse a case because it will not

298. Martin K. Dimitrov, *supra* n. 22, at 33 ff.
299. For more details on the rank relationship among authorities, *see* Martin K. Dimitrov, *supra* n. 22, at 51 ff.

suite its current political agenda, another to refuse to transfer a case to a higher authority but without leadership relation for mere pecuniary interest, still another may decide not to take a case or to blow an enforcement action by betraying the case to the infringer in advance due to bribes or personal relations and common business interests with infringers at local level. Also, an agency may have clear conflict of interests in a case: shutting down shops in a city market may damage the tax revenues of the same administration derived from the shops in that same market. In some cases, the market is owned by the municipality that administers the budget of the enforcing agency and would lose income if rent-paying stalls are shut down. The result is that in spite of the enforcement plans and investigative efforts of the brand owners, the implementation of their strategies is subject to uncontrollable, although predictable factors, at least to a certain extent. A good strategic enforcement plan should ideally take into account not only such factors, but also the collection of knowledge of the current "political" trends in that certain jurisdiction and the current state of the relations among the relevant agencies, so that this information could be effectively exploited to maximize the investigative and enforcement efforts in a certain region. This is however very difficult, if not impossible.

[B] The Vertical Structure of the Enforcement Agencies and Their Exposure to Local Factors

Even more critical appears the impact of decentralization of trademark enforcement on the efficacy of administrative enforcement in China, or better its lack thereof. While the central government in Beijing has long stepped up its efforts in improving IP laws and its guiding policies, everyday trademark enforcement and anti-counterfeiting actions in China still passes through the hands of local enforcement authorities. These authorities are physically far from Beijing, and may often be inclined to serve local economic and political interests, rather than follow national policies and the rule of law. Trademark enforcement authorities, including local judges and trademark administrative enforcement officials, are in fact appointed by the local governments and municipalities and receive their budget and salaries from these local authorities. A local AIC will be more for instance inclined to follow the directives and policies of the superior local agency or government authority rather than those of its direct superiors in Beijing.[300]

Another effect of decentralization is the loosened control of the conducts of public officials at a very local level and the low risk for them of being investigated and incriminated for corruptions by appointed supervisory bodies.[301] Enforcement officials often hold interests in local economic activities which may directly or indirectly profit

300. Martin K. Dimitrov *supra* n. 22 at 46 ff.

301. Martin K. Dimitrov *supra* n. 22, at 44 ff. In 2000, only 385 officials of SAIC were investigated for corruption and accepting bribes, less than a third of 1% of the total number of the employees of SAIC at that time. Only seven were transferred to the judicial authorities for criminal prosecution.

of the "business" generated by counterfeiters,[302] in spite of the fact that the law prohibits it.[303] Counterfeiting is in fact a business which creates "satellite industries" of lawful nature that benefit the local economy and labor market.[304] Local governments, especially those at municipal and district level, are therefore reluctant to fully and consistently implement anti-counterfeiting policies for fear of damaging local economies and the labor market.[305] In fact, AIC at local levels license and receive income from license granting works for local businesses and have often little incentive in enforcing the trademark law against such business relations. The result is that enforcement may depend not so much on the policies and agenda of the central government in Beijing, but on that of the local governments, their leaders and most of all on the specific individuals in charge of the field work and their local relations. Again, all this takes the wind off the sails of any brand enforcement strategy, which has to cope with often unpredictable external factors rather than the simple rule of law. This whole system is therefore characterized by inefficiency and random enforcement at the discretion of single public officials. In this complex environment, it is indeed difficult for foreign trademark owners to decide which objectives are achievable and

302. Since 2006, Mr. Li, former Sanya AIC official opened a company called Qingdao Co., Ltd. to produce "Hainan Tequ" wine which is very similar to the name and packing of "Haikou Daqu" manufactured by a famous local company "Yedao Co., Ltd." in Hainan. Fore reference, *see* http://bbs.news.163.com/bbs/shishi/4108010.html (June 2015). Former secretary of Tangxia village committee Mr. Liao was charged with the crime of illegally protecting counterfeiters for being the shareholder of the counterfeit cement factory and facilitated the counterfeiting activities. For reference, *see* http://news.ifeng.com/gundong/detail_2012_11/23/19477183_0.shtml (June 2015). Also, the major of Fengjiang Town, Guangdong province committed crimes by providing place, equipment and protection for cigarette counterfeiters under the pretext of attracting investment. As a return, he obtained over CNY 80,000 (about USD 13,000) per months as dividend from the illicit profit of the counterfeiters. For reference, *see* http://finance.sina.com.cn/x/46941.html (June 2015).

303. It is regulated in Article 53. 14 of China Public Servants law that: "Public servants shall observe discipline and are not allowed to commit any of the following acts: ... 14) engaging or participating in profit-making activities, and concurrently holding a post in an enterprise or other profit-making organizations...." Therefore, as public officials, no AIC officials have the right to involve in profit-making activities in China, otherwise they will incur in administrative and criminal liabilities.

304. Daniel C. K. Chow, *supra* n. 250. Local authorities in charge of trademark enforcement (AIC) are also in charge of local commercial activities and business promotion and investments. AICs often invest consistent sums in the construction and decoration of buildings used then by local markets where also counterfeits will be sold. The same AICs will charge and collect lease and management fees from the same counterfeiters for their space in the market. It is evident that to a certain extent AICs may have economic stakes in the operation of these markets.

305. In October, 2012, Mr Deng, former leader of No. 2 economic inspection team of Dongguan city, Guangdong province, China, was sentenced to two years and a half imprisonment for illegally releasing over 3,000 fake Crocs shoes during the on-spot raids and reducing the penalty for counterfeiters after taking bribes. For reference, *see* 2015http://news.ifeng.com/gundong/detail_2012_10/09/18112194_0.shtml (June 2015). On June 28, 2012, former deputy director of Chengdong AIC bureau, Wenling city, Zhejiang province, Mr. REN Hong Bing, was sentenced to ten-year-imprisonment for protecting counterfeiters in Wenling city after taking bribes. For references, *see* http://www.jcrb.com/sykd/201207/t20120701_894449.html (June 2015). Motived by economic benefit (tax and other revenue), Wuling AIC (Shandong Province) refused to raid a local counterfeit cement factory even upon several requests of the infringed entities. For references, *see* http://bbs.city.tianya.cn/tianyacity/content/80/1/588733.shtml (June 2015).

which legal means are most suitable for reducing the impact of counterfeiting on their brands and business. As this was not enough, further uncertainty is provided by two more important players influencing the way anti-counterfeiting is done in China: investigators and their informants.

[C] The Important Role of Investigators and Informants[306]

Trademark enforcement in China is characterized by two major forms of actions. One is the enforcement provided by administrative bodies upon their own direct initiative. A typical example is the seizure of fakes designated for export by the Chinese Customs in force of their institutional IPR functions.[307] Another example are the "Campaign-style" actions launched by an administration, often under external pressure of foreign lobbies or governments and institutions, like the recent SAIC campaign to tackle online counterfeiting,[308] or the special action to protect Disney trademarks ahead of the opening of the Shanghai Disneyland in June 2016.[309] Several provinces take active role in issuing special campaigns plans for IPR enforcement[310] and several campaigns have been launched by the Chinese police in the past against specific forms of counterfeiting in the fashion, toy and automotive industry, some of them within the frame of Interpol, like in the case of "Operation Real."[311] This form of enforcement derives from the policy commitments China takes at international level and from the external pressures on China to comply with its international obligations. These are a typical modus operandi of the Chinese administrative bodies in charge of enforcement in China. These operations are born from carefully negotiated policies and compromises between the different powerhouses in the Chinese administrative systems. Brand owners have no direct control on them and are mere passive spectators or at most have played a triggering role during the long and tiring pressure activities by their foreign governments and industrial associations. Furthermore, only famous brands benefit of such operations upon which no direct control by brand owners is allowed.

306. The information provided here derives in the first place from the almost ten years of field experience of the author in his role of IP attorney and investigator in China. He is recognized by reputation one of the current actual anti-counterfeiting experts in China. He has worked together with many investigators and investigative companies and leads himself one. All remarks and comments and considerations as well as provided facts derive from his direct experience of the matter and on some of these topics he has already written publications, some of which can be found in the web.
307. Custom Law of the People's Republic of China, Promulgated by SCNPC on January 22, 1987, and revised on July 8, 2000, effective as of the same day, provides the general legislative frame for the IPR functions of the Chinese Customs. Their effective powers are then regulated in the in the Regulation of the People's Republic of China on the Customs Protection of Intellectual Property Rights in their version promulgated in 2010 which amended and supplemented the previous version of 2004. For a copy of all the Custom Laws and Regulations reference is made to the database of www.ipkey.org (July 2016).
308. http://www.trademarksandbrandsonline.com/news/china-to-launch-anti-counterfeiting-campaign-in-july-4393.
309. http://www.law360.com/articles/723705/disney-receives-special-trademark-protection-in-china (July 2016).
310. *See* a list of such actions in English at http://www.qbpc.org.cn/list.php?cid = 102.
311. http://www.interpol.org/ (July 2016).

However, on a daily basis, brands are more directly involved on enforcement that starts from sightings their private investigators and lawyers dig out from the field and bring up to the attention of the various territorial ramifications of the trademark enforcement administrative apparatus. Private detectives specialized in IP enforcement employ investigators that continuously cover certain geographic areas looking for enforcement targets, and/or use informants and locals in different areas nationwide from which they buy information about possible enforcement targets. In a way or another, these investigators pass the information they acquired from an informant or through one of their employees direct sighting to their clients or to any involved brand and ask them whether the latter wishes to proceed with an enforcement action. The investigators and the informants normally get paid only when the brand owner agrees to have them help him arrange and conduct an administrative enforcement raid. Brands have developed a strong dependency on private investigators and rely on them to supply them with cases to meet their internal goals and objectives. Few brand owners could afford to employ in-house investigative teams for fieldwork that could deliver hundreds if not thousands of cases nationwide. Compliance considerations play also a critical role. Anti-counterfeiting investigations are a kind job requiring continuous lobbying with local enforcement agencies. It is in the best interest of brand owners not to have their employees involved directly in dealings with public officials. This modus operandi of foreign brands shows the central role private investigators play in the anti-counterfeiting business.

Private investigators build relations with local authorities in certain regions and specialize normally on product fields like fashion, consumer household goods, automotive and so on, in certain geographic areas. The number of private investigators and investigative firms has swollen to three-digit figures all over China. Officially, private eyes cannot legally operate as such in China, in that their job should be in the exclusive jurisdiction of administrative authorities. From a legal point of view, they are incorporated as business intelligence and consulting companies. This alone is a remarkable feature and foretells many of the apparent contradiction of the anti-counterfeiting system in China. Investigators should not do what they do, trademark enforcement agencies know that investigators do it nonetheless and are happy to tolerate this and to work along with these investigators, and often establish a system of reciprocal incentives that may ultimately affect the transparency and honesty of the trademark administrative enforcement system in China. At the same time, administrative enforcement agencies will never take the initiative of investigating 24/7 infringements of all registered trademarks owners in China. For one, this is materially impossible due to the sheer number of registered trademarks; for another, they are used to operate on a "campaign" style only, when ordered by their superior authorities. Manpower is indeed an issue here. Aside from few exceptions in regions such as Guangdong, in most cases, AIC and police officers in charge of enforcement have also many other tasks at hand and few people to accomplish them all. This helps explaining why investigative agencies have prospered in China. They are needed to fill that gap between the written law and the reality, by taking over the daily investigative work to dig out infringers, thus freeing public authorities from this takes and leaving them only the raiding and punishment functions only.

In the last decades, a number of investigative firms, some established by foreign specialists that have worked for decades in China as IP detectives, have developed a remarkable amount of know-how in handling infringers and public officials in a professional and transparent way. However, there is no investigative company in China that could have a complete control over the relations and the actions of their field investigators. Even less control can be exercised over their network of independent informants. However, reputed investigative firms try at the best of their abilities to scan and filter the people they work with and reduce the risk of fake sightings and illicit activities on the ground by setting tight checks and having direct hand on dealing with informants and administrative enforcement agencies to the highest possible extent. These are what we can call "tier-one" investigative service providers. These tier-one providers are normally the firms with whom foreign brands work in China and to whom they delegate the collection and filtering of sightings from all possible sources. In this way, the brand has never a direct contact with such sources and can efficiently screen itself from compliance risks. At the same time, brands and first-tier investigators, develop strong professional relationships and mutual trust. This is the engine that provides the "sightings" and the targets for trademark enforcement actions. Good investigative firms will be conservative as to the screening and forwarding of sightings to their stable clients. At the same time, these investigative companies need to make money and need cases that end up in enforcement so that they can collect their fees from the clients. In this respect, they play an important role in shaping and implementing the anti-counterfeiting strategies of foreign brands. There is no doubt that they can influence the agenda of the right holder as to what sightings will be privileged and what not. The stronger the relation between a first-tier investigator and its client, the more efficient their cooperation will be to the mutual benefit of both parties.

At the other end of the spectrum are the vast majority of the local Chinese investigative firms and informants scattered all over China. Many readers may likely recollect e-mails they received from never heard before investigative companies informing them that they had sighted a target with alleged fakes of the addressee's brand and that they could help them raid this target.[312] Some of these may even be in

312. Many local Chinese investigators and law firms are literally inundating the mailboxes of foreign company in China soliciting business for obviously bogus sightings. The author is witnessing an ever-increasing number of these cases, which follow a typical identical pattern. A local Chinese firm or investigator select a certain type of product, go online in popular e-commerce websites and identify likely counterfeits of all major foreign brands for that kind of product (they will judge this by comparing the price offered with the official sales price abroad for that same product). They will the write a letter to each of them soliciting further investigations and possible raids. What is interesting, and here is the scum, these letters are phrased so that at first you might have the impression they have obtained the information through an investigator who had physically visited the proposed target. However, this fiction is evident to the eyes of an expert, and it is easy for what they do not say about the infringement, to understand that their only source was the e-commerce website. It is a scum which looks similar to another one running already for a few years here in China, concerning letters from domain name registrars to foreign brand owners informing them that there is a company asking them to register a domain with the trade name or trademark of the addressee, and that they give the addressee of the solicitation the possibility to registered that domain in advance of the third party company. The author know by experience that in almost all these cases there is actually no third company

good faith, but normally this is the case only if they uncovered the fakes of a certain brand while officially working on a case on behalf of another brand that happened to be infringed as well by that same target. All other sightings could be ignored. The author has had direct experience of such solicitations and after trying to dig out and double check the shared information, it was found that there was no target at all.

Most of these smaller localized operations, which we normally call informants, supply tier-one investigative firms and brands with sightings. Informants are often groups of individuals or local investigative companies normally specialized on a certain types of products in a certain geographic area. They are an important, if not the most important, source of sightings for tier-one investigators. Informants represent conflicting interests in the field of anti-counterfeiting: they want to find infringers and have them raided by the AIC or the police, while at the same time they are the last people that would want to see counterfeiting defeated, for obvious business reasons. They are in this sense a knife with two edges. Thanks to their intensive work on a certain area and fields of industry, they are able to develop relations with the local public officials. These relations are often ambiguous and entail acts that would be at best considered to be in breach of compliance regulations (dinners and gifts to public officials), and in many cases are conditioned by criminally relevant conducts, such as the request and offer of monetary bribes. Some of the foreign and Chinese brands, and surely all their local lawyers and investigators involved in trademark anti-counterfeiting work in China are aware or at least strongly suspect that the fees they pay to Chinese informants to conduct administrative or police trademark enforcement contain something more than a service fees. Often Chinese officials involved in the protection of trademark rights, at all level and in all places in China, will take over responsibility for an enforcement action only after having cashed in some "extras" or incentives. Hidden "docketing fees," dinners, cash etc., are commonly requested by officials before deciding whether to take on a case. If, after bringing a complaint to an AIC office, the officer in charge informs you that due to Women's day they are short of personnel to carry out the requested action, then you know they need incentives to make up for that shortage! If they tell you that they are very busy for the next many weeks, you need to help your file to get faster on top of their pile by providing them incentives. In other cases, the request is more direct. For small cases, they will "order" your informant or investigator to "invite" them to a dinner on the raids' eve (we are talking here of a USD 1,000 or more dinner bills!). In larger cases, especially criminal cases a nonwritten tariff is imposed as a clear precondition for the case acceptance. It may be dressed in many literal ways as docketing fee, reimbursement of costs or whatever they may want to call it, if they call it some way at all, but it remains an illegal request and a bribe. The law does not require in fact any payment of money or docketing fees for a right holder to obtain administrative enforcement of his trademark rights. Failure to meet such demands results in their indifference towards the claimed act of infringement. Informants are that class of professionals that link the right holders to the enforcement bodies and take direct care of meeting the illicit demands of the public officials. In

involved, and the letter just aims at pressing the addressee to take a quick decision to entrust the sender's registrar to apply for a domain.

practice, given their local relations, informants will want to manage the preraid discussions with the police or the AIC officials of a given territorial station. Brand owners and tier-one investigators may want therefore to take over that relation and dismiss the local informant. However, this poses for all a practical dilemma. The official will still expect to be incentivized. If the local guy is sent away from the case, then the right holder has only a clear alternative choice: accept and pay the bribes themselves or abandon the idea of enforcement in that situation. Having this informant figure in between help brands wash away their liabilities and keep enforcing no matter the real costs of it.

This is an evil dilemma that afflicts us today. Governments give pressure on China to change the laws and step up enforcement; China complies and enforcement is more achievable as ever, but at the same time, the system is such that a virus is now inoculated in it that makes it ineffective. By enforcing, we feed this virus and we cannot break this vicious cycle unless we stop suing the system we have been lobbying for so long to have in place.

This is but one of the evils foreign brands must face. It has also been reported in the international press that not only products and trademarks are faked in China, but fake sightings of infringing counterfeiters are on the rise as well. The existence of fake sightings maybe some shocking revelations to foreign companies, but is not surprising for tier-one investigators. They have to cope with such issue on a daily basis. A good investigator can recognize nongenuine sightings and will normally refuse them. If this is the case, none of them will become a raid and make history. There is really no big news in that. The issue takes a more worrisome tinge if we explore the reasons of fake sightings and fake raids. There have been rumors for years that some local investigative companies and informants are themselves the genesis of counterfeiting activities. There may be informants that go as far as making arrangements with counterfeiters to create "artificial" sightings and raids. The infringer will benefit by receiving a portion of the fee claimed by the informant from the brand owner and will be back in business the day after the raid. Although the author has no direct evidence of such a case, his knowledge of the field and the people that populate it, makes him believe that these rumors may be true.

However, the author has had direct experience of another reason for local investigators to bring up fake sightings or provide inaccurate sightings, i.e., by providing untrue figures about the quantities of sighted counterfeits. In the last years, especially in some fields of business as luxury, brand owners have increased the quantity thresholds for having a sighting approved for raid action. They have also capped their fees driving down the price/raid ratio. This has reflected on the "market" in many negative ways. Low-raid fees have opened the market to many unchecked service providers, with low-quality services. At the same time, the low fee does not motivate even good investigators to do serious work and forced them to uniform to a very low-quality service market standard. For this reason, brand moneys for years have been invested in a lot of low-quality and low-deterrence work. Recent economic crisis have then prompted brands to revise such polices and to concentrate their budget on more added value cases. This explains their tighter conditions for the approval of a sighting. The counterfeiters, as very reactive and intelligent businessmen, have understood this very quickly and have reacted by using extra caution in order not to be caught red handed with large quantities in store. They have adapted their trading, manufacturing and storing systems to work on low quantities to stay under the radar, avoid as much as possible criminal liability and even AIC enforcement by keeping production and storing to small quantities. In this situation, informants find themselves in a difficult situation. They will still be able to dig out targets, but often such targets will store only small quantities below the acceptance threshold set forth by the right holder! That is why informants often resort to fake sightings or to tampering sightings by providing false info to the tier-one investigator. Again, it will have to be this professional in the first place to bear the risk of such fake sightings. He will have to exercise caution and refuse sightings that cannot be verified objectively.

Another unpleasantness of which the author has been often witness, is the unfair behavior of most aggressive Chinese local investigating company that refrain from nothing to stop foreign professionals to take over their clients and bring new ideas into this asphyxiating field of business. Sabotaging the case of a competitor is an unfortunate reality that both tier-one investigators and brand owners must take into consideration when enforcing trademarks in China. The lack of controls and ethic thresholds, especially at the local government level, makes it difficult to bring corrupted officials or illegal practices by private professionals before the criminal justice, and most of these phenomena will remain hidden to public scrutiny. Everybody knows but nothing is done. Such illegal conducts on all sides are accepted as part of the way business is done in China. Speaking out directly, i.e., bringing officials or fraudulent competitors before a court would risk becoming a boomerang, in that once the case is over, no informant would want to work with that tier-one investigator or with a right holder for fear of being sued as well.

All the bad things described above are the daily reality of anti-counterfeiting in China and everybody accept them as they are for lack of better alternatives. Stopping anti-counterfeiting and reset the whole system is not a viable solution in the short term. Stopping enforcing trademarks as a form of "protest" to bring the Chinese government to take serious steps to tackle the issues of officials' corruptions, is practically impossible. It would only benefit the infringers, at least in the short term. Considering China's state of political, economic and legal development, this may be the best of the systems available given the present circumstances. It is not the book's task to address these issues. What is important for this book is to provide right holders with as accurate information as possible about the way anti-counterfeiting works in China so that can take these factors under consideration when planning their enforcement strategies.

§4.07 THE LEGISLATIVE FRAME: AVAILABLE ENFORCEMENT TOOLS AND PROCEDURES

In China, trademarks can be enforced before a civil court or by filing complaints with certain administrative bodies (including the Police in case the infringement fulfills the conditions for criminal liability). Damage compensation can be obtained only from a civil court. Administrative enforcement proceedings are faster and cheaper but have a lower deterring effect compared to civil judgments (unless the administrative enforcement turns into a police/criminal case). Also, it is possible for a right holder to file a civil lawsuit to claim damage compensation after an administrative or police enforcement.

[A] Administrative Enforcement

According to Article 60 of the 2014 Trademark Law in case of an infringement of his registered trademark rights, the trademark registrant or any interested party may ask the administrative authority for industry and commerce (AIC) to handle the matter. Such administrative enforcement is provided by the trademark division of the AIC of the place where the infringer is located or the infringement is taking place. Article 60 Trademark Law further provides that upon determining that trademark infringement has taken place, the administrative authority for industry and commerce shall order the infringer to cease its infringing activity immediately, confiscate and destroy the infringing goods, and any instruments mainly used to manufacture the infringing goods and the counterfeit registered trademark. This provision was lightly modified from the previous version by deleting the expression "*(...) tools exclusively used for (...)*"[313] and replacing it with "*(...) any instrument mainly used to (...).*" This is a welcomed change in that reduces the room for the infringer to escape confiscation of the manufacturing tools by alleging that they were used also for other purposes. A larger array of manufacturing tools could then be confiscated.[314] Tool confiscation and destruction is actually of great deterrence in that it destroys the investment of the infringer and cripples his ability to repeat infringement until and if such tools are replaced. Considering the costs of certain tools, such confiscation could be alone sufficient to stop the infringer for a long period, especially if it is part of a small organization. Overall, it can be more effective than administrative fines. As to the latter, the law provides that a fine up to five times the amount of the illicit earnings may be imposed if the amount of illegal earnings is greater than CNY 50,000 (USD 7,500). If there is no illicit business revenue, or the total amount of illicit business revenue is less than CNY 50,000, a fine up to CNY 250,000 (USD 37,500) may be imposed. Such fines are still very discretional, and a critical role is played by the concrete method for the determination of business revenue.[315] Eventually, if trademark infringement occurs more than two times within a period of five years or other serious circumstances, a severe punishment shall be given.

313. Article 53 of China of the old Trademark Law provides that: "(...) If the matter is handled by an administrative department for industry and commerce and the department determines that infringement was committed, it shall order an immediate cessation of such infringement and shall confiscate and destroy the infringing goods and tools specifically used to produce the infringing goods and to counterfeit the labels of registered trademarks (...)."
314. Under the previous edition of the Trademark Law, AIC practice required the applicant to prove that the manufacturing tools could exclusively be used for the manufacturing of the counterfeits. In practice, only the molds with the impression of the infringed trademark could be destroyed, while molds or other manufacturing tools would remain untouched because they could also manufacture other licit products of the infringer.
315. Article 78 Implementing Regulations of the Trademark Law.

In practice, the administrative enforcement works as follows: Upon sighting an actually infringing target, the right holder can file a complaint with the territorially competent AIC. He will have to provide a notarized and legalized PoA to his acting agent, and evidence of his trademark entitlement and of the infringement. Normally, the AIC will conduct a raid on the premises of the infringer without any warning within 48 to 72 hours from receiving the complaint. During the raid, the AIC officials will seize the infringing goods and the relevant manufacturing tools and issue a fine against the infringer according to the figures listed in Article 60 Trademark Law. The procedure starts and ends within a few days from the complaint. The fact that it is started unknown to the target, helps bringing the infringement to a quick stop. The downside of such action, is that AIC will normally issue very low fines. Unless machinery and manufacturing tools are seized and confiscated on the spot, the action will unlikely deter the infringer from further violating the right holder's trademark rights. The low deterrence of an AIC raid can be offset by filing a follow-up civil lawsuit to obtain damage compensation from a civil court, thus increasing the degree and intensity of the punishment and consequently the deterring effect of the original AIC raid. The main evidence in the civil case will be the AIC raid itself (i.e., no specific evidence acquisition through notarized purchase will be needed).

Such action is suitable only when a counterfeiting venture is caught infringing. If a target is suspected of having infringed a trademark right, but it is not actually infringing it, such form of enforcement cannot be used, until the target is caught in the act of infringing again. In sum, such enforcement tool can only be used if, on the day of our pretext visit, the informant or investigator sees infringing goods in the factory, shop or warehouse. Placing an order of purchase under pretext and using that order to start an administrative enforcement will constitute what the jurisprudence in China calls an act of entrapment. Such evidence would be usable in court but likely could be held void in the administrative enforcement. The admissibility of entrapment in civil and criminal cases are generally accepted, while it is still disputed in administrative enforcement.[316]

As mentioned earlier, there are several other administrations with overlapping enforcement and raiding powers over counterfeiters. A most significant competitor of the AIC is the AQSIQ. In compliance with the Product Quality and the Standardization Law, AQSIQ is authorized by the State Council of PRC to use its inspection and quarantine organization to verify and remove from the market substandard and shoddy products which endanger or may endanger the life and health of people. AQSIQ is the product quality watchdog in China and the principal authority for investigation and recall of defective products and the punishment of their manufacturers, sellers and distributors. Since 1998, AQSIQ was given trademark enforcement powers, although limited to goods during production and transportation phases.[317] This was because of the focus of AQSIQ on manufacturing quality and standards. These powers were extended beyond such limit 10 years later. According to the "Regulations on Main

316. Dun Mingyue, Entrapment Evidence for IP Protection: Admissible or Not?, No. 18, China IP Magazine, http://www.chinaipmagazine.com/en/journal-show.asp?id = 160 (2007).
317. Zhongyang zhengfu zuzhi jigou 1998, 406, 426.

Responsibility, Internal Unit and Staffing of Administration of Quality Supervision, Inspection and Quarantine," issued on August 12, 2008 by the State Counsel of the PRC, AQSIQ is now authorized to organize and coordinate the fight against counterfeits in China, by employing its statutory inspection and quarantine organization and powers. In particular, AQSIQ has the power to raid and seize defective and low-quality products and their manufacturing tools and the related raw materials. This raiding and seizure power is quite remarkable, especially because it includes expressly the destruction of manufacturing tools of the shoddy products. Now these enforcement powers have been extended to the seizure and destruction of counterfeit products with shoddy quality. In practice, the organization internal to AQSIQ and the low ranking of the offices tasked with anti-counterfeiting work influence the lower volumes of interventions of this administration in the daily raiding activities compared to AICs.

[B] Criminal Enforcement

The Criminal Law of the PRC provides that the use of an identical trademark on the same merchandise without permission of its registered owner is to be punished with imprisonment or criminal detention of less than three years, with a fine, or a separately imposed fine if the case is of a "serious nature." An infringement of a "very serious" nature shall be punished with imprisonment of over three years and less than seven years, and with a fine.[318] The law then provides also that knowingly selling merchandise under a faked trademark with a "relatively large sales volume" shall also be punished with imprisonment or criminal detention of less than three years, with a fine or a separately imposed fine and in cases involving a "very large sales volume," with imprisonment of more than three years but less than seven years, and with fine.[319] Eventually, the law provides that forging or manufacturing without authority or selling or manufacturing without authority other's registered trademarks or identifications shall, for cases of a serious nature, be punished with imprisonment or criminal detention, or restriction for less than three years, with a fine or a separately imposed fine; for cases of an especially serious nature, with imprisonment of over three years and less than seven years, and with a fine.[320] The Criminal Law does not specify the thresholds of criminal liability generally indicated as "serious nature," and "large volume."

A 2004 Interpretation of the SPC provides clarification about these thresholds (hereinafter referred to as the "2004 Interpretation").[321] As to the use of another person's registered trademark, the crime is of a "serious nature" when the illegal

318. Article 213 of Criminal Law of the PRC adopted by the Second Session of the Fifth National People's Congress on July 1, 1979 and amended by the Fifth Session of the Eighth National People's Congress on March 14, 1997.
319. Article 214 Criminal Law of the PRC.
320. Article 215 Criminal Law of the PRC.
321. The Supreme People's Court and the Supreme People's Procuratorate, "Interpretation of the Supreme People's Court and the Supreme People's Procuratorate on Some Issues of Law Application in Handling the Criminal Cases Involving Intellectual Property," Fashi No. 19 (2004), of December 8, 2004.

business value is over CNY 50,000 (USD 7,500), or the illegal income surpasses CNY 30,000 (USD 4,500), or when the counterfeiter infringes two or more registered trademarks at the same time with an illegal business value of over CNY 30,000 (USD 4,500) or an illegal income of over CNY 20,000 (USD 3,000). The same Interpretation provides that infringement by use of another's registered trademark "of a very serious nature" as prescribed in Article 213 of the Criminal Law, is fulfilled when the counterfeiter obtained an illegal business value of over CNY 250,000 (USD 37,500) or an illegal income of over CNY 150,000 (USD 22,500). A very "serious nature" is fulfilled also in case the infringer violates two or more trademarks at the same time with a business value of over CNY 150,000 (USD 22,500) or an illegal income of over 100,000 (USD 15,000).

As to the definition of sold products, the 2004 Interpretation provides that "Sales volume" as prescribed in Article 213 of the Criminal Code refers to the amount of gained earnings and due income from selling goods that bear counterfeit registered trademarks. Any of the following cases shall be deemed as "committed knowingly" as prescribed in Article 214 of the Criminal Code: (1) selling goods that bear modified, transposed or covered registered trademarks; (2) selling goods that bear a counterfeit registered trademark after being subjected to administrative penalty or civil liabilities for such an act; (3) counterfeiting, or modifying the authorization file of the registered trademark owner, or knowing such counterfeiting or modification; (4) other circumstances where the actor knows, or shall know the goods that he or she sells bear counterfeit registered trademarks.[322]

A trademark holder can directly petition a criminal judge to take up a serious case of trademark counterfeiting; however, this is not what happens normally. Trademark criminal procedures start usually when the police decide to get involved in stopping an act of infringement. As already explained, the police act if involved in a "campaign-style" operation, or if convinced to do so by a brand owner providing evidence of an infringement. In the latter case, the police will organize and conduct a raid action. The infringer(s) will be detained and the goods seized. The police may conduct further investigative activities and issue and execute arrest warrants against infringers who are still at large. If evidence of further infringing companies and individuals are found during the raid, additional actions may be carried out within few hours against other targets. The efficiency of the police rations in such cases, depend also from the ability of the investigator to guide the officers in their field activities, especially because the latter are not necessarily familiar with the products in question, their manufacturing and distribution systems etc. The police have the power to seize documents, telephones and computers along with the infringing goods. Once the investigation by the police is completed, the case will then be transferred to a magistrate for criminal prosecution. During this phase, the right holder may try to obtain copy of the police investigation file. Such file is very precious for brand owners on that a lot of intelligence is contained therein that could help support damage compensation claims, and ramifying investigations to other possibly related targets. Recent amendments in the

322. *Ibid.* Article 9.

law appear to provide only the lawyer of the infringers with a right to copy such files.[323] However, the Public Prosecutor and the criminal judge retain discretion as to whether allowing the right holder's attorney to obtain copy of such documents as well. Generally, investigative companies lack the legal knowledge and sensibility to properly assist their clients in this phase of the criminal enforcement. Most investigative service providers would stay on the sideline after the police raid, waiting for the case to end up in an indictment judgment. This is kind of a waste of resources for the brand owner if it is considered that a criminal raid is many times more expensive for a brand than an AIC raid. Often, even a criminal raid may be of low deterrence to an infringer, if the people that got arrested were just the hands of the illegal business. Spending money to get a couple of underdogs arrested is surely not worth the effort. That is why it is strongly recommended that brand owners, once they decide to go for a criminal enforcement, they should do it with full commitment throughout its three phases (raid, prosecution and criminal trial). This includes being very active with the public prosecutor, obtaining copy of his file and related intelligence. Obtaining such documents is most critical for many reasons: it helps identify leads to potential ramification of the enforcement plan; it may provide support for damage compensation claims in the trial phase; it helps mapping out a geographical area; and it may actually reveal that the case was not well investigated and that sources of evidence were left untouched. In this latter case, the brand owner could file requests to the prosecutor to send the case back to the police for further investigations.

Eventually, the case may end with a request of indictment and land on the docket of a criminal judge for the trial phase. Although the Criminal Procedure does not exclude the possibility for the "victims" of the crime to file a request for damage compensation, most criminal judges in China would raise obstacles to such an attempt and invite the right holder to file a separate civil lawsuit. A way to get damage compensation and even more intelligence and information about an organization, without filing a separate civil lawsuit, is that of negotiating a settlement with the infringers before their indictment with the mediation of the criminal court. In such case, the brand owner can leverage a good settlement by promising a letter of clemency to the court which would help reduce the jail terms. This is a proven method for obtaining some compensation while still keeping the infringers in jail or on parole. The deterrent will be a mix between jail/parole and money payment. It is evident that strategic considerations must be made before deciding for a settlement. If the infringer is an important mastermind that was running a large network, it may be better to keep him in jail as long as possible, unless the damage compensation is so large that it deprives his organization of the means of repeating infringement (i.e., transfer property of buildings and machinery, pays a lot of money provides intelligence etc.). Alternatively, the right holder may decide not to negotiate and to recover the damages from a

323. Article 34 of the Law of the People's Republic of China on Lawyers as revised in 2012 provides that: "Where the is mandated by the defendant, he/she may consult, excerpt and copy filed materials of the case from the date of the review by the People's Prosecutor." The previous provision of 2007 was more generic and left room to the lawyers of both parties to request and obtain full copy of the prosecution's file.

separate civil lawsuit. Although a more expensive alternative, it still remains the best options in certain serious criminal cases.

Overall, criminal enforcement is difficult to obtain for a number of reasons. The "political" reasons explained in the preceding paragraphs the related high costs and the high discretion of the PSB offices in deciding which case to take on and which not. Furthermore, infringers are aware of such "political" issues and are strategically prepared to adapt to these circumstances in order to reduce their exposure to criminal liability. Therefore, police raids are less frequent also because infringers carefully organize production and storage so as to avoid accumulating large quantities of counterfeit products in the same place for a long time. Even if a factory produces large quantities, it may organize production so that delivery is done continuously in small batches (often at night or after PSB office hours), so as to reduce the time window in which a large number of finished goods could be found in the factory and/or warehouse. Even the deterring effect of the criminal punishment is to a certain extent questionable. In practice, punishment for IP crimes is not as harsh in practice as it appears to be in the written law.[324] Rarely criminals really spend long time in prison. Local PSB officers my even actively seek to help infringers.[325] Nonetheless, there have been recent cases in which counterfeiters have been severely punished with unusually highs terms of imprisonment.[326] It remains to be seen whether the counterfeiters will indeed serve these terms fully and, more importantly, whether such decisions were dictated only by internal political reasons specific to that single court and judge, or whether they foretell a new judicial trend in China.[327]

324. Daniel C. K. Chow, Anti-Counterfeiting Strategies of Multi-National Companies in China: How a Flawed Approach Is Making Counterfeiting Worse, Vol. 41, No. 4, Georgetown Journal of International Law, 757-758 (2010). Also, the author has personal experience of cases in which the Police has tried to mediate between the brand owner and the investigated counterfeiter, in order to have the criminal proceedings dropped upon payment of a monetary compensation by the counterfeiters.

325. In October, 2012, Mr Deng, former leader of No. 2 economic inspection team of Dongguan city, Guangdong province, China, was sentenced to two years and a half imprisonment for illegally releasing over 3,000 fake Crocs shoes during the on-spot raids and reducing the penalty for counterfeiters after taking bribes, http://news.ifeng.com/gundong/detail_2012_10/09/18112194_0.shtml (2012).

326. Chinese and US authorities have collaborated for the first time to shut down a major counterfeiting operation in the province of Guangdong. The goods included knock-off handbags that appeared to be brands like Coach, Hermes and Louis Vuitton. Authorities arrested 73 people who were planning to distribute almost a million bags to the Middle East and the United States, http://www.globalpost.com/dispatch/news/regions/asia-pacific/china/121120/china-counterfeit-bags-illegal-crackdown (July 2016).

327. In August 2012, the He Yuan Intermediate People's Court in the southern province of Guangdong, China sentenced Xiao Zhenjiang to life in prison after uncovering USD 15.7 million worth in fake Hermes bags in his underground factory. His three accomplices were also convicted to seven to ten years in prison and fined the equivalent of USD 79,000 to USD 126,000. An element of interest in the Hermes case is the fact that the court criminal judgment has not been granted on trademark law but on product quality law. The court indicted the infringer for manufacturing and selling poor quality and substandard product, without mentioning clearly the existence of a trademark infringement. In other words, this case cannot be legally classified as a case of trademark counterfeit. This again appears to confirm the

[C] Custom Protection

Chinese Customs are empowered by the law to stop the import or export of counterfeit goods. The 2004 Regulations of the PRC on Customs Protection of Intellectual Property Rights (hereinafter the Customs Regulations), were enacted to implement the general principles on Custom IPR protection laid out by the China Customs Law and were revised in 2010.[328] Customs Regulations include trademarks among the protected IPR in relation to import and export of goods,[329] and enunciate the principle that the State prohibits the import and export of counterfeit goods.[330]

The holder of a registered trademark can apply for custom protection against counterfeits goods imported into or being exported outside China. At the same time, the law imposes an obligation of consignees of import goods and the consignors of export goods to declare in good faith the status of the trademark rights related to their goods and provide ownership documents or other titles when requested by the Customs.[331] This provision is particularly important because it may affect official OEMs and suppliers of original products on behalf of the right holder. The latter should make sure to record all his suppliers with China Customs in order to avoid their shipment to be blocked at customs with the latter inquiring about the title of the exporter. This can happen once a right holder has recorded its trademark rights with China Customs and the latter start stopping suspicious cargos.

The most innovative part of this provision was the introduction of the recordation system.[332] By recording their IP rights with the GAC, it triggers the possibility of the customs to enforce the recorded right without need of a starting complaint by the right holder. A trademark recordation at custom shall be valid for 10 years from the date recordation was granted by GAC. A recordation for customs protection of an IP right shall cease to be valid immediately where no application is presented for renewal of the recordation for customs protection of the IP right upon expiration of its term of validity, or where the IP right is no longer protected under laws or administrative regulations.[333] This is a most recommended step for a more efficient protection of trademark rights by China Customs especially regarding counterfeiting goods exiting China for abroad markets.

uniqueness of this case. There will not be therefore any guarantee that at the next raid, under similar circumstances as in the case under scrutiny, the authorities will arrive to the same outcome.

328. Regulations of the People's Republic of China on Custom Protection of Intellectual property Rights, adopted at the 30th Executive Meeting of the State Council on November 26, 2003, promulgated by Decree No. 395 of the State Council of the People's Republic of China on December 2, 2003 and effective as of March 1, 2004 and revised by State Council on March 24, 2010 and effective as of April 1, 2010 (*see* www.IPKey.org for the English translation of this provision). This regulation amended and superseded the preceding 1995 regulations.
329. *Ibid.* Article 2.
330. *Ibid.* Article 3.
331. *Ibid.* Article 5.
332. *Ibid.* Article 7.
333. *Ibid.* Article 10.

China Customs can react to a request of enforcement from the right holder,[334] or can also proceed without such a request when acting a cargo in entry or exit suspected of infringing a recorded trademark right and then notify the right holder.[335] In both cases, the right holder who wishes to maintain the legal effect of the seizure will have to deposit a monetary guarantee not exceeding or equivalent to the value of the goods to cover the possible compensation for the losses suffered by the consignee or consignor due to an improper request for enforcement, and the payment of the expenses of warehousing, maintenance and disposal of the goods incurred after being detained by the Customs. This payment must be effected within three days from the relevant Custom notification. Additional regulations by GAC provide right holders with the possibility of providing a general guarantee of a minimum amount of the equivalent of USD 35,000. In this way, they will not be subject to the three-day deadline and will ensure a smoother process. The corresponding amount shall be deducted from the security where the holder of the IP right makes a direct payment of the expenses of warehousing and maintenance to the warehousing entity.

Customs of China are very efficient and surely make an effort to block fakes meant for export to Europe and the US. However, in order for a brand owner to enjoy custom protection, i.e., activation of custom IP protection at the borders done ex officio by the Chinese custom authorities (ex officio means that the custom takes the initiative to seize without need for the brand owner to be active in finding fake goods shipping data), two important things are required.

Thanks to this recordation, Chinese Customs will automatically stop fakes of a brand in exit of China's ports, so as they can find them. For each container stopped, the custom will request the payment of a guarantee equal to the value of the retail seized goods (the value of the fakes of course) plus warehousing fees up to three months time from the date of seizure. Such amount can be paid on a case-by-case basis (within three working days from the seizure notice), or a deposit of a minimum of USD 35,000 is made through bank guarantee to the account of China customs. In this case, the guarantee will cover the fees till the guaranteed amount is exceeded. This option is normally recommended if custom protection is stepped up as part of a comprehensive enforcement strategy.

After the customs notify the right holder and the latter has made the required application and guarantee payments, the custom starts an investigation, calling upon the right holder to provide a formal verification of the nature of the goods and declare officially whether they are counterfeits. To this purpose, the right holder has the right to obtain information about the goods and even inspect them.[336] After the verification process and within 30 days from the initial detention, the Customs will have to make a decision of whether the goods are counterfeits or not. If yes, the goods will be kept in a special warehouse of the China Customs at the port of detention. At this time, the

334. *Ibid.* Articles 12-13.
335. *Ibid.* Article 16.
336. *Ibid.* Article 20.

right holder can also request the territorially competent civil court to issue an injunction or an order for evidence preservation concerning the seized goods.[337]

A detention is lifted if the Customs cannot determine through investigation that the suspected infringing goods under detention have infringed the IP rights within 50 working days from the date of the detention; where the consignee or consignor of the goods suspected of infringing a patent requests the Customs to release his goods after providing to the Customs a security equivalent to the value of such goods; where the Customs is convinced that the consignee or consignor possesses ample evidence proving that his goods have not infringed the right of the holder of the IP right.[338]

Chinese customs are limited in their efforts by the small numbers of their officials compared to the cargos leaving China, by the vastness of the Chinese borders and the large number of ports of exit. This explains why the number of custom seizures ex officio each year is low compared to the cargos that are not seized. In order for a right holder to increase the chances of more "ex officio" seizures, is to train customs. Trainings allow brand owners to make the custom aware of their brand and more reactive on the field. There are thousands of foreign brands recorded at Customs, but Customs work in practice on the few they are familiar with, which are those that are more visible to them because of the brands' efforts in creating a concrete connection with the customs of China. Overall, Custom seizures are useful in that the procedure does not necessarily require the continuous involvement of the right holder and its informants network to uncover suspected cargos. In theory, it is the China Customs that can do that. In practice, leaving the Customs alone in doing the job results in the marginal impact this kind of enforcement tool has on the overall enforcement strategy in China. Few brands, the most famous actually, can at most enjoy a certain benefit from this legal tool, and this does not come at a cheap price either, given the efforts they make to lobby and work along with the major ports authorities.

§4.08 STRATEGIC ADJUSTMENTS

Administrative enforcement of IP rights, and in particular, of trademark rights in China is based on a set of legal provisions scattered among different laws, empowering special administrative bodies to enforce IP rights through raids and seizures, *inaudita altera parte*. This has become the most common form of trademark enforcement in China against counterfeiters. It is rather inexpensive and is fast. Most of all, administrative trademark enforcement is carried out without prior notice to or knowledge of the infringer, which will then normally be caught when still infringing. The most common brand protection strategy adopted by foreign enterprises in China focuses on stemming the counterfeiting tide by intense administrative enforcement, i.e., hitting counterfeiters by having administrative, and to a lesser extent, criminal enforcement bodies raid their factories and warehouses, in order to seize counterfeits, destroy manufacturing tools and, in case of criminal procedures, have the counterfeiters

337. *Ibid.* Article 23.
338. *Ibid.* Article 24.

convicted and jailed. This type of enforcement is normally realized through the cooperation of brand owners with a plethora of investigators which provide free sightings of counterfeiting targets ready to be raided. As already pointed out, the massive increase of administrative trademark enforcement in its most common form described above, along with more cooperative enforcement authorities, appear not to have any lasting impact on counterfeiting in China. In spite of the intensive short-term administrative enforcement, the counterfeiting business is objectively on the rise. Some experts even suggest that short-term enforcement may be counterproductive and make the problem even worse.[339]

However, ignoring or tolerating counterfeiting while waiting for epochal political and economic changes which may not take place any time soon, would be an even more serious mistake for foreign brand owners, with incalculable negative consequences. A passive stance towards counterfeiting would result in quick dilution of their brands maybe to the benefit of more careful competitors, loss of profit, jobs, market share, unjustified warranty costs and exposure to civil and even criminal liabilities for those cases in which counterfeits have been the cause of damages to property and to people. Renouncing daily brand protection is not an option, especially now that China is not only the world's factory but is also becoming the world's market as well. In this context, enforcement of IP rights against counterfeiters is not at issue. At issue is instead the determination by the brand owner of the real economic and commercial reasons that can justify enforcement as an IP management tool instead of resorting to other alternative forms of economic protection. At issue is also the implementation of IP management strategy to help the brand owner to choose the most suitable rights to be enforced and the method of their enforcement in each case.

[A] Seized Quantities versus Deterrence

In order to determine what strategies are most effective for a brand owner, namely, which strategies maximize his allocated budget and minimize the risks while allowing a consistent exploitation of the protected trademark registration, certain conceptual issues should be taken into consideration.

Quantity of seized goods has been for long the measure of a successful enforcement. The result has been for brands to focus on enforcement activities that could generate large volumes of seized goods. AIC suited such strategy in that AIC raids could produce large volume of cases and therefore large aggregated figures at a lower cost. In this respect, enforcement was focused on any possible target ranging from large factories to small shops, to market sweeps to clean up street markets in given regions. The result is the one cited a few lines above: a massive step up of fieldwork at the AIC level. What were the results? As we already know, the results were not satisfactorily for brand owners. Even without mentioning that counterfeiting is more rampant than it was before and in spite of AIC stepping up its fieldwork, quantity is per se a rather difficult parameter to measure a successful enforcement strategy. In fact, a successful

339. Daniel C. K. Chow, *supra* n. 250.

strategy based on quantities should be ultimately defined as successful if the raided quantities are dropping to "zero." In sum, a successful enforcement strategy based on the parameter of seized quantities of infringing goods should be represented by a graph in which quantities follow at the beginning an ascending curve, the curve extension determined by how much a brand has been counterfeited (i.e., how popular was among counterfeiters). However, if the curve is steadily climbing up, even with minor flections, it is evident that something is wrong with that strategy and with the selection of quantity as the parameter for success. We recall here the First Rule of Engagement: Goal setting. If the goals are impossible by definition, a strategy will always fail.

Once it is clear that seized quantities cannot be the sole parameter for determining a strategy and its success, what other parameters can be then taken into consideration? Furthermore, once other parameters are taken into consideration, how can AIC enforcement fulfill them? If it does not fulfill them, what are alternative strategies that can claim a higher success rate?

Before addressing these questions, it is remarked that the success of a strategy based on administrative trademark enforcement in anti-counterfeiting cannot be measured in general terms and assume that it is applicable to all enterprises in China. A certain type of enforcement beneficial to a certain group of products, may not result to be necessary so for others. Earlier in the preceding paragraphs, the book has highlighted this point by making a generalized distinction between types of brands and products according to the intensity by which a brand influence the purchasing behavior of the relevant consumer group for each specific product, how they are sold in the market etc. On the other hand, there are some traits of trademark enforcement that are common to all types of products due to the fact that unlike its commercial functions, the forms of legal protection of trademarks are limited in their form and are accessible by all right holders.

A fact is clear. Eradication of counterfeiting cannot be the goal of a brand owner's anti-counterfeiting strategy in China, not even elsewhere. This simple truth must be set straight by any brand manager at the beginning of any ant-counterfeiting strategy planning regarding China. Overloading trademark administrative enforcement of political functions will lead to a short-term erosion of the company resources and a failure in the mid-term. Further economic and technological development of the industrial and commercial infrastructure of China, together with the emergence of China's own world-famous brands on one side and radical changes in the political attitude of the enforcing authorities at local level on the other, will be necessary pre-conditions for a final and permanent reduction and eventual marginalization of the economic system based on counterfeiting. If China's economy is able to express its own genuine inventors, and it will be less dependent on foreign know-how, there will be fewer political and economic reasons for the Chinese enforcement authorities to tolerate counterfeiting. The more people will be employed in legitimate business activities, the less local economies will depend on submerged illegal enterprises and the easier it will be for the Chinese government to impose its national polices at local level. Such goal setting would be disproportionate to the legal and economic function of IP rights. The enforcement of IP rights against counterfeiters should not be put at the same level of national legislation and IP policies and consequently should not be evaluated and measured according to the extent it contributes to the achievement of public policy goals of a sovereign state, like the eradication of counterfeiting and the technological development of China.

Therefore, there must be more objective and realistic parameters aside from seized quantities of infringed goods that can be used to measure the efficacy of an anti-counterfeiting strategy and select the appropriate forms of enforcement given a limited budget. Considering that we are talking about enforcement, and therefore we are not focusing on prevention of a crime but with its punishment, one parameter that appears objectively relevant to an enforcement strategy is "deterrence." A trademark enforcement strategy can be determined as having succeeded or failed, if it does not deter the targeted infringer and others, at least in the neighboring area, to target again that specific brand.

[B] Degree of Deterrence of AIC Raids

As stated above, trademark enforcement in China is characterized by the prevalent recourse by brand owners to administrative trademark enforcement in the form of raids and seizures of counterfeit goods by AIC authorities. It rarely extends to criminal enforcement due to both legal and political difficulties of having the police involved in enforcement requests from a private party (the brand owner).[340] Compared to criminal or civil enforcement, administrative raids and seizures are easier to obtain and trademark administrative officials in charge of anti-counterfeiting are keener than PSB officials to initiate raids upon request of right holders, if the latter can bring a prima facie evidence of the infringement. This evidence is normally the result of the sighting by the local investigator, who in most cases will also negotiate the raid and seizure with the local authority on behalf of the brand owner.

However, administrative raids, so easy to obtain, may have a very low deterrent force due to the very limited legal consequences they have for the infringers. The major effect of an administrative raid is that it leads to a temporary shutdown of the infringer's activity and a monetary fine, normally just a low, symbolic amount. Although administrative bodies have the power to order the destruction of the counterfeit manufacturing tools, this rarely happens in practice, because the infringers have many ways to avoid such a punishment. For instance, it may convince and even bribe the AIC into leaving molds and other manufacturing tools untouched. In many

340. Police is normally engaged in ant-counterfeiting campaigns organized directly by the central or provincial governments. Police is an arm of the state in charge of public security and as such intervenes only in those cases initiated upon requests from private companies or individuals only where both the minimum quantitative requirements of the criminal law as well as the interest and prerogatives of the sovereign State are in danger. Enforcement of IP rights is on the other hand a legal instrument concerning the protection of commercial rights, and it is not normally concerned with public or state security. This explains why, aside from both legal or political unwillingness of the police enforcement units to be involved in anti-counterfeiting due to local protectionism, there is a more compelling institutional reason that helps us to explain why police raids are rare in the anti-counterfeiting arena and constitute an exception to the rule that IP rights are protected in first instance by either civil or administrative law and enforcement organs.

cases, such tools are indeed legally in a gray area with respect to the law distinction between essential and nonessential tools to the manufacturing of the counterfeits. In force of the Trademark law provisions, AIC could also seize computers or bookkeeping documents and contracts of the infringer. However, like for tools, the former must be mainly used in relation to the infringing activities. Therefore, computers and books could be seized only if they are in the same place where the raid is being conducted and are obviously visible and accessible to the AIC. Furthermore, from the letter of the law,[341] it seems that AIC cannot seize them before having determined whether they are relevant to the infringement. In practice, it will be difficult for an AIC official to determine on the spot, without seizing the computers and the books whether they are relevant to the case. The result is clear: it is rare to find computers and books in counterfeiter premises, especially factories, and it rarely occurs that AIC is able and even willing to seize computers and accounting books during a raid.

In sum, raid measures such as the seizure of the counterfeits and a low monetary fine, will cause but a temporary economic setback for the infringer but no durable consequences. As businesspeople, counterfeiters already take into account AIC raids as business-related risks. The loss of an order will be likely made good in few weeks or even days later by accepting more orders and having the illegally employed local workforce work double shifts! As we explained in the preceding chapters, counterfeiting organizations have the ability of absorbing such risks very easily and quickly. Lack of real economic damage and loss of manufacturing capacities, result therefore in AIC raid to be a low deterrence tool. Experienced investigators can easily recount how many times they have met an infringer at given intervals between an AIC raid and another!

[C] Conclusions

Seizing large quantities of counterfeits through AIC enforcement is therefore inefficient unless it has a strong deterring effect. If that were the case, the company statistics should see the curve going down at a certain point! If this does not happen, then the strategy must change and the parameter of quantity must be at least tempered, if not utterly substituted, by deterrence.

This does not mean that AIC raids are always useless. On the contrary, they can be very effective if they are aimed to certain targets and within a more complex strategy that mixes all the enforcement tools made available by the law. Hitting small targets such as online traders, small shops and sellers may indeed have little deterrent on both the target and the real sources of the infringement. However, an AIC campaign targeting for instance the factories in a certain geographic area may be an effective tactical move to send messages against those factories, in that same region, which have

341. Article 62 does not provide AIC with the same penetrating powers of PSB. AIC cannot order an infringer to disclose and produce accounting books and computers or other materials used for the infringement if not available on the spot. The general obligation of cooperation by the parties provided by the same norm is not more precisely defined and remains in most case a mere enunciation of principles.

not yet been uncovered and hit. A "carpet bombing" of targets concentrated in an area (a sweep of large dimensions not limited to a single street market), implies a more strategic use of the AIC enforcement tools and will require more time and resources compared to singled-out raids against isolated target. In sum, it is not the AIC enforcement way that is bad by definition, it is more the way it is used that can be defined as good or bad depending on the strategic goals set by the right holder. By reflection, a strategy made principally of small AIC raids targeting retailers, traders and shops may drain resources for enforcement of higher deterrence levels.

Using the parameter of deterrence we can also make remarks on PSB criminal raids. It is true that the deterring effect of a criminal raid is higher than an AIC raid.[342] However, this is not always the case for every criminal raid. For instance, if a criminal raid leads to the arrest of some of the infringers, and in particular, of the minute workers in a factory, but misses the owner of the factory, the deterring effect will be limited and maybe even comparable to that of an AIC raid. The owner will hide for as long as needed, and he may even continue to rebuild his counterfeiting activities with the support of other rings in the counterfeiting chain. Therefore, it is not the enforcement tool alone that determines the level of deterrence. It is the way it is planned, and used that makes the difference. In some cases, the raid will come out as planned, in others not, because many factors and situations are often not predictable or preventable. In this respect, strategic and tactical enforcement plans must retain flexibility and require a masterful ability to use them in a coordinated manner.

From the notes above, we can conclude that the deterring effect of enforcement tools is multilayered: (1) at the first level is the "natural" degree of deterrence of the enforcement tool as provided by the law. The deterrence here is measured by the statutory forms of punishment. It is evident that in general, the imprisonment foreseen by the criminal law is stronger than the fine of an AIC raid or the damage compensation by a court; (2) At the second level, the deterrence is influence by the use of the tool and by the specific circumstances of each case. An AIC strategy focusing on small traders and shops, or a criminal enforcement that misses the real masterminds, may be less effective of a civil lawsuit that liquidates some compensation; (3) Deterrence can be engineered to a certain extent by a flexible and combined use of the available tools, so as to defuse the negative impacts of specific case circumstances. For instance, we can think of the lawsuit against the wife of the boss who is still escaping arrest in a criminal raid, which will force him to surrender to help his wife out of trouble. In this last point, we can add any lawsuit that follows an AIC enforcement. It is evident that if an AIC raid is followed by a civil lawsuit collecting damages in addition to the fine, the deterrence action in that case will be much stronger than if the case ended with the AIC raid alone.

From a company's point of view, resorting to administrative enforcement derived from sightings reported by external investigators, although a valuable resource, it is

342. This is particularly the case in which administrative seizures of infringing products hit factories belonging to a wider and well-organized infringing network. In this counterfeiting constellation, it is very likely that either the raided factory will be replaced by another one, will be quickly relocated to a neighboring area, or it may even resume the infringing business within a few days from the enforcement.

also a source of concern, especially regarding the direction and control of such activities, their genuineness and their effectiveness. That is why all brand owners understand the importance of these sources of enforcement being subjected to a review process. The practical difference between a successful and an unsuccessful brand protection strategy will then depend on whether and how the brand owner can control and manage the work needed from external partners. The author believes that a successful approach to this managerial question lies first in the degree of awareness, knowledge and use of the company's legal as well as managerial resources to support brand policy. The more the brand owner will be able to integrate the more traditional control criteria based on the relation between available resources/seized quantities with IP management, the better it will be positioned in gaining control over and direct its brand protection strategy. In particular, when making the decision whether to authorize unsolicited sightings from independent Chinese investigators, the brand owner should not be guided solely by the natural urge of stopping each and every newly discovered infringing activity. This approach will lead even the most well-financed brand protection team to quickly use up financial resources in a very short time, or to require ever increasing resources without the palpable feeling of having really come close to tackle the problem, with the doubt always present of having in fact chosen the wrong cases.

In conclusion, an enforcement plan against trademark counterfeiters in China must be guided by clearly set strategic goals, and supported by clear knowledge of the law and the available enforcement tools and how they really work in practice. The measure for determining the goal achievement should be flexible and adapted to the business strategy of the company and its models of IP exploitation. Therefore, using seized goods quantities alone as criteria for choosing the enforcement tools at a tactical level may result in a continuous failure of any strategic plan. Deterrence should be a more suitable standard for selecting a proper enforcement strategy, ideally combined with the company IPR exploitation models and also to a certain extent with quantities (the latter as a budget refining tool rather than the principal goal). Deterrence will allow a better selection of the relevant trademarks to be enforced, will better identify the type of targets and set aside the appropriate budget to conceive and implement a successful enforcement plan.

CHAPTER 5
Learned Lessons and Take-Aways

§5.01 CHOP CHOP MOVE QUICK BEFORE ANY SIGN OF PROBLEMS

A right holder should prevent Trademark issues in China when possible. Knowledge of the system, of the China business and the related risks shall help them preventing a good part of the trademark challenges. Early filing of trademarks, tight selection of business partners and continuous control of the manufacturing and distribution chain, will help reduce both risks of trademark theft and trademark infringement.

For those risks that cannot be prevented or have not been prevented, quick reaction is the other golden rule. Postponing decisions may only make the problems bigger. It thus become very critical for any enforcement strategy that processes are in place that allow red flags to come up at the right time and for the right holder to recognize the danger and react quickly to reduce damages to the business and subside the infringement at the earliest time possible. If the infringer is left alone to make good money out of his illicit acts, it will be more difficult and costly to deter him from further infringing. For instance, failing to recognize the seriousness of the warning behind some activities of a business partner or a distributor may lead to the loss of the whole China market and very expensive lawsuits to rectify the situation. If an emerging brand has not prepared any budget or has not gained awareness of the importance of tackling counterfeiters at the source in China, he will be powerless once sightings of infringing factories will arrive and his reaction might be too slow and scattered to make any impact for a long time.

At the same time, reacting fast does not mean rushed reactions. Moving fast with efficiency and effectiveness against trademark threats will be possible only once the foreign right holders have started mastering the Rules of Engagement and have thus created an internal awareness system, and acquired the needed knowledge as to how to react effectively. Once such basics have been acquired, then moving fast will be the most natural consequence in that each reaction will be part of a well-thought and planned strategy in which speed will be but a tactical component. For example, once a right holder knows that in China trademarks are protected only after registration in force of the First-to-File Rule, they will never hesitate when filing a new brand and will also be very cautious about disclosing ahead of time.

§5.02 KNOWLEDGE IS THE KEY: STRATEGIC THINKING AND FACT FINDING

One thing that emerges clearly from the book is that foreign right holders must adapt to China and not China to them. Foreign right holders should stop blaming China and try to learn how Chinese see the same business and legal issues, so as to acquire a more effective view of the real game's rules and how to play it. Foreign investors seem in most cases to assume that Chinese laws and legal/business culture are similar to those in the West. The result is that most foreign brands trademark strategies in China were based on inaccurate knowledge, which has resulted in a consistent repetition of both legal and business mistakes and misunderstandings.

The book has thus introduced some basic rules of conduct that should allow foreign right holders to acquire knowledge and awareness of risks sufficient to prevent the usual mistakes and bad business decisions which have characterized many trademark protection and enforcement strategies in China. These are the Rules of Engagement. Rules of Engagement are strategic rules. They are the sum of legal and business knowledge about China trademarks. The mastery of these rules will help businesses, lawyers as well as businessmen and women to view trademark challenges in China in a comprehensive strategic manner that will supply them with effective business solutions to the most typical China trademark challenges. These rules are of general application and can positively help any kind of business to gain a more objective and factual knowledge of the trademark laws of China and their practical application and learn how to exploit them in their favor, finding practical, business solutions and avoid classic mistakes while preparing for new challenges. By adopting a strategic approach to trademark challenges in China, practitioners of all kinds will be in a better position to use and control their Chinese counsel, thus playing a really active and leading role in the creation, shaping and execution of trademark protection and enforcement strategies. Knowledge and use of the appropriate rules of engagement will show that there still are creative solutions to trademark challenges in China, without need to give in to resignation. Rules of Engagements start from the apolitical acceptance of Chinese law as it is and not as it should or could be. Rules of Engagements are not based on wishful thinking and start from the acceptance that westerners have made mistakes and that it is time they take new paths to correct them. Rules of Engagement are myth busters. This means that in certain cases, a consolidated and practically standard response to a trademark challenge may be abandoned for new, more business-oriented strategies.

There are in sum three major Rules of Engagements, and they are complementary and inseparable from each other:

- Know your strength: Set your Strategic/tactical goals before you take action and after you have collected all the needed information.

- Know the Enemy: Collect all the facts about the opponent and investigate him/her at 360 degrees. The solution of a case may lay in a small fact that you would ignore if you were to look only with the lenses of a lawyer!
- Know the battlefield: Acquire full knowledge of the local law and practices. Learn litigation tactics and exploit them in your favor. Accept the local law as it is without prejudice; this will help you make a better and more effective use of it.

Those who have consistently applied these rules to their trademark business in China have claimed also consistent and increasing successes. In particular, they have improved their business relations and set-ups in China, they have gained that awareness that allows them to recognize early signs of possible problems and challenges and have learned how tackle them at the earliest convenient time in a pragmatic and effective way, before they turn into complex legal issues.

§5.03 FEW SECRETS TO WINNING IN CHINESE COURTS

We should know by now that winning a case in court or raiding one counterfeiters' factory will not be alone the solution to a more complex problem. Legal issues are first and foremost business issues. However, winning a trademark infringement lawsuit is an important tactical milestone in an enforcement strategy, especially because it may absorb a good portion of a company's enforcement budget overall. Therefore, a few remarks on how to succeed in a civil lawsuit in China are very important for any right holder.

Transparency

Chinese courts are the most transparent among the State agencies in charge of IP enforcement in China. Although it is possible to corrupt a Chinese judge, it is normally much more difficult doing it successfully, as well as for the corrupted judge to go around the rule of law.[343] In fact, courts have less discretion than administrative bodies and are more strictly bound to the rule of law as a major criterion to decide a disputed claim. This is particularly true for IP Courts and IP cases involving foreign entities. Unlike normal tort or contractual cases, IP courts are more exposed to direct international scrutiny, the judges known to the right holders who may have many cases IP matters pending before the same IP court. The fact of an IP court being more under the spotlight has the benefit of reducing the risk of illicit dealings by its judges. Also, most trademark infringement cases today are engineered to be brought before IP courts far away from the infringer's domicile, which further contribute to reducing the impact of local factors on the judges. A civil lawsuit will therefore offer less excuses for

343. Judge corruption has been linked to the poor funding of courts and therefore the low economic incentives judges receive. An interesting study of judicial corruption in China is in Yuhua Wang, Court Funding and Judicial Corruption in China, Vol. 69 The China Journal 43-64 (University of Chicago Press 2013).

scapegoating and failure can find an easier paternity in the right holder's strategy and its execution.

Clear Goal Setting

A lawsuit in China should be won before filing it. This means that a lawsuit should be conceived and executed as to fulfill the tactical task assigned to it. This requires a further definition of "victory." If the only condition of success is obtaining for instance large damage compensation, such lawsuit will not be successful the moment this goal is not achieved in the exact way it was formulated. Also, if cessation of an infringement in the short term is the main goal, then winning the lawsuit may also not be sufficient to achieve it, or it may be achieved without need of winning a lawsuit at all. Goal setting is even more critical in China where court litigation is never a straightforward matter, where court pressure to settle is stronger than in Europe and surely much stronger than in the US. We should have learned that winning damage compensation in itself should not be the ultimate goal of filing a lawsuit. That could be considered at most as a tactical tool. Therefore, the lawsuit must be seen as a mere intermediary tool in the achievement of strategic goals that are business goals.

Once the strategic goals are clear, it will be easier for the right holder to conceive and execute a civil or criminal enforcement before a Chinese court in a pragmatic and flexible manner that supports its ultimate goals. In this context, just filing a lawsuit may achieve strategic goals. The filing of a well-structured lawsuit and enforcement strategy may induce the infringer to abandon the violation of the trademark rights straight away. For instance, if the counterpart is in the process of a merger or an IPO or any kind of restructuring, filing the lawsuit alone may damage the infringer and induce him to cease his illegal activities. In many other cases, the filing of a lawsuit with the advantage of surprise and together with other tactical moves, such a media exposure and market pressure on the relevant consumers of the disputed trademarked product, may also achieve a number of positive results before a judgment is issued. In such cases, how the lawsuit is concluded may become of secondary importance.

Intense Prelawsuit Investigation

Knowledge of the facts, including knowledge of the infringer and the right holder's own strengths and weaknesses are the most sensitive starting point in any lawsuit preparation. Company legal departments and board members should not hurry up a case preparation because of the immediate danger and damages caused by the infringement. Cool head and a lot of patience are required when preparing a winning case in China. Rushing into a lawsuit after a notarized purchase trap, strong of the certainty that there is an identity and similarity among the disputed trademarks, may not be enough to succeed in the strategic sense. Again, even winning that lawsuit may not solve the underlying business problem and deter the defendant from infringing. Preparation requires a careful fact-finding work that needs time. The emergence of new facts or clarity on others can change the direction of the initial strategy. Uncovering even a small crack in the enemy's wall may help tearing it down better and faster. Knowing the enemy will show where he may hit back and from which direction he may receive rescue. It will help the right holder shaping his strategy and goals and show him alternative paths to achieve them. Investigation will help determine the degree of political relevance of the case, and support the selection of a number of legal tools to build a strong enforcement that will put the infringer under a lot of pressure, i.e., engineering evidence acquisition and forum shopping, uncover additional infringements of any legal nature upon which parallel claims and actions could be triggered against the infringer at given time intervals etc.

Pressure and the Way to Build it Up

The chances of an infringer to stop infringing and doing it for good is proportionally equivalent to the level of legal and economic pressure he is subjected by the right holder. There are many tactical tools available to build up such pressure:

- Surprise
  A lawsuit in China should not be threatened or prematurely revealed by sending around warning letters. Warning letters do not work well in China. They are the legal tool with the lowest deterring force. Most infringers will ignore them. The only certain result of a warning letter in China is that of giving away the enforcement intention and its direction and allow the infringer to take protective measures that will surely soften the impact of the following lawsuit.
- Forum Shopping
  Another important element for pressure is forum shopping, e.g., the selection of a court that is far from the domicile and business relations of the defendant. This can be engineered through a formally and technically structured evidence acquisition strategy that will allow the right holder to involve a preselected court. Such strategy must be prepared carefully since the beginning because it will affect the way evidence selection and acquisition will be conducted. The golden rule is that the defendant should be brought before a court that has no direct relation with its businesses and it is physically removed from its place of domicile. Such a court will be less affected by local factors. This is very important in all cases in which the defendant is not a state-owned company or a company economically relevant at national level. In the latter cases, forum shopping alone cannot exclude political influence over the case. Forum shopping also forces the defendant to fight on unfamiliar ground, to find lawyers he is not familiar with, to spend more money to travel and monitor the case etc. In sum, forum shopping can help the right holder to make the defendant spend money and sweat a lot, thus weakening his will to fight.
- Damage Compensation
  If a case wants be taken seriously by a defendant and even a judge, damages are the way to attract this attention and increase thus the pressure on the infringer. This requires a big effort on the part of the right holder during the preparation phase. Resources and time will have to be spent in building up a strong evidence chain on damages. No efforts should be spared. The new

trademark law has come partly to the rescue of right holders in this very difficult task by imposing an obligation on the defendant to produce accounting books. This may be good, in that the right holder knows that in the worst of cases, the plaintiff will bear the consequences of not producing such books. However, it presents challenges as well. If a plaintiff relies only on this provision to fund his claims, his case may turn into a dramatic disaster. The worst that can happen is that the plaintiff does not formulate any specific demand of compensation and the defendant produces then only documents showing mere symbolic transactions. This will end up with a case dismissal or at most with ridiculously low damage compensation. This can derail the enforcement strategy and frustrate the achievement of the strategic goals. The message is clear on two counts: plaintiffs cannot rely only on the court or the law to prove damages. They must do their outmost best to find evidence of some sort and build up a believable calculation method supported by some facts. Second, plaintiffs should get always a figure down in that lawsuit. Leaving that part of the lawsuit blank will bring the case under the statutory damages umbrella, which will likely result in very low damage compensation and therefore in the lawsuit having a low deterring effect. The secret of success lies in the ability of the plaintiff's team to find the right damage figure and support it in a believable manner. This in turn will create credibility in the eyes of the court and will constitute a serious economic threat for the defendant.

- Injunctions and preservations

  It is important not to shy away from additional judicial tools such as interim injunctions and property preservation. Although it is not always easy to obtain them in China, they are an excellent tool to pressure the counterpart. By filing them, the counterpart will be forced to double its efforts and costs to defend against them. If a defendant is unsure about the outcome of the lawsuit and has already considered desisting from the infringement, these tools will likely accelerate that decision.

  In this group of activities, we can include also multilayered strategies in which enforcement is started with an AIC administrative raid and completed by an ensuing civil lawsuit. In this way, the two enforcement tools will pair and complement each other. The same can be done by combining enforcement at trade fairs and civil lawsuit.

- Parallel legal actions

  If a thorough investigation is conducted in the preparatory phase, other relevant facts may emerge to support additional legal claims and actions, even unrelated to the trademark infringement but related to the business of the infringer. For instance, labeling and product quality are issues that should never escape a good investigation. If the trademark is to be used on products that are subject to legal quality standards, labeling and warnings restrictions and obligations, all these facts become critical to the case. A substandard product or counterfeit can trigger criminal liabilities, forged or insufficient labeling will trigger administrative liabilities, and manufacturing products without required mandatory licenses can lead to both administrative and criminal liabilities depending on the products. All these actions may help the right holder increase the pressure on the defendant which will have to respond and defend on different fronts at the same time. Decisions in one action may help the other still pending and all sum up in an overall action of large and threatening proportions.

- Careful use of Media and Communication
  Announcing in a press release or in a press conference that a lawsuit has been filed by the right holder against the trademark infringer is not illegal and is generally shielded from unfair competition claims if the statements and information disclosed to the public are objective and openly verifiable. In sum, to state that a lawsuit for trademark infringement regarding a given product against a specific entity or person has been filed in a certain court in China, and that the right holder has full trust in the Chinese justice system, is objective and sufficient to convey to the relevant public the information that some of the consumer and customers of the right holder may have been buying trademark infringing products. If the products are sold to businesses, such messages are even stronger than those sent to consumers. Businesses, will be more sensitive to the risks of being considered as abetting an illegal conduct and may be willing to suspend transactions with the infringer once they know that a lawsuit is pending. This alone can be of great benefit to the right holder, already at a very early stage of the enforcement action.
  The same applies to the communication of the same facts to buyers and users of the trademarked products in dispute in a direct, one-to-one form. If the facts are objectively represented and at the same time a more general press release has been issued to which reference can be made, such communications can be particularly effective and reduce pressure on the commercial side of the business by having more buyers turning away from the allegedly infringing product.

§5.04 FIGHTING COUNTERFEITING AND BREAKING WITH THE SYSTEM

Chapter 4 has proposed new conceptual approaches to counterfeiting. These will help right holders to plan more effective and reasonable enforcement strategies against counterfeiters without the risk of wearing their budgets in actions that will ultimately increase only the frustration towards the Chinese trademark enforcement system. Aside from such pragmatic approaches, one other critical element has emerged: the inefficient administrative enforcement of trademark rights in China is founded also in the very unhealthy relations managed by the informants-centered business model. As long as third parties such as field informants are left with the power to write the enforcement agenda of the right holders, and to play the pivotal role in the relations with the enforcement agencies things will not change in better. Enforcement may increase in quantity but will not bring any real benefit to the brand owners. The perverse effect of such system will be for brand owners to invest even more on such a "system" and step up that kind of enforcement. The question is therefore, how to break this circle.

One way to reduce the impact of such system, would be for the brand owners to recognize that they may be working with untrustworthy partners and stop using them. Unfortunately, the perverse nature of the market and the relations between informants and public officials is such that it is not easy to clean up the market from the bad apples. Ideally, brand owners should work only with few reliable partners that have proved to be trustworthy. The latter would be in a position to dictated new rules to the market, which demand transparency and abidance with the rule of law. If AIC and PSB officials will end up dealing with strict and law-abiding investigators, they will have sooner or later to make a choice between enforcing and making their money the legal way, or not making money at all.

Another change should also occur to see an improvement in the system: brand should not shy away from denouncing illegal dealings to the criminal and civil courts. The rule that foreigners should adapt to China does not in fact mean should adapt to commit or even tolerate illegal acts. The rule of law should be the limit of the adaptation. It would be helpful if brands would unite in taking consistent action against corruption. At present, this does not happen on a regular basis. Everybody is scared to act alone, and this is understandable. Institutions should help brands coalesce and take over some of this burden by supporting direct legal actions against the widespread corruptions of the Chinese trademark enforcement apparatus.

Bibliography and Periodicals

Albanese S. Jay, The Causes of Organized Crime: Do Criminals Organize Around Opportunities for Crime or Do Opportunities Create New Criminals?, Vol. 16 Journal of Contemporary Criminal Justice, 409, 423 (2000).

Alexander J. Wurzer, IP Manager, (Carl Heymanns Verlag 2009).

Andrew C. Mertha, The Politics of Piracy, Intellectual Property in Contemporary China, 4 (Cornell Paperbacks 2005).

Bronshtein, Counterfeit Pharmaceuticals in China: Could Changes Bring Stronger Protection for Intellectual Property Rights and Human Health? Vol. 17, No. 2 Pacific Rim Law & Policy Journal Association, 439-466 (March 2008).

Daniel C. K. Chow, Counterfeiting in the People's Republic of China, Vol. 78, No. 1 Washington University Law Quarterly, 9, 10 (2000).

Daniel C. K. Chow, Lessons from Pfizer's Disputes over Its Viagra Trademark in China, Vol. 27 Maryland Journal of International Law, 82 (2012). *See also* Yahong Li et al., Viagra in China: A Prolonged Battle Over Intellectual Property Rights, Asia Case Research Center & Columbia Business School, 10 (2010).

Daniel C. K. Chow, Anti-Counterfeiting Strategies of Multi-National Companies in China: How a Flawed Approach Is Making Counterfeiting Worse, Vol. 41, No. 4, Georgetown Journal of International Law, 750 (2010).

Delener, Nejdet, International Counterfeit Marketing: Success Without Risk, Vol. 21, No. 1 Review of Business, (St. John's University March 2000).

Donald P. Harris, The Honeymoon Is Over: Evaluating The U.S.-China WTO Intellectual Property Complaint, Vol. 32, No. 1, Fordham International Law Journal, 96 (2008).

Dun Mingyue, Entrapment Evidence for IP Protection: Admissible or Not?, Issue 18 China IP Magazine, (2007).

Fang Yang, The Importance of Guangxi to Multinational Companies in China, Vol. 7, Issue 7 Asian Social Science, (July 2011).

Gordon G. Chang, The Coming Collapse of China, (Random House 2001).

Graeme B. Dinwoodie, Trademarks and Territory: Detaching Trademark Law From the Nation-State, Vol. 41 Houston Law Review 885, 892-893 (2004).

Guillermo Jimenez, Barbara Kolsun, Fashion Law, A Guide for Designers, Fashion Executives and Attorneys, 351 (Bloomsbury 2nd edition 2014).

Harry Yang, Is Counterfeiting a Part of Chinese Culture?, 19 China IP Journal, (August 2007).

Jessica Lin, *Fake Stuff*, Ruthledge 2011.

John Spink, et al, Defining the Types of Counterfeiters, Counterfeiting and Offender Organizations, 10 Crime Science, (Springer, December 1, 2013).

Kenneth Liebenthal, Michel Oksenberg, Policy Making in China: Leaders, Structures and Processes, (Princeton University Press 1988).

Kenneth Liebenthal, China's Governing System and Its impact on Environmental Policy Implementation, 1st Series China Environmental Series, 3 (Wilson Center's Asia Program First Series, 1995).

Kitsurong Sangusvang, Trademark Squatting, Vol. 37, Issue 1, Wisconsin International law Journal, 259 (December 2012).

Ling Jiang, Call for Copy–The Culture of Counterfeit in China, Vol. 2, No. 2 Journal of Chinese Economics, 73, 78 (2014).

Martin K. Dimitrov, Piracy and the State – The Politics of Intellectual Property Rights in China, (Cambridge University Press 2009).

Michael Silverstein, The $10 Trillion Prize, Captivating the Newly Affluent in China and India (Harvard Business Review Press 2015).

Mikahelle Schiappacasse, Intellectual Property Rights in China: Technology Transfers and Economic Development, Vol. 2, Buffalo Intellectual Property Law Journal, 164, 176 (2004).

Paul Jones, China: Bad Faith Registrations by Distributors, IBA Legal Practice Division, International Franchising Committee Newsletter (June 2008).

Paul F. Kilmer, The Value Equation of Trademark Oppositions: A Multinational Comparison of Costs and Perceived Benefits, Vol. 68, INTA Bulletin, (March 2013).

Peter Ganea, Thomas Pattloch, Intellectual property Law in China, (Kluwer International 2005).

Peter S. Sloane, Yijun Ge in their Article, Managing Trademark Investigations for Non-use in China: A Comparison with U.S. Practice, ABA Landslide Magazine (July/August 2013).

Qiang Ma, Jessica Chumen Ju, Lessons for Trademark Owners, China Law and Practice, (November 2014).

Randall Peeremboom, China Long March Toward Rule of Law, (Cambridge University Press 2002).

Samantha D. Slotkin, Trademark Piracy in Latin America: A Case Study on Reebok, International Ltd, Vol. 18 Loyola International & Comparative Law Review, 671, 671 (1996).

Tan, Loke Khoon, Pirates in the Middle kingdom: The Art of Trademark War (Thomson Sweet & Maxwell Asia 2004).

Turgut Guvenlu, Rajib Sanyal, Perception and Management of Legal Issues in China by US Firms, Vol. 32, No. 2 The Journal of Socio-Economics (May 2003).

Yang, Fryxell, Agnes K.Y. Sie, Anti-Piracy Effectiveness and Managerial Confidence: Insights from Multinationals in China, Vol. 43, Journal of World Business, 321 (2008).

Yu Hong, Reading the Twelfth Five-Year Plan: China's Communication-Driven Mode of Economic Restructuring, Vol. 5, International Journal of Communication (University of Southern California 2011).

Yuhua Wang, Court Funding and Judicial Corruption in China, Vol. 69, The China Journal (University of Chicago Press 2013).

Yu Hui, Preliminary Research on the Judicial Judgment of Similar Goods in Trademark Infringement Cases, Vol. 14 IP China Intellectual Property Magazine, (October 2006).

Wiedmann, Hennigs, Siebels, Measuring Consumers' Luxury Value Perception: A Cross-Cultural Framework, Vol. 2007, No. 7, Academy of Marketing Science Review, (2007).

Index